JUSTICE
WILLIAM JOHNSON

After the Miniature by Charles Fraser

WILLIAM JOHNSON

JUSTICE
WILLIAM JOHNSON
THE FIRST DISSENTER

THE CAREER AND CONSTITUTIONAL PHILOSOPHY
OF A JEFFERSONIAN JUDGE

By
DONALD G. MORGAN

UNIVERSITY OF SOUTH CAROLINA PRESS
Columbia, South Carolina

Published in South Carolina by the
UNIVERSITY OF SOUTH CAROLINA PRESS, COLUMBIA

International Standard Book Number: 0–87249–060–2
Library of Congress Catalog Card Number: 54–14788

Suggested Library of Congress classification furnished by
McKissick Memorial Library of the University of South Carolina:
KF8745.J

Manufactured by JENKINS-UNIVERSAL CORPORATION

FOREWORD

For almost everyone, American historians included, Chief Justice John Marshall was the Marshall Court. His colleagues seem shadowy figures, none of whom did much more than echo his chief. Though Marshall was clearly the dominant figure of that Court, as he is the leading judge in our entire history, he is certainly not the only member of his Court worthy of careful study. The Presidents before Andrew Jackson appointed no fewer than twelve associate justices to the Marshall Court, yet these judges have suffered almost complete neglect at the hands of modern biographers preoccupied with Marshall.

Few persons remember even the names of most of the judges concerned, but most will probably remember that John Adams saw to it that the federal judiciary, including the newly established courts, was staffed exclusively with Federalists. All of the justices appointed to the Supreme Court by Washington and Adams were of that party.

Jefferson was fully aware of the dangers inherent in the Federalist control of the courts. He had been in office less than a year when he wrote, in a letter to John Dickinson: "The Federalists [having been defeated at the polls] have retired into the judiciary . . . and from that battery all the works of republicanism are to be beaten down and erased."

During his first three years in the Presidency, Jefferson had no opportunity to redress the balance on the Supreme Court. When in 1804, his first chance came, he chose with great care, and his choice was William Johnson of South Carolina. Johnson was young even in an era when men often came to high office early in life. He was but thirty-two, whereas the average age of those appointed to the Court before him was forty-eight. He was a graduate of Princeton; he had served his state as judge for four years; and he was believed by the President to be a sound Republican, one who would assert his independence of the domineering Chief Justice.

Associate Justice Johnson was a man of unusual independence. Not only was he, as Professor Morgan has shown, the first dissenter in the Court's history, he was, upon occasion, independent even of the state he loved and the President he tremendously admired and to whom he was deeply devoted. But he asserted his independence only when principle made it necessary, not for the sake of dissenting. Agreeing as he did with many of the tenets of Marshall's economic conservatism and with his belief in a strong union, Johnson dissented infrequently in cases dealing with those great questions.

He was not a forerunner of the secessionists or the Populists, even though he did write almost as many dissenting opinions as all the rest of the justices who were on the Court during his thirty years. In particular, he did not go all the way with Marshall so far as concerned the scope and nature of the judicial power. There is more than a trace, in certain of these dissents, of the point of view expressed in the twentieth century by Justice Holmes, as there is evidence that he here was influenced by the philosophy of Jefferson.

Professor Morgan has written a biography which is a work of careful scholarship, not of myopic piety. He is, as a biographer ordinarily should be, sympathetic with his subject, but his concern is for the discovery and statement of the truth, not the production of an apology. He has searched out local records and unpublished manuscripts, as well as the Reports of the Supreme Court and all relevant secondary materials. The product is a book which goes far toward rounding out our knowledge of the Marshall Court. Though the Chief Justice was the greatest figure of that Court, as of American jurisprudence, he was never without the necessity of convincing his brethren, and, almost certainly, of adapting his views to theirs, when he could not persuade them to his.

Since the period of thirty years in which Johnson served on the Court is the one in which the American doctrine of judicial review was first applied in a series of major causes, the period in which the Supreme Court became a great, instead of a lesser, power in the government of the Republic, this first thorough study of his life and his judicial career is a contribution of considerable importance to the literature of American history.

BENJAMIN F. WRIGHT

ACKNOWLEDGMENTS

At the outset I should like to express a word of grateful tribute to the memory of an eminent and discerning jurist, Louis D. Brandeis. In an interview at Chatham, Massachusetts, some years ago, he spoke of William Johnson's as one of the outstanding minds of the early Supreme Court. This comment by Mr. Justice Brandeis first suggested to me the writing of this book.

In preparing this study, I have relied to only a limited extent on private papers. Libraries near and far have furnished, in all, two large folders of Johnson's correspondence. A list of the holders of those letters thus far discovered appears in Appendix I. To all I extend my sincere thanks for their assistance and cooperation. Mention should be made here particularly of the Library of Congress, the National Archives, the Historical Societies of New York and Pennsylvania, and the South Caroliniana Library at the University of South Carolina. At all of these, the directors and the staffs in charge of manuscripts have lent valuable aid. If other letters exist, in private collections or in some long-forgotten family trunk, this work, it is hoped, may cause them to be brought to public attention. Where I have quoted from that early correspondence and other manuscript sources, I have tried to make the reading easier by the use of modern capitalization.

Especially helpful have been the newspapers of Johnson's time. These have been consulted at many places, but two libraries have proved of outstanding assistance. At the Charleston Library Society, Miss Ellen M. FitzSimons and her assistants gave liberally of their time to make materials available; and for many items from the press of Johnson's native city, I am especially indebted to Miss Anna Wells Rutledge. At the Georgia Historical Society, in Savannah, the librarian, Mrs. Marmaduke Floyd, gave generous help in locating newspaper materials—a process greatly facilitated by an index compiled by a WPA Historical Records Survey project.

While prospecting in both these cities I found another rich vein. I refer to the manuscript journals of the early federal circuit courts. At some hazard to health and limb, Mr. Justice Johnson, like his fellow-justices, rode circuit; there in the lower courts, with no large bench of associates to satisfy, he set down his own convictions with clarity and conciseness. To the Clerks and their staffs at the United States District Courts in Charleston and Savannah, who gave convenient access to these records, I offer my thanks. Since most of these opinions remain unpublished, I trust that they may some day reach the public in a form more complete and systematic than that provided here.

Other materials, chiefly of a documentary form, appeared in the collection garnered by the Historical Commission of South Carolina. At its headquarters in Columbia, both the former director, Mr. A. S. Salley, and his successor, Dr. J. Harold Easterby, contributed not only valuable materials, but also many helpful suggestions.

To the descendants of Judge Johnson and to others of the family I express my thanks. Advice and encouragement as well as a number of important original papers were generously provided by Mrs. I. G. Ball and Mrs. William Henry Johnson, of Charleston; the late Mrs. L. A. Denson, of Raleigh; Miss Gertrude M. L'Engle and Mrs. C. W. Camp, of Jacksonville; Miss Jane McCrady, of Boston; and Dr. William B. Johnson, of Washington, D.C. The directors of the South Carolina Historical Society gave useful advice. At Savannah, Mr. Alexander A. Lawrence, the biographer of Johnson's successor, Mr. Justice Wayne, and in Washington, D.C., Mr. Thomas E. Waggaman, until recently Marshal of the Supreme Court, furnished valuable help and suggestions. For the never-failing courtesy and assistance given by my friends at the libraries of Harvard University, Trinity College, and Mount Holyoke College, where most of the work of compilation and composition was done, I am eternally grateful. A grant from the Social Science Research Council has aided in the completion of the project. The frontispiece is reproduced by the courtesy of Mr. Bradley T. Johnson, of Charlottesville, Virginia, whose daughter, Mrs. Joseph B. Ryan, of Mount Tremblant, Canada, is the owner of the miniature.

My Chapter X appeared, with slight changes, in the *William and Mary Quarterly* for July, 1953; thanks go to the editors of the *Quarterly* for permission to republish here. A similar acknowledgment is due the editors of the *George Washington Law Review* for permission to reproduce material from my article entitled "Justice William Johnson on the Treaty-Making Power." This article, of December, 1953, examined at greater length than was possible here the "Philonimus" correspondence of 1823.

Many have tendered counsel and help in the preparation of the final manuscript. From the very outset, Professor Benjamin F. Wright of Harvard, now president of Smith College, was unsparing in time and energy in offering advice, criticism, and encouragement; this study was originally prepared under his direction as a doctoral dissertation and accepted at Harvard in 1942. Others who have read the manuscript include Dr. Easterby, who furnished detailed suggestions on the sections on local history, Professor Mark DeW.

Howe, of the Harvard Law School, who offered valuable criticism in the field of legal history, and Professor Roger W. Holmes, of the Mount Holyoke Department of Philosophy, who gave a wealth of helpful criticisms on both style and content. Mr. John Lofton, formerly of Charleston, read portions of Chapter VIII, and the late Professor Joseph E. Ledden, of Mount Holyoke College, Chapters IX and XII. For the help and advice of all these I am indeed grateful. In the progress of the work, Miss L. E. Reggio, of Boston, gave untiring help. To others who have helped I can offer here only a blanket vote of thanks. For the presentation both of evidence and conclusions I, of course, accept full responsibility.

DONALD G. MORGAN

South Hadley, Massachusetts

CONTENTS

PROLOGUE

THE Republic was young. It was in a village fresh cut from the forest that Thomas Jefferson, the Virginian, on March 4, 1801, repeated the words of the President's oath. Avenues of mud reached out, finger-like, from the unfinished Capitol, as if further to isolate the rude shops and dwellings that clustered about it. The raw appearance of Washington, the nation's capital, was such as could inspire only the confirmed patriot. Those who had planned the city had with foresight marked out streets and located the seat of Congress and the home of the President, but it remained for the architects of later generations to fix other building sites and, by elaborating the generalities of the plan, to transform a village into a metropolis.

Like the blueprints for the capital, the Constitution of 1787, in spite of a dozen years of Federalist party rule, remained to a considerable extent a paper plan. The Philadelphia convention had drafted the system in general terms, locating and describing the constitutional landmarks and tracing out the connections between them only in rough outline. The administrations of Washington and Adams had begun the process of implementation, but Jefferson and his Republican Congress might go far toward completing it and converting into concrete practice the abstract formulas of the Constitution. The system of government over which he was about to assume executive headship was still in a highly malleable state.

There could be little doubt about Jefferson's intentions. The tall, slender figure who stood up for the inaugural ceremony was in earnest, and the eccentric garb and soft-spokenness could not disguise the spirit of mission which animated him. Scarce twenty-five years had passed since this same man had drafted for his countrymen a political credo which had asserted the rights of individuals to be paramount to governmental power and had grounded the exercise of authority on the consent of the people. Now the American people had bestowed on Jefferson and his Republican party a mandate to rule, and the philosopher-statesman would seek to build into the design and operations of the new government the principles of the Revolution.

If Jefferson and his followers aspired to the role of institutional architects, the problems they faced were manifold and important. What should be the tasks of the Chief Executive and the degree of his subordination to the legislature? What parts should the central and state governments play in the delicate balance of Union? To precisely what rights might the individual lay claim in his age-old

xiii

struggle against authority? What prerogatives were proper for the national judiciary, which up to now had lingered in the background of the constitutional stage? These questions have ever since baffled American officialdom. In 1801 they still had the appearance of novelty. It was Jefferson's objective to settle these issues with finality on the firm footing of Republican doctrine. The broad popular support which the Third President enjoyed strengthened his hand as he approached the challenge of constitutional implementation.

Across Jefferson's path, however, stood one notable obstacle, personified by the very man who on that March day administered the Presidential oath. The Federalist party had gone down to defeat in the late elections and, in fact, was destined soon to expire, but the Adams administration, which the people had repudiated, had engineered a rare stroke of political skill—the appointment of forty-five-year-old John Marshall to the Supreme Court. Thus it was that Jefferson took from the mouth of his perennial Virginia adversary the words of his oath to support the Constitution, and no doubt the new President felt dismay at the prospect. Not only was the Supreme Court's presiding officer a young and able leader of the opposition, but the entire judiciary lay in the control of Federalists, and the life tenure of judges gave them sanctuary from popular control.

Indeed, Marshall would soon be asserting for his Court the high prerogative of judicial review, of construing the meaning of the fundamental law, and it seemed that the Federalists might keep in their hands the opportunity which the Republicans coveted. As things turned out, it was Marshall who took the lead in expounding the meaning of the Constitution during that formative period; Marshall, whose ringing sentences spoken over a period of more than a generation would echo and re-echo from the bench and bar down to our own time; Marshall, whose decisions on constitutional issues would seldom, if ever, meet with serious questioning by later judges.

That this would happen Jefferson could scarcely have realized, although it was obvious from the beginning that Marshall and his Federalist associates would constitute a serious barrier. Jefferson was not the last President to encounter a hostile judiciary, but in none of the subsequent periods of conflict would the stakes be so high or the oppostition from the bench so unanimous as during the opening years of his administration. Small wonder, then, that during three years of mounting tension, the President awaited anxiously a vacancy in the Supreme Court, an opportunity to send a tried and true Republican to the high bench.

At last in 1804, the opening appeared. In his search for a likely candidate, the President turned to South Carolina. What he sought was not merely a good lawyer and an honest man, but a Republican zealot. He found his man. Party leaders from the state offered the name of William Johnson, Jr., a thirty-two-year-old state judge who, they insisted, possessed "good nerves in his political principles." This was the man whom Jefferson picked.

Johnson was to sit with Marshall for thirty years. Unlike his associates, he would break with the Chief Justice on many occasions. The opinions which he was to express would furnish not only a running commentary on the decisions of Marshall, but also the outlines of an alternative interpretation of the fundamental law. To a degree they would provide a reading of the Constitution in the spirit of Jefferson and of the Revolution.

JUSTICE
WILLIAM JOHNSON

Chapter I

A COLONIST DISSENTS

ONE day in the autumn of 1766 William Johnson, blacksmith, made his way to a great oak in the outskirts of Charlestown. A little knot of men was gathering under its foliage; and, like his fellows, this young newcomer from New York found much to discuss. London had devised restrictions and regulations that bore heavily on this bustling capital of His Majesty's Province of South Carolina. A sense of grievance had produced demands for relief and assertions of rights. Nearly a full decade before open revolution, the oak tree rang with shouts of American resistance to British tyranny.[1] The debate was on. Johnson, with the rest, was exploring the structure of political power and within it the role of the individual—problems which in different guises would absorb his son and namesake throughout his public life.

This "Liberty Tree" was a familiar feature of the colonial agitation. Charleston, to use the later form for this chief port of the South, was not the only American city to boast of such a forum. To the shade of similar trees in other colonies His Majesty's American subjects early betook themselves to condemn imperial restrictions and taxes and to voice their rights. Often the harangues which enlivened these sylvan gatherings had two objectives. They explored the propriety of British rule over the colonies, and they expressed the strivings of a new middle class for a voice in affairs. It was not merely home rule, but also popular participation in government that led radicals like Johnson to raise their cries of protest.

Such considerations doubtless impelled the Charleston group to call its autumn meeting. A few months earlier, on May 6, news of Parliament's repeal of the Stamp Act had broken on the port, producing a wave of general rejoicing. The new enactment represented a compromise agreeable to the dominant class. In June the planter and merchant aristocracy had united with Crown officials to celebrate a royal birthday; a banquet had taken place in honor of the event and the evening had ended "with illuminations and other

[1]Edward McCrady, *History of South Carolina under the Royal Government, 1719-1776* (New York, 1899), pp. 589-90.

demonstrations of joy and gratitude for the many blessings enjoyed under his Majesty's most auspicious reign."[2]

Yet Parliament had added a joker to its repealing measure in the form of a declaration that Parliament might adopt laws "to bind the colonies in all cases whatsoever."[3] It was this provision, overlooked or disregarded by the elite of Charleston, that precipitated the gathering at the Liberty Tree.

At the head of the little group stood the impetuous Christopher Gadsden, a young merchant, planter, and political leader who had already declared himself on the issue of British rule. The year before, he had gone to the Stamp Act Congress with convictions about the trade regulations of the mother country.[4] In correspondence he had traced out the argument which he thought the colonists should employ in resisting oppression: "I have ever been of opinion," he had written, "that we should endeavor to stand upon the broad and common ground of those natural and inherent rights that we all feel and know, as men and as descendants of Englishmen, we have a right to."[5] It was on John Locke's theory of natural rights, therefore, that Gadsden sought to build his case. Moreover, the men of all the colonies should act together if they would save themselves. "There ought to be," Gadsden had insisted, "no New England men, no New Yorker known on the Continent, but all of us Americans."[6] In thus linking national unity with protection for the rights of man he stood in the front ranks of the colonial agitators. The advice would not be lost on Johnson, nor in subsequent decades on his son.

In renewing his argument at the oak tree, Gadsden now warned his radical followers of the folly of relaxing their opposition to British measures. He drew their attention to Parliament's claim to absolute power, and the argument hit home. According to one account, "The address was received with silent but profound devotion, and with linked hands, the whole party pledged themselves to resist."[7] Like his friend and counterpart, Sam Adams of Boston,

[2]From a quoted press notice, *ibid.*, p. 587.

[3]Declaratory Act of March 18, 1766, in William MacDonald, *Select Charters and Other Documents Illustrative of American History, 1606-1775* (New York, 1899), pp. 316-17.

[4]R. L. Meriwether, article on Gadsden, in *Dictionary of American Biography*, VII, 82-83.

[5]Gadsden to Charles Garth, Agent of the Colony, Dec. 2, 1765, in R. W. Gibbes, *Documentary History of the American Revolution, Consisting of Letters and Papers Relating to the Contest for Liberty, Chiefly in South Carolina, from Originals in Possession of the Editor and Other Sources, 1774-1776* (New York, 1855), p. 8.

[6]*Ibid.*

[7]William Johnson, *Sketches of the Life and Correspondence of Nathanael Greene* (2 vols.; Charleston, 1822), I, 266 n.

Gadsden was a skillful leader of the humbler sort of men; and, like Adams, he repudiated compromise, doubted the possibility of reconciliation, and early endorsed a total freedom from Crown and Parliamentary domination.[8]

The twenty-five men who took such delight in Gadsden's oak-tree harangue occupied modest stations in this community of eleven thousand souls. Among the radicals stood three house carpenters, a retail merchant, a boatbuilder, a painter, an upholsterer, three coach-and chairmakers, a bookkeeper, a butcher, and a schoolmaster.[9] Here were mechanics, artisans, and men of the middle class generally, who saw in Gadsden, despite his considerable properties and business interests, a spokesman for their desire to rise in the colonial society. Charleston would long maintain an aristocratic cast. Its society of a later time would compare well in refinement, says Henry Adams, "with that of any city of its size in the world."[10] The spirited yeomen of Gadsden's company stood ready to press their claims not only against the British, but also against the dominant elements at home.

Such was the group with which the young Johnson had allied himself. By 1766 he had already made himself one of Gadsden's chief lieutenants among the mechanics, and he would stand by the leader to the end. John Rutledge, a later convert to the revolutionary cause, has reportedly assigned to Johnson a key role in the agitation; by this testimony, the Charleston blacksmith was the first in the city to call for separation from the mother country.[11] Whether or not this be true, Johnson's role became that of a zealous aide to Gadsden.

Like most of the radicals, Johnson came from the humbler social strata. He was later described as of that class of "men who enjoying neither the advantages of hereditary social position, nor liberal education, nor great wealth, yet wielded a large influence among the people, and contributed not only to the success but to the character of the Revolution."[12]

[8] *Ibid.*, p. 265 n.

[9] From a list compiled in 1820 by George Flagg, a member of the original group, and recorded in Joseph Johnson, *Traditions and Reminiscences Chiefly of the American Revolution in the South* (Charleston, 1851), pp. 28, 31-34.

[10] Henry Adams, *History of the United States of America* (9 vols.; New York, 1891-1898), I, 149.

[11] To Rutledge is attributed the statement that Johnson was "the man who first moved the ball of the revolution in Charleston . . . he was an upright, influential and intelligent mechanic, and at his own instance, two or three individuals assembled with him under an oak tree somewhere in Hampstead, on the Neck, and there freely discussed the aggressions of the mother country." Letter from Charles R. Carroll to Dr. Joseph Johnson, Johnson, *Traditions*, p. 30.

[12] John Belton O'Neall, *Biographical Sketches of the Bench and Bar of South Carolina* (2 vols.; Charleston, 1859), I, 72.

In addition, Johnson was a relative newcomer in Charleston. He was born in New York in 1741,[13] where his father, John, and seven members of the family had served in 1738 in the troops of that city. The first Johnson to reach the continent had evidently left Holland for New Amsterdam in 1659.[14] William Johnson, of New York, had arrived in Charleston at the age of twenty-three.[15]

What had brought him here can only be conjectured, but the opportunity of bettering his fortune may have been a factor. That Charleston had offered hope of advancement is the implication of a glowing account set down in later years by Johnson's son:

> The years that elapsed between 1728 and 1763, were years of unprecedented prosperity. The increase of population was immense, and in the enjoyment of unexampled happiness, the people became gay, polished and devoted to hospitality. Among those who passed the meridian of life during that period, it was always affectionately remembered by the appellation of *the good old times.*[16]

Johnson's advent to Charleston coincided approximately with the end of this golden age, but this stranger had few ties to the ruling class of his adopted city and accordingly might have little compunction about assailing the principle of British regulation.

However vocal may have been his political dissent from the established order, his status improved rapidly during the decade after the meeting of 1766 under the Liberty Tree. In 1768 he dissolved an earlier partnership and went into the blacksmith business for himself.[17] Soon he was advertising for trade in the following language:

> William Johnson, having taken a convenient shop, on Mr. Charles Elliot's wharf, acquaints all his friends, merchants, ship masters, planters and others that may have occasion for any kind of blacksmith's work, that they may depend upon

[13]Notes, presumably from the Johnson Family Bible, furnished by Miss Jane McCrady, of Boston.

[14]A recent work traces the family to Jan Meindersen Van Jever, an immigrant from the Netherlands. His son, Michiel Jansen, was apprenticed after his father's death in 1695. In 1702, he married Maria Stevens, and their son John, who changed the name from Jansen to Johnson, married Jane Haywood; William Johnson was their son.—Bernard H. M. Vlekke and Henry Beets, *Hollanders Who Helped Build America* (New York, 1942), p. 150. An earlier member of the family, a brother of Mr. Justice Johnson, supposed that the Johnson family had originated in England, but immigrated to New York by way of Holland; see Johnson, *Traditions,* pp. 373-75.

[15]William Henry Johnson, M.D., Johnson Genealogy (MS; Charleston, 1931), loaned to the author by Mrs. I. G. Ball, of Charleston.

[16]Johnson, *Greene,* I, 255.

[17]*South-Carolina Gazette* (Charleston), Supplement, May 2, 1768; Johnson had entered partnership with Tunis Tebout in 1765.—*Ibid.,* August 10, 1765, cited in Alston Deas, *The Early Iron Work of Charleston* (Columbia, 1941), p. 28, n. 42.

the same being done, at his shop, exactly agreeable to directions, with the greatest dispatch, and upon reasonable terms.[18] A strong arm gripping a sledge hammer was his sign of trade, and the owner of the growing business would win praise and patronage for his ironwork.[19] Sometime during this period he acquired that *sine qua non* of the Charleston gentleman, a plantation. The location was in the Parish of St. James Goose Creek in the country, some thirteen miles from the city.

In 1769 Johnson was married.[20] It may have been a mutual concern with horses that brought the parties together. In any case the bride was a desirable match, for Sarah was the daughter of Thomas Nightingale, the owner of the Newmarket race track and of several famous race horses.[21]

From Yorkshire this Thomas had entered the colony many years earlier and had set up a cowpen near what was then the frontier.[22] From cow-driving he had turned in time to horse racing and had chosen Charleston as the site for his project. A newspaper notice of March, 1768, holds out to devotees of the sport "A PURSE, value upwards of TWO HUNDRED POUNDS, given by the MECHANICKS of Charles-Town," and directs those who would enter their horses to submit their entrance fees to Nightingale. An added attraction promised,

> IF two parties will show each fifteen COCKS a side, and fight as many as will fall in, not less than nine BATTLES, according to the rules of cocking in England . . . he that wins the odd battle shall have £50, giving notice to Thomas Nightingale as above.[23]

The new bride, Sarah Nightingale Johnson, was the only surviving child of Thomas and Sarah Amory Nightingale. The Amorys were of the upper middle class in England.[24] An Isaac Amory, uncle of the bride, had sailed from England to the colony in 1764 to serve as rector of a small parish near Charleston. Through an over-zealous pursuance of the instructions issued to him by the Society for the Propagation of the Gospel, Amory entered enthusiastically into the religious instruction of the slaves of his parish. This policy

[18]*South-Carolina Gazette,* Feb. 23, 1769, quoted in Deas, p. 29.

[19]W. H. Johnson, Johnson Genealogy; Deas, pp. 66, 28-29.

[20]The ceremony took place May 15, 1769, and was conducted by the Reverend James Harrison, of Goose Creek.—Notes from the Johnson Family Bible.

[21]The course was first projected in 1754. First races were held there in 1760. For a description of the course and races, see McCrady, pp. 521-22.

[22]*Ibid.,* p. 296.

[23]*South-Carolina Gazette,* March 7-14, 1768.

[24]Jonathan Amory, great-grandfather of Sarah Nightingale Johnson, served for a time as Treasurer of the Province of South Carolina.—"Memoir of the Family of Amory," *New England Historical and Genealogical Register,* X (1856), 59-65, 59-60.

evidently antagonized his parishioners and occasioned his return to England the succeeding year.[25]

In a will dated and proved in November, 1769, Thomas Nightingale, "Sadler," specifically disposed of £1,500, a town lot in Beaufort, and 450 acres of land; the rest he assigned to his son-in-law, William Johnson, blacksmith, naming him executor.[26] Subsequently Johnson announced an auction for the disposal of some of the property, including "cattle, sheep, hogs, horses, breeding mares, some colts of the *English* breed, all the household furniture—also sixteen valuable slaves, amongst which are a good *driver,* a very good *ploughman,* a fellow that has been *bred entirely to attend on race horses,* and some house wenches." In a display of caution, Johnson called for cash payment for small items, and for items above £20 the terms were twelve months "upon bond bearing interest, with security if required. But the property is not to be altered till these conditions are complied with."[27] Doubtless it was partly out of gratitude that William and Sarah Johnson named their first child after Thomas Nightingale.[28]

Twenty-two months later, on December 27, 1771, the Johnson family was increased by the birth of a second son, William. The baptism was delayed until the succeeding Christmas. The ceremony was held by the Reverend James Harrison, Rector of the parish of St. James Goose Creek, where the Johnson plantation was situated.[29] By 1796 six more sons and three daughters would be born to the Johnsons.[30]

But the young New Yorker had ambitions that went beyond the blacksmithy in the town and the plantation in Goose Creek to which he and his growing family were fond of resorting. He aspired to a role in public affairs. A meeting held in St. Philip's Church in April, 1774, elected Johnson one of five Commissioners of the Markets and Workhouse.[31] Although the influence which this post bestowed upon its occupant may have been slight, greater honor came his way the next year. By now his holdings enabled him to meet the weighty property qualifications exacted of candidates for

[25]Johnson, *Traditions,* pp. 272-73; Frederick Dalcho, *An Historical Account of the Protestant Episcopal Church, in South Carolina, from the First Settlement of the Province, to the War of the Revolution* (Charleston, 1820), pp. 361-62.

[26]Charleston County Record of Wills, XII (1767-1771) (MSS; Probate Judge's Office, Charleston), p. 641.

[27]*South-Carolina Gazette,* June 27, 1771.

[28]Thomas Nightingale Johnson was born Feb. 18, 1770.—Notes from Johnson Family Bible.

[29]*Ibid.*

[30]*Ibid.*

[31]*South-Carolina Gazette,* April 11, 1774.

the South Carolina assembly;[32] and in 1775 he took his place as one of thirty delegates from the Charleston parishes to the Second Provincial Congress, the body which was to resolve itself a year later into the General Assembly of the state.[33] In the state legislature Johnson was to remain, except for a brief interval, until the early 1790's.[34]

While Johnson steadily rose in the city of his adoption, the Liberty Tree had continued to be a favorite rendezvous. Meetings there were especially frequent during the summer of 1769. The British Townshend Acts had levied import duties on glass, painter's colors, lead, paper, and tea and had thereby provoked resistance at the North, and in Charleston, Gadsden called for action. The mechanics promptly met at the Liberty Tree and approved an agreement to stop all importations from Great Britain, excepting certain necessities such as blankets, workmen's tools, nails, ammunition, books, salt, and coal. They resolved to purchase no Negroes brought into the colony, and promised to promote domestic manufacturing. Two hundred thirty persons signed the agreement. With aid from the planting class, the mechanics soon brought pressure on the merchants, who somewhat grudgingly acceded to a modified form of the agreement. Through unity, the force of numbers, and the threat of boycott, the Charleston workingmen had won concessions from the mercantile wing of the ruling group.[35]

A committee of thirty-nine, drawn in equal numbers from the planters, mechanics, and merchants, pressed the execution of the agreement. So effective were these measures that British imports the succeeding year were down by more than half.[36] At the peak of the controversy a nonsigner skillfully assailed the agreement as illegal. In the press, Gadsden replied with heat, basing colonial resistance to the measures of the corrupt and oppressive British rulers on the old argument; in such an extremity, men might assert, he declared, "those *latent* though *inherent* rights of SOCIETY, which *no climate, no time, no constitution, no contract,* can ever destroy or diminish."[37]

[32]In 1722, the qualifications for membership in the assembly had been fixed at ownership of a plantation or freehold of five hundred acres of land and ten slaves or personal property to the value of £1000.—McCrady, p. 37.
[33]A. S. Salley, Jr., ed., *Journal of the General Assembly of South Carolina, March 26, 1776—April 11, 1776* (Columbia, 1906), p. 73.
[34]Johnson, *Traditions,* p. 31.
[35]Arthur M. Schlesinger, *The Colonial Merchants and the American Revolution, 1763-1776* (New York, 1918), pp. 140-47; W. H. Johnson, *Johnson Genealogy.*
[36]Schlesinger, p. 208.
[37]Letter signed "A Member of the General Committee," in *South-Carolina Gazette,* Oct. 18, 1769, in Schlesinger, p. 205.

Radical measures called for radical doctrine, and William Johnson undoubtedly stood among those who embraced Gadsden's program. In time the mother country relaxed its duties, only to renew its pressure on the colonies on other scores, even to the closing of the port of Boston. Again, the radicals called for non-intercourse. William Johnson was soon sitting with a general committee of ninety-nine to correspond with other colonies and enforce colonial rights, and Gadsden was off to attend the first Continental Congress.[38]

Events were coming to a head. Retaliation was proving as fruitless in resolving the conflict as conciliation. The moderates were now joining the resistance forces. The Rutledges and the Pinckneys were assuming posts of command, with men like Johnson filling the ranks. Yet much of the energy and the ideological content of the resistance movement came from the radicals. Christopher Gadsden continued to personify the extremists' theory. As late as March, 1776, he was horrifying his fellow-members of a legislative committee chosen to draft a new constitution for South Carolina by demanding immediate separation from Great Britain. For his text he chose Tom Paine's flaming pamphlet, *Common Sense*.[39] The American cause, he reportedly declared later, was the "cause of liberty and of human nature."[40] By summer the break was made. Johnson and his fellow-mechanics returned to the Liberty Tree for an imposing ceremony. A Declaration of Independence, lately drafted by a young Virginian, Jefferson, and approved by colonial delegates at Philadelphia, was read to the company.[41] Its doctrine was that broached by Gadsden a decade earlier:

> We hold these truths to be self-evident, that all men are created equal, that they are endowed by their Creator with certain unalienable Rights, that among these, are life, liberty, and the pursuit of Happiness. That to secure these rights, Governments are instituted among Men, deriving their just powers from the consent of the governed. That, whenever any form of Government becomes destructive of these ends, it is the Right of the People to alter or abolish it, and to institute new Government, laying its foundation on such principles, and organizing its Powers in such a form, as to them shall seem most likely to effect their Safety and Happiness.

In the war which ensued, Johnson took a modest though resolute part. As hostilities approached, he went one night with others

[38]See P. Force, comp., *American Archives* . . . , 4th series (6 vols.; Washington, 1837-1846), I, 527; Schlesinger, p. 378.

[39]John Drayton, *Memoirs of the American Revolution* (2 vols.; Charleston, 1821), II, 172-73.

[40]David Ramsay, *History of South Carolina* (2 vols.; Charleston, 1809), II, 463.

[41]Edward McCrady, *History of South Carolina in the Revolution, 1775-1780* (New York, 1901), pp. 178-79.

to the State House and broke in; from the building the men removed British arms, for possible use by the colonial forces. On another mission he sailed in a small flotilla to Beaufort to salvage a store of powder captured on a British sloop.[42] The blacksmithy itself served not only as a convenient cache for munitions but likewise as a repair depot for American arms.[43]

Charleston, a coveted prize for the British, on three occasions suffered attack. In 1778 Johnson enlisted in the local artillery and several times saw service.[44] It was only after a third siege that Charleston, in May, 1780, capitulated. The bombardment was intense. Johnson stood in the lines as they bent slowly back. The pressure was excessive and after six weeks the city fell.[45]

The fall of Charleston saw a corresponding fall in the fortunes of the family of William Johnson. The first months of occupation brought a brief respite. Although technically a prisoner of war, Johnson enjoyed the freedom of the city on a pledge that he would refrain from acts "prejudicial to the success of his majesty's arms."[46] Yet the policy of conciliation which underlay the parole soon gave way to one of severity and pressure. Sarah Johnson one day found herself under arrest when an irate butcher charged her with passing a counterfeit shilling in payment for the family provisions.[47] Her husband was harried by threats of detention and by offers of a monopoly of the blacksmith's work for the British navy—all of it calculated to bring him to disavow the American cause.[48]

The end of the summer, however, abruptly terminated this period of uneasy liberty. The British commander ordered sixty-seven of the most obdurate citizens to go aboard a prison ship, and Johnson had the distinction of being included. The ship soon weighed anchor and departed for St. Augustine, Florida. There Johnson, Gadsden, and the rest of the Charleston notables were to remain as exiles until the following summer.[49]

Years later Johnson's son Joseph wrote down an account of the exile, based, no doubt, on his father's testimony. Johnson, it seems, although politically irreconcilable, had remained on friendly terms with certain Charleston Loyalists. From one of them he had

[42]Johnson, *Traditions*, pp. 54-58.
[43]*Ibid.*, pp. 55, 120.
[44]*Ibid.*, pp. 210 ff.
[45]*Ibid.*, pp. 246-65.
[46]*Ibid.*, p. 267.
[47]*Ibid.*, p. 271.
[48]*Ibid.*, pp. 314-15.
[49]*Ibid.*, pp. 316-17; for an account of the exile by a participant, see Mabel L. Webber, annotator, "Josiah Smith's Diary, 1780-1781," *South Carolina Historical and Genealogical Magazine*, XXXIII (1932), 1-28, 79-116, 197-207, 281-89, XXXIV (1933), 31-39, 67-84, 138-48, 194-210; Johnson, *Greene*, I, 278-79.

received a letter of credit for £200. With these resources and permission to circulate in the city of exile, Johnson could scarcely have found his imprisonment physically unbearable.[50] Gadsden, alone of the prisoners, remained intransigent; refusing every concession, he stayed in his "dungeon" a full ten months.[51] When July 4, 1781, arrived the little company unfurled the Stars and Stripes, held prayers, and struck up the new hymn:

God save the thirteen States.
Thirteen united States.
God save them all.[52]

Within a week, official news of their release reached the exiles. British prisoners were being exchanged for American. Soon a ship was readied for their return. A petition for an additional vessel to sail at the expense of the Carolinians met with British favor, and Johnson and his inseparable servant, Stephen, sailed on the hired brig. A fortnight later the brig, bound for Philadelphia, was entering the Capes of Delaware.[53]

Another ship had preceded the company up the bay. When the brig moored at Newcastle, Johnson hailed the other from a distance. The returning voice of the captain had a familiar ring. Johnson shouted his name and received this reply: "Aye, is that you William Johnson? we have your family on board." During the "pious effusions of their gratitude" that greeted this reunion, Johnson talked with Sarah and learned what had happened. In June the British commander had notified the families of those Charlestonians who had refused to take protection that within six weeks they must leave the state. Along with other victims of the decree, Sarah had accordingly bundled her five children off to a ship and with them several slaves and some state and federal securities purchased earlier by William. In case of destitution the slaves and stock might be sold in Philadelphia at a good price. By coincidence her ship had met with William's on the northerly voyage.[54]

Shortly thereafter the little party of American refugees disembarked at the capital of the new nation. The Philadelphians struck the southern guest as "cold and formal," but soon displayed generous hearts. The Johnsons were fitted out with a cottage on the Schuylkill, and there the boys spent the fall in a state of excitement. A quarter of a mile away lay a French encampment, and one day the boys witnessed a whole division of American and French troops crossing a floating bridge "with their baggage wagons and

[50]Johnson, *Traditions,* pp. 316-17.
[51]*Ibid.,* p. 317.
[52]*Ibid.,* p. 320.
[53]*Ibid.,* p. 330.
[54]*Ibid.,* pp. 331-33, 386.

heavy artillery."[55] One night that autumn the astonished family beheld the illumination of Philadelphia and soon learned the cause —the surrender of Yorktown.[56]

As winter drew on, this idleness began to pall on the elder Johnson, and accordingly he inquired for quarters in the city. Both purse and conscience, it would seem, furnished motives. A house was soon rented on Loxley's Court; two slaves trained for the blacksmith's trade were rented out, and with the proceeds Johnson put his three oldest boys in school. Employment was not to be had for himself, but as conditions to the southward improved, his plans for a homeward migration took shape.[57]

In the spring or summer of 1782 the Johnsons departed from the seat of government of the infant Republic. William must have painted a bright picture of Charleston for his New York kin, for the caravan that set off on the upland journey included not only the seven Johnsons and their slaves, but William's aged mother, his brother John, and his widowed sister as well. Sarah's forethought was rewarded, for with the wages from the slaves and proceeds from the securities the group was outfitted with a wagon and team, a stage and two horses.[58]

After a hard journey, aggravated by a shortage of food, the party reached Charlotte, North Carolina. William, who in the words of his son "could not bear to be idle, while so near to his home," mounted, and, in the company of his faithful Stephen, set off to volunteer with General Greene. This plan was never executed, for he soon met with General Charles Cotesworth Pinckney, who assured him that the fighting was virtually over. The British had retired to Charleston, and so the caravan took up its march and pressed on towards the plantation. The Carolina patriots had fought not only the British but also the Loyalists, and the ravages which this internecine warfare had caused to their native state dismayed the returning refugees. Young Joseph was then but five, but years afterward he could still remember the "ruined settlements and deserted habitations." The problem of water supply raised difficulties, and at each encampment the boys scoured the woods for a spring.[59]

After many delays William Johnson brought his family safe to the plantation on Goose Creek. The slaves left behind had remained loyal and had thwarted British searching parties by hiding the farm equipment in the woods. Most of the stock, however, had

[55]*Ibid.*, p. 370.
[56]*Ibid.*, p. 370.
[57]*Ibid.*, p. 371.
[58]*Ibid.*, pp. 372-73, 387.
[59]*Ibid.*, pp. 378, 380.

been captured. The sentiments of the Johnsons are preserved in
Joseph's words:

> It was a humble dwelling, but afforded peace, rest, and
> competence to the exiled wanderers. It was a joyful home
> to us—far beyond our expectations in many of the dark and
> gloomy periods of our absence. It was a reunion with our
> family, and our affectionate faithful servants, after an ab-
> sence of eighteen months, and of my father's absence two and
> a half years.[60]

Soon the British evacuated Charleston itself. The family returned
to the Charleston house, and Johnson to the blacksmith shop. Hap-
pily, the smithy was intact, for its owner had adjured a friendly
British officer to look after it during his absence.[61] He got some coal
and iron with his dwindling resources, and he soon had his slaves
tending his fires.[62] Charleston had returned to peace.

Yet the true state of the city could hardly be described as "nor-
malcy." The planters of the "low country" in which it lay were
beginning to feel the pinch of a depression which was to continue
until the nineties, when a new variety of cotton and Whitney's gin
would restore their prosperity.[63] With prices rising, debtors calling
for relief, and a returning soldiery demanding opportunity, the city
entered a period of genuine distress. The Liberty Tree was gone,
for in a fit of vindictiveness the enemy had burned it to ashes.[64]
The victorious remnants of Gadsden's radicals faced serious problems in the stabilization of their new-won independence.

In this work Johnson played an active part. When a minor crime
wave struck the city he stood his ground; on one occasion a visitor
to the shop, Commodore Gillon, the radical leader, expressed concern over two suspicious-looking pursuers, and Johnson "took a
heavy stick, 'convoyed the Commodore into port,' and returned
without annoyance."[65] As early as 1784 the city council had named
Johnson one of its "Fire Masters"; when later a fire destroyed a
large section of the city, Johnson added his name to an appeal for
contributions, addressed to the country people, "whose interest
and whose affection are bound up with ours, and who share in our
prosperity and our adversity."[66] As a city commissioner in later
years, he saw to it that the streets were kept in order, the lamps

[60]*Ibid.*, pp. 384-85.
[61]*Ibid.*, p. 316.
[62]*Ibid.*, p. 386.
[63]Ulrich B. Phillips, "The South Carolina Federalists," *American Historical
Review*, XIV (1909), 529-43, 731-43, at 539.
[64]McCrady, *History of South Carolina Under the Royal Government,* p. 590.
[65]Johnson, *Traditions,* pp. 400-1.
[66]*Gazette of the State of South Carolina* (Charleston), April 22, 1784; *Columbian Herald; or, the New Daily Advertiser* (Charleston), June 22, 1796.

lit, and a wall around the jail constructed.[67] He continued to play a modest but effectual part in his community.

It was in the service of the emerging State of South Carolina that Johnson encountered broader issues. Back in the legislature he was soon deliberating measures to restore order and to relieve the economic distress of those postwar years. A dearth of financial institutions led to an abortive effort to establish a state bank. More important, the plight of debtors evoked laws for the expansion of the currency and for the postponement of debt payments.[68]

These were stopgap measures. In March, 1787, the lawmakers took a step of more enduring significance. Shortcomings had developed in the organization of the United States, and the weaknesses of the Confederation persisted despite attempts at patchwork reform. Some of these reforms this state had already supported.[69] Now the legislature adopted a bolder measure. Its purpose was "to render the Federal Constitution entirely adequate to the actual situation and future good government of the confederated States."[70]

The task of representing the state at the convention summoned to meet that May in Philadelphia was given to five delegates. On the elite of Charleston fell the assignment, for the group selected included John Rutledge, Charles Cotesworth Pinckney, Henry Laurens, Charles Pinckney, and Pierce Butler.[71] They were frequent contributors to the debates that took place behind the closed doors of Independence Hall. Of four blueprints which served as bases for the work of the convention, one came from the pen of the junior delegate from Charleston—Charles Pinckney. By September the South Carolina agents were ready to embark for home with a final draft of the Constitution in their luggage.

When the state lawmakers convened again, a proposal for a ratifying convention was the prime order of business. Young Charles Pinckney led off in support of the new charter. Admitting that it was an "experiment," he nonetheless portrayed its advantages in glowing terms.[72] On the vote to summon a convention there was unanimity. On the proposal to meet in Charleston, however, there was genuine opposition, and that feature of the summons car-

[67]*City Gazette and Daily Advertiser* (Charleston), Dec. 16, 1795; *Times* (Charleston), March 26, 1806.
[68]John Harold Wolfe, *Jeffersonian Democracy in South Carolina* ("The James Sprunt Studies in History and Political Science," Vol. XXIV, No. 1 [Chapel Hill, 1940]), pp. 14-18. Cf. Johnson, *Traditions,* p. 400.
[69]Wolfe, pp. 21-22.
[70]*Ibid.,* p. 22, quoting from *South Carolina Statutes at Large,* V, 4.
[71]Laurens declined because of ill-health.—Wolfe, p. 22.
[72]*Ibid.,* pp. 26-27.

ried by a margin of only one vote.[73] William Johnson cast an affirmative vote on each motion.[74]

In April those Charlestonians privileged to vote filed into St. Michael's Church, to cast ballots for delegates to the state convention.[75] Thirty-two delegates were chosen from the two Charleston parishes, among them Christopher Gadsden and William Johnson.[76] In another month the convention was in session. There the Charleston bloc furnished the principal leadership in support of the Constitution of Philadelphia. To judge by the extant records, Charles Pinckney, the brilliant young planter-aristocrat, spearheaded the argument for approval of the charter, appealing primarily to the planters and farmers, and secondarily to men of the professions. A third economic group, commercial men, would, in his opinion, never attain dominance.[77] The main opposition came from the "up country": that section of small farmers, debtors, and others had misgivings about the seaboard aristocracy and the new government it was supporting. Had any proportionate system of representation prevailed, the opposition would doubtless have succeeded.[78] Yet the coastal area, having the advantage, carried the ratification by better than two to one.[79] The men from Charleston voted solidly for approval; among them, influenced perhaps by Gadsden's enthusiasm over the commercial features of the document, was William Johnson.[80]

The humble dissenter of 1766 had joined a privileged class in 1788 to help launch the new American Union. To him it doubtless appealed as a practical solution to practical problems. The firmer system of defense, the protection from commercial restraints, the safeguards against inflated currency, the restoration of order—all of these would come as useful measures for meeting keenly felt needs.

The same years were bringing problems of a domestic sort to Johnson the blacksmith and citizen of a young republic. His sons were growing up. To fill posts of leadership and responsibility in the Charleston of that day they would need education, a resource

[73]*Ibid.*, p. 33.
[74]*Debates Which Arose in the House of Representatives of South-Carolina, on the Constitution Framed for the United States, by a Convention of Delegates Assembled at Philadelphia. Together with Such Notices of the Convention as Could Be Procured* (Charleston, 1831), p. 56.
[75]*State Gazette of South Carolina*, April 7, 1788.
[76]*Columbian Herald, or The Independent Courier of North-America*, April 17, 1788.
[77]Wolfe, p. 34.
[78]*Ibid.*, pp. 37-39, especially p. 37, n. 71.
[79]*Ibid.*, pp. 36-37.
[80]Letter from Gadsden to Jefferson, Oct. 29, 1787, cited in Wolfe, p. 25; *Debates Which Arose in the House of Representatives*, p. 80.

which Johnson himself had lacked. A few weeks after the close of the ratifying convention, we find him renewing ties with Sarah's English uncle, Isaac Amory:

REV. SIR:
. . . It was with the greatest pleasure we received your favor of the 15th October last. We often talked about you but could not tell wither you was in the land of the living or not nor had we any method of enquiring about you not knowing where to apply. Your information respecting our removall from this place in the time of the war was vary true. After the fall of Charleston I was sent a prisoner to St. Augustine their remained till exchanged and then was sent to Philadelphia were I met Mrs. Johnson & my children who was banished on my account, but by Gods blessing we returned home in health and safety. We enjoy our health still and are blessed with seven as promising children as any in South Carolina. Our eldest son Tho. is with a merchant, a man grown, our second William is at his studies in Princeton Colledge and has a good character. The rest is with us at school. I mention this to lett you know what a number of relations you have in this country and believe me we shall always be glad to hear from our good unkle. . . .[81]

Of the seven children, Thomas was soon to receive a gubernatorial appointment as tax collector.[82] It may be left to speculation whether William employed his influence as legislator to procure this position for a son just arrived at his majority.

On his second son, William, of the "good character," Johnson lavished his attention. Alone of Johnson's sons, this one attended college in the North.[83] Clearly the Revolution and the turmoil that accompanied it placed barriers in the way of formal instruction, and the sojourn at school in Philadelphia must have been brief. In Charleston the exigencies of defense and the disturbance of British occupation doubtless forced the existing academies to close their doors. It is likely, however, that by 1785 young William was again in the classroom. In that year a new academy of the English grammar school type opened its doors. The head of this school, the Reverend Robert Smith, was a stanch supporter of the Revolution; he was also an Episcopalian. On both counts he would suit the Johnsons. Under him William would associate with students

---

[81]Letter to Reverend Isaac Amory, June 10, 1788, from a collection of eleven letters in the possession of Dr. William B. Johnson, of Washington, D.C., and generously furnished the author by his son, William B. Johnson, Jr. Extracts from this and other letters appear in Minnie L. Radcliffe, comp., *Genealogical Records* (Woodland Hills, Calif., 1950), pp. 6-8.

[82]*City Gazette*, March 22, 1791.

[83]Joseph Johnson attended the medical school at the University of Pennsylvania and James S. Johnson, another son, the Litchfield, Connecticut, Law School.

from many walks of Charleston life; the diet furnished included "the English, Latin, Greek and French Languages—Writing, Arithmetic and Geography."[84] Whatever may have been the obstacles to learning, the father evidently persevered, for the son's schooling, especially in the classics, carried him successfully through the oral examinations required for college admission and on to scholastic honors.

It was in 1786 or 1787 that William Johnson packed his son and namesake off to the College of New Jersey at Princeton.[85] Two decades earlier the Scotch Presbyterian divine, John Witherspoon, had sailed for the colonies to assume control of the institution, which languished for want of direction. He had poured his rich resources of energy and scholarship into the undertaking and had raised the college to a position of eminence.[86] Not the least factor in his success was a talent for raising money; on one occasion the Charleston press carried accounts of a lottery in behalf of the New Jersey institution.[87] The president himself made several expeditions to the South.[88] This publicity coupled with moderate tuition fees helps explain Johnson's choice of the northern college.[89]

In addition, the follower of Gadsden must have known something of Witherspoon's role in Revolutionary politics. Witherspoon had served in his state assembly and for six years in the Continental Congress, and in both he had devoted his talents to the American cause. Many a politician of the new confederation had sat in his classes; the Philadelphia convention is an example in point, for of twenty-five college graduates in that body, nine were Princetonians and five of these Witherspoon men.[90]

The investment which Johnson made in his son's education was money well spent. Among the assets of the college were a cosmopolitan atmosphere, with students enrolled during those years from many of the states and the West Indies, and from diverse social classes; a rare intimacy in relations between faculty and students, the maximum enrollment being well under one hundred; and a rich curriculum, grounded in the first two years in the classics,

[84] J. H. Easterby, *A History of the College of Charleston* (New York, 1935), p. 27.

[85] The Faculty Minutes (MSS), on file at Princeton University and cited for the author by Professor Thomas J. Wertenbaker of Princeton, refer to Johnson's entrance into the college in 1789; the passage quoted from the letter to Amory, dated June, 1788, and the reference, below, to sophomore honors received in 1788, would seem to indicate an earlier matriculation.

[86] Varnum Lansing Collins, *Princeton* (New York, 1914), pp. 299 ff.

[87] *South-Carolina Gazette,* Supplement, Oct. 25, 1773.

[88] Collins, p. 93.

[89] John Maclean, *History of the College of New Jersey, from its Origin in 1746 to the Commencement of 1854* (2 vols.; Philadelphia, 1877), I, 356.

[90] Collins, p. 95.

mathematics, geography, and English, and leading to philosophical and literary studies introduced chiefly at Witherspoon's instigation.[91] Witherspoon not only strengthened old subjects—English, public speaking, and history; he went further, by delivering to the seniors lectures on ethics, politics, and government.[92] Princeton by now had built a tradition of free scholarly inquiry; in addition, the public orations and debates which Witherspoon encouraged taught the student to think straight and speak his thoughts clearly. The Revolution had served to heighten the boys' spirit of independence and afforded ample material for public discussions.[93] The lad from Charleston evidently applied his mind to contemporary affairs, for at a disputation in his senior year he responded to the question: "Is the present system of education so remote apparently from the ordinary business of the world a proper discipline to train young persons for its active employment?"[94] The college was alert to its mission in society.

In Witherspoon the young man with political ambition found a mind steeped in the books and mellowed by a weighty experience in the practical problems of government. In his lectures on politics, the president devoted much time to the writings of Montesquieu; accordingly, young Johnson, like Madison before him, must have formed many of his concepts from the president's analysis of *L'Esprit des lois*.[95] Beyond this, the tenets which Witherspoon taught his students cannot be definitely known. One can readily imagine, however, with what zest Johnson and his classmates must have applied their lessons to events of the day. During these very years, 1787-1790, the people of America framed and adopted their new Constitution. These occurrences must often have provoked discussions at Nassau Hall.

Of all these opportunities the blacksmith's son took full advantage. At commencement in his sophomore year he received a prize for translation from English into Latin.[96] And when in the autumn of 1790 he returned to Charleston he could submit an even brighter report. At the September exercises he had received the degree of Bachelor of Arts; and he had been awarded a cer-

[91]*Ibid., passim.*
[92]*Ibid.,* p. 300.
[93]Thomas Jefferson Wertenbaker, *Princeton, 1746-1896* (Princeton, 1946), pp. 97, 100.
[94]Taken from the Faculty Minutes (MSS) and furnished to the author by Professor Thomas J. Wertenbaker.
[95]See William Seal Carpenter, "Political Education in the Time of John Witherspoon," *Princeton Alumni Weekly,* XXVIII (Feb. 10, 1928), 489; Johnson, however, was in later years to give a somewhat limited application to Montesquieu's best publicized doctrine—the separation of powers.
[96]John Rogers Williams, comp. and ed., *Academic Honors in Princeton University 1748-1902* (Princeton, 1902), p. 12.

tificate (in which, rendered from the Latin, he was "guaranteed as to morals and approved in the pursuit of his studies") from the American Whig Society, an organization established "for encouraging friendship among free-born young men and especially for encouraging the liberal arts."[97] Best of all, from among the fourteen seniors he had been chosen to deliver the Latin Salutatory—a privilege, which custom assigned to the student having the highest rank in scholarship.[98]

Like so many other leaders of the ensuing decades, the younger Johnson owed a heavy debt to Witherspoon and to Princeton.[99] To the president's activities in behalf of a stronger central government the young Johnson was one day to pay tribute in a leading judicial opinion.[100] Concerning Princeton he was to confess in a letter to a fellow-graduate: "I have now passed the meridian of life, and I shall die in the conviction that to minds which acquire a taste for intellectual improvement the days of a college life are among the happiest spent on earth."[101] The tool which the untutored blacksmith had furnished his son would serve well in the fashioning of a career.

In preparation for that career William Johnson soon had his eighteen-year-old namesake reading law. By this time the bar had become the main gateway to politics. Moreover, there was work aplenty for the practitioner in Charleston. The luxury which gave a unique flavor to this American port grew out of a flourishing foreign trade.[102] The miniaturist Charles Fraser, himself a student of the law during the nineties, has described the business then crowding the courts. It included commercial cases arising out of insurance, charter party, bills of exchange, and foreign claims; likewise, admiralty causes with an occasional rich prize case. In addition there were domestic issues, such as those concerning land titles and those

[97]The Princeton diploma and certificate of membership were furnished by the late Mrs. L. A. Denson, Raleigh, N.C.
[98]Williams, p. 12; Maclean, I, 349. By coincidence, two other South Carolinians ranked high that year—John Taylor gave the English Salutatory, and Ezekiel Pickens, the Valedictory Oration.—Williams, p. 12.
[99]Collins, pp. 96 ff., includes in a list of Witherspoon's graduates one President, one Vice President, nine Cabinet officers, twenty-one U.S. Senators, thirty-nine U.S. Representatives, three justices of the U.S. Supreme Court, twelve governors, six members of the Continental Congress, and thirty-three judges. The President was James Madison, the Supreme Court justices, Johnson, Henry Brockholst Livingston, and Smith Thompson.
[100]In his concurring opinion in Gibbons v. Ogden, 9 Wheat. 1, 224-25 (1824), Mr. Justice Johnson described Witherspoon as one of the "most enlightened men" of his time.
[101]Letter to the Reverend George S. Woodhull, Oct. 30, 1817 (MS in files of the Presbyterian Historical Society, Philadelphia, quoted through the courtesy of the Society.)
[102]For a characterization of post-Revolutionary Charleston, see Wolfe, pp. 8-13.

produced by the sharply defined classes of debtors and creditors.[103] The disorder characterizing the laws of the state intensified the demand for competent attorneys. A prominent jurist had earlier insisted: "the laws of this country, on which depend the lives and property of the people, now lie concealed from their eyes, mingled in a confused chaos, under a stupendous pile of old and new law rubbish." He doubted whether all the laws were known to more than a few lawyers, and stated that even the ablest of them could not in all cases "have separated the grain from the immense heap of chaff" without a heavy expenditure of effort.[104] As for the profits that might accrue to the competent, one report has it that four leading Charleston lawyers were reaping from their practices annual incomes ranging from $18,000 to $23,000.[105]

Charles Cotesworth Pinckney was one of the four, and it was under his tutelage that Johnson placed his son William.[106] In Pinckney, Johnson found one whose Revolutionary career in state and nation had won for him high eminence, who had recently served in the Philadelphia convention, and who, at the very time the younger Johnson was receiving his instruction, could turn down an appointment to the Supreme Court of the United States out of preference for his practice and his seat in the state legislature.[107]

Not the least of Pinckney's qualifications for the task was his own legal learning. He had enrolled at Oxford in the sixties and had pursued the reading of law at the Inns of Court. William Blackstone himself had taught him, and before returning to the colony he had ridden the English circuit in order to broaden his experience.[108] Pinckney was not the only lawyer in the city to boast an English training; the bar of Charleston at that epoch included many another. Of 115 Americans who had studied at the Inns of Court during the generation prior to 1783, two-fifths, or 47, were South Carolinians.[109] Like the others, Pinckney was well qualified to conduct his charges through the labyrinth of the common law and constitutional practice of Great Britain. One day the student would laud the teacher for his "profound law-knowl-

[103]Charles Fraser, *Reminiscences of Charleston* (Charleston, 1854), p. 71.
[104]O'Neall, I, 35, citing Mr. Justice Burke, one of three commissioners appointed in 1785 to investigate the condition of the laws.
[105]Fraser, pp. 71-72.
[106]O'Neall, I, 73.
[107]J. G. deR. Hamilton, "Charles Cotesworth Pinckney," *Dictionary of American Biography*, XIV, 614-15; Wolfe, p. 62.
[108]Hamilton, p. 614. Cf. Fraser, p. 69.
[109]Charles J. Stillé, *The Life and Times of John Dickinson, 1732-1808* (Philadelphia, 1891), pp. 26-27. Stillé reports that 21 went from Virginia, 16 from Maryland, 11 from Pennsylvania, 5 from New York, and but one or two from New England.

edge," and for "every quality that can render man amiable and estimable."[110]

About 1792 William Johnson, blacksmith, withdrew from the South Carolina House of Representatives. With his son plying his books in preparation for admission to the bar the succeeding year,[111] Johnson could sit back and enjoy his family, supervise his busy shop, and content his public conscience with occasional sojourns in municipal offices.

The dissenter of Liberty Tree days had made his mark. To his death in 1818 he continued to play his modest role in the life of Charleston. When at last he was laid to rest in the churchyard at St. Philip's, his family continued to enjoy his bounty. To his wife and surviving children he left £10,000 and, in addition, many slaves, several plantations, and a number of Charleston houses. In behalf of his minor children he bequeathed a large sum for "as good an education as can be given, suited to their capacities and the profession they seem inclined to pursue."[112] Johnson's most important bequest was the example he had provided of personal integrity and of citizenship in a free society. Of this the children have left a tangible expression. In memory of William Johnson, blacksmith, they had these words inscribed above his grave:

> . . . Through a long and active life he enjoyed the uninterrupted confidence of his country and the esteem of all who knew him. Few men have lived more respected or died more happy. Among the earliest and most strenuous assertors of American Independence his name stands recorded in the annals of his country. The duties of an honest man and a good citizen were the cherished lessons which he taught to his children. Sincere and unostentatious in his piety he walked with God in secret. An unaffected adherent of those opinions which open the Kingdom of Heaven to all believers.[113]

[110]Johnson, *Greene*, II, 345.

[111]O'Neall, II, 601.

[112]Will dated Oct. 25, 1808, and proved April 9, 1818, Will Book E (1807-1818) (MSS; Probate Judge's Office, Charleston), p. 710.

[113]From a plaque in Western Churchyard, St. Philip's Church, Charleston, S.C.; the death occurred March 21, 1818; obituary notices appeared in the *Southern Patriot* (Charleston), April 17, 1818, and in *City Gazette* (Charleston), April 18, 1818.

Chapter II

A REPUBLICAN ASPIRES

SOON after his father's retirement from the South Carolina legislature, William Johnson, Jr., at twenty-two, was running for election to the lower house. For a decade he was to occupy public posts in his state. For the tasks he was to confront his preparation had been broad. There was the example of the father—honest, thrifty, public-spirited; there was the Revolution, for the exiled Johnsons had witnessed the effects of that upheaval on widely scattered parts of the new union; there was Witherspoon's Princeton and the intellectual ferment which the schooling there had initiated; and finally, there was C. C. Pinckney's erudite introduction to the law. At a time when opportunities for public careers beckoned to youth, the younger Johnson stood ready to embrace them.

Between the day late in 1792 when Johnson returned his Blackstone to its shelf and received his final instructions from the dignified Pinckney, and that in October, 1794, when his name appeared before the voters of Charleston, crucial events had occurred. Some of these were personal, some national. For one thing, the fledgling lawyer had tested his professional wings. As early as the spring of 1793, a few months after his admission to the bar, he assisted another counsel in a civil suit in the Cheraw District; in this, Johnson's first reported effort, his client won the case.[1] The next year he defended two alleged criminals; one was accused of murder, the other, of horse-stealing. At the second trial he was sole counsel for the defense and lost the verdict.[2] By 1796 he was carrying appeals to the highest courts of the state. Of five causes which Johnson argued in the Constitutional Court, three were actions for debt, one an effort by the widow of a banished Loyalist to recover dowry, and one an action in land title.[3]

Soon thereafter Johnson was presenting briefs in the recently established courts of the United States. His mentor Pinckney, who

[1]Smith v. Stinson and Ellison, 1 Brevard 1 (S.C., 1793).
[2]State v. Simmons, 1 Brevard 6 (S.C., 1794); State v. Briggs, 1 Brevard 8 (S.C., 1794).
[3]Wells v. Martin, 2 Bay 20 (S.C., 1796); Thompson v. M'Cord, 2 Bay 76 (S.C., 1796); Sessions v. Barfield, 2 Bay 94 (S.C., 1797); Wallace v. Rippon, 2 Bay 112 (S.C., 1797); Brown v. Frost, 2 Bay 126 (S.C., 1798).

had enrolled as a "charter" member of the bar of the Circuit Court at its first sitting in 1790, had become a familiar sight in the federal courtroom.[4] Johnson, however, had to postpone his appearance until 1797, since the court had stipulated, in addition to a "fair" character as qualification for counsel, two years of practice in the state courts of Common Pleas.[5]

The abbreviated reports of those early cases give scant opportunity for passing judgment on the skill of the young lawyer. Yet in the words of the judicial biographer, John Belton O'Neall, Johnson enjoyed in his professional career "signal and almost unparalleled success."[6] Significantly, by 1798 the United States Secretary of State, Timothy Pickering, was approaching Johnson for aid in promoting a federal claim. The Duke of Luxembourg had loaned a ship to South Carolina during the Revolution, and the State Department was prepared to rely on Johnson to support the Duke's cause in the legislature and in the courts. Pickering later withdrew the request when he discovered that the federal prosecutor in Charleston had been assigned the case,[7] but the incident is suggestive of Johnson's advancement in the bar of South Carolina.

The opening months of 1794 witnessed two additional events important to the young Johnson's developing plans. Increasingly for over half a century the South Carolina Society had been drawing leading Charlestonians into its membership and enlisting their support for philanthropic causes. At thirty-eight the elder Johnson had made his way into its circle. Now, at only twenty-two, William, Jr., received a like honor.[8]

On the sixteenth of March of the same year Johnson was married to Sarah Bennett.[9] Sarah's father, Thomas, an architect of some reputation in the city, like the Johnsons had supported the Revo-

[4]Justices John Rutledge and James Iredell opened court on May 12, 1790, and admitted to practice John Julius Pringle, Charles Cotesworth Pinckney, Elihu Hall Bay, John Ewing Calhoun, Henry William DeSaussure, and James G. Hunt, Esquires.—Minutes of the Circuit Court for the District of South Carolina (MSS), Bk. A (1790-1809), pp. 1-2. Pinckney's name appears among counsel as follows: 1790, p. 2; 1791, pp. 9, 10; 1792, pp. 15, 20, 21; 1793, pp. 32, 42, etc. The collection of the minutes of this court is incomplete: Bk. B (1809-1821) has been lost, but Bks. A (1790-1809) and C (1821-1836) and later volumes are available at the U.S. District Court offices in Charleston.

[5]Ibid., Bk. A, p. 1. The cases in which Johnson appeared were Grayson v. Wayne (1797), p. 129; DeGraffindert v. Adair (1797), p. 129; Booth & Co. v. Miller (1799), p. 165.

[6]O'Neall, Biographical Sketches of the Bench and Bar of S.C., I, 73.

[7]Pickering to Johnson, Dec. 29, 1798, referring to a communication sent by Pickering, Nov. 30, 1798; Pickering to Johnson, Jan. 5, 1799.—Pickering Papers (MSS; Massachusetts Historical Society).

[8]J. H. Easterby, ed., The Rules of the South Carolina Society (Baltimore, 1937), p. 124. In subsequent decades at least fourteen other members of the Johnson family were enrolled in the Society.—Ibid., p. 41.

[9]City Gazette, March 20, 1794.

lution, and her brother, Thomas, Jr., was to prove a lifelong friend and associate of Johnson; but there is a family tradition to the effect that the groom's mother opposed the match and accordingly remained at home during the ceremony, pacing the floor.[10] Perhaps the explanation of her disapproval lies in the sphere of denominationalism, for the wedding reportedly took place at the Scotch Presbyterian Church.[11] Certainly the age of the bride, who was only seventeen, would have caused no misgivings in those days.[12] At any event, the groom evidently had a mind of his own.

The match succeeded in spite of the mother's doubts, yet the years ahead of the young couple would not be without their sorrows. Of the eight children to be born to the young Johnsons, only two, Anna Hayes and Margaret Bennett, would live beyond childhood.[13] When in 1805 the first-born, William Henry, died at the age of nine, a press notice expressed in brief words, probably from the father's pen, the grief of the family: "The opening character of this interesting child, promised everything that a parent's heart could desire."[14] By that time, however, two other children would have come to the Johnson home through adoption. In answer to a plea for homes for refugees from the servile revolt in Santo Domingo, William and Sarah would receive John and Madeleine L'Engle into their family.[15]

In 1794, however, all this was in the future. By the fall of that year young Johnson could well take satisfaction in his situation. He had acquired a wife, social standing, and the beginnings of a reputation at the bar. Likewise he had secured the quota of property required of candidates to the House of Representatives—five hundred acres of land and ten slaves, or real estate to the value of one hundred fifty pounds. With these resources he approached his public career.

Yet the politics of 1794 were a different matter from those of 1792, when he had finished reading law. A king had been guillotined in France, and the thunder of the French Revolution was having its echoes in America. In April, 1793, the French minister, Citizen Genêt had landed in Charleston, to be greeted with enthusiasm by

[10]William H. Johnson, Some Notes on the Johnson Family (MS furnished by Mrs. William H. Johnson, of Charleston).
[11]Ibid.
[12]The Saunders Family Bible, owned by the late Mrs. L. A. Denson, Raleigh, N.C.
[13]Ibid.
[14]City Gazette, Oct. 9, 1805, reprinted in S.C. Hist. and Gen. Mag., XXIX (1938), 156.
[15]The Saunders Family Bible. Cf. Will of William Johnson, Will Book H (1834-1839), Probate Judge's Office, Charleston. John L'Engle attended West Point and was subsequently named by Johnson one of the executors of his will; Marie Madeleine was an especial favorite of the judge.

the populace. Even a year after Genêt's departure for Philadelphia the tricolor cockade could everywhere be seen, and the "Marseillaise" heard, in the streets of Charleston.[16]

Enthusiasm was not all that Genêt left in his wake. As early as August, 1793, one hundred and more Charlestonians had formed themselves into a "Republican Society," with a platform of democratic principles and pro-French sentiments. Soon four more of these "self-created" societies had taken root in the state. Many a conservative thought the groups menacing. Some moderates, like C. C. Pinckney, took no part in them, and Johnson himself evidently remained aloof from the Charleston club.[17]

In cities and towns throughout the nation the mushrooming of these democratic societies served to hasten the emergence of rival political parties. The rift had already appeared in President Washington's cabinet. From the Treasury, Hamilton had been manipulating the financial interests of the North and East into a Federalist party; and Jefferson, the Secretary of State, had been welding agrarians and city mechanics into a Republican party to block Federalist measures. Although the lines were blurred and Jefferson hesitated to avow his policies, the elements were there for a party in power and a party in opposition. The resignation of the Secretary of State on the last day of 1793 signalized the trend. The French question had only widened the gulf, as the rival factions hurled at each other the epithets "Monocrat" and "Jacobin."

In an atmosphere charged with incipient party feelings, the voters of Charleston cast their ballots on October 15, 1794, for the state legislators. For the Senate they chose C. C. Pinckney; for the House of Representatives, fifteen members, including William Johnson, Jr.[18] At the little town of Columbia, in the South Carolina back country, the legislature gathered some six weeks later, and the youthful neophyte took his seat.

For three terms, totaling twice that in years, Johnson was to remain in the state assembly. His legislative career will receive treatment in due course. It is relevant here briefly to explore two preliminary subjects—the structure of the government in which he participated, and the growth of statewide political parties then taking place.

At the state constitutional convention of 1790 the planter aristocracy had erected a form of government well calculated to bul-

[16]Wolfe, *Jeffersonian Democracy in South Carolina*, p. 76.

[17]Eugene P. Link, *Democratic-Republican Societies, 1790-1800* ("Columbia Studies in American Culture," No. 9 [New York, 1942]), *passim*. Johnson's name is not to be found in the extant list of members of the Charleston Society.—Republican Society of South Carolina (Charleston) Correspondence, list dated April 14, 1794, No. 1436, p. 11 (MSS in Boston Public Library).

[18]*Columbian Herald*, Oct. 17, 1794.

wark that class against the threat of mob rule.[19] In some respects this was an excellent charter, for, like the Federal Constitution, it embodied only fundamental provisions and left details to the legislature. That it was to remain in effect for seventy-five years proves that it retained the support of the dominant land-owning element.

The planters who devised it feared democracy and embodied their apprehensions in many features. There was no provision for popular ratification. Not merely the legislators, but the voters as well, had to satisfy heavy property qualifications. The net result could only be a conservative lawmaking body.

In addition, by making the executive and judicial departments in large measure dependent on the legislature, the constitutional framers had guaranteed the dominance of that body. Governor and judge alike took office as the direct choice of the lawmakers. The governorship was to be a position of honor rather than of power; it lacked a veto, its incumbent was re-eligible only on the lapse of four years from the close of his two-year term, and its powers were narrowly defined.

Other states had experimented with this system of legislative supremacy only to forsake it. In South Carolina the plan worked well, perhaps because men of high caliber sought public stations. The planters, eager that government should protect their interests, saw to it that their ablest sons aspired to office. To a government career they attached prestige; hence, competence rather than mediocrity ordinarily characterized the legislators, governors, and judges of that state. To the businessmen, and even more to the small farmers of the up country who raised a constant clamor for equal representation, the planters assigned subordinate roles.

It was in such a "parliament" that Johnson found his seat. In a sense it was an extension of Charleston. Of that busy port, the peripatetic Yankee journalist Ebenezer Thomas has left this characterization:

> Charleston was the most aristocratic city in the Union notwithstanding her Jacobin club, with her red liberty caps, and fraternal *hugs*. There was a complete nobility in everything but the title, and a few with that appendage.
>
> The political professions of her leading men in those days, were of the Jefferson school, but their practice was aristocracy complete.[20]

[19]For material on the Constitution of 1790 the author has relied heavily on David Duncan Wallace's excellent *History of South Carolina* (3 vols.; New York, 1934); see especially II, 350-51, 454-55.

[20]E. S. Thomas, *Reminiscences of the Last Sixty-five Years* (2 vols.; Hartford, 1840), I, 33, 34.

This picture is overdrawn, as is shown by the elder Johnson's rise in status, yet it is suggestive of the tone of Charleston society.

Thomas' reference to Jefferson's influence is pertinent. Political parties were emerging in the state as well as in the nation. Into the Federalist party of Hamilton trooped such leaders as Thomas Pinckney, William Smith, and Robert G. Harper. C. C. Pinckney, although a moderate partisan, gradually rose in the party and in time ran for President on its national ticket. Many of these planters and Charleston merchants, in alliance with northern finance and commerce, had worked for the ratification of the Federal Constitution. The party was to dominate the state for several years, and to prevent more than one effort at reform.[21]

Yet a growing opposition was asserting itself. The commercial policy of the Washington administration, epitomized by the Jay Treaty of 1794, seemed to threaten the state's growing prosperity. The policy aroused even conservatives like John Rutledge to protest. The luxuriant growth of democratic clubs, too, had its effect; the disturbing ideas they fomented struck responsive ears among the humbler elements in Charleston and among the small farmers of the up country. All that was needed to weld this opposition into an effective party organization was a vigorous and skillful leader.[22]

The man primarily responsible for the successful prosecution of this task was Charles Pinckney. A second cousin of the brothers Charles Cotesworth and Thomas Pinckney and a member of the same conservative class, Charles was a planter in his own right. He held vast areas of land and reportedly owned nearly two thousand slaves,[23] and he was an ardent devotee of literature and the arts. As "Blackguard Charlie," the traitor to his class, Pinckney has been treated roughly by historians until recently. The supposition is common that his abandonment of Federalism resulted from pique over his failure to secure a federal appointment; and, indeed, his forceful part in the framing and ratification of the Federal Constitution would have warranted such a reward. Moreover, his less spectacular cousins had frequent recognition from the Washington administration.

A recent student, however, has explained this change of heart on other grounds. According to this view, Pinckney foresaw that the steady expansion of the plantation system over the state would eventually supply a safeguard against the more democratic ideas of Republicans. At the same time he felt that policies of the Fed-

[21]See especially U. B. Phillips, "The South Carolina Federalists, II," *American Historical Review*, XIV, 731-43, *passim.;* and Wallace, II, 339-57.

[22]For a careful account of the rise of the Jeffersonian party in the state, see Wolfe, pp. 21-44.

[23]Wallace, II, 340.

eralist regime at the nation's capital jeopardized the prospects of his state and section. Pinckney saw less to fear from the small farmer and the urban mechanic than from the northern financier and man of commerce.[24] As for the charge that Pinckney belonged socially and culturally to the class of Washington and Hamilton rather than to the rank and file of Republicans, the same might be said of Jefferson himself.

As early as 1788, the elder Johnson had heard Pinckney appeal for a national control by landed interests supported by professional men and the educated, arguing that commerce should remain the servant of agriculture and that a fair distribution of money would avert the extremes of wealth and poverty.[25] Charles Pinckney had, as governor, appointed William Johnson's elder brother to be tax collector in 1791, and within two years of Johnson's advent at Columbia, Pinckney was to return to the governorship on a platform supporting reforms agreeable to the up country.[26]

When Johnson took his seat Pinckney's star was beginning its ascent. Around this thirty-seven-year-old aristocrat clustered many youthful aspirants for public office and among them doubtless was Johnson. It was under Charles that he eschewed the politics of Charles Cotesworth Pinckney and "attached himself warmly" to Jefferson's rapidly growing party.[27] Political ideas were in full ferment and the great parties in rapid formation when Johnson began his first two-year legislative term.

Despite his youth, Johnson applied himself with vigor to the work of the assembly. An initial honor came his way in the form of the post of "Cashier of the House."[28] Possibly his reputation at the bar explains his appointment at the outset of his opening term to a nine-man committee to revise the judicial system of the state.[29] The problem agitated the legislature for several years, and Johnson was to play a vital part in the movement for reforming the antiquated county courts. Even in his first term, Johnson voiced his convictions on court affairs; on one occasion he helped fix the salary of the chief justice of the state at £600 per annum; on an-

[24]See Wolfe, especially pp. 63-65.
[25]See above, p. 18. See also Jonathan Elliot, ed., *The Debates in the Several State Conventions, on the Adoption of the Federal Constitution* (2d ed.; 4 vols.; Washington, 1836), IV, 318-32.
[26]J. Harold Easterby, "Charles Pinckney," *Dictionary of American Biography*, XIV, 612.
[27]O'Neall, I, 73.
[28]Journal of the House of Representatives, Nov. 29, 1794 (MSS at Historical Commission of South Carolina, Columbia). Material from this source was generously furnished by Mr. A. S. Salley and Dr. J. Harold Easterby.
[29]*City Gazette*, Dec. 11, 1794.

other he attempted to defeat a bill which would have vested in petit juries power to impose fines and terms of imprisonment.[30]

The assembly took advantage of Johnson's legal skill in other ways. To a three-man committee which included Johnson it gave the task of examining "what laws are near expiring" and of formulating a "revival bill."[31] Moreover, at the second sitting of this term, the body named him to a joint Senate-House committee to inspect the printing of legislation.[32]

Again, when the House received a petition from the Elders and Vestry of the Hebrew Synagogue in Charleston praying for permission to raise funds by a lottery, it assigned consideration of the request to a committee on religion of three members, including Johnson.[33]

On other committees the young legislator encountered a wide range of problems, social, economic, and political. Among these subjects were the settlement of claims against the state and of debts due it, the importation from other states of cannon and slaves, the disposal of confiscated estates, and the alteration of laws concerning illegitimate children.[34] Here was the abundant experience in the practical affairs of government for the student of Witherspoon.[35]

The votes which Johnson registered at this session reflect the influence of the dominant planting conservatives. On one occasion an effort was launched to assign the governor a salary of £900, a stipend that would have enhanced the independence and popular appeal of an office essentially one of dignity. Johnson sided with the majority on this issue and helped defeat it by a vote of sixty to thirty-two.[36]

At both sessions of this first term the men of the up country demanded a reapportionment of seats. That section suffered from a long-standing underrepresentation. Out of a total white population of 140,178, the three low-country districts of Beaufort, Charleston, and Georgetown could boast in 1790 only 28,644, while the streams of Scotch-Irish, German, and other immigrants from Pennsylvania, Virginia, and North Carolina had swelled the number in the up country to 111,534.[37] Yet the coastal planters had exacted a total

[30]Journal of the House, Dec. 15, 1794, Dec. 7, 1795.
[31]*Ibid.*, Nov. 28, 1794.
[32]*Ibid.*, Dec. 15, 1795.
[33]*City Gazette*, Dec. 6, 1794.
[34]Journal of the House, 1794, *passim.*, Dec. 18, 1795.
[35]At adjournment, Johnson was elected a "Justice of the Quorum."—*City Gazette*, Jan. 14, 1795.
[36]*Ibid.*, Dec. 12, 1794.
[37]Wolfe, p. 5, citing census figures for 1790.

of 70 of the 124 seats in the assembly; and in the 37-man Senate their share was 20.[38]

In 1794 thirteen aggrieved counties united in demanding reform, but the House by a vote of 58 to 53, with Johnson on the majority side, announced that no change was expedient. In support of its stand the majority declared that the arrangements had been constitutionally established in 1790 in an "equipoise of interests between the different parts of the state," and with a rare complacency, the low-country rulers called the existing system "well calculated to preserve the tranquility, and advance the prosperity of these sections."[39] When a like request made its appearance next year, the majority adopted a new mode of resistance. After receiving the report of a special committee, the body, again by a plurality of five, decided to postpone its consideration until December 27. It so happened that that date fell on a Sunday after adjournment. Again, Johnson helped balk the reform.[40]

The leading incident of the term and one which helped dispel this intersectional friction was a vote on the Jay Treaty. The Federalists had engineered that agreement with Britain in the interests of peace; but to the South it looked like a threat to its growing export trade, and to the Republicans it appeared to be an insult to France. In the legislature the Committee of the Whole considered a resolution denouncing this measure as "highly injurious to the general interests of the United States." The odium in which the treaty appeared was mirrored in the vote: sixty-nine members, including Johnson, favored the resolution, and only nine opposed.[41] It was an oratorical assault by Charles Pinckney that played a substantial part in carrying the vote by such a margin,[42] and the event was a milestone in Pinckney's political ambitions. Likewise, it illustrates the developing party lines and the allegiance of William Johnson to the policies of Jefferson.

Above the bustle accompanying the opening of the next term of the assembly, 1796-1797, Johnson frequently heard mention of the names of Thomas Jefferson and Charles Pinckney. The one had a growing popularity in both parts of the state; in choosing presidential electors at this sitting, the legislature registered, as against John Adams, the Federalist, an overwhelming endorsement of the Virginia Republican.[43] The other now won his third term as governor.[44] The election which returned Johnson for his second term

[38]*Ibid.*, p. 47.
[39]*City Gazette*, Dec. 19, 1794.
[40]*Ibid.*, Dec. 22, 1795.
[41]*Ibid.*, Dec. 21, 1795.
[42]News dispatch from Columbia, printed in *City Gazette*, Dec. 22, 1795.
[43]Wolfe, pp. 96-98.
[44]*City Gazette*, Dec. 12, 1796.

was to a considerable extent a victory for the new Republican party.[45]

If committee assignments be a fair index, the blacksmith's son rose steadily in the esteem of his colleagues when the legislature sat for the new term. The 1796 session found Johnson on the Committee of Ways and Means and on a committee to report a bill "to prevent the appropriation of money otherwise than by an act of the legislature." On the latter group Johnson evidently sat as chairman, for it was he who formally reported out the bill.[46]

Next year Johnson found his way to a kind of steering committee of three, whose function was to "report what business was to be taken up in the . . . session."[47] He likewise served with units which received the report of the state treasury and reported on unfinished business of the preceding session.[48] Through the committee mill poured petitions on a wide variety of problems.[49]

Throughout the term, committee assignments also kept Johnson in touch with affairs of the judiciary. Not only did he continue to study court reorganization, but specific reforms came before him in the form of bills.[50] On a recess committee he took up penal reform. The legislature, pursuing a popular trend of the times, had charged this body with investigating the penal code and recommending changes to provide a system of punishments "less sanguinary and more proportionate to the crime and better calculated to answer the great ends of justice" than those then in effect.[51]

Several of Johnson's votes at this session are instructive. On one occasion he again helped defeat a move by the up country for equal representation.[52] On another, he supported an unsuccessful

[45]Wolfe, p. 99.
[46]*City Gazette,* Dec. 8, 12, 1796.
[47]*Ibid.,* Dec. 4, 1797.
[48]Journal of the House, Nov. 27, 1797.
[49]These matters included improving the navigability of certain "runs," receiving a statement of the state's foreign debt (*City Gazette,* Dec. 6, 8, 1797), granting land in Columbia to the Agricultural Society of the state for carrying on experiments, regulating weights and measures, administering the system of land grants, granting land-owners protection against hold-over tenants, and authorizing a college in Beaufort District to raise funds.—Journal of the House, 1797, *passim.*
[50]*City Gazette,* Dec. 11, 1797. He considered one bill to suspend and remove magistrates from office, and another, which he reported, to regulate trial by special juries.—Journal of the House, Dec. 5, 12, 1796. When a master in equity sought permission to leave the state and appoint a temporary substitute, Johnson's committee opposed favorable action on the score of "the importance of that office in the administration of justice, being endowed with powers which should not be delegated to a deputy."—*Ibid.,* Nov. 27, Dec. 2, 1797.
[51]*City Gazette,* Dec. 19, 1796.
[52]By a vote of 57 to 50 the assembly defeated a motion declaring the existing apportionment "unequal and unjust."—*Ibid.,* Dec. 21, 1796.

attempt to incorporate the "Bank of South Carolina."[53] This vote was noteworthy; it suggests that Johnson was willing to see the commonwealth supplement the Charleston branch of the United States Bank by a financial institution of its own. It was prophetic of his later tolerance for state credit institutions and for state economic regulations generally.

Of equal interest is his position on a state income tax. This bill set forth that "there are many wealthy citizens of this State, who derive very considerable revenues from monies which produce an interest, and who do not contribute a due proportion to the public exigencies of the same." It added income from investments to land and slaves as subjects of taxation and set the rate at twenty-five cents for every hundred dollars. This effort by the dominant planters to extend the burden of supporting government to investors carried, with Johnson's support.[54] Years later, Johnson would come to think income taxes undesirable, but nevertheless would insist that the states retained power to enact them, even against federal-security-holders.

As his second term drew to a close, a new subject drew Johnson's attention. A foreign war was threatening, and the state was preparing to meet an attack. The scrawled journal of the House gives the cryptic disclosure that a "Capt. Johnson" and five other officers sat as a committee on a petition from Charleston inhabitants who sought to enroll as a cavalry troop. The committee responded with speed, and Johnson, in its behalf, brought in a bill embodying a detailed reorganization of the artillery and cavalry of the state.[55] In due course "Willm. Johnson, Jr. Capt.," of the "Republican Artillery," was certifying a statement of a debt incurred by his unit for labor and materials.[56]

In the crisis the legislature took up an appropriation of $100,000 for arms, ammunition, and supplies. This measure, if passed, would have directed the governor to request the President of the United States to reimburse the state for the amount "as a just claim on the general government for defenses." Johnson disliked this procedure; on a motion to substitute for the appropriation a bid for a direct grant from the United States he voted "aye," and the mo-

[53]The vote was 52 to 45.—*Ibid.*, Sept. 20, 1796.
[54]The bill exempted interest paid out, and likewise income received by widows and orphans. The vote was 60 to 26.—*Ibid.*, Dec. 25, 1799.
[55]Journal of the House, Dec. 11, 1797.
[56]From a copy of a bill for £40 16s. rendered by John Reid, Dr., dated July 3, 1798, certified by Johnson, Sept. 24, 1798.—Military Affairs, Acc'ts., No. 20 (MSS; Historical Commission of South Carolina, and furnished by Mr. A. S. Salley).

tion carried by a plurality of four.[57] To Johnson the task of defending the nation was primarily the responsibility of the nation's government.

At twenty-six, and with four years of legislative experience to his credit, Johnson in 1798 ran for his third and final term. At the nation's capital Jefferson, from his vantage point as Vice President, was quietly organizing his party for the great campaign of 1800. The enthusiasm for France had waned. In warm defense of Jefferson's attachment to France, Johnson was one day to declare: "it was no mere partiality to France which had enlisted the feelings of the American people in the cause of France . . . . It was a sacred sympathy with an awakened nation, breaking its chains, and asserting the common cause of oppressed man. It is true, it was driven to madness, but by whom? Let those who combined to make a common cause of kings against people, of hierarchies and despotism against the liberties of mankind, bear the odium of the folly and misery of that period."[58] In the rising tide against Federalism, there was a similar fear of oppression. To mention only one source of grievance, there was the Alien and Sedition legislation, with its severe measures for restricting foreign-born agitators and for repressing political criticism.

In Charleston party feeling ran high. A Charleston paper enclosed the election results of 1798 in a heavy black bar and mourned the departure from public life of the "best citizens of our country, those in whom are combined talents, integrity and patriotism."[59]

At Columbia Johnson, again a successful candidate, won a signal honor. On convening, the House balloted for speaker, and William Johnson, Jr., carried the day and took the rostrum. At the same session Charles Pinckney won an appointment as United States Senator. This was evidence of the statewide popularity of the Republicans, for according to customary practice the Senate seat this year should have gone to a leader from the up country.[60]

As moderator, the young Republican was relieved at this term of much of the onerous labor of committee deliberations and debates. Yet his vote found a regular place in the records. Soon after his installation the assembly received a resolution adopted by the legislature of Massachusetts. This was a proposal, inspired doubtless by the spirit of the Alien and Sedition Acts, that the Federal Constitution be amended so as to restrict the offices of President,

[57]Journal of the House, Dec. 14, 1797. Johnson took a like stand on a proposed appropriation of $20,000 to fortify an island near Charleston.—Ibid., Dec. 15, 1797.
[58]Johnson, Eulogy on Thomas Jefferson (pamphlet; Charleston, 1826), p. 16.
[59]South Carolina State Gazette, Oct. 12, 15, 1798, quoted in Wolfe, p. 123.
[60]Wolfe, p. 123.

Vice-President, Senator, and Representative to natural-born citizens of the United States or residents at the time of the Declaration of Independence.[61] To this the South Carolina House replied in blunt terms. An overwhelming majority, which included the speaker, resolved that only "the most urgent necessity" would sanction an innovation in the Constitution, that no such necessity existed, that it would be "inconsistent with the Constitution to deprive any citizen of his eligibility to office in the United States," and that Congress, in regulating the admission of aliens, was competent to prescribe all proper restrictions on their eligibility to hold office.[62]

At this session the leading topic of debate was judicial reform. The investigating committee, on which Johnson had served so long, at last submitted a report, and the bill incorporating its findings received legislative approval. This far-reaching measure was one of three great early reforms of the judicature.[63] By instituting circuit courts in each district it brought to every citizen convenient access to tribunals with a full civil and criminal jurisdiction. The judges rode on the several circuits in rotation and then met to form an appellate Court of Common Pleas, or Constitutional Court. The four places on the highest bench were increased to six—a change that was to work to Johnson's benefit.[64]

In later debates on proposed amendments to the new law Johnson took an active part. When, for example, the House resolved that a judge who should refuse to perform any duty required of him by law should be deemed to have violated good behavior, Johnson's vote helped carry the declaration.[65]

In all of this the exalted legislature of South Carolina was demonstrating its authority over the courts, and in the process Johnson was acquiring attitudes that later associates were to challenge. The youthful legislator was serving his apprenticeship in a system where the legislature played the star role in the governmental drama.

This legislature not only remodeled the courts but selected the judges to serve in them. In the closing days of Johnson's final term the houses had three vacancies to fill on the appellate court—one

[61]*City Gazette,* Dec. 7, 1798.
[62]Journal of the House, Dec. 10, 1798. The vote was 62 to 19.
[63]Wallace, II, 459. An act of 1767 had provided for the holding of circuit courts in seven places, and an act of 1785 had set up county courts, which, however, were allowed to suffer ruin by inadequate personnel.
[64]*Ibid.,* p. 460.
[65]The vote was 77 to 15.—*City Gazette,* Dec. 19, 1799. Johnson brought in an amendment to create a separate judgeship for Charleston, a reform which, though much needed, was defeated.—Letter from Columbia, *City Gazette,* Dec. 11, 1799. Cf. O'Neall, I, 73. He also helped defeat another proposal, for vesting in the common-law courts an equity jurisdiction.—*City Gazette,* Dec. 19, 1799. Accordingly equity remained in separate tribunals until 1868.— Wallace, II, 459 ff.

resulting from a retirement, the other two from the recent court act. On December 18, 1799, William Johnson, Jr., was chosen to fill one of the places. Two other young Republicans, Lewis Trezevant and Ephraim Ramsay, were assigned to the others. Trezevant was Johnson's senior by only a year and like him had read law with C. C. Pinckney.[66]

For the expansion of the higher state court there may have been several motives. For one thing, the dockets of the court called for additional judges. Even after the reform, an observer at the Charleston sitting deplored the burden of cases and cited figures to prove his point. He was fearful that the horse races might interrupt the proceedings, and proposed a double shift of juries and judges in order to expedite matters.[67] Again, the court reformers may have had political considerations in mind. Johnson, Trezevant, and Ramsay, might serve to counterbalance conservative older justices, possibly tinged with Federalism.[68]

In a sense, the reform burdened, more than it relieved. In addition to semiannual sessions of the Constitutional Court at Charleston and at Columbia, the judges had to undertake the onerous task of circuit-riding. Twice a year each was obliged to go among the districts in his circuit and hold local court. In a day of primitive roads and coaches, travel was anything but recreation. For Johnson, circuit-riding was to become a lifelong hardship.

Doubtless Johnson had won this appointment not merely for his politics, but for his legal learning and his legislative service. There must have been traits of character and of temperament, too, that induced Charles Pinckney and his Republican associates to work for Johnson's selection.

At twenty-seven he had found a career that was to absorb his energies for the remainder of his life. It was as judge that he would acquire his reputation and make his principal contribution. Johnson was, however, to serve less than five years on the bench of his state. Of his role there, little is known. The terse reports of that era admit meager light on his actions and views.

[66]*City Gazette,* Dec. 23, 1799; O'Neall, I, 68. Trezevant appears to have been a close friend of Johnson, for at the former's death in 1808, Johnson became an executor of his will and accepted guardianship of Trezevant's infant son.—Charleston County Probate Records, Bk. 1, 32, cited in A. S. Salley, Jr., "Daniel Trezevant, Huguenot, and Some of his Descendants," *S.C. Hist. and Gen. Mag.,* III (1902), 43 n.

[67]Letter from "A Subscriber," *Carolina Gazette,* Feb. 12, 1801. The correspondent found that when the court met in Charleston 863 cases were pending, and that at the current rate of 15 per day 400 would remain undecided at the end of the five-week session.

[68]The hold-over judges were John F. Grimké, Thomas Waties, and Elihu Hall Bay; the death of Ephraim Ramsay occasioned the election of Joseph Brevard in 1801.—2 Bay (S.C.), p. v.

Two conclusions, however, are warrantable. First, in marked contrast to what he confronted later, the court on which Johnson now sat tolerated a healthy difference of opinion and expression. The judges were agreed, it is true, on most decisions.[69] Nevertheless each judge had full freedom to voice his own views; a study of Brevard's *Reports* shows that out of fifty-two decisions rendered, twenty, or nearly two-fifths, appeared in the form of seriatim, or separate, opinions.[70] Under John Marshall, Johnson was to encounter a different practice, and in time to protest against it.

In the second place, he now had convictions as to the proper construction to be applied to the Federal Constitution. In 1801, in Sumter District, Johnson wrote an opinion in the case of State *v.* Pitman.[71] This was an indictment under a state law for uttering and publishing counterfeited bills of the Branch Bank of the United States. The defense sought habeas corpus and argued in part that the offense was not triable in state courts, since it was an offense only under federal laws. Over such cases, the argument ran, the federal courts had exclusive jurisdiction.

Johnson, however, denied the objections of the defendant. The opinion bears so heavily on the two issues of implied federal power and concurrent state power as to merit quotation:

> The national government may pass such laws as may be proper and necessary to avoid the mischiefs arising from the counterfeiting, and passing, as true, the forged bills of credit of the bank of the nation; but it cannot be maintained that the several State governments may not also pass such laws, as they shall deem necessary, to the welfare of their internal concerns, in relation to the same subject. The power and authority which may be used and exercised by each, in this behalf, is by no means incompatible, but perfectly reconcilable and consistent.[72]

The passage on the one hand, seems to express a tolerance for a definite range of discretion in the federal government. The Constitution had authorized Congress to punish those who might counterfeit the "Securities and current Coin of the United States."[73] Johnson would sanction the extension of the punishing power to counterfeiters of the bills of the United States Bank. On the other hand, the statement expresses a solicitude for state power and an anxiety to permit states to act in the absence of definite constitu-

[69]The Court was in agreement in 80 out of 87 cases reported.—2 Bay (S.C.), *passim.*
[70]1 Brevard (S.C.) *passim.* A few of these decisions were handed down in the lower courts; it should be noted also that at this period the Constitutional Court had no chief justice.
[71]1 Brevard 32 (S.C.).
[72]*Ibid.,* p. 34.
[73]Art. I, sec. 8.

tional prohibitions or obvious conflicts of power. Here in embryo was a unique approach to the Constitution; Johnson was soon to have abundant opportunity to explore the subject further.

In donning his judicial robes, the young Republican by no means forsook other interests. Politics, for one thing, continued to claim his attention. In the elections of 1802, the Republicans scored notable successes in the state and nation. At that time Johnson penned to his sister a brief note in which he pays his respects to John Adams and his Federalists. He mentions an excursion then being projected by Sarah, his wife, and says, "For my part like a very obedient spouse I will follow where she leads." He then continues:

> I congratulate you heartily on having thrown Adams & Co. over the bridge. I suppose the old gem-man drifted down the stream like an eggshell. While his male-friends tritonlike sounded their conchs around him and petticoat politicians in the character of sea nymphs softened the din by their treble notes. Should the group reach the ocean, let them beware of the whale and codfish who may perhaps recognize their inveterate destroyers.[74]

Another event marked the closing years of his state career. Like William the elder, this William Johnson, even while in public office, took an active part in community and state undertakings. In Charleston he helped organize a mutual fire insurance company; and as chairman of the school committee of the venerable South Carolina Society, he was subsequently advertising for a "Principal Teacher" to serve at the Society's charity school.[75] But it was to a project of state-wide significance that the young judge devoted most of his attention while off the bench. The founding of a state university for many years absorbed the wide-ranging interest of Thomas Jefferson, and in South Carolina William Johnson, Jr., took part in a like innovation.

Various motives produced the charter of the South Carolina College in 1801. Some leaders objected to the prevailing practice of sending students to the North for their education; others, particularly of the low country, found in a publicly supported college a means of uniting the conflicting sections of the state. In this latter respect, the decision to situate the institution at Columbia was astute di-

[74]Letter dated Dec. 10, 1802, in possession of the author. The identity of the sister is not indicated.

[75]*City Gazette,* July 6, 1799. Johnson was chosen a director of the insurance company.—*Ibid.,* July, 19, 1799. He served as a director of a local water company.—*Ibid.,* May 4, 1803. Besides promoting the Society's school (*Charleston Courier,* Jan. 9, 1806), Johnson served as one of nine commissioners of the Orphan House.—Negrin's *Directory and Almanac for the Year 1806,* p. 121 (Charleston Library Society).

plomacy. Many, however, must have sincerely desired to extend to the abler youth of the state the advantages of a higher education.[76]

As state judge, Johnson acquired an ex officio position on the Board of Trustees of the college, and as a member of a three-man committee of trustees, Johnson helped digest and report plans. In another capacity he busied himself with the problem of the style of the building and advertised for bids by contractors. Perhaps it was his initiative and judgment that led the trustees to elect him board president late in 1802.[77] This was a post of dignity, but also of exacting duties.

With a fund of $20,000 at his disposal Johnson carried through the construction program, and by January, 1804, he was appealing to friends at the North for candidates for his faculty. Columbia, he insisted, was a wholly desirable locality, whether one looked to "health, beauty, convenience or society." Living accommodations would be provided, and in addition the president would receive a salary of $2,500, and the professors salaries of $1,500 and $1,000.[78] The proffered income must have sufficed for the needs of the academic profession of that day, for a faculty was soon appointed. By January, 1805, formal instruction began. The new professors drove hard. Within a year a Charleston newspaper could proclaim that the college scholars had demonstrated before a "numerous and brilliant assembly," including the trustees, the governor, and the legislature, and that "the performances would have done honor to the alumni of any institution in *America*."[79]

The South Carolina College was in time to become the state university. Johnson was to see it expand and serve effectively the purposes for which it had been established.

While his mind was thus absorbed, Johnson received a summons to a new post, in the national judiciary. His acceptance brought to a close the decade of fruitful activity in state offices and placed him in a position offering greater opportunities and greater hazards.

The preparation of William Johnson for that post was as rich as it was brief. In time it measured a mere thirty-two years. In content, however, it was worth double that in the life of many another man. The example of the modest, forthright blacksmith was incalculable. His childhood was lived close to the struggles of the

[76]Wallace, III, 27.
[77]Edwin L. Green, *A History of the University of South Carolina* (Columbia, 1916), pp. 16-20. Extant records show that Johnson served as trustee till 1808. During this period he sat on twelve separate committees of the Board. —Minutes of the Board of Trustees of South Carolina College, I, *passim.* (MSS in Treasurer's Office, University of South Carolina, information generously furnished by Professor R. L. Meriwether).
[78]Johnson to the Reverend Ashbel Green, Jan. 31, 1804 (a printed form letter; Chamberlain Collection MSS, Boston Public Library).
[79]*City Gazette,* Dec. 11, 1805.

Revolution; from them Johnson learned that the nation and the states were interdependent, especially in the area of defense. Witherspoon and his Princeton colleagues implanted and cultivated a zest for intellectual inquiry and doubtless furnished the groundwork for a rounded political philosophy. Charles Cotesworth Pinckney taught him the principles of Anglo-Saxon jurisprudence and impressed him, if not by his politics, at least by his integrity.

And all this was topped by a decade in state offices. The son took the father's place in the state assembly precisely at the first blossoming of Republican idealism. There, he acquired a direct familiarity with the processes of lawmaking for a rapidly developing society. At first, as investigator of the machinery and operation of courts, and later, as judge, he learned at first hand the function of the judiciary. This schooling lasted little more than three decades. In the remaining three allotted to William Johnson, the result would emerge in a vigorous and challenging philosophy of the Federal Constitution.

Chapter III

JEFFERSON RECRUITS A JUDGE

O N AN April day in 1804 Judge Johnson of South Carolina turned from the briefs of counsel and his blueprints for the state college to read a communication from James Madison, United States Secretary of State. The letter announced Johnson's appointment as a justice of the federal Supreme Court; with it came a commission duly signed and sealed. Would Johnson accept the position?

The choice was not an easy one. Both the President who had made the appointment and the judge to whom it was offered were fully aware of the gravity of the event and the difficulties the new judge would encounter. The message from the nation's capital, although tendering a post of honor was, in effect, a summons for military induction.

A contest for power was in full process between the Supreme Court and the President. In the elections of 1800 and 1802, "Adams & Co." had, in Johnson's words, been thrown "over the bridge." After more than a decade in office, the Federalist party had suffered ignominious defeat. Hamilton, Adams, Marshall, and the rest had seen their hopes for strong national power, for a vigorous and pretentious executive, and for special safeguards for property inundated by a tide of votes. The triumphant Jefferson had pitched his inaugural address to the theme of unity among all elements of the population; yet he had gone on to declare the principles that would govern his administration:

> Equal and exact justice to all men, of whatever state or persuasion, religious or political; peace, commerce, and honest friendship with all nations, entangling alliances with none; the support of the State governments in all their rights, as the most competent administrations for our domestic concerns and the surest bulwarks against antirepublican tendencies; the preservation of the General Government in its whole constitutional vigor, as the sheet anchor of our peace at home and safety abroad; a jealous care of the right of election by the people—a mild and safe corrective of abuses which are lopped by the sword of revolution where peaceable remedies are unprovided; absolute acquiescence in the decisions of the

41

majority, the vital principle of republics, from which is no appeal but to force, the vital principle and immediate parent of despotism; a well-disciplined militia, our best reliance in peace and for the first moments of war, till regulars may relieve them; the supremacy of the civil over the military authority; economy in the public expense, that labor may be lightly burthened; the honest payment of our debts and sacred preservation of the public faith; encouragement of agriculture, and of commerce as its handmaid; the diffusion of information and arraignment of all abuses at the bar of the public reason; freedom of religion; freedom of the press, and freedom of person under the protection of the habeas corpus, and trial by juries impartially selected.[1]

This to Jefferson was a fitting American political creed and a "touchstone" by which to measure the performance of officials. Congress might be expected to follow this lead, for the Republicans had also succeeded in capturing that branch of the government. Whether the Supreme Court would conform was another matter. That tribunal remained a citadel of Federalism; to overcome it would be the aim of Jefferson and conceivably the duty of any Republican who might accept an assignment to enter it.

The conflict that began with Jefferson's advent to power had deep roots. The wave of public sentiment that had swept out Adams and the Federalist Congress had resulted in no small measure from hostility to the conduct of the federal courts. The judiciary under the Federalists had shown a disconcerting appetite for jurisdiction and a readiness to apply with vigor unpopular measures of the party. As early as 1793, the Supreme Court had ruled that a state— Georgia—could be hailed to the bar of the court as defendant in a private suit.[2] Only a constitutional amendment had sufficed to overrule this decision. The courts had enforced British debts in opposition to confiscation laws of the states; they had maintained to the letter the obligations of neutrality in the teeth of a pro-French sentiment; they had held a tax on carriages a valid indirect tax despite the opposition's insistence that such a tax was direct and hence should have followed the constitutional rule of apportionment; and they had sustained the English common law in denying the natural right of expatriation so dear to the Republicans. Without a specific authorization from Congress the courts had furthermore asserted a jurisdiction to try persons for crimes at the common law. Finally, the lower courts, where the Supreme Court justices sat while riding circuit, had supported the Alien and Sedition Acts and had enforced these measures with a flourish that smacked of vindictive-

---

[1] Inaugural Address, March 4, 1801, in James D. Richardson, ed., *Messages and Papers of the Presidents* (10 vols.; Washington, 1896-1899), I, 323-24.
[2] Chisholm v. Georgia, 2 Dall. 419 (1793).

ness. In the course of these trials the judges had lectured the juries in a partisan and even reactionary tone.[3]

Thus the Federalist judges themselves had created much of the odium directed against the courts. In fact, the judiciary had taken on a political aspect. The courts had overridden the laws and the settled policies of several of the states; they had shown a tendency to decide for themselves to what limits to extend their jurisdiction, notwithstanding the constitutional authority of Congress and the Judiciary Acts passed in consonance with this authority. Their jury charges attacking Republicans and Republican doctrines sounded like campaign oratory. While insisting on their independence from Congress in the matter of jurisdiction, they had kept in intimate contact with the executive. Two Chief Justices, John Jay and Oliver Ellsworth, had sailed on foreign missions during their terms on the bench.[4]

But the election of 1800 had given pause to the Federalists and thrown them on the defensive. Accordingly they took steps to consolidate their position in the one branch of government remaining in their control. The strategy was clear. Members of the repudiated party sought by a variety of actions to strengthen their hold on the judiciary and to enhance its prestige, its power, and its independence.

The first moves were made on the eve of Jefferson's inauguration. In the lameduck Congress the party pushed through an act reorganizing the courts; this act of February, 1801, provided for the reduction of the Supreme Court from six to five justices at the next occurring vacancy, eliminated circuit-riding, and set up six circuits to be manned by sixteen new judges. Before his retirement on March 4, Adams filled all these positions with safe Federalists.[5]

A timely vacancy on the Supreme Court gave Adams his major opportunity. Late in 1800 the President learned of the resignation of Oliver Ellsworth from the Chief Justiceship; he thereupon nominated John Jay of New York for the position and urged him to accept:

> This [station] is as independent of the inconstancy of the people as it is of the will of a President. In the future administration of our country, the firmest security we can have against the effects of visionary schemes or fluctuating theories will be in a solid judiciary; and nothing will cheer the hopes

[3]Charles Warren, *The Supreme Court in United States History* (Rev. Ed.; 2 vols.; Boston, 1926), I, 190-92.
[4]*Ibid.*, p. 191.
[5]*Ibid.*, pp. 185-89.

of the best men so much as your acceptance of this appointment.[6]

The offer failed to inspire Jay, and Adams turned next to John
Marshall. In his search for an able and vigorous Chief Justice,
Adams passed over William Paterson, a member of the Court and
a favorite with many party leaders.[7] Paterson was fifty-five and
was to live until only 1806. Whether or not his age disqualified him
is not wholly clear; in any event Adams told one correspondent
who had suggested that Adams himself take the appointment that
he was seeking "a gentleman in the full vigor of middle age, in
the full habits of business and whose reading in the science is
fresh in his head."[8] Accordingly, a month before Jefferson's inauguration Marshall assumed the leadership of the Court, where his
gentle but firm hand was to shape the construction of the Constitution for more than a generation. The tall, erect, dark-haired
Virginian brought to the Court rare qualities of character and personality. His clarity and logic of thought, his simplicity and amiable
persuasiveness of manner, and his modesty and equability of disposition made him first of the six justices in more than rank.

Even after Jefferson's installation the courts continued the campaign of resistance. The aim was the enhancement of the judiciary
vis-à-vis Congress and the President. The lower courts made decisions contravening actions of the executive and attempting to suppress public criticism of the judiciary.[9] More significant was a ruling
of the Supreme Court. In December, 1801, a Federalist appointee
sought a mandamus to secure his commission from the new Secretary of State. The Supreme Court under Marshall promptly accepted
the petition and called for arguments on the merits.[10] The action
irritated the Republicans and provoked a clamor for retaliation, yet
Marshall proceeded undaunted to a decision in the case.

The opinion of the Chief Justice in Marbury v. Madison[11] was
an offense to the dominant party. Besides officially proclaiming the
power of the courts to annul acts of Congress, it excoriated the
administration for its failure to deliver up the desired commission.
It was this latter aspect of the decision that especially antagonized
Jefferson and his party.

The President's resentment against Marshall appears in a letter
which he was one day to send to William Johnson:

[6]Letter dated Dec. 19, 1800, John Adams, *Works,* ed. C. F. Adams (10
vols.; Boston, 1851-1856), I, 91.
[7]Warren, I, 175.
[8]Adams to Elias Boudinot, Jan. 26, 1801, Adams, *Works,* IX, 93-94.
[9]Warren, I, 194-200.
[10]*Ibid.,* pp. 200-3.
[11]1 Cranch 137 (1803).

The court determined, at once, that, being an original process, they had no cognisance of it; and there the question before them was ended, but the Chief Justice went on to lay down what the law would be, had they jurisdiction of the case, to wit, that they should command the delivery. The object was clearly to instruct any other court having the jurisdiction, what they should do, if Marbury should apply to them. Besides the impropriety of this gratuitous interference, could anything exceed the perversion of law? . . . Yet this case of Marbury and Madison is continually cited by bench and bar as if it were settled law, without any animadversion on its being merely an obiter dissertation of the Chief Justice.[12]

Yet it was the assertion of judicial review rather than the criticism of the President for which the opinion had long-term significance. Although in refusing jurisdiction he appeared to be exercising self-restraint, Marshall buttressed the independence of the judiciary with the implied claim of a right to determine the limits of the constitutional powers of Congress and the executive. For the time being, not Republicans but Federalists would enjoy the prerogative of constitutional revelation.

Jefferson's denunciation of Marshall's "obiter dissertation" in the Marbury case suggests a new role which the Chief Justice came to play and a new procedure which he brought to the Court. Now that the Court was shorn of its close relations with a friendly executive and its political support in Congress, it would have to look elsewhere for prestige and strength. Marshall saw that to gain effectiveness the Court must speak with a single voice. Unanimity, or the appearance of unanimity, would enhance the authoritativeness of its decrees. With Marshall's advent on the Court came a striking innovation in the mode of opinion-giving. The change reflected his generalship and diplomacy.[13]

The reports of decisions before 1801 give clear proof that the judges of that period had enjoyed a rare freedom in the expression of their views.[14] With few exceptions each justice of the primitive Court expressed himself in at least one decision each year. Some of the opinions admittedly were unanimous and were distributed rather widely among the several members of the Court. When the Court divided and a majority opinion was presented, individual justices were at liberty to dissent. Out of sixty-three cases reported

[12]Jefferson to Johnson, June 12, 1823, Jefferson Papers (MSS; Library of Congress), published in *S.C. Hist. and Gen. Mag.,* I (1900), 9-10.
[13]Admittedly there is no proof that Marshall would not have followed this policy even in the event of continued Federalist control of the political branches. His appointment and the advent of the new administration were almost simultaneous.
[14]The data that follow were compiled by the author from the *Supreme Court Reports.*

for the period twelve appeared as seriatim opinions; thus nearly one-fifth of the adjudications found all the justices expressing their individual convictions, and among the number were such pivotal cases as Chisholm v. Georgia, Hylton v. United States, Ware v. Hylton, and Calder v. Bull.[15]

With the advent of Marshall to the Chief Justiceship this, freedom ceased. Up to the date of William Johnson's nomination the Court decided with opinion some twenty-six cases. The benign but firm hand of Marshall cut a deep impression on the reports, for every one of them came forth as the decree of a unanimous Court. In fact Marshall himself wrote all but two of the total. The two exceptions came up from Marshall's own circuit; since he had sat on the decisions below, he now felt constrained to absent himself.[16] Only once was a separate concurring opinion delivered.[17]

Table 1 gives graphic evidence of the departure wrought by Marshall. In presenting the number and types of opinions for three periods between 1791 and 1804, it reveals the total demise of the

TABLE 1

FREQUENCY OF SERIATIM AND MAJORITY OPINIONS
FOR THREE PERIODS, 1791-1804

PERIOD AND CHIEF JUSTICE	TOTAL NUMBER OF CASES*	SERIATIM OPINIONS		MAJORITY OPINIONS BY CHIEF JUSTICE	
		Number	% of Total	Number	% of Total
1791-1795—Jay and Rutledge	17	5	29.4	2	11.7
1796-1800—Ellsworth	46	7	15.2	12	26.1
1801-1804—Marshall	38	0	0	24	63.2

* Includes decisions given per curiam as well as those with opinions ascribed to specific judges.

[15] A full list of the twelve cases follows: Georgia v. Brailsford, 2 Dall. 402 (1792); Chisholm v. Georgia, 2 Dall. 419 (1793); Bingham v. Cabot, 3 Dall. 19 (1795); Penhallow v. Doane's Administrators, 3 Dall. 54 (1795); Talbot v. Janson, 3 Dall. 133 (1795); Hylton v. United States, 3 Dall. 171 (1796); Ware v. Hylton, 3 Dall. 199 (1796); Fenemore v. United States, 3 Dall. 357 (1797); Calder v. Bull, 3 Dall. 386 (1798); Cooper v. Telfair, 4 Dall. 14 (1800); Priestman v. United States, 4 Dall. 28 (1800); and Bas v. Tingy, 4 Dall. 37 (1800).
[16] Stuart v. Laird, 1 Cranch 299 (1803); Ogden v. Blackledge, 2 Cranch 272 (1804).
[17] Head v. Providence Insurance Co., 2 Cranch 127 (1804).

seriatim opinion. It depicts furthermore an increasing resort to unanimous or majority opinions rendered by the Chief Justice.[18] Marshall perceived that the Court would increase the conclusiveness and fixity of its constructions of the Constitution and statutes by speaking in unison. He himself would be the mouthpiece, even if it meant expressing ideas at variance with his own convictions.[19]

Although by this procedure Marshall's Court may have gained prestige with the public, it must have intensified the resentment of the Republican leadership. The Federalists had not been content with packing the courts; not only had their judges issued decisions hostile to the Jeffersonians, but, as the first volume of Cranch's reports in 1804 gave proof, they had rallied into a phalanx under an iron discipline. Thomas Jefferson had earlier deplored the capture of the courts: "the Federalists have retired into the judiciary as a stronghold . . . and from that battery all the works of republicanism are to be beaten down and erased."[20] And now the precise and simultaneous firing of Marshall's guns increased the power of the fortress.

While the Federalists were thus busily entrenching themselves in the judiciary, the Republican camp, too, was astir. Backed by the people's mandate, Jefferson's forces sought in one way or another to bring the third branch into line with prevailing political sentiment. Their difficulties were substantial. The Constitution itself presented several obstacles in the form of the safeguards which it threw around the independence of the courts. Of these the principal was the guarantee of life tenure for judges, which could be set aside only by the tedious and difficult process of impeachment.

In this situation Jefferson's first expedient was a move to reorganize the courts. Soon after the Supreme Court had accepted for consideration the Marbury mandamus petition, his lieutenants in Congress moved a repeal of the Federalist Judiciary Act of 1801. A heated debate ensued in which the sides took divergent positions on the issue of judicial independence; but the Republicans were successful, and the bill became law in March, 1802.[21]

[18]Actually the trend toward the elimination of separate opinions had already set in during Ellsworth's Chief Justiceship, for the number of seriatim opinions declined steadily from the date of his appearance on the Court. The judges then reverted to the more liberal practice during Ellsworth's French mission in 1800. Yet the complete break with the former mode came with Marshall's advent.

[19]See Little v. Barreme, 2 Cranch 170, 179 (1804). Cf. Johnson's later comments to Jefferson, below, pp. 181-82.

[20]Jefferson to Dickinson, Dec. 19, 1801; quoted in Warren, I, 193.

[21]Warren, I, 204-9. Cf. Charles Grove Haines, The Role of the Supreme Court in American Government and Politics, 1789-1835 (Berkeley, 1944), pp. 227-45.

By this stroke the triumphant party killed the Federalists' court-packing measure; for the new act cancelled the projected reduction in the membership of the Supreme Court and eliminated the sixteen new judgeships created in the Circuit Courts. Congress then enacted a new law creating six circuits, to each of which one Supreme Court justice was permanently to be assigned.[22]

By other measures the Republicans sought to affect the personnel of the courts, either through actual removal or through intimidation. The impeachment in 1803 of Judge John Pickering of New Hampshire, whose insanity could hardly be embraced within the constitutional "high crimes and misdemeanors," established a precedent available for application elsewhere.[23] Of the justices of the Supreme Court the most obnoxious to the Republicans was Samuel Chase. Almost on the eve of Johnson's confirmation by the Senate, the House of Representatives appointed a committee to determine whether impeachment proceedings should be initiated against Chase because of his partisan conduct of earlier trials.[24] Had the move to oust Chase succeeded, his Federalist brothers on the Court would doubtless have shared his fate.[25] At the trial, however, the administration failed to secure the requisite majority, and the party accordingly abandoned this device.[26]

Yet the struggle continued. On several occasions Jefferson's backers in Congress introduced constitutional amendments to facilitate the removal of judges.[27] At no time was the conflict more violent than in 1804 when Thomas Jefferson sent the name of William Johnson, Jr., to the Senate.

[22]Warren, I, 209. In 1803 the Supreme Court in the case of Stuart v. Laird, 1 Cranch 299, upheld the repeal act and the act reinstating circuit duty for judges. The report of the case conveys the impression that the Court was unanimous. This endorsement of a detested Republican measure has been treated as a benevolent and nonpartisan action on the part of the Federalist Court. It should be borne in mind, however, that Marshall had earlier expressed doubts as to the constitutionality of the requirement of circuit duty for those commissioned as members of the Supreme Court and that in this case he absented himself because of his role in presiding over the case in the lower court. In addition, Mr. Justice Chase here appears to have joined with his colleagues in upholding the act, although previously he had expressed a private view that he regarded the circuit assignments as unconstitutional. Had the decision been rendered seriatim and had each justice expressed his personal convictions, the vote presumably would have been three to one. The Court evidently acted on the assumption that unanimity even in the support of a measure deemed invalid by some was preferable to a division. For a favorable view of the decision and the correspondence among the justices that preceded it, see Warren, I, 269-73. Cf. Albert J. Beveridge, *The Life of John Marshall* (4 vols.; Boston, 1916-1919), III, 130-31.

[23]Beveridge, *Marshall,* III, 164-68.
[24]Warren, I, 273-82.
[25]Beveridge, *Marshall,* III, 157-60.
[26]Warren, I, 289-95.
[27]*Ibid.,* pp. 295, 298, 313.

Jefferson's last recourse in the transformation of the Court was the slow process of replacement. After three years the long-sought vacancy occurred. Ill-health prompted Justice Alfred Moore, who had been riding the Sixth Circuit, to resign.[28] As one wit put it, "Judge Moore, from a full conviction of a speedy removal by writ of habeas corpus returnable to Heaven's Chancery, has resigned his office."[29] Moore's departure meant that the states comprising two circuits, the Second and the Sixth, would lack representation on the Court. Since the new judge would serve in the latter, Jefferson sought a native of Georgia or South Carolina for the post.

It is no matter of surprise that Jefferson looked not merely for an honest man and a good lawyer but also a loyal Republican. Albert Gallatin, at the Treasury, expressed to Jefferson a preference for a Republican of "sufficient talents to be useful." Confessing an ignorance of proper candidates in the southern Circuit he counseled further inquiry and added: "I am told that the practice is as loose in Georgia as in New England and that a real lawyer could not easily be found there. But South Carolina stands high in that respect, at least in reputation."[30]

Jefferson followed this advice and proceeded with dispatch to the investigation. Charles Pinckney was then serving as Minister to Spain; hence that Republican stalwart's advice was unavailable if the matter were to be closed promptly. Two days after Gallatin's note went to the President, two trusted members of Congress from South Carolina, Senator Thomas Sumter and Congressman Wade Hampton, were busy preparing for the President a statement of the "Characters of the lawyers of S.C."[31] Sumter and Hampton were Republicans of prominence; both had served in the Revolution and both had been active in the politics of the state.

Among the five candidates whom they described for Jefferson there was no secret as to their choice. By reputation, they said, the two leading Republican lawyers were John Julius Pringle, state attorney-general, and Thomas Waties, an associate of Johnson on the state court. But Pringle had once wavered and sided with the Federalists. "Both are so moderate that they only vote with the Republicans; they never meddle otherwise." Furthermore, Pringle

[28] Moore resigned on account of ill-health after five years on the Court.— Charleston *City Gazette*, March 5, 1804; Warren, I, 156, 286.

[29] W. Plumer to Dr. John Parton, Feb. 14, 1804; letter of J. Smith, Feb. 28, 1804, Plumer Papers, MSS, quoted in Warren, I, 286 n.

[30] Gallatin to Jefferson, Feb. 15, 1804, Gallatin, *Writings*, ed. H. Adams (3 vols.; Philadelphia, 1879), quoted in Warren, I, 287.

[31] Archives of the Department of State, reproduced in Gaillard Hunt, "Office-Seeking during Jefferson's Administration," *American Historical Review*, III (1898), 282.

was "so rich that he confines his practice to Charleston," and would probably not care to leave that place. Waties was "so sickly that he would not be able to ride [circuit]. Neither would possess the confidence of the Republicans."

Another candidate, Theodore Gaillard, a former speaker of the state assembly, met the same treatment as had Pringle. His "connections" had sided with the British in the Revolution and had accordingly lost most of their American properties. He had studied abroad and had returned hostile to the dominant governing group; hence, his allegiance to the rising Republicans. In the assembly he had been "uniformly firm, almost vindictive; yet in an instance or two, from family influence or interest he has swerved a little from sound principle."

Fourth on the list was Lewis C. Trezevant, Johnson's friend, who, like him, had studied law with C. C. Pinckney and had later gone to the state bench. The memorandum spoke warmly of his qualifications but found him too feeble in body to serve. While traveling on circuit Trezevant had been thrown from his carriage and suffered knee injuries which may have increased his general feebleness. He drove himself hard, burning the lamp at the courthouse until after midnight.[32] When death overtook him in 1808 it was William Johnson who became guardian of his four-year-old son.[33]

For Johnson the memorandum expressed unqualified praise: "a state judge. an excellent lawyer, prompt, eloquent, of irreproachable character, Republican connections, and of good nerves in his political principles about 35 years old. was speaker some years."[34] The statement erred in its estimate of Johnson's age. He was thirty-two, not thirty-five; yet experience and responsibility may have given him the bearing of an older man. At any rate, Sumter and Hampton gave the President no ground for mistaking their preference.

Whether or not Jefferson made additional inquiries is unknown. The estimate he had received of Johnson's ability, character, associations, and, above all, loyalty to the party faith doubtless determined his choice. On March 22 the Senate took up a list of nominations to office and among them was the name of William Johnson for Associate Justice of the Supreme Court.[35] The same day Senator William Plumer of New Hampshire, who at that time was a Federalist, wrote a friend that Johnson was a "democrat, but I am assured, a man of fair moral character, & not destitute of talents." In

[32]O'Neall, *Biographical Sketches of the Bench and Bar of South Carolina*, I, 68.
[33]*S.C. Hist. and Gen. Mag.*, III (1902), 43 n.
[34]See Memorandum cited in note 31.
[35]*Executive Journal of the United States Senate* (Washington, 1828), I, 466.

another letter Plumer described the nominee as "a zealous democrat but . . . honest & capable." He continues, "He has without the aid of family, friends, or connections, by his talents and persevering industry raised himself to office."[36] This estimate from the opposition camp gives further evidence of Johnson's devotion to the doctrines of Jefferson.

A few days later the Republicans in the Senate reported notice of confirmation to Jefferson and without delay the President ordered a commission prepared.[37] Thus it was that the Republicans after three years of delay gained promise of a foothold on the Supreme Court. All that remained was to secure Johnson's acceptance. Accordingly, Madison dispatched his tender of the offer together with the commission to the new recruit in South Carolina.

Toward the middle of April this communication overtook the rising young state judge in the midst of his state activities, judicial and otherwise. Would he accept? Or would he, like his mentor C. C. Pinckney before him, turn it down out of preference for a local career? He was doubtless aware of the struggle over the federal judiciary, then at its height, and of the difficulties he would encounter there. He would occupy an outpost on the front and would be called on, in the interest of Republicanism, to resist singlehanded the aggressions of Marshall and the Federalists. In any event, he made his decision promptly. His letter of acceptance follows:

CHARLESTON, APRIL 18, 1804

SIR.

I have the honor to acknowledge the receipt of your communication of the 30th & 31 March accompanying a commission constituting me one of the Associate Justices of the United States, together with the President's arrangement of the Circuits. I will trouble you sir to present my acknowledgements to the President for this mark of attention and confidence, & to communicate my willingness to accept the appointment. But sir as the offer of this commission was to me totally unexpected I shall be under the necessity to postpone the resignation of my present commission as a judge of this state until the 1st May next. A debt of gratitude to a state which has honor'd me with its confidence, and an anxiety to promote the Interests of the So. Carolina College of which I am a trustee only ex officio, will I flatter myself excuse this delay to the President. Nor sir can it be productive of any ill effects in the adminis-

[36]Plumer to James Sheafe, March 22, and Plumer to Jeremiah Smith, March 23, 1804, Plumer Papers (MSS; Library of Congress).
[37]*Executive Journal of the Senate*, I, 466-67. The commission was dated March 26, the day Jefferson received the notice of senatorial approval.

tration of justice on this Circuit as the Court at Savannah will
not sit until the 6 May so that I shall be in full time to attend it.

> I remain sir
> With the highest respect
> Yr very h'le ser't
> WILL'M JOHNSON, JR.[38]

Thus did Johnson register his willingness to leave the service
of South Carolina for the more distant and precarious service of
the nation. His comment that the offer was "totally unexpected" is
noteworthy. Jefferson had evidently taken the word of his ad-
visers, assumed that Johnson would accept, and pushed the appointment through to completion in haste.

In Savannah in May Johnson took the oath and in the presence
of the District Judge officially assumed his new post in the federal
judiciary. Had he been a Federalist he might have grasped this
opportunity to illumine the grand jury of the Circuit Court on the
principles of true political wisdom and the folly and wickedness of
the opposition. In a sense the reverse happened. At this very moment he listened, doubtless ruefully, to a presentment by that body
attacking the conduct of a Georgia judge. The people felt "deep
abhorrence" and "bitter indignation" at a judge who had so completely forgotten the dignity of office, obedience to the law, and
gratitude to the people as "to wish to violate those laws which he
had sworn to support, to ruin that people whose rights he had been
appointed to watch over, and to desolate that country whose guardian he was."[39]

After this outburst the jurors made a bow to Johnson:

> The grand jury beg leave to tender their high respect to the
> Honble Judge Johnson & assure him of the sincere pleasure
> they feel at meeting in a judicial capacity a gentleman who
> from having been born and bred up in the midst of those
> people to whom he is to administer the law, is acquainted with
> their wants, their habits, & their opinions.[40]

The greeting typified the change from the Federalist judicial regime.
Judges, instead of constituting a separate caste remote from the
people and imposing with solemnity their judgments upon them, now
would have a new role. Their selection if not by the people was
at least from among them; to serve the people the judge should

---

[38]Records of the Department of State, Miscellaneous Letters (The National
Archives).

[39]Minutes of the Circuit Court for the District of Georgia (MSS), Bk. C
(1798-1806), pp. 404-5, 410-11. The following additional volumes of these
records have been used in this study: Bk. D (1806-1816), Bk. E (1816-1823),
and Bk. F (1823-1834). These and other volumes in the series are available
at the U.S. District Court offices in Savannah.

[40]Minutes C.C. Dist. of Ga., May 8, 1804, Bk. C, pp. 411-12.

know "their wants, their habits, & their opinions" and consider these in making decisions. The voluble Georgia jury was merely registering its belief in the new gospel of Republicanism.

What fortunes would befall Johnson in his work on the court of Marshall? In February next he took his seat at Washington. Of his loyalty to Jefferson and his intentions to sustain Jeffersonian doctrine there is little doubt. After the close of his first session we find him addressing a letter of introduction to Monticello in behalf of a friend who had been "an active and useful promoter of the Republican interest in our country from its earliest revival; and on this account as well as his other public services possesses a respectable rank in the confidence of his fellow citizens." Johnson ended his note with "the most profound respect, sir."[41] This "Republican interest" had importance for Johnson even in his new judicial station.

Johnson now faced formidable hurdles. At the time when he entered the courtroom in Washington he was but one against five. Furthermore, his modest origins might be regarded with disdain in Federalist circles. Youth was another liability, for at thirty-three he came to sit alongside men who were by years his seniors. The Court in 1805 included in addition to Johnson, William Cushing, seventy-two, Samuel Chase, sixty-three, William Paterson, fifty-nine, John Marshall, forty-nine, and Bushrod Washington, forty-two.[42] To his venerable brethren the newcomer must have appeared a mere stripling.

Moreover, the rule of unanimity, now so firmly fixed, and the virtual monopoly of expression which had drifted into Marshall's hands would set up serious obstacles to the voicing of Republican sentiments. Although Johnson parted company with the others in his conceptions of sound political principle, he had to contend with the smothering effect of Marshall's practices of opinion-giving. Johnson's was an unenviable position in 1805.

These considerations coupled with Marshall's subtle dominance— so much acclaimed by biographers—[43] left to Johnson three alternative courses of action. First of all, Johnson on entering the Federalist fortress might desert to the enemy. By shaping his ideas to fit the Federalist pattern he would win the acclaim of his fellow-judges and become a court spokesman. That would, of course, gain

[41]Johnson to Jefferson, May 25, 1805, Jefferson Papers (MSS; Library of Congress).

[42]From data cited in Warren, II, 757-58. In 1806 Henry Brockholst Livingston was appointed at the age of forty-nine and the following year, Thomas Todd at forty-two.

[43]See Beveridge's reference to the "master of the Supreme Court," *Marshall* IV, 443. Cf. Edward S. Corwin, *John Marshall and the Constitution* (New Haven, 1919), pp. 115-16.

for Johnson the everlasting enmity of the party and of the President who had appointed him. His judicial independence would, however, furnish a protection.

In the second place, he might adopt the strategy of the open attack; a determined drive against Federalist rulings would protect his intellectual integrity and his fame with the party but would place him in a position of virtual ineffectiveness on the Court. A Court which operates by compromise and on which the Chief Justice exercises a limited but material sway in guiding consultations and assigning opinions places the rebel in a position of voluble impotence.

Finally, he might have recourse to infiltration. A cautious policy of limited acquiescence in majority rulings and of protest at strategic points would afford opportunity to influence decisions and to retain status. In time like-minded associates might come to his side and perhaps even create a new majority. Meanwhile, a careful weighing of the issues and a disinterested effort to combine the salutary features of the doctrines of Marshall and of Jefferson might in the end produce a rounded American philosophy of law and government. This campaign might satisfy neither camp.

Such was the predicament faced by Jefferson's youthful appointee on the day of his advent to the Court. Whatever course he might adopt would entail risks. Yet to "minds which acquired a taste for intellectual improvement" the contest would offer its challenges and its gratifications. Johnson was not long waiting for an opportunity to explore his principles and assert his own position. The thrust was to come from an unexpected quarter.

Chapter IV

THE PRESIDENT GETS A CHIDING

By A singular stroke of fortune it was with Thomas Jefferson that Justice Johnson had his first major encounter. Sitting on circuit in May, 1808, he received a petition for mandamus which put to question embargo orders issuing from the administration—the very administration, in fact, which four years earlier had elevated Johnson to the federal bench. At the time, Johnson's decision and subsequent bearing in the controversy won wide publicity and general acclaim from the Federalists. In later years his action was to receive praise as one of the "most striking illustrations of judicial independence in American history" and, alternatively, blame as a "meddling" intrusion into matters properly administrative.[1] Was this decision a sound correction of presidential waywardness or an inept betrayal of true Republicanism?

The issues at stake in the Embargo Mandamus case continue to cut deep into the American legal order. Fundamentally they are two: First, what is the range of power properly assignable to administrators? That is, what is the law which governs the "bureaucrat" and to what extent may it control him? How may the elected and responsible Congress insist on a strict devotion to the letter of the statute on the part of the appointed and often permanent administrator? Second, when should the independent judge interfere? Is he by nature fitted to call to question the administrator and review that official's actions? Is the judicial process inherently the safest brake to apply to the executive juggernaut?

"Executive tyranny" and "judicial treason" were the epithets which the country used in discussing these issues in 1807, a year before Johnson's audacious ruling. Jefferson had caused the arrest of Aaron Burr and others supposed to be plotting a war with Spain and the secession of the western states. Burr himself came to trial in Virginia, only to receive his freedom as the result of decisions by John Marshall. Federalists hailed Marshall's stern defense of individual liberty against arbitrary power; Republicans excoriated this frustration of efforts by the government to punish traitors.

---

[1]Warren, *The Supreme Court in United States History,* I, 324; Louis B. Boudin, *Government by Judiciary* (2 vols.; New York, 1932), I, 260-63.

Also in 1807, Johnson himself had a share in a parallel decision. Justus Bollman and Samuel Swartwout, two accomplices of Burr, were taken in New Orleans and brought to Washington, where in the Circuit Court they were committed for treason. They appealed to the Supreme Court for a writ of habeas corpus, counsel arguing vehemently for their right to the writ and against the depredations of the executive.

Marshall and the majority granted the writ. In his opinion the Chief Justice asserted the power to issue the writ and grounded that power on precedent and on a liberal construction of the Judiciary Act of 1789.[2]

Johnson protested the action of the Court and gave voice to his convictions in a strong dissenting opinion.[3] Explaining his silence in another case of habeas corpus the previous year,[4] he said:

> The gentleman who argued that cause confined himself strictly to those considerations which ought alone to influence the decisions of this court. No popular observations on the necessity of protecting the citizen from executive oppression, no animated address calculated to enlist the passions or prejudices of an audience in defense of his motion, imposed on me the necessity of vindicating my opinion. I submitted in silent deference to the decision of my brethren.[5]

Now, with the executive clearly challenged, Johnson felt it necessary to deny the Court's power to interfere. His closely reasoned opinion rejected, first, a general power to issue the writ of habeas corpus, and, second, a power to issue it in this case after the commitment by the lower court. The Court possessed only the jurisdiction and power given by the Constitution and laws and what was necessarily incident to the exercise of these. For support Johnson referred ironically to Marshall's own opinion in the Marbury case. The Court exercised its original jurisdiction—the grant of the Constitution itself—free from legislative interference, but lacked the power to exercise its appellate jurisdiction unless "expressly authorized to do so by the laws of Congress."[6] At the risk of antagonizing Marshall, Johnson thus in effect demanded that the Court possess a search warrant duly authenticated by the Constitution or Congress before it should enter the executive's premises.

Jefferson's first appointee had, to the summer of 1807, stood by the party in power and its program. There is no reason to suppose that the President had Johnson in mind when in April he wrote:

[2] *Ex parte* Bollman and Swartwout, 4 Cranch 75 (1807).
[3] He was joined in dissent by another, presumably Chase.
[4] *Ex parte* Burford, 3 Cranch 448 (1806).
[5] 4 Cranch 107.
[6] *Ibid.*, p. 103.

The fact is that the Federalists make Burr's cause their own, and exert their whole influence to shield him from punishment . . . . It is unfortunate that Federalism is still predominant in our judiciary department, which is consequently in opposition to the legislative and executive branches and is able to baffle their measures often.[7]

Jefferson's resentment against Marshall's conduct of the Burr trials, however, spurred him to appeal to Congress for relief. In his annual message he promised to lay before the legislature all the evidence of the Burr case; Congress might then judge "whether the defect was in the testimony, in the law, or in the administration of the law," and apply whatever remedy seemed necessary.[8] What that remedy might be was left to the judgment of the lawmakers. Jefferson's outburst could stand by itself as a warning against further machinations by politically hostile judges.

As the year 1807 drew to a close, a weightier problem confronted the Chief Executive and the Congress. Ship seizures by the belligerents in the European war formed the jaws of a vise threatening to immobilize American trade. In order to avoid involvement and to preserve the nation at peace Jefferson in December secured passage of the Embargo Act, with the intent of banning from foreign trade all vessels, American or foreign, and all exports.

Enforcement of that well-intended statute proved a serious matter. Infractions were numerous, and during the opening months of 1808 Congress passed three supplementary acts to plug loopholes in the embargo system. The new provisions strengthened the penalties for violations and raised additional barriers to evasion by vessels pretending to engage in the coastwise trade. It was under the third of these amending acts that the Embargo Mandamus case would come before Johnson. Section 11 authorized the collectors of the several ports "to detain any vessel ostensibly bound with a cargo to some other port of the United States, whenever in their opinions the intention is to violate or evade any of the provisions of the act laying an embargo, until the decision of the President of the United States be had thereupon."[9]

Yet Jefferson soon found this provision in and of itself unsatisfactory. In spite of the recent changes, evasions of the embargo especially by "coastal" ships continued. A New York journal slyly reported:

[7]Jefferson to James Bowdoin, Jr., April 2, 1807, Temple-Bowdoin Papers (MSS; Massachusetts Historical Society Collection), quoted in Warren, I, 315 n.

[8]Thomas Jefferson, Seventh Annual Message, Oct. 27, 1807, Richardson, *Messages and Papers of the Presidents*, I, 429.

[9]Act of April 25, 1808, 2 Stat. 499, 501.

> Since the permanent embargo laid on by Mr. Jefferson there
> seems to be a radical change in the Heavenly bodies. Al-
> most every vessel employed in the coasting trade, has, the
> moment she got to sea (no matter what port bound to in
> the United States) met with a head wind and continual and
> violent gales, sprung a mast, or started a butt, and been
> obliged to put into some of the West-India Islands in *great
> distress, very much to the prejudice of the interests of the
> owner of course.*[10]

In the face of these violations Jefferson acted with dispatch. First,
he enlisted the cooperation of the state governors in a plan to supervise the flow of necessary commodities from one state to another.
His purpose was to "ensure a supply of the real wants of our citizens, and at the same time prevent those wants from being made
a cover for the crimes against their country, which unprincipled ad-
venturers are in the habit of committing."[11]

Second, he had the Treasury dispatch a circular to the collectors
of the ports to guide them in making detentions. This order, dated
May 6, warned the port officers to be on the alert for excessive ship-
ments of certain commodities, such as flour, and named such ship-
ments adequate cause for the detention of vessels loaded with them.
The order required weekly reporting of vessels and cargoes:

> As it was the great leading object of the Legislature in giv-
> ing the power of detention, he [the President] considers it his
> duty in the execution of it, to give complete effect to the
> embargo laws. He recommends, therefore, that every shipment
> of the above articles for a place where they cannot be wanted
> for consumption, should be detained.[12]

Whereas the statute had given the collectors discretion in determining what vessels should be detained, the President in his anxiety
to curb suspicious commerce had sought by an express rule to control that discretion. In other words, an act made discretionary by the
statute was made ministerial by the Treasury order.

Such were the instructions which in May reached Simeon Theus,
Collector of the Port of Charleston. Hardly had that official digested
the orders before certain merchants and shipowners applied to him
for clearance papers; their ships laden with cotton and rice were
bound, they alleged, for Baltimore. Theus refused their request
and the petitioners carried their case to the Circuit Court then sitting in Charleston. Their appeal was for a writ of mandamus to
compel the collector to issue the clearance and was addressed to the

[10]*New York Herald,* republished in the *Charleston Courier,* May 25, 1808.
[11]Jefferson to the Governors of Orleans, Georgia, South Carolina, Massachusetts, and New Hampshire, May 6, 1808, *Charleston Courier,* May 25,
1808.
[12]Circular signed by Albert Gallatin, *Charleston Courier,* May 23, 1808.

judges composing the Court—the District Judge and William Johnson, Jr.

In an affidavit the shippers argued their cause. The ships would be damaged by worms unless moved; in lieu of ballast two hundred barrels of rice had been taken on board, freight free for shipment to Baltimore; and the collector had refused clearance on the sole ground that his instructions bound him to refuse it, although he could find no reason for suspecting an attempt to violate the law.[13]

With all of this Theus was in full agreement. When the Court ordered him to show cause why a mandamus should not issue, he confessed the quandary in which he found himself. Under the law he saw no justification for detention; it was only under the instructions that he had acted, for as a "public officer" he thought himself "bound to obey" them. ". . . being unwilling on the one hand, to injure individuals; and on the other, equally so to commit a breach of his duty, he submits the question to the court, upon the cause . . . ."[14] In going to the Court, Theus was doing the obvious thing. Had he disobeyed the orders he was subject to removal by the Executive; had he obeyed them he might be liable for damages, since by an earlier decision Marshall's Court had held a subordinate executive officer financially responsible for enforcing illegal orders of a superior.[15]

The circuit judge met the issue with dispatch. There is a family tradition among the Johnsons that the justice on learning of the controversy took his walking stick, put on his hat, and "boarded each of these vessels in turn and surprised the captains upon requesting to see their orders for he tore them up and issued an order in their stead permitting them to sail."[16] The anecdote is suggestive of the directness with which Johnson acted.

Three days after the filing of the petition Johnson and his colleague issued their decision. Since the case was presented without argument it is likely that no issue was made of the jurisdiction of the Court. In his haste Johnson almost ignored that question: "It is not denied that if the petitioners be legally entitled to a clearance, this Court may interpose its authority, by the writ of mandamus to compel the collector to grant it."[17] Thus was the whole issue of judicial intervention put to one side.

[13]The petition was filed May 25, 1808, Minutes C.C. Dist. of S.C., Bk. A, p. 339.
[14]Gilchrist v. Collector, 10 Fed. Cas. 355, 356, No. 5420 (C.C. Dist. of S.C., 1808).
[15]Little v. Barreme, 2 Cranch 170 (1804).
[16]William Henry Johnson, A Partial Genealogy of the Johnson Family (MS; 1931), reproduced here through the courtesy of Mrs. I. G. Ball and the kind assistance of Miss Anne King Gregorie, of Charleston.
[17]10 Fed. Cas. 356.

Johnson moved on to the merits of the case to determine whether the act of Congress authorized the detention and, if not, whether the instructions unsupported by statute would justify the refusal of clearance. He found no doubt on the latter question:

> The officers of our government, from the highest to the lowest, are equally subjected to legal restraint; and it is confidently believed that all of them feel themselves equally incapable, as well from law as inclination, to attempt an unsanctioned encroachment upon individual liberty.[18]

The instructions could operate only as recommendations, for Congress according to Johnson had clearly vested in the collectors the determination of the question.

> Congress might have vested this discretion in the president, the secretary of the treasury, or any other officer, in which they thought proper to vest it; but, having vested the right of granting or refusing in the collector, with an appeal to the president only in case of refusal—the right of granting clearances remains in him unimpaired and unrestricted.[19]

Furthermore he observed that the shipment appeared proper even under the terms of the instructions.

This was a clear assertion of the rule of law. Executive officers even at the highest level must conform to the spirit and letter of the statutes of the Congress. As a rebuke to Jefferson the decision won instant acclaim from the Federalist press. In Charleston itself the *Courier* hailed its salutary effect on trade and found it a "memorable example" of the need of an independent judiciary.[20] Republicans on their part deplored this fresh instance of judicial irresponsibility and renewed the cry for political control over judges.[21]

Soon the President himself was voicing alarm over the decision; his dismay was greater, he confessed to Charles Pinckney, because of the place from which the opinion had come, since it could scarcely be explained by any "political waywardness." In this same letter Jefferson set forth at length the reasons which had made the instructions seem essential. A central control of the clearance of vessels would make for greater uniformity in enforcement, the elimination of favoritism by individual collectors, and avoidance of temporary detentions. He warned that this decision had "too many important bearings on the constitutional organization of our government to let it go off so carelessly."[22]

[18]*Ibid.*
[19]*Ibid.*
[20]May 30, 1808, Warren, I, 326-28.
[21]Warren, I, 328-29.
[22]Jefferson to Governor Charles Pinckney, July 18, 1808, Jefferson, *Writings,* ed. A. A. Lipscomb (20 vols.; Washington, 1903), XII, 104.

And the President made good on his threat. An opinion rebutting Johnson's ruling went out from the Attorney-General, Caesar A. Rodney, to all collectors and marshals. The statement, widely published at the time, was meant in a sense to overrule the Mandamus decision insofar as it might apply to future cases.[23]

Rodney opened his argument by an attack on the weak point in Johnson's decision—the matter of jurisdiction. The writ of mandamus was a prerogative writ which in England only the Court of King's Bench might issue. In America, he stated, courts acquired jurisdiction only through the Constitution or statutes. As Johnson had done in the Bollman case the previous year, Rodney called for an express showing of authority to issue the writ and found none in the statutes. Since the Circuit Court had lacked jurisdiction, consent of the parties could not confer it, and much less could "the mere tacit acquiescence of a party, in not denying their [the Court's] authority."[24]

Rodney warned of the dangers which might flow from judicial intervention in the operations of the executive.

> It might perhaps with propriety be added, that there does not appear in the constitution of the United States any thing which favours an indefinite extension of the jurisdiction of courts, over the ministerial officer within the executive department. On the contrary, the careful discrimination which is marked between the several departments should dictate great circumspection to each, in the exercise of powers having any relation to the other. . . . there appears to be a material and obvious distinction, between a course of proceeding which redresses a wrong committed by an executive officer, and an interposition by a mandatory writ, taking the executive authority out of the hands of the president, and prescribing the course, which he and the agents of any department must pursue. In one case the executive is left free to act in his proper sphere, but it is held to strict responsibility; in the other all responsibility is taken away; and he acts agreeably to judicial mandate . . . . If in a case like the present, where the law vests a duty and a discretion in an executive officer, a court can not only administer redress against the misuse of the authority, but previously direct the use to be made of it, it would seem that under the name of a judicial power, an executive function is necessarily assumed, and that part of the constitution perhaps defeated, which makes it the duty of the president to take care that the laws be faithfully executed.[25]

[23]"Letter from the Attorney General to the President of the United States, relative to the proceedings of the Circuit Court of South Carolina in the case of The Resource," 10 Fed. Cas. 357.

[24]*Ibid.*, p. 358.

[25]*Ibid.*, p. 358-59.

Such a practice, said he, if pursued by the courts would result only in confusion. Rodney pointed out that the lower courts might differ in their applications of executive instructions to citizens of the different states and thus destroy "that unity of administration which the constitution meant to secure by placing the executive power for them all, in the same head."[26] Likewise this interference by judges would destroy the accountability of the executive to Congress and the nation.

This was less a defense of the executive than an assault on the judge. To soothe the feelings of the latter Rodney expressed respect for the Charleston Circuit Court with one of the members of which he was "personally acquainted" and for whose character he felt the "sincerest regard."[27]

That this opinion of the government's chief counsel questioning the legality of the judicial decision should have reached the press was unprecedented. The judge at whom it was aimed replied in kind. On August 26 Johnson completed his rejoinder, and in October this voluminous statement appeared in the press.[28] He returned Rodney's words of personal esteem but declared that the publication of the opinion had spurred him to defend himself before the public. The whole affair, he felt, might have been handled with greater dignity in another way.

The bulk of Johnson's argument dealt with the orders of the executive to the port collectors. Every inhabitant of the United States had a right to carry on commerce from one port to another unless restricted by law. He had as much of a right to this freedom, said Johnson in language reminiscent of Christopher Gadsden's, as "to the air that he breathes, or the food that he consumes."[29] No officer of the executive could restrict that right except under express statutory authority. Hence the collector was bound to grant clearance when the shipper had complied with the letter of the law. Johnson could find no authorization to the executive under the act to lay down general rules to govern in advance the conduct of collectors. The mandamus therefore merely secured to the collector the exercise of the power vested in him by law and to the citizen the benefit of the collector's being released from an illegal restraint.

In defense of his jurisdiction Johnson explained that he had expressly questioned the United States Attorney in Charleston to de-

[26]*Ibid.*, p. 359.
[27]*Ibid.*
[28]Judge Johnson's remarks on the publication of the Attorney General's letter to the President, on the subject of the mandamus issued by the Circuit Court of South Carolina to the collector, in the case of The Resource," published in the *Charleston Courier*, Oct. 15, 17, 18, 1808. 10 Fed. Cas. 359. The reply was republished widely in the northern press, Warren, I, 335.
[29]10 Fed. Cas. 360.

termine whether that official wished to dispute the power to issue the writ. The official had made no objection; and Johnson found a suitable apology in the "high respect in which that gentleman's talents and information are held" for proceeding with the case.[30] That Rodney had gone to the press with his argument constituted proof for Johnson that the executive regarded its orders as commands rather than as recommendations to collectors.

Johnson then set up three arguments to support his assumption of jurisdiction. First, the judicial power vested in the courts might itself draw with it a power to deal with such a case as this. Where law governs, courts necessarily serve as intermediaries between the government and the governed. This requires "a judiciary sufficiently independent to disregard the will of power, and sufficiently energetic to secure to the citizen the full enjoyment of his rights."[31] Power to issue the writ could be inferred from jurisdiction granted to the courts by Congress and from the nature of judicial power itself.

Second, the Circuit Court itself possessed the right to issue the writ. The statutes presented uncertainties, however, and Johnson favored "the introduction of philological correctness into our laws at some stage of their progress . . . ."[32]

Third, mandamus was proper in the case in question. The Court might protect the right of the collector to the exercise of personal judgment from illegal interference. Under the law the President could interfere only where specific detention orders were appealed. Congress might have bestowed on the President broad power to govern the matter, but that it had failed to do. Against the collector mandamus would lie.

Rodney's charge of judicial interference received a retort from the judge:

> The courts do not pretend to impose any restraint upon any officer of government, but what results from a just construction of the laws of the United States. Of these laws the courts are the constitutional expositors; and every department of government must submit to their exposition; for laws have no legal meaning but what is given them by the courts to whose exposition they are submitted. It is against the law, therefore, and not the courts, that the executive should urge the charge of usurpation and restraint: a restraint which may at times be productive of inconveniences, but which is certainly very consistent with the nature of our government: one which it is very possible the president may have deserved the plaudits of his country for having transcended, in ordering detentions not

[30]*Ibid.*, p. 361.
[31]*Ibid.*
[32]10 Fed. Cas. 363.

within the embargo acts, but which notwithstanding it is the duty of our courts to encounter the odium of imposing.[33]

To Rodney's insistence upon executive accountability to Congress Johnson objected. To hold the President responsible only to Congress and all his subordinates responsible only to him, with impeachment or action for damages the sole recourse of the citizen, would be "organizing a band, which in the hands of an unprincipled and intrepid president (and we may have the misfortune to see such a one elevated to that post) could be directed with an effect, but once paralleled in history."[34]

Johnson returned to his belief in the supremacy of law. The law assigned rights and duties to all, and courts existed to deal with both.

Yet he was ready to admit qualifications to the sweeping doctrine of judicial omnicompetence. The courts had no controlling power over the executive. They could not interfere where a discretion was constitutionally vested in an officer or where an agent was a mere instrument of a superior. There, only action for damages was appropriate, for such an action examined only the motives of an officer, to determine whether his acts had been prompted by "express malice or daring disregard to propriety."[35] For an elaboration of this idea Johnson directed Rodney to the Marbury case.

Moreover the judge now wavered in his confidence in his own jurisdiction. The Court might have acted differently had the collector raised the issue of the Court's authority to proceed or stated merely that he had acted in accordance with his statutory discretion. That would have saved the judge from the thankless task of deciding the legal questions at stake in the case. Johnson insisted that his own motives were pure:

It is very possible that the court may have erred in their decision. It is enough, however, and all that a judge, who has understanding enough to be conscious of his own fallibility, can pretend to, that there existed grounds at least specious for the issuing of the mandamus. Though the laws had not vested the power, the submission of the officers of government would, at least, excuse the act of the court. There never existed a stronger case for calling forth the powers of a court; and whatever censure the executive sanction may draw upon us, nothing can deprive us of the consciousness of having acted with firmness, impartiality and an honest intention to discharge our duty.[36]

[33]*Ibid.*, p. 364.
[34]*Ibid.*, p. 365.
[35]*Ibid.*
[36]10 Fed. Cas. 366.

In short, Rodney had gone to the public not to prove that the executive had been right but to argue that the judiciary lacked power to prevent its doing wrong. That, at least, was Johnson's summation of the position of the executive. In the course of his reply Jefferson's first appointee had voiced opinions of court power not unlike those of Marshall himself. In contrast to his circumspect stand in the Bollman decision, he had assumed jurisdiction without a clear showing of express constitutional or statutory authority. Courts ought, he insisted, to interfere where officials lacked legal power to act or where their action sprang from improper motives. That the executive had erred he had no doubt. The President and his subordinate officers could do only those things which the law sanctioned.[37]

Whatever may have been Johnson's true motives—concern for the rights of traders, confidence in the soundness of the rule of law, or mere pugnacity—he had risked his reputation with the Republican party in resisting the express will of the President. And the blunt ruling in the Embargo Mandamus case had several important effects. Two of these were immediate.

When Johnson next showed his face in the Circuit Court rooms in Georgia he faced a grand jury agitated by his recent conduct. This time the outspoken jurors leveled a strongly worded presentment at Johnson himself. They stated as a grievance his "daring precipitancy" in meddling with the execution of the embargo system; his arguments they denounced as inconsequential; the government should increase its exertions to halt foreign trade.[38]

The target of this attack showed no hesitancy in voicing an answer. Johnson told the jury he felt only a sense of regret at seeing so many upright citizens impelled into this action by a "delusion, which a little inquiry would have effectively removed." He defended his decision by disclaiming any wish to embarrass the carrying out of

[37]The supremacy of statutes over administration Johnson confirmed in several later cases. Concurring in Gelston v. Hoyt, 3 Wheat. 246 (1818), he found that a neutrality act had failed to empower the President to authorize the seizure as illegal. In the Apollon, Minutes C.C. Dist. of Ga. (1822), Bk. E., p. 335 (or see newspaper copy of the opinion accompanying a letter from Richard W. Habersham to J. Q. Adams, Jan. 10, 1823, Records of the Dept. of State, Miscellaneous Letters, Jan. to Feb., 1823, National Archives), Johnson held invalid seizure of a French vessel under a tonnage act; no instructions from any department transcending "those laws which are equally obligatory upon all our public functionaries" could justify the seizure. This was affirmed by the Supreme Court in the Apollon, 9 Wheat. 362 (1824). In Herbert and Morel v. the Post Master General (C.C. Dist. of Ga., 1824), published in Savannah Republican, Jan. 11, 1825, he held unauthorized by postal statutes an official bond exacted of the Savannah postmaster; to justify the taking of such bonds would require from Congress a "delegated and specific power."
[38]Minutes C.C. Dist. of Ga., Bk. D, pp. 125-41, published in the Charleston Times, Jan. 17, 1809; for other references see Warren, I, 338 n.

the embargo laws; the only question before the Court had been whether the law or the executive order was to govern. He then admonished his critics:

> If you are prepared, gentlemen, to waive the government of the laws and submit without repining to every errour or encroachment of the several Departments of government, avow it to your fellow citizens, and prevail on them to abolish the Constitution, or get into office a feeble and submissive Judiciary. For what cause are we now reproached? For interposing the authority of the laws in the protection of individual rights, of your rights and the rights of succeeding generations.[39]

More noteworthy than the jury presentment and the blast it provoked from Johnson were events which took place in Washington after the circulation of Johnson's reply to Rodney. When the Attorney-General had finished reading that rejoinder, he addressed to the President a sharp criticism of the judge.[40] Johnson had caught the "leprosy of the Bench" and was now championing all the "high-church doctrines" so prevalent there. Rodney mentioned a rumor that Johnson had "made a question with the Bench whether the Judges should wait upon the President" at the time Jefferson had laid the evidence in the Burr trial before Congress and hinted at remedial legislation. This allegation Rodney now believed correct, and Johnson's evident hostility to the administration was indicative, Rodney felt, of "some plan concerning the election of a future president." The elections of 1808 would soon take place, and Rodney saw significance in the timing of Johnson's publication. The writer offered to reply to Johnson, either officially or in his private capacity, but thought that the matter did not demand it and that the action might be considered improper. Whatever Jefferson may have thought of Rodney's insinuations, he evidently saw no use in protracting the controversy, and the public airing of the contest between the executive and the judge ended with Johnson's defense.

As a matter of fact, Johnson's protests soon elicited from the administration tacit admission of its own illegal conduct. Jefferson now deemed new legislation essential in order to furnish express authority for controlling collectors' decisions and for regulating the use of mandamus by the courts in such cases.[41] Secretary Gallatin, who had issued the original orders, now admitted that his instructions could operate merely as opinion, not as command. On this point Johnson, declared Gallatin, had been wholly correct.[42]

---

[39]Warren, I, 337-38.

[40]Rodney to Jefferson, Oct. 31, 1808, Jefferson Papers (MSS; Library of Congress).

[41]Jefferson to Gallatin, Oct. 25, 1808, Gallatin, *Works,* cited in Warren, I, 339 and 338, n. 2.

[42]Gallatin to William Giles, Nov. 24, 1808, Gallatin, *Works,* I, 434.

Changes which the administration sought soon passed Congress. The new amendments clearly empowered the President to issue general rules governing detentions and set forth the mode by which individuals might proceed in the district courts.[43]

Thus had the executive followed Johnson's advice and gone to the Congress for a broader grant of power. This transfer of discretion from the collectors to the central agency had regularized procedure and clarified the lines of authority. The stickler for legality had won his point. The Embargo Mandamus decision had unquestionably served as a prime factor in evoking the legislative action.

Yet this incident of the clearance papers and all that accompanied it should not be overemphasized. Johnson had thrown himself impetuously into the controversy, but, as later cases show, cool afterthoughts must have caused him to question the assumptions on which he had built his argument. At any rate, views which he expressed earlier and would express later help to put his decision in the Embargo Mandamus case in proper focus.

Even before the collector of Charleston had placed in his lap the thorny problem of the clearance papers, Johnson had confronted the questions of executive accountability to the law and of judicial intervention. The first of these questions carried subordinate issues with it, among them the circumstances in which administrative officers should enjoy a range of free discretion to make decisions on their own information, and the extent to which Congress might vest such discretion in the executive.

In Charleston, in 1807, William Crafts and other taxpayers had taken to the Circuit Court their grievance over the manner in which certain direct taxes had been assessed. As applied to them the federal tax on dwelling houses, slaves, and land had, they contended, been illegally and unfairly enforced, and they asked Johnson for a writ of injunction to restrain the tax supervisor from making collections. The judge, they hoped, would rescue them from assessments they thought excessive.[44]

Johnson refused the injunction. He agreed that the tax had been badly managed in South Carolina and that something should be

[43]See sec. 10, Act of Jan. 9, 1809, 2 Stat. 506, 509.
[44]Johnson summarized their position as follows: "that no proprietor of slaves is liable to pay his assessment until every slave in the state is assessed—that no proprietor of dwelling houses is liable to pay his assessment until every dwelling house shall be returned and correctly valued—and that no proprietor of lands is liable until upon the return and assessment of every dwelling house and slave and the correct valuation of the former, a deficiency shall appear—Or in other words that the act imposing a direct tax may lose its efficacy either thro' the fraud of individuals or the neglect or ignorance of the subordinate officers employed in the collection of it." Crafts v. Stevens, Supervisor, Minutes C.C. Dist. of S.C. (1807), Bk. A, pp. 297-98.

done to correct assessment on defaulters or to punish their neglect. Yet it was not his province to inquire whether the defect lay
in the act or in incompetence and dishonesty in carrying it out.
The parties should have based their claim of a violation of their
rights either on the unconstitutionality of the act, or on the exercise of an undelegated power by the supervisor. This they had
not done, and the Court was no proper protection against unequal
taxation. It was to Congress that the appeal should be made.

Johnson's confidence in the administrative machinery that Congress had provided here was notable. Congress had by law authorized taxpayers to appeal from assessment to a board of commissioners in each state, and Crafts had failed to make use of this
opportunity to have his assessment reviewed. The problem was complex and the legislature might devise special machinery to meet it:

> Congress foresaw that in the immense detail of transactions
> necessary to carrying this law into effect, questions of real
> merit and interest might occur in which the judicial power
> could not interfere, or certainly could not reach the justice
> of the case—they therefore gave a right of appeal to the
> principal assessor with power to vary each particular valua-
> tion; and to the commissioners they gave a further power to
> *revise, adjust and vary* the valuations, retaining only the ratio,
> and to oblige the assessors *to correct* their returns, and even
> to order a new valuation if they thought it necessary—To these
> boards with peculiar propriety the subject was referred, they
> possessed all the information necessary, and not being re-
> stricted in their decisions by the strict rules which govern
> courts of justice might upon proper representation have re-
> dressed every grievance now complained of—The citizen there-
> fore has not been left without the means of obtaining justice,
> but has neglected to make use of the opportunities afforded him
> and must bear the consequences—Their last remedy is by a
> remonstrance to Congress—That body may perhaps think it
> advisable to vest the supervisor with powers to afford them
> relief, but I certainly cannot.[45]

In refusing to interfere with the determinations of administrative
agencies Johnson went a long way toward recognizing authority in
Congress to provide whatever machinery it deemed necessary for
carrying out an important domestic power. Although he nowhere
stated that the courts were powerless to intervene after administrative appeals had been tried unsuccessfully, he seemed to suggest
that the citizen who felt himself injured could resort only to a petition to the legislature. He thought the regular courts lacked the
information and procedure necessary for efficient action.

[45]*Ibid.*, p. 299.

In the field of foreign relations, too, Johnson saw an unavoidable necessity for assigning discretionary powers to the executive. The "daring precipitancy" of 1808 was gone in 1810 when the seizure of the schooner *Swift* came before the Circuit Court for judicial scrutiny. That vessel had sailed from England in 1809, and federal officials had taken it for an alleged violation of the Non-intercourse Act of that year. The statute was an effort to cope with the restrictions which the rival belligerents—Great Britain and France—had clamped on neutral commerce. The act authorized the President, in case either of these powers should remove its restrictions on American commerce, to proclaim such a withdrawal and consequently to permit trade to be renewed with the complying state.[46] The British ambassador had led President Madison to expect that Britain would revoke its restrictive orders, and the President had accordingly issued a proclamation authorizing renewal of commerce with that country. But the British government had remained adamant, and Madison had revoked his earlier proclamation.

The ship had sailed and undergone seizure after the later proclamation, and the rival counsel argued ingeniously on the point of seizure.[47] The government lawyer insisted that the first proclamation was invalid as based on an incorrect supposition by the President that Britain would comply. On his part the opposing counsel defended the first proclamation on the ground that the Chief Executive had been constituted the "sole judge" of the question and that his decision was final; but the second proclamation was void since there was no power given him, or that constitutionally could be given him, to re-enact or revive the law imposing trade restrictions. Each counsel cut his conceptions of presidential power to suit his own ends.

Johnson held the seizure valid. This was a "very interesting" question and one which had been the subject of wide discussions and conflicting decisions. Both proclamations of the President he found legal. The power given the President was a "suspending or dispensing power commensurate with the possible state of things and which he was to exercise with reference to a change in our foreign relations with regard to the occurrence or deviation of which he alone could be an adequate judge."[48]

The phrasing of this passage is scarcely impeccable but its burden is clear. The case required a broad delegation to the President and reliance on his examination of supporting conditions. Courts of law were inept in these situations, for the grounds on which they

[46]Act of March 1, 1809, 2 Stat. 528, 530-31.
[47]United States *v.* Schooner *Swift*, Minutes C.C. Dist. of Ga. (1810), Bk. D, p. 247.
[48]*Ibid.*, pp. 247-48.

would have to act would depend on developments in diplomacy which only the President could comprehend. Again, to permit the President to suspend the operation of the law, without power to revive, would enable the British government to restore to effect orders earlier revoked and prevent our government from retaliating until Congress might convene; this was a "state of things to which the legislature of the United States could never have intended to have exposed themselves." The words of the act were not explicit on this point but were open to such a construction. Johnson would infer an intention in the legislature to permit the revival of restrictions.

The owners, no doubt dazed by the conflicting orders, had lost their ship, and Johnson had tolerated a broad grant of power to the President. A President who had been wrong must be deemed by the judge to have been right. Furthermore, the executive without express authority might revive as well as suspend a whole system of restrictions on commerce. In spirit at least, this was a retreat from the bold stand in the Embargo case.

Within three years these ideas received confirmation in the Supreme Court. There another vessel, the brig *Aurora,* and another statute were involved, but the issues paralleled those in the *Swift* case.[49] This time Congress had empowered the President to revive the earlier restrictions against one belligerent whenever he should find that the other had lessened its interferences with American commerce.[50] Madison had found France cooperative and accordingly had restored limitations on trade with Britain. Counsel deplored the statute as an unconstitutional delegation of legislative power; for the President to revive a law was to give his decrees the force and status of law. Yet Johnson, here speaking for the Court, found no such objections to the proclamation.[51] He stated tersely that there was good reason why Congress should exercise its discretion in reviving the act of 1809, "either expressly or conditionally as their judgment should direct."[52] Without elaborating the point, Johnson had tolerated a wide latitude of discretion in Congress to make the President the supreme spokesman in foreign relations. Under suitable authorization the Chief Executive might act without restraint in determining those conditions in which the legislative policy should take effect.

The rebel of 1808 had acquired a healthy respect for the demands on the executive. On one occasion during this same period

[49]The brig *Aurora,* 7 Cranch 382 (1813).
[50]See Act of May 1, 1810, 2 Stat. 605, 606.
[51]The opposing counsel denied that any delegation of legislative power had been made; he felt that Congress had only prescribed the evidence requisite for determining a fact upon which the law should go into effect.
[52]7 Cranch 388.

he spoke of the President in his capacity as Commander-in-Chief as having extensive control over privateers.[53] On another he intimated that Congress might give to executive orders the same legal "ubiquity" that attached to statutes; hence the requirement of notice might be waived.[54] Finally, in three instances he told persons aggrieved by his decisions in their cases to go to the executive for clemency; because of the administrative official's familiarity with conditions and because of the flexibility of his powers, he was often better fitted than the judge to make exceptions.[55] Hence the executive, although bound by law, nonetheless might require a breadth of discretion in which to move. And on no occasion did Johnson impose limits on Congress in its provisions for that discretion.

On the second question in the Embargo Mandamus case Johnson likewise had more to say in subsequent years. The judge had boldly attacked Jefferson and Gallatin for overstepping the law, yet what of the power of the judge himself? In rebutting Rodney's argument Johnson had denied that individuals on whose rights the executive had trampled could find sufficient security in impeachment of the offending officer or in an action for damages. Rodney's contention would lead to disaster:

> If these arguments have any force at all, as directed against the correctness of the circuit court's issuing the writ of mandamus, they would have equal weight to prove the impropriety of permitting them to issue the writ of habeas corpus;

[53]United States v. the *Thomas Gibbons*, Minutes C.C. Dist. of Ga. (1812), Bk. D, pp. 332, 334. A vessel which had sailed from Europe after the outbreak of war was claimed by both the capturing privateer and the government. At issue were presidential instructions to privateers to let such vessels pass in order to permit seizure for violation of the Non-intercourse Acts. Johnson awarded the vessel to the government and upheld the instructions. He said he would feel no difficulty in resting his opinion on the general powers that must exist in the "Supreme Executive Magistrate and Commander in Chief of the Army and Navy of the United States." He continued, "It would be melancholy indeed if he did not possess the power of staying the ravages of war whenever the interests of the country required it and singular if the vessel of war of the U.S. could be restrained by his orders in exercising the right of capture whilst the privateers were left at large to pursue their enterprises without control in opposition to executive authority." Yet Johnson also discovered express statutory authority in a recent prize act.

[54]The *Mary and Susan*, 1 Wheat. 46, 58 (1816).

[55]United States v. 1960 Bags of Coffee, 8 Cranch 398, 405 (1814); United States v. the Brig *Charles*, Minutes C.C. Dist. of Ga. (1809), Bk. D, p. 157; United States v. the Sloop *Philadelphia*, Minutes C.C. Dist. of S.C. (1809), Bk. A, p. 376, in which Johnson, speaking of a boatload of slaves arbitrarily taken in Cuba, stated: "This case is one, in which were the Court at liberty to consult its feelings it could not hesitate for a moment—But the Constitution of our government is calculated to shelter the judgment from the delusion of sensibility, the pleasant offices of humanity are delegated to the executive and legislature, while to us is committed the sole power of adjudging what the law imposes."

which is but an analogous protection to another class of individual rights, and might be urged to show that the whole executive department, in all its ramifications, civil, military and naval, should be left absolutely at large, in their conduct to individuals.[56]

For relief from oppression individuals should resort to the courts; their means of protection were the hoary writs of injunction, habeas corpus, and mandamus. The Charleston shippers had won their mandamus from Johnson and their benefactor had been hard put to it later to discover an authority to issue that writ.

In a sense, however, Johnson's action in the Embargo Mandamus case had been atypical. In 1807 the taxpayers had failed in their attempt to win an injunction against a tax they deemed unfair. The same year Burr's accomplices, Bollman and Swartwout, had secured a habeas corpus over a vigorous dissent by Johnson; for Johnson had there demanded an unequivocal showing of jurisdiction either in the Constitution itself or in statutes of Congress. The dissenting justice had found in the statutes suitable remedies for individuals without the Court's interposing its will through a strained construction.[57] To this position Jefferson's appointee clung, with rare lapses, to the end of his career.[58] The judge who would venture

[56]Johnson continued: "What benefit results to the ruined citizen from the impeachment of the President, could we suppose it in the power of any individual to effect it? or what security from an action against a public officer whose circumstances may be desperate? But such is not the genius of our constitution. The law assigns every one his duty and his rights; and for enforcing the one and maintaining the other, courts of justice are instituted." "Judge Johnson's remarks," 10 Fed. Cas. 365.

[57]Referring to a section of the Judiciary Act other than that applied by the Court, Johnson stated, "if the power of the several courts and individual judges be referred to their respective jurisdictions all clashing and interference of power ceases, and sufficient means of redress are still held out to the citizen, if deprived of his liberty; and this surely must have been the intention of the legislature. It never could have been contemplated that the mandates of this court should be borne to the extremities of the States, to convene before them every prisoner who may be committed under the authority of the general government." *Ex parte* Bollman and Swartwout, 4 Cranch 75, 106-7 (1807).

[58]See Johnson dissenting, in *Ex parte* Watkins, 7 Pet. 568 (1833). The majority, speaking through Story, awarded habeas corpus to a former treasury official whom the Jackson administration had prosecuted for defalcations and who had been held in jail beyond the termination of his sentence. The marshal had failed to respond to certain writs issued by the lower court; the prisoner had then appealed to the Supreme Court. Johnson contended that it was a case of false imprisonment against the officer, not of error in the lower court. He said, "The truth is, that this is a direct interference by means of the writ now moved for, between a court of the United States and the executive officer of that court; and upon the principles of this decision, I see no reason why we may not next be called upon to issue the same writ to our *Ultima Thule,* the mouth of the Oregon, to bring up a prisoner under a *capias ad satisfaciendum,* in order to examine whether he has paid the debt or not. Is this appellate jurisdiction; or is it the proper employment of this tribunal?" 7 Pet. 580-81.

to question the acts of the executive should consult the expressed will of Congress before moving ahead.[59]

This was just as true of mandamus as of habeas corpus. Five years after he had signed the mandamus to the Charleston collector he confronted the old problem in the Supreme Court. This time the case concerned the Circuit Court in Ohio and the power of that court to issue the writ to compel a federal land officer to deliver over certificates of purchase.[60] Johnson, now speaking for the Court, agreed that mandamus might serve well in many cases where individual rights called for satisfaction through some ministerial act. But now he denied that the lower court had power to issue:

. . . although the judicial power of the United States extends to cases arising under the laws of the United States, the legislature have not thought proper to delegate the exercise of that power to its circuit courts, except in certain specified cases.[61]

Congress had failed to endow the judges with such a power, and Johnson took this occasion to explain the decision of 1808. The "notoriety" of that decision justified a reference to it. Without question the earlier mandamus could not have been granted "but upon a supposition inconsistent with the decision" in the present case. Johnson had evidently undergone a change of mind, although he could not restrain a parting comment to justify his earlier conduct.[62]

The appointee of 1804 long retained his sensitiveness to the assault made on his ruling in the Embargo case. Doubtless he felt the cause had been a righteous one, that his insistence that the executive abide by the rule of law had rested on firm ground. It was a full year after his reply to Rodney that he phrased a formal note to Jefferson tendering the retired President a collection of seeds. Acacia, Egyptian grass, and benne grass might grow in

[59]In Elkison v. Deliesseline, 8 Fed. Cas. 493, 497, No. 4366 (C.C. Dist. of S.C., 1823), where a writ of habeas corpus was sought against a state officer, Johnson intimated that Congress was empowered to set forth the cases in which the writ should issue and the situations in which its suspension should occur; said he, "We [the Court] cannot undertake to judge when that crisis has arrived which the constitution contemplates; nor are we to undertake to define or limit that meaning of those words, 'the privilege of the writ of habeas corpus.' " Provision for the writ differed in the several states and Johnson asserted that it could only be for Congress to give a "uniform and national operation" to this provision of the Constitution.

[60]M'Intire v. Wood, 7 Cranch 504 (1813).

[61]7 Cranch 506.

[62]He continued: "But that mandamus was issued upon the voluntary submission of the collector and the district attorney, and in order to extricate themselves from an embarrassment resulting from conflicting duties. *Volenti non fit injuria.*" 7 Cranch 506. Cf. Johnson, for the Court, in M'Clung v. Silliman, 6 Wheat. 598 (1821), where it was held that Congress had failed to grant jurisdiction to state courts to issue the writ of mandamus to federal land officials.

Virginia if the recipient would follow his directions. Would the former President accept Johnson's "warmest assurance of respect and esteem?"[63]

Another six months elapsed before a reply came from Monticello. Jefferson apologized for the delay, thanked the judge for the gifts, returned some seeds of his own, and said he would be "happy to administer to your taste for the care of plants in any way you can make me useful." He closed with expressions of "high esteem and respect."[64] Years would go by before the correspondence would be renewed. Relations had probably cooled as a result of Johnson's conduct.

Yet the whole affair had significance beyond the personal. The President, rebuffed by his own appointee, had gone at last to Congress for a clear assignment of power; and, a century and more later, the growth of executive power would give added point to Johnson's bold insistence on legality.

In a sense, the judge had followed the same route as Jefferson. More and more, Johnson saw in Congress the true source of legitimate authority. Where conditions, domestic or foreign, required it, that assemblage might confer on its executive agents a broad discretion to act.

Although justice demanded remedies by which individuals might gain redress from executive wrongdoing, Johnson increasingly saw Congress rather than the courts as the branch most competent to devise those remedies. Precipitancy moderated into caution as the judge came to insist on a definite assignment of jurisdiction. On this subject of courts and court power Johnson was soon to have ample opportunity for argument. A new appointment to the Court would face him with an antagonist who would engage him in conflict on this point for the rest of his career.

[63]Johnson to Jefferson, Sept. 20, 1809, Jefferson Papers (MSS; Library of Congress).
[64]Jefferson to Johnson, March 17, 1810, *ibid.*

Chapter V

COURTS AND COURT POWER

JOHNSON'S uneasiness over his impulsive assumption of jurisdiction in the Embargo case in 1808 remained with him in 1812. The strong will was still there: to one observer at this period he seemed "bold, independent, eccentric, and sometimes harsh."[1] Yet the argument of Jefferson's Attorney-General had hit the mark. Henceforth, before embarking on decisions, Johnson would pass a searching eye over the jurisdictional charts furnished by the Constitution and statutes, and would steer close to the Jeffersonian course insofar as courts and their power were concerned. A criminal libel case in 1812 gave Johnson an opportunity to score a victory for Republican doctrine.

This session of 1812 had importance for another reason. A new appointee—ambitious, energetic, industrious—one whose conceptions of the role of courts stood poles apart from Johnson's—appeared on the high bench. Only two nominal Federalists remained there now, Marshall and his fellow Virginian, Bushrod Washington, nephew of the first President. Alongside these were five Republicans. With Johnson now sat another Princetonian, the earnest and genial Henry Brockholst Livingston, of New York, the modest and reticent Thomas Todd, of Kentucky, and the angular Gabriel Duvall, of Maryland. Of these three, Livingston was to prove easily the most articulate. But the last of the five Republicans would surpass all of the others in activity and perhaps in influence. He was the lawyer and politician from Massachusetts, Joseph Story.[2] The arrival of Story in 1812 brought to Marshall's side a sympathizer of considerable talents; from now on, Marshall and Story would form a team seldom in disagreement on constitutional issues. And on no subject was Story's influence greater than on that of the place of the judiciary in the American constitutional system.

Like Johnson, Story came to the Court at the age of thirty-two. Like Johnson, again, his fame at the time of his appointment was

[1]Charles J. Ingersoll, *History of the Second War between the United States of America and Great Britain* (2d series; 2 vols.; Philadelphia, 1852), I, 74.
[2]Livingston was appointed in 1806, Todd in 1807, and Duvall and Story in 1811.

confined in the main to his home state. Unlike Johnson, however, Story had no judicial experience to his credit.[3]

In temperament and interest the two men had marked differences. Johnson was proud, aloof, and impulsive; the law was but one among many pursuits to which he bent his active mind. Story was genial and urbane; and the study of the law was the absorbing passion of his life, as his reasons for accepting his judicial post indicate:

> The high honor attached to it, the permanence of the tenure, the respectability, if I may so say, of the salary, and the opportunity it will allow me to pursue, what of all things I admire, juridical studies, have combined to urge me to this result.[4]

The contrast between Johnson and Story extended even to their appearance. In 1824 a newspaper man said Story looked old because of baldness and glasses. "Below medium size, of light, airy form, rapid and sprightly in his motions, and polished and courtly in his manner; his countenance indicates genius, affability, versatility of thought, and almost anything but the patient research of the scholar and the gravity and wisdom of the judge."[5] This same observer found Johnson a "large, athletic, well built man of sixty or upwards, with a full, ruddy, and fair countenance, with thin white hair, and partially bald."[6] If Story's demeanor was sprightly, Johnson's was grave. The face that looks out from extant portraits of Johnson is arresting. Its features are regular; the eyes, which are set under heavy brows and a high forehead, are stern, even piercing. The face, like Johnson's writings, is more serious than gay, more reflective than genial.

The two young judges both came from the ranks of the Republican party. Yet Story's devotion to the creed of Jefferson was suspect: President Madison had offered the appointment to three other candidates before turning to Story; and Jefferson, even at this early date, had called the new appointee "pseudo-republican."[7] Story's subsequent rulings on the problem of court jurisdiction and other matters would do little to quiet these misgivings.

The precise role which the courts should play was a matter of hot debate between Republicans and Federalists. Who should determine the range and the nature of judicial power? Federalists, seeking inviolable safeguards for property rights against the attacks of Congress and the state legislatures, tended to exalt the

[3]Warren, *The Supreme Court in United States History,* I, 415-17.
[4]Story to Nathaniel Williams, Nov. 30, 1811, William W. Story, *Life and Letters of Joseph Story* (2 vols.; Boston, 1851), I, 201.
[5]Warren, I, 468.
[6]*Ibid.*
[7]Warren, I, 406, n. 2.

judiciary and particularly its independent control over its own
scope of authority. Jeffersonians, with a greater confidence in the
elected and responsible representatives of the people, commonly
insisted that judges take their cue from the political branches. Rodney's rebuke to Johnson in the Embargo Mandamus case was in
a sense typical of the Republican standpoint, for it had proclaimed
the rule that judges before proceeding with cases must discover at
the outset a clear assignment of authority to proceed either in the
Constitution or in laws of the Congress. True, that position sprang
in part at least from a concern for state autonomy. Nevertheless,
it also reflected a preference for control in the representative Congress rather than in the judiciary.

Accordingly, it was over a crucial political issue that the justice
from Salem and the justice from Charleston were soon to grapple.
Indeed, it was more than that, for the outcome would have a critical
bearing on the enduring role of the courts. The reading which the
Marshall Court would give to Article III of the Constitution would
freeze for generations the particular scope to be given judicial
power. The problem has two facets. The first relates to jurisdiction—
the kind of cases which courts may legitimately decide. In a technological age the issue has presented serious complications. To cite
but one example: Is Congress compelled by Article III to vest in
the regular courts a final and sweeping review over the findings of
administrators, or may Congress create special administrative tribunals to deal with special forms of regulation?[8] The second problem is that of judicial power proper: Within their acknowledged
jurisdiction, do the courts possess any inherent powers? Are the
powers to issue injunctions and broadly to punish for contempts
inherent in courts and hence beyond legislative interference? Here,
as elsewhere, the Court of Marshall would go far toward setting
the stage.

The case of Hudson and Goodwin in 1812 raised for decision the
first of these issues—that of jurisdiction and its control.[9] Did the
Constitution authorize the federal courts to try offenses made criminal under the English common law? Or, alternatively, must the
courts look to statutes of Congress for the establishment of offenses? Before the election of Jefferson, most of the federal judges
appointed by Washington and Adams had asserted such a jurisdiction. With the advent of the Republicans to power, public sentiment and the responsible leaders of the party had repudiated this

[8]Cf. Crowell v. Benson, 285 U.S. 22 (1932), in which the Court intimated
that Congress is barred by force of Article III from vesting the determination
of "jurisdictional facts" in administrative bodies.
[9]United States v. Hudson and Goodwin, 7 Cranch 32 (1812).

independent power in judges. Jefferson and his associates had discountenanced the resort to prosecutions at the common law.

Yet despite the President's precautions, prosecuting officers in Connecticut had secured from the Circuit Court indictments against certain critics of the new administration.[10] Although most of these were soon quashed, one against Hudson and Goodwin, editors of the *Connecticut Courant,* reached the Supreme Court. The defendants had printed an article attacking the President, and the prosecution had contended that, since libel was a crime under the English common law, the lower court had jurisdiction over the offense.

Although counsel appeared for neither side, the majority of the Supreme Court proceeded to a decision. Johnson on this occasion was their spokesman. In a terse opinion he denied that the federal courts could take jurisdiction over such crimes. The question, he felt, had been long settled in public opinion and the legal profession. He voiced his convictions on the control of jurisdiction in forthright terms:

> The powers of the general government are made up of concessions from the several states; whatever is not expressly given to the former, the latter expressly reserve. The judicial power of the United States is a constituent part of those concessions; that power is to be exercised by courts organized for the purpose, and brought into existence by an effort of the legislative power of the Union. Of all the courts which the United States may, under their general powers, constitute, one only—the Supreme Court—possesses jurisdiction derived immediately from the constitution, and of which the legislative power cannot deprive it. All other courts created by the general government possess no jurisdiction but what is given them by the power that creates them, and can be vested with none but what the power ceded to the general government will authorize them to confer.[11]

Thus Congress was supreme not only over the creation of inferior federal courts but also over the scope of their authority. Whether Congress might in its discretion vest in the courts a jurisdiction over common-law crimes, Johnson declined to decide. It was enough that no statute had attempted to do so. Power to create courts implied a power to restrict their jurisdiction to specific objects. And Johnson asked with what "propriety" a court, so created and restricted, could "assume to itself a jurisdiction— much more extended; in its nature very indefinite; applicable to a great variety of subjects; varying in every state in the Union— and with regard to which there exists no definite criterion of dis-

[10]Warren, I, 436.
[11]7 Cranch 33.

tribution between the district and circuit courts of the same district?"[12]

The principal argument for such a jurisdiction was that of implied powers—the power of every political body to preserve itself and promote the object of its creation. But Johnson declared that this doctrine by itself could not justify the courts' taking jurisdiction over even a single act alleged to be against the peace and dignity of the sovereign power: "The legislative authority of the Union must first make an act a crime, affix a punishment to it, and declare the court that shall have jurisdiction of the offense."[13] Thus did the Jeffersonian judge set forth what has become the cardinal rule of federal criminal jurisdiction.

Courts might possess some limited inherent powers essential to their proper functioning, but Johnson was emphatic that the jurisdiction over acts made criminal by the common law was not among them.

Justice Story, however, remained unconvinced. Sitting on circuit, he was soon disregarding the Hudson ruling and was considering an indictment for the forcible rescue of a ship on the high seas—an offense punishable at the common law but not under any statute of Congress. As a result, the question of common-law crimes again beset the Supreme Court.[14] Government counsel declined to argue the case. Johnson and Story split over the binding effect of the Hudson decision; and in 1816 after deliberation the majority, through Johnson, refused to reconsider the earlier ruling.[15] Johnson had been the leader in carrying the day for a legislative control over federal criminal jurisdiction.

Story, however, stood his ground. This very year he wrote William Pinkney, the lawyer and diplomat, that a broad criminal jurisdiction was indispensable.[16] In a peroration on national power, Story stated as a maxim that the "Government of the United States is intrinsically too weak, and the powers of the State Governments too strong . . . ." The time was ripe, he argued, for the establishment of "a great national policy, and of great national institutions,

[12]*Ibid.*
[13]7 Cranch 34.
[14]United States *v.* Coolidge, 1 Wheat. 415 (1816).
[15]Justices Washington and Livingston expressed a willingness to hear arguments on the question—a concession repeated in the Court's opinion. Had there been argument, it is conceivable that the offense might have been treated as one in admiralty, instead of common-law jurisdiction.—Cf. Peter S. Du Ponceau, *A Dissertation on the Nature and Extent of the Jurisdiction of the Courts of the United States* (Philadelphia, 1824), p. 62. The author is indebted to Professor Mark DeW. Howe for calling this point and Du Ponceau's comments to his attention.
[16]Letter dated 1816, Story, *Story,* I, 293.

in respect to the army, the navy, the judicial, the commercial, and the internal interests of the country."[17]

Would Pinkney, Story asked, take the lead by giving favorable consideration to a bill expanding the jurisdiction of the federal courts? Story had personally drafted the bill and had submitted it to his fellow-judges for their criticism and suggestions. All had approved save Johnson; the South Carolinian had objected, evidently on grounds of policy, to the section which conferred on the courts a common-law criminal jurisdiction. Yet Story believed the courts competent, even without a legislative grant, to try such crimes. Down to 1804, he asserted, every judge on the Supreme Court, except one, had thought such a jurisdiction constitutional; since that time there had been a difference on the Court, and the question was still unsettled.[18]

The first brush had ended in a victory for Johnson. Until Congress should act, the common law, subject to statutory correction, would remain within each state the law of that state. Story had failed to engraft on the legal system of the country a limited national common law; and the result must have appeared in his eyes to be a setback to the prestige of the federal courts. Story a generation later, it is true, would achieve a minor success in an analogous field; it would take a century to correct his precedent,[19] and Johnson's stand would prevail in the end.[20]

The contest over jurisdiction spread to other theaters. One of these grew out of the constitutional inclusion within judicial power of "Cases of admiralty and maritime Jurisdiction."[21] This indeterminate sphere of power Congress had vested in the district courts in the first instance, with a provision for appeals.[22] The vagueness of the clause left a wide area for construction. Should the federal courts, in interpreting their own power, restrict or amplify the scope of these cases? An expansive reading might in effect remove numerous cases from state courts and from trial by jury.

Story embarked on the problem with customary zest. One who then frequented the bar of the Court reported that this ardent, indefatigable student, "more of a reader than a thinker," was digging

[17]*Ibid.*, p. 296.
[18]*Ibid.*, pp. 299-300.
[19]Swift *v.* Tyson, 16 Pet., 1 (1842), overruled in Erie Railroad Co. *v.* Tompkins, 304 U.S. 64 (1938).
[20]Johnson was solicitous to give effect to the law of the state, even in diversity of citizenship cases, see below, pp. 225, 238, and his comment in Holmes *v.* United States (C.C. Dist. of S.C., 1832), Charleston *City Gazette,* June 9, 1832: "That section [sec. 34 Judiciary Act of 1789] enacts nothing but what would have been law without it, to wit that: the Lex loci should be the law of the courts of the U.S. distributed over the Union."
[21]Art. III, sec. 2.
[22]Judiciary Act of 1789, 1 Stat. 73.

to the roots of the English admiralty law for precedents.[23] And in 1815 Story on circuit handed down a decision holding that a policy for marine insurance came properly within admiralty jurisdiction.[24] The opinion was learned and elaborate. After tracing the history of the admiralty courts in England, it insisted that the constitutional grant included all cases originally within the English admiralty unlimited by later acts of Parliament.

In 1821 this question—whether admiralty comprised commercial contracts of a maritime nature—reappeared in Johnson's circuit in a suit on a bill of lading against the master and owners of the ship *Amanda*.[25] When counsel, arguing for jurisdiction, cited as precedent Story's earlier decision, Johnson expressed embarrassment at reviewing the decision of a brother judge, but his opinion showed little mercy for Story's arguments. He urged two considerations as significant here; because of them, he said, he had always set his face against the progress of this form of jurisdiction. One was the menace which it held over the state courts of common law. To expand the admiralty would put it in the power of Congress to remove to federal courts a wide range of cases. The other was a threat to trial by jury. Admiralty courts, save in criminal cases, operated without benefit of juries, and accordingly he feared an infringement on the constitutional right of jury trial.

Furthermore, said Johnson, Story's reliance on ancient British practice was both unhistorical and insidious. The Lord High Admirals of Britain had acquired in the course of years "an accumulation of power, wealth, prerogative, and jurisdiction which rendered them formidable and intolerable to the British people." Those officials had lost their vast powers through statutes and the extension of common-law jurisdiction, for the British had preferred the more liberal procedures and rules of the common-law courts. The true limits of the admiralty jurisdiction were those in effect at the time of the American Revolution. The states had granted only that jurisdiction which they themselves had exercised at that period.[26]

Story's tendency to inflate admiralty jurisdiction caused Johnson increasing irritation. In 1819, according to Wheaton's report of the case, Story had stated it as the conviction of the Supreme Court that admiralty embraced generally cases of material men, that is, suits by those who had repaired vessels for wages and the like.[27] In a separate opinion in 1827 Johnson denounced this as a mere

[23]Ingersoll, I, 92.
[24]DeLovio v. Boit, 7 Fed. Cas. 418, No. 3776 (C.C. Dist. of Mass., 1815).
[25]The *Amanda*, Minutes C.C. Dist. of S.C. (1821), Bk. C, p. 15.
[26]Cf. Johnson's opinion in Stevens v. Schooner *Hornet*, Minutes C.C. Dist. of S.C. (1822), Bk. C, p. 69.
[27]The *General Smith*, 4 Wheat. 438, 443 (1819).

dictum.[28] It was none too early to halt "this silent and stealing progress" of the admiralty in usurping jurisdiction; false doctrines and dicta deserved prompt repudiation.[29] The British had seen fit progressively to narrow the original sweep of admiralty in the interest of the common law and jury trial. Following Story to the sources and citing precedents to support the contrary position, he could find no satisfactory precedent on Story's side in the "whole library of law books—and God knows we have enough of them already, 'camel loads.' "[30] He saw danger in the trend of Story's decisions:

> The study of the history of the admiralty jurisdiction in England, in common with that of all the courts of that kingdom, except the common law courts, presents an instructive lesson on the necessity of watching the advancement of judicial power, in common with all power; inasmuch as it shows in what small beginnings, and by what indirect and covert means, aided by perseverance and ingenuity, originated the mighty structures against which, ultimately, the legislative and judicial power of the country had to exert the full force of their united efforts.[31]

Not merely the subject matter, but the territorial scope of admiralty as well caused Johnson misgivings. It would take a constitutional amendment, he thought, to extend the power of admiralty courts to controversies on vessels plying the inland waters of the United States.[32]

Yet Johnson met frustration in his efforts to restrict the admiralty, and Story's labors brought fruit. Story's views, both as to the content and the territorial scope of that form of jurisdiction ultimately prevailed in the Supreme Court; and the result has been more than a little confusion and difficulty for the federal judiciary.[33]

The debate over admiralty jurisdiction had brought defeat for the South Carolinian. He suffered a second reverse in connection with the place of corporations as litigants in the lower federal courts. Corporations, then beginning their fantastic growth in numbers and power, might well wish for sanctuary in the national tribunals

[28]Ramsay v. Allegre, 12 Wheat. 611 (1827). Marshall gave the opinion of the Court. The case involved a suit on a promissory note for work and materials furnished the owner of the vessel.
[29]Ibid., p. 614.
[30]Ibid., p. 629.
[31]Ibid., p. 616.
[32]Steam Boat Edgefield v. Brooks, Minutes C.C. Dist. of S.C. (1828), Bk. C, pp. 278, 279.
[33]Westel Woodbury Willoughby, The Constitutional Law of the United States, (2 ed.; 3 vols.; New York, 1929), III, 1341-58. But cf. the Thomas Jefferson, 10 Wheat. 428 (1825), in which Justice Story ruled for the Court that admiralty did not extend above the ebb and flow of the tide; overruled in the Genessee Chief, 12 How. 443 (1852).

from hostile state laws and courts. Yet the words of Article III offered them slight promise; in enumerating the kinds of cases and parties to which the judicial power of the United States might extend, that part of the Constitution made no mention of corporations. Despite this fact, Johnson's fellow-judges, notably Marshall and Story, were fully able to make the Article fit the need.

As early as 1808 the question of corporations as litigants in the lower federal courts appeared before Johnson on circuit.[34] Officers of the United States Bank brought an action for trespass against a sheriff and a tax collector of Georgia for damages resulting from the forcible collection of a state tax.[35] Under Article III and the judiciary acts the court had jurisdiction over suits between citizens of different states. Did the bank corporation come within the term "citizen of a state"?

The judge rejected jurisdiction. The party here must bring suit either as individuals or as a corporation. In the former case it would have to sue in the "baptismal" names of the members; in the latter, Johnson said, the members were so completely immersed in the corporate existence that, even if they were all citizens of Pennsylvania, still they could not "communicate their right of suing in this court to the corporate body of which they are members. . . ." The Constitution made no mention of corporations in its enumeration of parties, and Johnson refused to stretch those clauses:

> A corporation cannot with propriety be denominated a citizen of any state, so that the right to sue in this court under the constitution can only be extended to corporate bodies by a liberality of construction, which we do not feel ourselves at liberty to exercise.[36]

The Bank, nevertheless, carried its case to the Supreme Court and there won a partial reversal.[37] Speaking for the Court, Marshall agreed that a corporation—"That invisible, intangible, and artificial being"—was not a citizen in the meaning of the Constitution.[38] Yet the Court made an important concession in permitting the individuals composing the corporation to sue in the corporate name. Unlike Johnson, Marshall was ready to look behind the name of the corporation at the individuals who composed it; as citizens, these individuals were entitled by Article III to bring suit, provided the state citizenship of all of them was different from that

[34]Bank of the United States v. Deveaux, 2 Fed. Cas. 692, No. 916 (C.C. Dist. of Ga., 1808).
[35]Warren, I, 389-92.
[36]2 Fed. Cas. 693.
[37]Bank of the United States v. Deveaux, 5 Cranch 61 (1809).
[38]Ibid., p. 86.

of the defendants. The principle underlying the decision failed to win Johnson's approval.[39]

The movement which Marshall had launched reached completion in after years. Story, alone of the judges of the early Marshall Court, remained in 1844 when the Court undercut the requirement of diversity of citizenship.[40] At that time a fiction served the purpose: the judges felt that a corporation chartered in a state, although not a citizen of that state, might be deemed a citizen within the meaning of Article III.[41] The judiciary thus went all the way in endowing corporations with a constitutional status. Justice Story exulted over the result:

> It gets rid of a great anomaly in our jurisprudence. This was always Judge Washington's opinion. I have held the same opinion for very many years, and Mr. Chief Justice Marshall had, before his death, arrived at the conclusion, that our early decisions were wrong.[42]

Despite the plain words of the Constitution, the ingenuity of judges had opened the national courts to private corporations, which might thus escape the application of state regulations by unfriendly state courts.

But the diverse citizenship clause was unavailable to the Second Bank of the United States, and it was under another jurisdictional provision that this institution, chartered by Congress in 1816, sought access to the national courts.

When a wave of hostility to the Bank caused Ohio to impose an annual $50,000 tax on its branches there, the corporation sought injunction protection in a federal circuit court. Article III, it was pointed out, had extended the judicial power to "all Cases, in Law and Equity, arising under this Constitution, the Laws of the United States, and Treaties. . . ." Was not this such a case, since the bank charter was a federal law and since Congress had there authorized the Bank to sue or be sued in state courts having jurisdiction and in

[39]See Johnson, dissenting in Bank of the United States v. Planters' Bank of Georgia, 9 Wheat. 904 (1824), in which he denied that the Court could take jurisdiction of a suit against a state bank. The Eleventh Amendment barred suits against a state, and according to the Deveaux rule the presence of the state among the stockholders would serve to withdraw the party from suability. Johnson here indicated lack of agreement with the Deveaux decision. 9 Wheat. 913.

[40]Louisville, C. & C. R. Co. v. Letson, 2 How. 497 (1844).

[41]*Ibid.*, p. 555.

[42]Story to Chancellor Kent, Aug. 31, 1844, Story, *Story*, II, 469. Mr. Dudley O. McGovney doubts Story's assertion of a change of mind on the part of Marshall. He believes that Story "lacked the analytical mind essential to comprehension and correct reporting of the expressions and ideas of Marshall." See his "A Supreme Court Fiction: Corporations in the Diverse Citizenship Jurisdiction of the Federal Courts," 56 Harvard Law Review (1943) 853-98, 1090-1124, 1225-60, at 877.

the federal circuit courts? In 1789 Congress had extended a general original jurisdiction over cases arising under federal laws only to the state courts with the possibility of appeal by writs of error.[43] Hence the claim of jurisdiction must rest, first, on a showing that a case involving the Bank was a case arising under federal law, and, second, that Congress by the charter provision had intended an exception to the prevailing rule favoring the state courts.

John Marshall and the majority were equal to the task.[44] The Chief Justice rested his argument, not so much on an intention in Congress to grant the jurisdiction claimed, as on a constitutional competence' of Congress to do so. He reached this conclusion by a general discussion of judicial power and the need of every government to protect itself. Original jurisdiction, as far as the Constitution was concerned, was "co-extensive with the judicial power"; Marshall found in the fundamental law no prohibition to its exercise in every case in which the judicial power could be exercised.[45] The existence of the charter made this a case arising under a federal law—in other words, the charter itself furnished a federal question. Every act of the Bank grew out of this law and hence was reviewable by the lower federal courts. Furthermore, the existence of the charter need be but one among many ingredients of a case to bring it within the sweep of Article III.

Against this assumption of jurisdiction, Justice Johnson directed a lengthy and forthright dissent.[46] He acknowledged the Bank's constitutionality and the urgent necessity of furnishing it every possible protection. Yet access to lower federal courts was both unnecessary and unconstitutional. Congress had not intended a right to sue there. The right to sue or be sued, provided in the charter, was merely an incident of the new creation, not an express enactment; this was but one of those ordinary acts in which the corporation might impersonate a natural man.

Congress, in Johnson's mind, had intended that most cases should come up through the state courts; the provision for appeal on writ of error to the Supreme Court was adequate guarantee of a uniform construction of national laws. Beyond that the federal government "had no interest in stripping the state courts of their jurisdiction."[47]

The dissenter hammered on the point that a genuine federal question was totally absent:

Why, then, should it [the general government] be vested with jurisdiction in a thousand causes, on a mere possibility of

[43]Judiciary Act of 1789, sec. 25, 1 Stat., 86-88.
[44]Osborn v. Bank of the United States, 9 Wheat. 738 (1824).
[45]Ibid., p. 821.
[46]Ibid., p. 871.
[47]Ibid., p. 886.

a question arising, which question, at last, does not occur in one of them? Indeed, I cannot perceive how such a reach of jurisdiction can be asserted, without changing the reading of the Constitution on this subject altogether. The judicial power extends only to "cases arising," that is, actual, not potential cases. The framers of the Constitution knew better than to trust such a *quo minus* fiction in the hands of any government.[48]

Congress might, if it saw fit, vest original jurisdiction in lower federal courts over cases actually arising under federal laws; but this was not such a case. This case in fact had arisen, not under a federal law, but under a state law. It was the law of the state that governed contracts. Under that law this bank carried on its business. And the resort to the corporate charter to discover a federal question was against "sound philosophy."[49] The federal law had merely created the Bank; it was the state law that took it up and made it what it was.

Not even the national legislature itself could constitutionally vest the jurisdiction claimed. Johnson forsook his customary deference to the national lawmakers in making this assertion. "No one branch of the general government can new model the constitutional structure of the other."[50] It was absurd to argue for a coordinate power in the courts, for under our Constitution the "judicial power so very far transcends both the others, in its acknowledged limits."[51] Johnson here had in mind the power of judicial review over state laws, a power not assigned to Congress.

Yet the argument was more with Marshall than with Congress. The Chief Justice had read the charter in such a way as to push the jurisdiction of the courts beyond its constitutional limits. It was Johnson's leading rule to construe strictly grants of jurisdiction, whether constitutional or statutory.

In thus opposing the inflation of jurisdiction in relation to common-law crimes, admiralty cases, and corporations, the South Carolinian reiterated his concern for the state judiciaries. The courts of the several states should occupy a primary position in the American judicial system. For this reason, he insisted on restraint on the part of the federal judges and demanded that those judges look to the representative body for an authority to proceed.

It is no matter of surprise, then, that a case putting in collision the United States Supreme Court and a state court should elicit in clearest contrast the philosophies of Johnson and Story. When a land title based on a treaty had come before it for settlement, the

[48]*Ibid.*
[49]*Ibid.*, p. 890.
[50]*Ibid.*, p. 896.
[51]*Ibid.*

Supreme Court, in deciding the controversy, had ruled against the law of Virginia as determined by the highest court of that state, and had thereupon issued a mandate to the state court ordering execution.[52] That mandate the Virginia tribunal had refused to carry out; its opinion had denied an appellate jurisdiction in the Supreme Court.

Virginia's defiance came before the United States Supreme Court in Martin v. Hunter's Lessee. The Supreme Court was unanimous in asserting its jurisdiction to compel respect for its prior decision and in upholding the twenty-fifth section of the Judiciary Act.[53] To Justice Story fell the task of writing the opinion. Thus, in 1816, the very year he was urging upon Pinkney the necessity of establishing a great national judiciary, he was expounding judicially the import of Article III.

To Story that provision, with its enumeration of the areas of national judicial power, was a mandate to Congress. Under its terms Congress was obligated to create federal courts, not merely the Supreme Court, but also inferior courts, and vest in them the whole range of power delegated by the Article:

> The judicial power must, therefore, be vested in some court by Congress; and to suppose that it was not an obligation binding on them, but might, at their pleasure, be omitted or declined, is to suppose that, under the sanction of the constitution, they might defeat the constitution itself.[54]

Perhaps on the insistence of his brethren, however, Story concluded that, even if one felt that the Article was not mandatory, "it cannot be denied that when it [judicial power] is vested, it may be exercised to the utmost constitutional extent."[55]

The points actually decided in the Martin case won Johnson's approval. But in Story's reasoning he found little to commend. "Few minds," said Johnson, "are accustomed to the same habit of thinking, and our conclusions are most satisfactory to ourselves when arrived at in our own way."[56] His concern was more with the Judiciary Act than with the Constitution. He seemed to be contending that the Court could not issue compulsory process to the state courts and that the Constitution in its solicitude for state judicial independence had authorized modes of appeal less obnoxious to state sensibilities. Congress had reflected this concern by specifying execution of a decree by the Supreme Court itself when state courts failed to comply therewith. Johnson appealed for the exercise of comity and forbearance; he denied that the Court on which he sat

[52] Fairfax's Devisee v. Hunter's Lessee, 7 Cranch 603 (1813); Johnson dissented on the merits.
[53] 1 Wheat. 304 (1816). Marshall abstained.
[54] Ibid., p. 329.
[55] Ibid., p. 337.
[56] Ibid., p. 362.

possessed "more infallibility than other courts composed of the same frail materials. . . ."[57]

To this Jeffersonian judge, the judicial article was merely permissive; it was not mandatory upon Congress. How to assign jurisdiction was well within the discretion of Congress. In the constitutional phrase "The Judicial Power shall extend" the key word was "shall." Johnson found little benefit in a "hypercritical severity" in considering the specific force of words. Language was defective in precision to an extent that might surprise those not habituated to submitting it to "philological analysis." The word "shall" here was used in the future sense and had nothing imperative about it. Continuing, he insisted:

I, therefore, see nothing imperative in this clause, and certainly it would have been very unnecessary to use the word in that sense; for, as there was no controlling power constituted, it would only, if used in an imperative sense, have imposed a moral obligation to act. But the same result arises from using it in a future sense, and the constitution everywhere assumes, as a postulate, that wherever power is given it will be used, or, at least, used as far as the interests of the American people require it, if not from the natural proneness of man to the exercise of power, at least from a sense of duty, and the obligation of an oath.[58]

In Johnson's opinion, Congress had assumed, for federal courts, only a part of the jurisdiction delegated by Article III. There was no reason why Congress could not leave the remainder to be exercised in the first instance by state courts. By virtue of the "necessary and proper" clause, Congress had acted; and that action bound the courts. Congress, not the courts, bore the responsibility for implementing the Constitution by passing necessary laws.

Here Johnson's doubts stood in contrast to Story's confidence concerning the infallibility of the Supreme Court. In Story the Federalist appetite for jurisdiction continued to live on long after the demise of the party. Johnson, on the other hand, showed a lively respect for state judges and accordingly interpreted strictly grants of jurisdiction that threatened inroads on the free action of those officials.[59] Indeed, Johnson discovered certain controversies that by nature must be excluded from judicial examination. Such was the petition for injunction which the Cherokee Indians filed with the Supreme Court in 1831; its object was to restrain the State of

[57]*Ibid.*, p. 364.
[58]*Ibid.*, pp. 374-75.
[59]Cf. Weston *v.* Charleston, 2 Pet. 449 (1829), in which Johnson, dissenting, denied that a motion for prohibition came within a strict reading of the Judiciary Act. In Cohens *v.* Virginia, 6 Wheat. 264 (1821), Johnson acquiesced in silence in the opinion of the Court upholding the appellate jurisdiction of the Supreme Court over state tribunals.

Georgia from enforcing certain laws in contravention of treaties.[60]
In denying jurisdiction Marshall relied in part on the inadequacy
of the tribe as a party in the meaning of the judicial article: the
Indians, it was held, were not a foreign state and hence could not
sue. Johnson, in concurring, found the case wholly political. As an
issue of conflicting sovereign rights, as a dispute which verged upon
a state of war between the parties, as a controversy in which the
President had already refused to intercede in behalf of the Indians,
this case was inappropriate for judicial consideration. Said Johnson:

> Courts of justice are properly excluded from all considera-
> tions of policy, and therefore are very unfit instruments to
> control the action of that branch of government which may
> often be compelled by the highest considerations of public
> policy to withhold even the exercise of a positive duty.[61]

Despite a native pugnacity, Johnson was capable of exercising restraint. The term "unfit instruments" suggests the skepticism with
which he regarded the role of courts. He had read strictly the acts
of Congress in the earlier cases; in the Cherokee case he applied the
same reading to the Constitution itself, for that case had entered
the Court under the original jurisdiction granted directly by Article
III.

In most instances, however, for Johnson it was Congress that
governed the jurisdiction of the court. Moreover, the legislature might
withdraw jurisdiction it had earlier granted. As he declared judicially
in 1819: "The forms of administering justice, and the duties and
powers of courts as incident to the exercise of a branch of sovereign
power, must ever be subject to legislative will, and the power over
them is unalienable, so as to bind subsequent legislatures."[62]

As a member of the assembly of his state, William Johnson had
helped carry through a comprehensive reform of the courts of
South Carolina. As a justice of the national Supreme Court he
insisted that the national legislature retain a broad power over the
national tribunals. In his mind the Constitution, through Article
III, had established only the framework of a judicial system. Through
the "necessary and proper" clause it had assigned to Congress the
task of creating, abolishing, or modifying the lower federal courts
and their jurisdiction. While Joseph Story saw the judicial article
as a directive to Congress, Johnson saw it as a guidepost. Crimes
punishable by the common law could be tried in federal courts

[60]Cherokee Nation v. Georgia, 5 Pet. 1 (1831).
[61]5 Pet. 30: Story concurred with Thompson in dissent. Cf. Johnson's separate opinion in Fletcher v. Peck, 6 Cranch 87, 146 (1810), in which he contended that a question of conflicting claims of a state and an Indian tribe to
lands was "more fitted for a diplomatic or legislative than a judicial inquiry."
[62]Johnson for the Court in Bank of Columbia v. Okely, 4 Wheat. 235, 245
(1819). Cf. a statement to the same effect in his dissenting opinion in Yeaton
v. Bank of Alexandria, 5 Cranch 49, 54 (1809).

only when Congress had expressly authorized it. The cases cognizable in the lower federal courts and those appealable from the state courts were for Congress to determine. Changes in the system were fit subjects for legislative and not judicial determination. This, then, was a "congressional" theory of jurisdiction.[63]

If Congress governed the channels of access to the courts, might it not likewise control their proceedings and decisions? Or might not the judges claim, as of right, certain inherent powers essential for their proper functioning? Here the writ of injunction is in point. If courts possess no such power, and if legislatures through apathy or intention fail to confer power to issue injunctions, then individuals may suffer. If, contrariwise, courts possess that power by right, then irresponsible and biased judges may award it in the face of a hostile public sentiment.

In this delicate matter of inherent powers, judicial self-restraint was at a premium. The Embargo case had taught Johnson a lesson, and from 1808 on he sought for congressional authority before considering mandamus or habeas corpus. Typical of this stand was his endorsement as late as 1831 of a strong dissent repudiating an inherent power in the Supreme Court to issue mandamus to lower courts.[64] So it was with injunction, a writ which Johnson intimated Congress alone could authorize the courts to issue.[65]

Nevertheless, even Johnson found some powers essential to judicial bodies. A dictum to this effect occurs in the Hudson and Goodwin opinion:

> To fine for contempt, imprison for contumacy, inforce the observance of order, &c., are powers which cannot be dispensed with in a court, because they are necessary to the exercise of all others; and so far our courts no doubt possess powers not immediately derived from statute. . . .[66]

Through resort to the indeterminate "&c." Johnson left uncertain the exact scope of inherent powers. Yet in finding that courts required certain powers "necessary to the exercise of all others," he gave a formula for determining them. This was strict construction applied to courts.[67]

[63]Cf. Robert Jennings Harris, *The Judicial Power of the United States* (Baton Rouge, 1940), pp. 87 ff.

[64]*Ex parte Crane,* 5 Pet. 190 (1831). Johnson concurred in a dissent by Baldwin.

[65]See 1 Wheat. 381-82.

[66]United States *v.* Hudson and Goodwin, 7 Cranch 32, 34 (1812).

[67]Elsewhere Johnson suggested the limits of the contempt power: "On this principle [implied powers], it is, that courts of justice are universally acknowledged to be vested, by their very creation, with power to impose silence, respect, and decorum, in their presence, and submission to their lawful mandates, and, as a corollary to this proposition, to preserve themselves and their officers from the approach and insults of pollution." Johnson in Anderson *v.* Dunn, 6 Wheat. 204, 227 (1821).

Throughout his long contest with Joseph Story, Johnson stood firm on that mode of interpretation. Where the New Englander sought to inflate the prestige and authority of the judges, the South Carolinian sought to preserve the dominance of the representative legislature. Where the former would expand jurisdiction, the latter would restrict it in the interest of the states and of a legislative surveillance over the judicial system. Courts of justice existed not only to protect individuals against arbitrary power, but also, equally, to discharge an essential function of the people's government—the administration of justice.

Admittedly, courts were to some extent exempt from legislative control. Safely beyond interference by the lawmakers were the original jurisdiction of the Supreme Court, possibly also admiralty cases, and a limited number of powers inherent in courts. The author of the Embargo Mandamus decision would have been the first to resist encroachments of the Congress on the actual process of decision-making. These were exceptions to the rule.

Johnson's stress on legislative surveillance would rule out a rigid and traditionalistic structure of courts. His view would have recognized the need for experimentation and the adaptation of judicial institutions to new conditions. Applied to our own time, for example, that view would leave it to Congress to improvise tribunals for administrative justice and to decide to what extent appeal should be allowed to the Supreme Court.

The resistance to Story in the matter of judicial power paralleled the resistance to Jefferson in the Embargo case. Over judge and executive officer alike, Johnson upheld the arm of Congress. Where a direct constitutional grant was lacking, each must look to Congress for power. In the matter of the Embargo case, at least, this was turning Jefferson's ideas against their author. It was giving the popular branch the role of leader in the constitutional triumvirate.

In his later years Johnson articulated this conception. Jefferson himself, he wrote, had defended legislative supremacy while a member of Washington's cabinet. Johnson asserted that without express statutory authorization, some organs of the early government had exercised executive and judicial powers on the theory that the Constitution had directly granted such powers or had implied them in the creation of those organs.[68] This reflected an "imperfect" view of the constitutional distribution of powers. In Johnson's view Jefferson had stood on sound footing:

> The precedent was dangerous in the extreme: it made the judicial and executive departments independent of the legislative, where the constitution did not sanction that independ-

[68]*Eulogy on Thomas Jefferson* (Charleston, 1826), p. 16.

ence; and left few limits to their power besides their own moderation or discretion in assuming it. On this ground it was opposed; and in the discussions arising out of that opposition, commenced the altercations which distracted the cabinet. To Mr. Jefferson's well known opinions on this subject we appeal for the doctrines which he espoused.[69]

His essential Jeffersonianism led Johnson to linger behind while Marshall and Story carried the doctrine of separation of powers to an extreme. The dominant faction on the Court took the Federalist path. Nationalism and economic conservatism alike impelled them to exalt the judiciary; due to political considerations, they had less concern for executive power.

On his part, Johnson on one occasion called the separation of powers into three departments "natural" and "necessary . . . to individual security."[70] Yet he applied the principle narrowly. Wherever possible, whether in relation to executive or judiciary, Jefferson's appointee of 1804 sought to preserve as wide a range of control as possible to the national legislature. How would this Jeffersonian construe the great substantive powers of that legislature? This problem of strict versus broad construction of congressional powers would face him at the midpoint of his career, and the manner in which he would meet it would result in no small part from events outside the judicial chambers.

[69]*Ibid.*, p. 17; cf. *ibid.*, p. 16.
[70]Johnson, for the Court, in Lessee of Livingston *v.* Moore, 7 Pet. 469, 546 (1833).

Chapter VI

CITIZEN AND PLANTER: 1809-1819

BY THE summer of 1814 the office of federal judge had lost its glamour for William Johnson. At three full sittings of the Court he had sparred inconclusively with his younger and more methodical brother from Salem. Beyond the doors of the courtroom history was being made; the United States had once again gone to war with Great Britain. The tidings of Napoleon's defeat and exile had just reached America, and Mr. Justice Johnson had a favor to ask of President Madison:

CHARLESTON, June 16th ——14

MY DEAR SIR

I have taken the liberty to address this directly to yourself under cover to Mr. Monroe because the subject is one which for many reasons cannot be confined to the knowledge of too few—and because I would not have it appear as if I had attempted to make an interest in your cabinet to obtain what I would wish to owe to yourself alone.

The wonderful events which have recently occurred in Europe will I apprehend impose on you the necessity of sending another minister to Paris. If it comports with the views of the administration, I beg leave to make you a tender of my services in that capacity.

It is my wish to retire from the bench, and I only await a decent apology to my friends for doing so.[1]

The incumbent then at the Paris legation was the Republican politician and erstwhile Senator from Georgia, William H. Crawford. Johnson argued in further support of his bid:

Crawford would no doubt be gratified with an appointment to my place, as I suspect it would comport both with his wishes and convenience. No man could be more agreeable to the circuit over which he will preside if appointed.

I know there is no subject on which we are so apt to deceive ourselves as with regard to the peculiar cast or character of our own talents, but I have thought myself into the opinion that I can be at least as servicable [sic] in the capacity to which I aspire as in that which I fill.[2]

[1] Madison Papers (MSS; Library of Congress).
[2] Ibid.

Whatever the President thought of this unorthodox bid, he did nothing about it. That the bid was made at all, however, was noteworthy. Why had Johnson grown dissatisfied with his judicial station? Evidently the lure of an active political career had potency; but why should he leave the judiciary, with its permanence of tenure and its remoteness from party machinations?

A full decade had passed since Johnson had entered the Court, and by now the Republicans there outnumbered the Federalists by five to two. Had John Marshall relegated the South Carolinian to a new minority by converting the other Republicans to Federalism, and did Johnson deem further resistance futile? As a state judge Johnson had kept alive his interest in politics and had actively promoted the South Carolina College. The allusion now to Crawford suggests relations of intimacy with that leader and perhaps a continuing interest in party politics. Was the note to Madison symptomatic of a congenital restlessness—a desire to leave the study and enter the arena of active affairs?

A review of Johnson's activities out of court may suggest an answer to these questions. Furthermore, such a survey will disclose something of the wealth, and variety of unofficial duties assumed by the early judges. The federal justice of that day was more than a lawyer and arbiter of controversies; he was in fact a channel of communication at a time when the movement of intelligence was sporadic and lumbering. In linking together government and people, Washington and the state capitals, he served as a key adjunct to the press and post office.[3]

Finally, it may appear that Johnson's unofficial interests and activities served to some extent to color his construction of the Constitution. In reading that document, the judge in one sense applies a body of law, fixed, consistent, systematic. In another, however, he serves as mediator in the tug of interests and approaches his work with values and presuppositions shaped by non-legal forces. The currents of thought and action with which Johnson associated

---

[3]A news item in 1809 suggests the point. A Savannah newspaper reprinted from a Washington paper an advertisement for a newly patented substance known as impenetrable stucco. The dispatch holds out as a proof of claims made for the new product a signed certificate by nature of a testimonial. The signatories describe the stucco as a roof-covering capable of withstanding fire. They continue: "as we have viewed an experiment made on it, as well by Aquafortis, as by a coal of fire, neither of which seemed to have complete power of destruction; we are therefore of opinion, that the same Cement is a very useful invention." After a concluding bid for the patronage of the public, the certificate bears the signatures of Justices Marshall, Washington, Johnson, and Livingston. *Columbian Museum and Savannah Advertiser,* May 4, 1809, reprinted from *Washington Monitor.* Evidently no dissent was rendered!

himself during the War of 1812 and the peace that followed may furnish clues to his subsequent utterances on the bench.

Two addresses which Johnson made during this period are significant. One of these was delivered in Charleston on July 4, 1812. At Washington a fortnight earlier, Congress had adopted the declaration of war with Great Britain, an event long awaited by the nation. Madison's continuance, with modifications, of Jefferson's policy of trade restrictions had served more to aggravate interests at home than to curb the depredations of the belligerents abroad. Young "war-hawks" like Calhoun of South Carolina and Clay of Kentucky had berated their fellows in Congress for their passivity. The South and, even more, the West had pressed for action, and Madison had been pushed into war. New England and neighboring states, however, denounced the war as they had the restrictions. Politicians there attacked the measures of the administration and even talked of secession. The old Federalist, John Marshall, was disturbed by the course of events and hoped for a union of peace advocates to bring about an end to the war.[4] Marshall confided his opinions to a friend: Johnson would declaim his from the platform.

Would the young South Carolinian support the war? As early as 1809, when Pennsylvania and states in New England were defying national measures, he had sat with a committee of leading Charlestonians for the purpose of public protest. These men had drafted resolutions setting forth their "confidence in the general government and their determination to support the union, constitution and rights of the country."[5] When news of the declaration of war reached Charleston, only a week before the Fourth, a meeting was hastily called at Wood's Hotel at which Justice Johnson took the chair. This "numerous and respectable" assemblage proceeded to embody its members as "Alarm Men" for the defense of the port.[6]

On July 4, Charleston glowed with even more than the customary patriotic warmth. The members of the '76 Association celebrated the anniversary of independence with "unusual demonstrations of joy."[7] A procession wound noisily from the Exchange past St. Michael's Church and on to St. Philip's, where the patriots heard divine service, sat through the traditional reading of the Declaration of

[4] See Marshall to Robert Smith, July 27, 1812, Beveridge, *Life of John Marshall*, IV, 35 ff.
[5] The *Republican and Savannah Evening Ledger,* Sept. 2, 1809. Among the fifteen on the committee were Charles Pinckney, Langdon Cheves, Peter Freneau, Theodore Gaillard, William L. Smith, Major Thomas Pinckney, and William Lowndes.
[6] *City Gazette* (Charleston), July 1, 1812.
[7] *Carolina Gazette* (Charleston), July 11, 1812.

Independence, and then awaited the annual oration. Johnson's opening pronouncements set the tone for his address. Those who had
filed into St. Philip's expecting a declamation in the ornate style of
the day would not be disappointed.

> The heart, my Fellow-Citizens, that dilates not with ex-
> traordinary emotion on the return of this day, must be insen-
> sible to some of the finest feelings that animate and give dig-
> nity to our nature. . . .
> Sacred to the recurrence of the most ennobling recollections,
> be the return of this day! Ominous will it prove to the cause
> of liberty, whenever its first dawn shall no longer be an-
> nounced by the cannon's voice, and the exhilarating sounds of
> martial music, when it shall cease to be hailed as a day of
> rational festivity, or the orator refuse a well-meant effort to
> contribute to its celebration.[8]

The American Revolution, Johnson proceeded, was an event
that had rocked the world. The ancients had slumbered in ignorance
of the western continents. Only in modern times had the discoverers
torn away the veil which concealed the Americas. The result had
gladdened the downtrodden of Europe, who had taken heart at
the prospect of a new world beyond the reach of tyrants, "where
one great effort might yet be made for ameliorating the condition of
man."[9] At length Americans had resorted to revolution. That occurrence was a "pillar of fire" to guide men toward a realization
of their highest powers, and the example of the patriots of '76 should
inspire their sons in the present crisis.

The men of Charleston would find heroes enough in the record
of South Carolina without importing them from other states. M'Donald, Jasper, Hume, Hayne, and Moultrie, all stood out as worthy
of emulation. And then there was the orator of the Liberty Tree:

> Who can forget the patriot Gadsden? Boldness and deci-
> sion marked his every thought, energy and firmness character-
> ized his actions.—His elevated soul had fixed on freedom for
> its object, and his ardent mind sprung to the goal of his
> wishes, with a celerity that distances the ordinary concep-
> tions of man.[10]

Johnson himself could remember many of the "appalling scenes"
of the Revolution. Doubtless he spoke from personal experience
when he described the exile of the citizens, including his father, to
St. Augustine. The men of South Carolina had stood firm. "Where
else," Johnson asked, "was it deemed necessary to tear the father

[8]*An Oration delivered in St. Philip's Church: before the Inhabitants of
Charleston, South Carolina, on Saturday, the Fourth of July, 1812, in Com-
memoration of American Independence: by Appointment of the '76 Association and published at the request of that Society* (Charleston, 1813), p. 3.
[9]*Ibid.*, p. 6.
[10]*Ibid.*, p. 13.

from his weeping family, and in contempt of the most solemn pledge of faith, in war, to incarcerate him in a distant land . . . ?"[11]

Now the old enemy was again threatening. Great Britain was throttling commerce and impressing American seamen. British gold, Johnson was ready to allege, had persuaded the frontier Indians to attack. In this crisis Americans must unite. Dangers there were, but these would not alarm the patriot. Lack of unity, distrust of the elected rulers, and unwillingness to contribute to the needs of war were pitfalls which the nation would avoid. Johnson saw only one menace ahead. The "wily serpent of disunion" had crept into the cradle of the Revolution, but Johnson was sure that in the crisis Massachusetts would stand by the Union.[12]

Patriots might take courage from the struggle of the Poles and Swiss to regain their liberty. Americans had their heroes and their memory would never be forgotten. With a flourish Johnson ended his appeal:

> Long may the love of country be the animating principle of the sons of Carolina. May her untarnished laurels descend to ages of virtuous posterity, and canopied by Almighty Power, may she remain the consecrated abode of Rational Liberty.[13]

As an orator, the judge had met the standards of his time. The local press acclaimed his address at St. Philip's for its "elegance, erudition and patriotic warmth."[14] In appealing to the memory of the Revolution and in casting scorn on opponents of the war party, Johnson had proved himself a propagandist of vigor and skill.

Yet the easy confidence he had felt over the outcome of the war vanished within a year. By July, 1813, he was voicing his fears to the Secretary of State in an urgent plea for help; he acted from two motives, an interest in "whatever affects the present administration," and a wish to further the security of Charleston.[15] That city and the surrounding coast lay exposed to the enemy. The militia commander—the Federalist Jacob Read—and many of Charleston's residents, Johnson asserted, deplored the present administration and would welcome its repudiation. He said he would hide his apprehensions from his fellow-townsmen and would busy himself with providing fortifications around the port; but only a new, trustworthy commander and additional troops from Washington would suffice to ward off an attack. Yet, despite Johnson's entreaty, no ade-

[11]*Ibid.*, pp. 9, 12.
[12]*Ibid.*, p. 17.
[13]*Ibid.*, p. 22.
[14]*Carolina Gazette*, July 11, 1812.
[15]Letter dated July 25, 1813, Monroe Papers (MSS; New York Public Library).

quate aid came from the north, and South Carolina fought out the war on her coast virtually single-handed.[16]

The next year, 1814, saw Johnson making his futile request for the Paris mission. That he felt pique over the outcome of that bid and regret over the prominence given to Federalists in military posts is likely. When peace was at last concluded he was able to accept with exultation the congratulations of a Georgia friend over "the Eclat justly acquired by the Republicans" during the war.[17] But in Johnson's view, it was the spirit of the Republicans and not their administration that had brought victory. It was a case of "excellent materials miserably applied." Perhaps this damning of Madison's conduct of the war had justification in the facts. Johnson evidently thought it had. When the President was about to leave Washington at the close of his administration, the justice sent an impassioned farewell note to his friend, Dolly Madison, with only a "respectful adieu" for her husband.[18]

The judge had followed the war with keen interest. At the February terms of Court in Washington and in his regular swings around the Georgia and South Carolina circuit he had kept himself informed on trends and opinions. He had felt the nation in genuine danger, and he had used what influence he had to avert the peril. But the first flush of enthusiasm which had evoked the *Oration* had disappeared. Republican principles might remain untarnished, but to him the Republican leadership had failed in the crisis. The war had produced much misery and, at the Hartford Convention, threats of a northern secession. Perhaps the return of peace would restore the nation's unity.

The ceremony at St. Philip's had enabled Johnson to express to his fellow-citizens his views on the war. The restoration of peace soon brought an opportunity to set forth a reasoned scheme for meeting some of the problems of the aftermath. One Saturday in October, 1815, the intellectual elite of Charleston gathered at the hall of the South Carolina Society for the regular monthly meeting of the Literary and Philosophical Society. The speaker of the day was its senior vice-president, "The Honorable William Johnson."[19]

[16]Wallace, *History of South Carolina*, II, 385-95.
[17]Johnson to Charles Harris of Savannah, May 3, 1815 (Miscellaneous MSS; New-York Historical Society; courtesy of the Society).
[18]Johnson to Dolly Madison, March (?), 1817, Maud Wilder Goodwin, *Dolly Madison* (New York, 1896), p. 198. Johnson wrote: "be assured that all who have ever enjoyed the honor of your aquaintance, will long remember that polite condescension which never failed to encourage the diffident, that suavity of manner which tempted the morose or thoughtful to be cheerful, or that benevolence of aspect which suffered no one to turn from you without an emotion of gratitude." *Ibid.*, pp. 197-98.
[19]*Charleston Courier*, Oct. 19, 1815.

The moment was auspicious. The nation was entering the "Era of Good Feeling." The machinations of Federalists in New England had brought the final decline of their party and with it an end to party bickering. Wartime depression had given way to prosperity. Men in all sections were turning their thoughts to measures that might sustain and carry forward the national well-being. Along with others, statesmen from South Carolina would soon be advocating a new national bank, protective tariff, and improvements for internal communications and transportation.

For the moment that state would spearhead the nationalist forces. Yet the policy was destined for a short life. Cotton planting, with its usual counterpart, slavery, was inundating the state and was spilling over into new lands to the southwest. General business depression and the competition of the more fertile acres of Alabama and Mississippi would in time produce resentment. South Carolina would then seek safety by retreating from nationalism and by standing defiantly on state rights.

But in 1815 that lay in the future. As Johnson drove to the hall, manuscript in hand, prospects must have seemed bright. Behind him in Cannonsborough was a new home with ample rooms, decorated in the classical cornices and friezes of the period, spacious and hospitable.[20] There on his large lot lived Sarah, the growing children, and a retinue of ten slaves.[21] By this date Johnson had begun to acquire property in town and country which later included several plantations.[22] These were but a few of the perquisites of the Charleston gentleman to which Johnson, at forty-three, could lay claim. The essay he was about to present would be the advice of one gentleman-planter to others of his kind.

This time, Johnson's style was restrained; yet, as before, his tone was didactic:

> If I can succeed in exhibiting an imaginary view of the man
> of education and competence, in the retirement of his own

[20]Johnson had purchased this lot, measuring 80 x 220 feet, in May, 1812, the cost being $7,000.—Conveyance at the Mesne Conveyance Office, Charleston. By 1813 he had moved from his former residence, at 1 Anson St., to the new home.—Richard Hrabowski, *Directory of the District of Charleston for 1809* (Charleston, n.d.); Joseph Folker, *Directory of the City and District of Charleston . . . for . . . 1813* (Charleston, n.d.). The house still stands at 156 Rutledge Ave.

[21]Population Census Schedules, 1820, South Carolina, Vol. II, Charleston District (MSS; National Archives), p. 309.

[22]Johnson was a frequent party to transfers of land and other properties, as shown by a survey of Direct Indices of Real Estate Transactions, Mesne Conveyance Office, Charleston; at his death he left several town lots, slaves, personal property, and several plantations, one totaling 1700 acres. See Johnson's will, in Will Book H (1834-1839), p. 32, Probate Judge's Office, Charleston; and a Deed of Sale, dated Sept. 21, 1835, Mesne Conveyance Office, Charleston.

farm, dividing his time between necessary cares and philosophical amusement; and if I can thereby direct the attention of my auditors to a few subjects on which enlightened taste may be amused; and a few objects not unworthy the care of him who would add something however small to the stock of public wealth or happiness, it is all that I am permitted to aspire to.[23]

As its title, *Nugae Georgicae,* suggested, Johnson's discourse dealt with agriculture. The speaker's mood changed from modesty to complacency as he drew a portrait of the southern plantation-owner. No one was so well fitted as the planter, blessed as he was with leisure time, to attain the only legitimate source of human happiness, that is, "moral and intellectual improvement."[24] He lived remote from the corruptions of the city. He indulged in hunting, riding, and the pleasures of the table only in moderation. He had little in common with that farmer whose only enjoyment lay in acquiring wealth. Indeed, his was a high calling:

> Surrounded by his family, his dependents, his flocks and his herds, with all around him looking to him for food, for comfort, for protection or instruction, he cannot but form a high estimate of his own importance in the scale of creation. Then it is too that he must feel most forcibly the weight of that responsibility which his station forces on him, and be daily and hourly urged to the faithful discharge of the great duties of life.[25]

Johnson's ideal planter would devote himself to the history of agriculture. That would furnish valuable lessons for the present. From Rome, for instance, came a warning to the modern farmer. At the height of Rome's prosperity her farms exhibited three features—moderate size, the immediate supervision of the owner, and the liberal use of manures and irrigation. To Johnson, the decline of agriculture—and already he professed to see signs of such a decline in his state—showed itself in the disappearance of small units and the use of hired overseers.

He exhorted the Carolina planters to consider what crops to raise. One of the oldest products, rice, should be more widely planted; rice land increased in fertility—a fact of political importance, since it gave a "fixed state to society, and a permanence to public resources."[26] Cotton, too, merited study; not only might the

---

[23]*Nugae Georgicae; an Essay, delivered to the Literary and Philosophical Society of Charleston, South Carolina, October 14, 1815.* By the Honorable William Johnson, Senior Vice-President. (Charleston, 1815.) At the Boston Public Library is a copy of this pamphlet presented by Johnson to Jefferson. See below, p. 104.

[24]*Ibid.,* p. 4.

[25]*Ibid.,* p. 5.

[26]*Ibid.,* p. 15.

species be improved, but other reforms were in order. South Carolina should manufacture textiles, since the proximity of raw material and the availability of water power gave her an advantage over distant states.

The speaker warned his hearers against a reckless destruction of the soil: he hoped that "the present ruinous mode of clearing and exhausting, will give place to the more rational and ultimately beneficial plan of planting less and manuring more."[27] A careful rotation of crops would likewise help to conserve the soil.

Furthermore, South Carolina would do well to diversify her products. "Immense other countries," Johnson asserted, would soon be producing cotton, and the price of rice fluctuated with the political condition of Europe. Some should improve and extend the raising of cattle, sheep, and horses. Others might experiment with fruits, such as apples, pears, oranges, peaches, and apricots. Peach brandy was already in production and offered a profitable export. To hope to eliminate the taste for this and other spirits was useless; the next best recourse was to improve the product. Some of these articles Johnson had grown himself. His auditors received a detailed account of his experiments.

Still other crops would serve to free South Carolina from dependence on foreign sources. Olives would furnish oils, as would also the seed of the benne plant. The oil of benne seed had eminent supporters: "Amidst that concourse of strangers, which is drawn together at the Seat of Government, even at the President's table, it has been rigidly tested, and the decision was universally favorable."[28] These and other products would make for national self-sufficiency. This was in Johnson's opinion a justifiable objective.

> When a nation can no longer be cut off from her usual supplies; when the wants which nature or our habits have created, can be gratified from sources that set at nought the hostility of other nations, the weak, the timid, the luxurious or effeminate, can be roused with the more facility at national indignity. A consciousness of independence invigorates the public mind; and independently of the wealth and comfort which flow from such acquisitions, the nation becomes strengthened in the spirit of the people.[29]

Three great objects stood out above others as urgent. The first was a proper care of the soil to prevent its total destruction. The second was a judicious management of slaves. The justice and policy of slavery Johnson hesitated to consider. In such a place as this,

[27] *Ibid.*, p. 18.
[28] *Ibid.*, p. 30.
[29] *Ibid.*, pp. 30-31.

only a fanatic, he thought, would agitate that subject. Johnson evidently had mixed feelings on the question:

> Whether the soil of Carolina will ever be cultivated by the hands of freemen, is a question on which philanthropy will muse with painful emotion, whilst the Christian, who considers all conditions with a view to a state of probation, will often see more to be envied in the life of the slave than in that of the master.[30]

The inquiring planter would find that his own interest in the labor and increase of the slaves conformed precisely with the dictates of humanity. Masters and slaves alike would benefit from a careful regard to the health and comfort of the slaves, the education of their children in habits of industry, and a firm and uniform, yet reasonable discipline.

All this was eminently practical. Nevertheless, Johnson put in a word of sympathy for the slave. He denounced as a vulgar prejudice the idea that the black man was incapable of generous or grateful feelings. It was absurd to expect from the slave that "elevation of soul" found in the freeman. What could be expected from one "who has so little to lose, so little to gain, so little to hope, so little to fear, and to whom character is of so little importance?"[31] Yet everyone was acquainted with faithful slaves.

Johnson's third object was a cheap and efficient form of transportation. The rivers and streams which crisscrossed the state offered the best possibilities. Johnson suggested three canals to connect these watercourses. The work called for clearing the rivers and constructing locks, and Johnson, deploring the manner in which private promoters had handled the tasks, called for governmental control. The state should set up a board of inland navigation with ample funds to disburse. This board should survey river courses and then proceed to their clearing. As a result, permanent and efficient farms would in time line their banks, and the system of internal navigation would bring rich rewards to the state and the port of Charleston.[32]

In pursuing this program the state should avoid two pitfalls. Speculators had earlier obtained charters from the state government for the clearing of streams. Some of these were still in force, and the state should either buy them up or legally vacate them in order to protect from all embarrassing obstructions "the interest of the public at large." The State of New York furnished another example of monopoly which South Carolina should avoid. New York had granted an exclusive franchise for the steam navigation of her

[30]*Ibid.*, p. 33.
[31]*Ibid.*, pp. 36-37.
[32]*Ibid.*, pp. 37-40.

rivers. Johnson, predicting that steamboats would soon provide swift and safe transportation between all parts of South Carolina, cautioned against a similar mistake:

> it is to be hoped, that we shall not be tempted to the adoption of that short-sighted policy which renders a whole community liable to be severely assessed by the cupidity of a few individuals.[33]

After uttering these warnings, Johnson apologized to his fellow-planters for his prolixity and turned away from the lectern. Despite its verbosity the essay was suggestive and a fitting sequel to the more ornate *Oration*. The 1812 piece had appealed for national unity and had sought to implement that unity through a revival of the political principles of 1776. The failure of Republicanism during the succeeding crisis to produce competent leaders seemed to Johnson no reflection on the party creed. The goal was still national well-being. Now, however, instead of emphasizing political principle, Johnson turned to means that were in the main economic and technological. Through the manufacture of cotton textiles, diversified agriculture, and protection of the soil, he sought to assure a balanced and stable economy. National self-sufficiency would, he thought, promote national independence. Improvements in transport under state auspices would serve the same purposes.

There were others, it is true, who in those years were promoting similar reforms, and in much of this, of course, they and Johnson were fighting a losing battle. King Cotton and its ally, the system of slavery, which even Johnson regarded as a necessary evil, were here to stay; and, by a singular irony, several of the problems treated in the essay of 1815 were to confront Johnson in other forms in later years.

Throughout the pronouncement on agriculture Johnson had insisted on a scientific method. Time and again he had referred to researches of his own and of others, and had called for experimentation and a free exchange of knowledge. A friend and associate of Johnson would one day characterize the judge as "habitually and from choice a student." In a library which must have housed not only law books, but works of history, philosophy, and science, Johnson supplemented his own researches with the wisdom of other observers in his approach to the concrete problems of the hour.[34]

The objectives which this erudite judge had set forth in his two Charleston addresses continued to absorb his energies. An exchange

---

[33]*Ibid.*, p. 40.
[34]"He [Johnson] felt that in reaching the highest distinctions at which all of us should aim, that it was necessary to avail himself of all the lights of history and philosophy, and that a vast circle of science must be traversed."— Resolutions adopted after Johnson's death at a meeting of the Literary and Philosophical Society, *Charleston Courier*, Aug. 18, 1834.

of letters with Thomas Jefferson in 1817 gives evidence of his sustained interest. Along with his letter Johnson sent the aging leader of the Republicans two gifts. One was a tortoise-shell walking stick. The head of the stick bore an engraved legend, "We will resist," and was made of oak taken from the remains of the Liberty Tree. Johnson related that he had dug up the root and had used it in various ways to "keep alive the sacred flame of '76."[35] The second gift was a copy of *Nugae Georgicae*. The author of that essay considered it a humble effort and hoped it would stimulate further inquiry. He intended to follow it up with some home-grown olives for Jefferson to sample.

Jefferson's reply to all this glowed with appreciative camaraderie. The founder of the Republican party took delight in the walking stick, because of its associations with the early discussions which he thought would in time change the face of the world.[36] And Jefferson had this to say of Johnson and of the party which both had long ago helped to organize:

> We have been associated in times and labor covered with awful gloom and painful anxiety for the destinies of our country, and we have lived to see those our labors and anxieties issue in the happiest forms and principles of administration which man has ever yet seen; and acquire, through a course of 24 years . . . a force of habit which will protect them from change. These scenes, which we have witnessed, leave endearing impressions on fellow-laborers, which I can assure you with sincerity have lost none of their strength with me and which I am happy in this occasion of expressing.[37]

The essay on agriculture Jefferson thought reflected a praiseworthy zeal. The interests of agriculture were the "happiest we can follow, and the more important to our country." He hoped that through Johnson's efforts and example, South Carolina would abound in wine and oil. Agriculture and party loyalty had furnished common bonds to reunite the antagonists of the Embargo case.

Johnson's leisure hours were by no means confined to agricultural improvements. Transportation, which would facilitate business and commerce as well as planting, also remained an object of interest. It is significant that Johnson's brothers were by this time not only acquiring plantations of their own, but were seeking their livelihoods in business and the professions. One had until recently been managing the largest textile factory in the state, another would soon enter the hay and grain business, and two others jointly combined

[35]Johnson to Jefferson, March 2, 1817, Jefferson Papers (MSS; Library of Congress).
[36]Jefferson to Johnson, May 10, 1817, Jefferson Papers (MSS; Library of Congress).
[37]*Ibid.*

the practice of medicine with the sale of drugs. One of these last, Joseph, would in 1818 be elected president of the Charleston branch of the United States Bank.[38] Thus, through family affiliations, Johnson came into contact with the interests of finance and commerce.

Improvements in communications and transport vitally affected those interests. That Johnson continued to occupy himself with steamboat navigation in general and the New York monopoly in particular is the testimony of John Quincy Adams. These two met on a voyage from New York to New Haven in 1818, and after a lengthy conversation Adams confided to his diary that the judge was very "ingenious and learned." Johnson had defended his opinions with so much force that Adams had found it advisable after a time to abandon the subject. He had then left Johnson "philosophizing with another of the passengers upon the construction of the steamboat and the conflicting pretensions of Fitch and Fulton."[39] Johnson's interest, however, was not confined to water transportation: when a railroad was projected for South Carolina, Johnson tendered to Joseph Johnson and Thomas Bennett, both directors of the company, suggestions concerning the most advisable route.[40]

The voyage to New England noted by Adams had importance in another connection. Johnson by this date had begun preparations for his *Life of Greene*. Marshall's *Washington* had served that Federalist biographer as a valuable medium for expressing his views on national affairs, and Johnson's *Greene* might serve the same purpose for its Republican author. Two years previously Johnson had offered to complete a biography of Andrew Jackson, hero of New Orleans, which would be worthy of "the occasion and the nation."[41] A mutual friend had then endorsed Johnson's offer

[38]John, the eldest of William's brothers, prior to 1816 had been president of the South Carolina Homespun Company in Charleston.—Wallace, II, 408. James, after completing his studies at the Litchfield Law School in Connecticut, entered the hay and grain business in Charleston.—Early files at the Litchfield Law School building, Litchfield, Conn. The other two, Joseph and Isaac, shared an office as physicians and druggists.—Abraham Motte, *Charleston Directory and Stranger's Guide for the Year 1816* (Charleston, 1816). Joseph served as president of the branch bank from 1818 to 1825.—Article by J. G. deR. Hamilton, in *Dictionary of American Biography*, X, 108.

[39]Adams described Johnson as "one of the anti-classical despisers of Homer and Virgil and admirers of Ossian, Falconer, Walter Scott, Lord Byron and Southey." Entry for Sept. 2, 1818, *Memoirs* (12 vols.; Philadelphia, 1874-1877), IV, 128-29.

[40]Samuel Melanchthon Derrick, *Centennial History of South Carolina Railroad* (Columbia, 1930), p. 28. In 1821 Johnson absented himself from the bench during a lower court case involving the Santee Canal Company, in which conceivably he had an interest.—Minutes C.C. Dist. of S.C., Bk. C, p. 2. It is evident that Johnson was also interested in better roads.—Wallace, II, 400.

[41]Col. Arthur P. Hayne to Jackson, March 27, 1816, John S. Bassett (ed.), *Correspondence of Andrew Jackson* (7 vols.; Washington, 1926-1935), II, 238.

although he hinted to Jackson that the biographer's motive was love of literary fame.[42] That project, however, had fallen to the lot of another.[43] Johnson had then adopted General Greene as his subject and in 1818 had gone to New England in quest of materials. Doubtless he envisaged the project as a vehicle for propagating his opinions, political, economic, and social.

Finally, Johnson sought to achieve his objectives on the stage of national politics. That he should voice his views on candidates and issues conforms fully with the tenacity with which he held convictions and the vigor with which he expressed them. Monroe's austere Secretary of State, John Quincy Adams, is once again the witness. Early in 1820 Adams related in his diary that William H. Crawford, then Secretary of the Treasury, had shown him a strongly worded attack on Adams which had appeared in a Charleston paper. Someone had attributed it to Johnson, although Crawford agreed with Adams that Johnson was probably not the author. Adams, however, leveled this charge at Johnson: "Judge Johnson at the last presidential elections canvassed with great ardor in favor of Crawford and against Monroe. He has been warmly canvassing for Crawford since. . . ."[44]

By nature Adams was suspicious, but there is no ground for doubting Johnson's espousal of the cause of Crawford, who could boast a considerable following in 1816. Johnson had probably consulted Crawford before suggesting to Madison in 1814 that the Minister to France and the justice trade places, and the assumption suggests relations of intimacy between the two Southerners. Almost of an age, they had much in common. The towering Georgian was studious and sagacious. He had assailed Madison's vacillating preparations for war in 1810, had worked for coast fortifications, and favored the national bank and tariff protection.[45] Much in this program would have won the approval of the Charlestonian.

Adams had further grudges against Johnson. Speaking of a verbal thrust which he supposed Johnson had made at him during a meeting of the Supreme Court, he complained:

[42]Hayne to Jackson, March 27, 1818, *loc. cit.*; Hayne to Jackson, March 31, 1816, Bassett, II, 238, n.

[43]The book appeared in 1817 under the title, *The Life of Andrew Jackson, Major-General in the Service of the United States,* completed by John Henry Eaton (Philadelphia). The book had been begun by John Reid.

[44]Entry for Jan. 26, 1820, *Memoirs*, IV, 513. The letter critical of Adams appeared in the Charleston *City Gazette,* for Jan. 17, 1820, over the signature of "Sagittarius"; it defends Spain in the negotiations over the cession of Florida and assails Adams's conduct of those negotiations. Although Johnson was keenly interested in Florida and was no supporter of Adams, it seems unlikely that he could have written this letter. Its anti-republican tone is the strongest reason for attributing it to someone else.

[45]Article on Crawford by U. B. Phillips, *Dictionary of American Biography,* IV, 527-30.

This Judge Johnson is a man of considerable talents and law knowledge, but a restless, turbulent, hot-headed, politician caballing Judge. He has been an ardent canvasser for Crawford, and, though a Judge flaringly independent, a place-hunter for himself and his brother, a carpenter in Charleston. He obtained, through Crawford's influence, the appointment of Collector of the port of Charleston, kept it two or three months, in doubt whether he would accept it or not, and then declined, attempting to bargain his brother into it in his place. This is the man whose judicial virtue was so much alarmed at the suspicion of Executive interference with his duties. Termagant virtue![46]

The charge was probably a compound of truth and personal venom. In all likelihood the justice was sincere in his intention of resigning. A leading newspaper, in February, 1819, took notice of this intention and stated that Johnson would obtain a post of less dignity but higher pay than that of judge.[47] In March, Johnson's name appeared in a list of presidential appointees, the office being that of Collector of the Port of Charleston.[48] At the same time, however, Johnson was quoted as denying a purpose to resign.[49]

Fortunately, Johnson himself has shed some light on the activities of which Adams complained. In April, a Raleigh newspaper published an unsigned attack on the judge. Was it true, this writer demanded, that Johnson's brother Joseph, "a druggist in Charleston," owed his elevation to the presidency of the Charleston branch of the national bank solely to the "personal attentions and solicitations of the Judge in Philadelphia?" Joseph's election had taken place a few months earlier. Was it true, continued the letter, that the judge had used similar methods in obtaining the collectorship for himself? It would certainly lower the dignity of the Court for a judge "to descend from that exalted station for the purpose of grasping a few more dollars behind the counter of a custom house." Finally, was it true that the judge had brought pressure on the President to have another brother substituted in his place in the coveted post?[50]

These hints of place-hunting and nepotism brought forth a vitriolic disclaimer from Johnson. He denounced the Raleigh editor for

[46]Entry for March 27, 1820, *Memoirs*, V, 43.
[47]*National Intelligencer* (Washington), Feb. 1, 1819.
[48]*Columbian Museum and Savannah Daily Gazette,* March 22, 1819.
[49]*Ibid.,* March 16, 1819.
[50]Washington *Gazette,* April 24, 1819, reprinted from the Raleigh *Star,* April 9, 1819. In spreading out the correspondence in his pages, Jonathan Elliot, editor of the *Gazette,* expressed pleasure at Johnson's decision not to resign, for the judge, "if he has not been marked for a fascinating exterior, has been always distinguished for integrity and capacity. . . ." To Mr. Thomas E. Waggaman, former Marshal of the Supreme Court, the author is grateful for calling this correspondence to his attention.

spreading calumnies and denied that he had helped Joseph win
his bank presidency. The allusion to him as a druggist was con-
temptible, in view of his standing in Charleston.[51] Although silent
on how he had come by the appointment as collector, Johnson
called a falsehood the statement that he had brought pressure on
the President in the other brother's behalf. He was proud of the
talents and achievements of both brothers and accordingly said that
the actions charged against him, even if true, would have been
justified.[52] As for his own appointment as collector, there is little
doubt that his intimacy with Crawford, who as Secretary of the
Treasury made the selection, was a telling factor.

With the above letter Johnson caused to be published another,
to Crawford, dated March 31. Here he gave his reasons for de-
clining the new appointment and remaining on the Court:

> My unaffected fondness for retirement, and the interests and
> wishes of my family have long kept my mind in suspense;
> but I have finally, and upon the maturest deliberation satisfied
> myself, that I should not be able to silence my own reproaches,
> were I to suffer my interests or wishes to prevail. I feel most
> sensibly, and whether the feeling be suggested by imagination,
> by vanity or by principle, is immaterial as long as it in fact
> exists, that under existing circumstances my duty is to remain
> where I am.[53]

One of the causes of Johnson's uneasiness had, he said, been the
smallness of the judicial salary. Joseph Story had made a similar
complaint earlier, and doubtless the whole Court felt relieved when
Congress at this juncture raised the salary of associate justices from
$3,500 to $4,500.[54] Thus, we find Johnson asserting that he no
longer felt "neglected by the government." Another reason for his

[51]Johnson to the editor of the Raleigh *Star,* reprinted in Washington
Gazette, April 24, 1819: "He [Joseph Johnson] had been nominated a direc-
tor on the first establishment of this Branch, was then looked to as the
President, had Mr. Faber declined; repeatedly acted as President pro tem.;
was elected as such on the demise of the President; and unanimously elected
President when the late election took place."

[52]While defending the members of his family, Johnson said he had made
known his opposition to his brother John's appointment as collector. He
added that John's chief backer for the post was a member of Congress. That
his brother was at least interested in the post is suggested by a statement
found among papers of the Johnson family. This attests to the character and
fitness for the post of collector for Charleston of Col. John Johnson, Jr.; the
statement is signed by Justice Johnson's colleague on the Circuit Court, District
Judge John Drayton.—Paper in possession of Mr. J. Reid Johnson, New London, Conn. The attempt, however made, was unsuccessful. John was listed in
1819 as blacksmith and director of the P. and M. Bank, in 1822 as blacksmith and founder, and in 1829 as owner of an iron foundry.—From early
city directories (Charleston Library Society).

[53]Johnson to the Secretary of the Treasury, March 31, 1819, reprinted from
the Raleigh *Star,* in Washington *Gazette,* April 24, 1819.

[54]See Story to Stephen White, Feb. 17, 1819, Story, *Life and Letters of
Joseph Story,* I, 326-27. Cf. *ibid.,* pp. 301-3; Act of Feb. 20, 1819, 3 Stat. 484.

remaining was the long experience which he had accumulated on the high bench, an asset which he called irreplaceable. Many friends, he said, had urged him to stay, and this led him to feel that he had the confidence of government and people. A final motive which Johnson gave hinted that he had come by 1819 to look on the work of the Court in a new light:

> The interesting aspect also that the business of the Supreme Court has lately exhibited, its acknowledged importance and weight in the Union, and the responsibility which it has been called on to assume, satisfy me that I ought not to appear to steal away from the discharge of those duties or from my share of that responsibility, in order to fill a station of less general and determinate importance to the Union, and susceptible of being discharged, with perhaps more ability, by so many others.[55]

The Court, as we shall see, had through a series of epochal decisions, leaped into prominence. This must have offered a gratifying stimulus to this restless mind. Thus did William Johnson at the midpoint of his judicial career decide to remain.

The decade which had opened in 1809 with a public appeal for national unity had closed with a voluble endorsement of a favored Presidential candidate to whom Johnson probably owed a lucrative though unacceptable appointment. Restive in his judicial robes, he had followed intently events of the battlefield and market place. He had steadily agitated for reforms. His repeated threats to resign from the bench sprang both from a desire for activity and from a wide-roving interest. As a citizen and as a unique combination of planter and promoter of commerce, he had sought to bestir men in state and nation to act. Not till our own century would many of his proposed reforms, especially those in agriculture, reach fruition.

Throughout all this, national unity was a prime objective. That was essential for defense; likewise it had associations in Johnson's mind with economic self-sufficiency. For the most part, he sought to achieve his goals through local initiative. His appeal for fortifications, improved crops, soil conservation, and amelioration of the conditions of slaves called in the main for voluntary private action. Yet some of these and other measures might demand public attention. Government alone could protect the community from abuses such as monopoly or wasteful exploitation.

And the government to which Johnson looked for most of these measures was that of the state. Would he tolerate the adoption of like measures by the national government and, by thus endorsing implied powers, create doubts about his Republican orthodoxy?

[55]Johnson to the Secretary of the Treasury, March 31, 1819, *loc. cit.*

Chapter VII

THE HERESY OF IMPLIED POWERS

At THE session of 1819 the Supreme Court entered a new era. Although important questions had been decided before, the fundamentals of the Constitution were to be resolved. What was novel was the volume in which such questions flooded the Court, the intense public interest they commanded, and the confident air with which the Court approached them. A handful of judges would seek to settle for good the major premises of the American constitutional order. At this very term they announced three decisions asserting far-reaching powers in the national Congress and judiciary.[1] In the face of a challenge like this, small wonder that Mr. Justice Johnson had determined to stay on the bench!

No decision of this term, nor of any other for that matter, was of higher importance than McCulloch v. Maryland, which involved the attempt of that state to levy a tax on the notes of the Second Bank of the United States. To this ruling the usually articulate justice from Charleston nodded his silent approval. The Chief Justice declared the Union to be the creation of the whole American people, not simply the instrument of separate sovereign states. To serve the people effectively, Congress required a broad choice among measures in carrying out the powers granted it by the Constitution. By virtue of the nature of the Constitution and that clause permitting Congress to pass "all laws which shall be necessary and proper for carrying into execution" the enumerated powers,[2] Congress was entitled to exercise implied powers. Notwithstanding the framers' silence on the subject, the government could validly establish a bank; since national laws were supreme, the attempt by Maryland to tax the operations of the Bank of the United States was unconstitutional. Such was the unanimous opinion of the Court.

To all of this, leaders in Virginia registered a powerful dissent. From his plantation the aging Jefferson called for resistance. Years before, as a member of Washington's cabinet, Jefferson had opposed the incorporation of a bank. Taking issue with Hamilton, he

[1]Sturges v. Crowninshield, 4 Wheat. 122; McCulloch v. Maryland, 4 Wheat. 316; and Dartmouth College v. Woodward, 4 Wheat. 518.
[2]Art. I, sec. 8.

had found no need for such an institution. The Constitution, he had asserted, tolerated only means that were necessary, not those which were convenient, for effectuating the enumerated powers. The argument of convenience had dangers, for it could also apply elsewhere: "It would swallow up all the delegated powers, and reduce the whole to one power. . . ."[3] Jefferson had lost the argument, and the bank of 1791 had done business for twenty years. Congress had chartered, with some modifications, a second bank in 1816. Now Marshall's opinion simply restated the nationalistic contentions of Hamilton. Behind that opinion Jefferson saw lurking the specter of a consolidated government: "The constitution," he complained, ". . . is a mere thing of wax in the hands of the judiciary, which they may twist and shape into any form they please."[4] Others rallied to Jefferson's side, among them Judge Spencer Roane of the Virginia Court, Thomas Ritchie of the *Richmond Enquirer,* and John Taylor of Caroline, statesman and publicist. Centralized power was their common enemy; against the federal judiciary they leveled the charge of attempting to convert the compact of sovereign states into an all-powerful central government.

These Virginia agrarians conceived of implied powers as peculiarly favorable to a hostile economic interest. In his many writings, John Taylor was especially incisive and thorough in his depiction of the menace. To him, finance and manufacturing were the villains of the piece, since only through the assertion of implied powers could they secure their favored instruments, the bank and protective tariff. National laws of that kind would lay the groundwork for a privileged money power. Hence, the scruples of the Virginia Republicans against Marshall's construction in the Bank case. Hence, too, the simultaneous insistence of another Virginian, President James Monroe, that the federal government lacked an implied power to construct internal improvements. Political principle and economic interest alike moved Jefferson and his friends to excoriate the resort to implication.

Yet the precedent of the Bank decision would in the course of time serve other interests. In time, the federal government would require broad powers to cope with the needs of a complex and interdependent society. Only on the basis of implied powers could the lawmakers of another century erect a Federal Reserve System, a controlled currency, and a Tennessee Valley Authority.

In approving Marshall's opinion in the Bank case, William Johnson parted company with Thomas Jefferson. What reasons and

[3]*Writings,* ed. P. L. Ford (10 vols.; New York, 1892-1899), V, 287.
[4]Jefferson to Judge Spencer Roane, Sept. 6, 1819, *ibid.,* X, 141.

motives led him to espouse Hamiltonian views and adopt the chosen weapon of the moneyed interests?

Not until 1821 was Johnson to express at length his own convictions. Long before that, however, even before his elevation to the federal judiciary, he had started down the path to broad construction. From the state bench he had declared that Congress might support the United States Bank through suitable means. "The national government," his statement ran, "may pass such laws as may be proper and necessary to avoid all the mischiefs arising from the counterfeiting, and passing, as true, the forged bills of credit of the Bank of the nation."[5]

As a federal judge, too, Johnson tolerated departures from strict construction. At his very first term he evidently joined with Marshall in upholding a discretion in Congress.[6] Marshall's opinion insisted that Congress, in regulating bankruptcy, might employ any means which were "in fact conducive" to the exercise of the enumerated power.[7] A few years later on circuit, Johnson rejected jurisdiction of a case involving the national bank. Although no question was made of the constitutionality of the Bank, Johnson there took occasion to praise this "valuable institution" and acknowledge its importance to the nation.[8]

In 1812 Johnson came closer to the central issue. As has been shown, the immediate question at stake in the case of Hudson and Goodwin was whether the federal courts possessed a jurisdiction to try crimes at the common law,[9] and Johnson and the majority found no sanction for such a jurisdiction in the Constitution or statutes. But the assertion had been made that courts possessed the power by implication. Johnson began with language reminiscent of Jefferson: "The powers of the general government are made up of concessions from the several states; whatever is not expressly given to the former, the latter expressly reserve."[10]

On this premise Johnson repudiated the jurisdiction attributed to the courts. Nevertheless, he seemed to concede that the power of the government in general as wielded by the legislature might embrace a wide discretion. It was contended, he said, that "upon the formation of any political body, an implied power to preserve its own

[5] State v. Pitman, 1 Brevard 32, 34 (S.C., 1801).
[6] United States v. Fisher, 2 Cranch 358 (1805). The reporter listed Johnson as present at the decision. Marshall said his opinion was that of a majority of the Court. Justice Washington delivered a dissenting opinion.
[7] 2 Cranch 396.
[8] Bank of the United States v. Deveaux, 2 Fed. Cas. 692, 693, No. 916 (C.C. Dist. of Ga., 1808). See above, pp. 83-84.
[9] United States v. Hudson and Goodwin, 7 Cranch 32 (1812). For a fuller discussion, see above, pp. 77-79.
[10] 7 Cranch 33.

existence and promote the end and object of its creation, necessarily results to it." That principle was not peculiar to the common law. Johnson declared, "It is coeval, probably, with the first formation of a limited government; belongs to a system of universal law, and may as well support the assumption of many other powers as those more peculiarly acknowledged by the common law of England."[11]

In saying that courts lacked this criminal jurisdiction even though the doctrine of implication might "communicate certain implied powers to the general government,"[12] Johnson showed a willingness at least to consider the existence of implied powers in Congress. Thus by 1812 Johnson had found some basis for broad construction in the principles of political theory.

The War of 1812 afforded the judges the first clear opportunity for examining the war powers of the national government. In this field, admittedly, Johnson was interpreting not the implied, but the express powers. Furthermore, Jefferson himself in his first inaugural had called the federal government the "sheet anchor of our peace at home and safety abroad," and later had acquired an empire in the West and cut off foreign trade, all in the name of national power. If Jefferson could employ powers over foreign relations in this way, Johnson without giving offense could interpret broadly powers over the related subject of national defense. Yet the manner in which Johnson would approach these powers might suggest, if not determine, his approach to others of a more dubious character.

Two of Johnson's responses to war problems are noteworthy. In 1814 it fell to him to write the Court's opinion in the case of the *Rapid*.[13] An importer had purchased goods in England in peacetime and tried to sail them into Boston after the outbreak of the war. Johnson regretfully held the goods forfeited and legally condemned. One must see war for what it was. He spoke strongly of the dehumanizing effect of war and of the way it completely severed the ties that bound together the citizens of rival belligerents. "The whole nation," he concluded, "are embarked in one common bottom, and must be reconciled to submit to one common fate."[14] This meant the cessation, not merely of trade, but of all intercourse with the enemy.

If the war power imparted to Congress control over commercial activity, it also gave Congress wide discretion in the raising of troops. What Johnson had to say on this subject has pertinence to twentieth-century discussions of compulsory military service. War-

[11]*Ibid.*, pp. 33-34.
[12]*Ibid.*, p. 34.
[13]8 Cranch 155 (1814).
[14]*Ibid.*, p. 161.

fare by militia had nearly failed during the War of 1812, and in the aftermath men questioned this system of raising troops. After living through two wars and after completing the researches for the biography of Greene, Johnson thought the militia inept for protracted combat. Nor was the standing army any better. The nation that forgot the use of arms and employed mercenaries to do its fighting invited foreign and domestic attacks.[15]

More satisfactory modes of raising troops were open to Congress. One of these was the method of enlistment—preferably for the duration of the war. Here, there was little danger of habituating the citizenry to a military way of life, Johnson asserted, for men of a superior sort would "leave the service resolved afterwards rather to try any other pursuit in life."[16] The best of all, however, was the method of conscription. It was rapid, it furnished the best personnel, and it offered no danger either in the maintenance of forces or in their demobilization. Nevertheless, the "genius, the easy life and free habits" of Americans were hard to reconcile with the sacrifices which conscription would call for.[17]

Virginia, under its Revolutionary governor, Thomas Jefferson, had resorted in its extremity to conscription. Johnson praised that action, but said the recourse to it had been tardy.[18] It was not during a period of war or poverty that the government should adopt this system, nor should it attempt in a hasty fashion to transform the habits of the community. Said Johnson:

> If the imagination of man can suggest one method more prompt than all others, of raising an efficient and virtuous army, it is that of conscription. It would bear in its vitals the corrective of the dangers apprehended from a standing army. . . . And a judicious system for training our militia would qualify our youth, ere they attained the age which qualifies them to participate in their country's sovereignty, to stand forth when called upon, as disciplined soldiers in their country's defence.[19]

So sure was Johnson of the merits of the system that he predicted that it would "one day be adopted by the United States, and after that day, she need never fear a foreign war."[20]

To later times it would be reserved to challenge the constitutionality and the democratic character of forced military service. Johnson was willing to extend the power of the national legislature to

[15]Johnson, *Sketches of the Life and Correspondence of Nathanael Greene*, I, 213.
[16]*Ibid.*, p. 212; see also *ibid.*, pp. 214 and 443.
[17]*Ibid.*, p. 214.
[18]*Ibid.*, p. 442.
[19]*Greene*, II, 56-57.
[20]*Ibid.*, I, 442.

meet the predictable contingencies of war. At the same time, be it noted, he thought the states, by virtue of their own militia powers, might supplement federal militia orders. As a later chapter will show, Johnson diverged from his brothers in insisting that the states possessed concurrent power in the raising of militia.[21]

After the close of the war, Johnson was soon declaring himself again on the subject of implied powers. In a separate opinion in 1816 he grounded the congressional control over jurisdiction squarely on the "necessary and proper" clause.[22] In this same opinion he stated his own conception of the constitutional compact. Against the state-rights contention that the document was a compact of sovereign states, Justice Story had declared it solely the creation of the whole people.[23] The former conception led logically to strict construction, the latter to liberal. Johnson strove for a middle ground:

> To me the constitution appears, in every line of it, to be a contract, which, in legal language, may be denominated tripartite. The parties are the people, the states, and the United States. It is returning in a circle to contend that it professes to be the exclusive act of the people, for what have the people done but to form this compact? That the states are recognized as parties to it is evident from various passages, and particularly that in which the United States guaranty to each state a republican form of government.
>
> The security and happiness of the whole was the object. . . .[24]

In a period of growing tension between advocates of state and federal power such a theory would have few supporters. Yet it furnished a basis on which to erect a doctrine conducive both to state autonomy and national discretion.

When at last the United States Bank sought in the Supreme Court protection from the Maryland tax, it found in Johnson not only a sympathizer but one whose conceptions of congressional power had for years verged on liberality. John Marshall spoke the "unanimous and decided" opinion of the Court in upholding the constitutionality of the Bank's charter.[25] The Chief Justice laid down in powerful terms the argument for a choice of means. This power to incorporate a bank he inferred from several of the enumerated powers. The doctrine of implied powers itself he based on two grounds: first, general principles and, second, constitutional provisions—notably the "necessary and proper clause." "Let the end be legitimate," he proclaimed, "let it be within the scope of the con-

---

[21]Houston v. Moore, 5 Wheat. 1 (1820); see below, pp. 243-46.
[22]Concurring opinion in Martin v. Hunter's Lessee, 1 Wheat. 304, 377 (1816).
[23]Ibid., p. 324.
[24]Ibid., p. 373.
[25]McCulloch v. Maryland, 4 Wheat. 316, 424 (1819).

stitution, and all means which are appropriate, which are plainly adapted to that end, which are not prohibited, but consist with the letter and spirit of the constitution, are constitutional."[26] As a valid agent of the national government, the Bank was immune from state taxation.

The voluble South Carolinian remained silent. Hence, he had tacitly acquiesced in views raising to the zenith powers of the nation and circumscribing those of the states. Was this inconsistent with his earlier position?

What of Johnson's private interests? Two months earlier, his brother had assumed headship of the Charleston branch of the Bank. This might conceivably furnish a ground for bias. Critics of the judiciary had pointed with suspicion to the effects which an interest in their stations had on federal judges; and Johnson, by the testimony of Adams, was negotiating at this very time to secure either for himself or for his brother a lucrative federal appointment.[27] Was this not ample inducement to inflate the power and prestige of the government that provided his salary?

Or, again, did not the opinion comport with Johnson's own economic views? Admittedly, he had long favored the Bank as a financial institution, and opinions he had uttered in 1815 supported government action as a means of promoting economic progress. He was soon to engage in correspondence with his friend, Mathew Carey of Philadelphia, and Carey, who wrote voluminously in behalf of the Bank, protection for manufactures, and internal improvements, stood in the vanguard of nationalistic economists.[28]

Other South Carolinians, however, had supported the Bank. John C. Calhoun had drawn up the charter in 1816; residents of Charleston had subscribed heavily to the stock; and when mismanagement threatened the Bank with insolvency, Langdon Cheves, of Charleston, assumed the presidency of the national institution.[29] Economic distress and a defensive attitude toward slavery would soon convert South Carolina to state rights and its corollary, strict construction. At the moment, the tide of nationalism still ran strong.

[26]*Ibid.*, p. 421.

[27]See above, pp. 106-8.

[28]Among copies of extant letters written by Johnson are seven to Carey: three dated 1821, one 1822, one 1825, and two 1826. In 1826 Johnson urged Carey to issue a new edition of his famous *Olive Branch* on the subject of bankruptcy legislation. See below, p. 118, note 37. The first of many editions of the *Olive Branch* appeared in 1814 from Carey's publishing firm in Philadelphia; the work was a plea for harmony between the contending political parties to win the war and secure support for a national program of economic encouragement. See article on Carey by Broadus Mitchell, in *Dictionary of American Biography*, III, 490.

[29]Wallace, *History of South Carolina*, II, 473.

The supposed economic interests of nation and states served only to reinforce this Republican's liberal conception of federal power. Johnson had long since applied strict construction to the powers of executive and courts; but Congress he put in a class by itself. What, one may ask, would forestall that department from usurping power? Might not broad construction enable the national lawmakers to make the Constitution, in Jefferson's words, a "thing of wax"?

On the question of congressional power, Johnson soon had three opportunities to state his views. The first came in 1820 when Americans far and wide were debating the extent to which Congress might go in legislating under its express power to pass bankruptcy laws.

Postwar prosperity had by this time given way to panic and depression. Businesses were failing on all sides. Debtors in increasing numbers were praying for relief, and their creditors were seeking some satisfactory method of making collections. Charleston was hard hit; the business slump would continue there for many years, and Joseph Johnson, new president of the local branch of the United States Bank, would soon be signing a memorial to Congress to enact a national bankruptcy system.[30]

With mounting fervor men called on Congress to act, since the Constitution, it seemed, effectively barred the separate states from meeting the crisis. Had not Justice Washington, sometime since, decreed on circuit that the bankruptcy power was exclusive and implied that the subject was withdrawn from state cognizance?[31] And had not the Supreme Court in the case of Sturges in 1819 completed the restrictive process?[32] That decision had held invalid, as applied to existing contracts, a New York law for insolvent debtors. Marshall's language had affirmed a concurrent state bankruptcy power, but had exalted the constitutional contract clause as a barrier against relief legislation. Strictly speaking, the decision had held void only retrospective state laws; and the opinion actually had the blessing of only three of the seven judges composing the Court, but this fact only time would expose.[33]

Accordingly the national lawmakers had set about framing a national system. That the quest proved fruitless resulted largely from constitutional scruples. The Constitution gave Congress the

[30]Joseph Johnson was one of a committee of five elected by a meeting of citizens to draft the petition.—*Charleston Courier*, Jan. 24, 1822.

[31]Golden v. Prince, 10 Fed. Cas. 542, No. 5509 (C.C. Dist. of Pa., 1814).

[32]Sturges v. Crowninshield, 4 Wheat. 122 (1819).

[33]Todd was absent. Livingston failed to concur in the opinion.—W. Story, *Life and Letters of Joseph Story*, I, 326. Washington still deemed the bankruptcy power exclusive in Congress; see Washington, J., in Ogden v. Saunders, 12 Wheat. 213, 264 (1827). Johnson later termed this a "compromise" decision in which the minority had "thought it better to yield something than risk the whole." Johnson, J., in Ogden v. Saunders, *ibid.*, pp. 272-73.

power to establish "uniform laws on the subject of bankruptcies throughout the United States."[34] But many thought the clause sanctioned laws applying only to those engaged directly in commerce; the notion that others besides merchants and traders might come within the system and that these debtors might themselves initiate proceedings aimed at their relief appeared novel and dangerous. These widespread doubts would inhibit congressional action for twenty years.[35]

But Johnson did not share these doubts. In 1820 he drafted and circulated in pamphlet form a national bill of his own.[36] Johnson was proud of his effort, and when some years later he loaned his last copy to his friend, Mathew Carey of Philadelphia, he still believed its general features the best available to Congress.[37]

This elaborate plan, running to thirty-seven sections, sketched out an advanced system. For one thing, it envisaged a broad power in the federal lawmakers to furnish relief. The special bankruptcy officials whom it would have attached to the district courts would have served not merely the creditor but the debtor as well. In fact, all debtors would have had resort to relief; these bankrupts would have retained necessary furnishings, clothing, and implements of their trade, and, in addition, an allowance for subsistence during three months following discharge. As a compulsory program available to creditors, the system could apply only to defaulting merchants and traders. Moreover, if Congress possessed an amplitude of power, so did the states. By specific provision, Johnson made it clear that the states retained a power over the subject.[38]

[34]Art. I, sec. 8, cl. 4.

[35]See Charles Warren, *Bankruptcy in United States History* (Cambridge, 1935), pp. 24-68. A national law of limited scope had existed from 1800 to 1803.

[36]*A Bill to Establish an Uniform System of Bankruptcy in the United States* (Washington, 1820). The printed copy appeared without the author's name, but a copy at the Harvard Law School library bears the following in Johnson's hand: "drawn by the Hon'ble Willm. Johnson."

[37]He wrote: "As to a bankrupt-law the country needs it very much; but I would rather never see one, than one upon the old plan of commissioners & assignees. I compiled one some years since on the plan of the Scotch & French systems—the best in the world; but we must have everything English. I send you by mail the last copy I have of my projèt, it admits of improvement, but the outline is the best we could adopt. Be so good as to return it to me to Washington with your remarks. I wish you would give us a postscript to the Olive-branch on the subject." Johnson to Carey, Jan. 17, 1826, Chamberlain Collection (MSS; courtesy of Boston Public Library).

[38]Section 33 of Johnson's bill provided: "That nothing herein contained shall be construed to impair the right of the states to legislate and adjudicate on subjects of insolvency or bankruptcy, so far as no provision is made for such cases by this act, except only so far as relates to persons declared involuntary bankrupts in pursuance of this act." Johnson, *Bill to Establish an Uniform System of Bankruptcy*, p. 15.

In the course of time Johnson would again support a broad power over bankruptcy.[39] Yet as early as 1820, as shown by his bill, he conceived of the national power in sweeping terms.

A year later, in 1821, Jefferson's first justice declared himself again on congressional power. Here he spoke openly, officially, and directly on the question of implied powers. At the same term, be it observed, Johnson also agreed silently with his brothers in Cohens v. Virginia. In the Virginia courts, one who had sold lottery tickets in the state had been found guilty of violating a state law forbidding such sales. Defendant had appealed to the Supreme Court on writ of error, arguing that a law of Congress for the District of Columbia had in effect authorized such sales outside the District. In the end Marshall, for the Court, decided against such a construction of the statute, but in the course of his opinion reasserted the jurisdiction of the Court to hear appeals from state courts. Johnson acquiesced in a ruling which raised national powers, legislative as well as judicial, to the zenith.[40]

In another decision, however, Johnson at last emerged from his retreat. This was Anderson v. Dunn, familiar to later times for its establishment of the contempt power of Congress.[41] The facts in the case were trivial almost to the farcical. One Colonel John Anderson had certain claims he sought to press on the government. To secure favorable consideration by Congress, he tendered a "gift" of five hundred dollars to a member of the lower house for the trouble which the matter might entail. The House thereupon ordered its sergeant-at-arms, Thomas Dunn, to arrest Anderson and bring him before its bar. Dunn complied, and the Speaker reprimanded Anderson for his contempt of the Congress. Anderson was thereupon discharged from custody. Subsequently he brought an action of trespass against Dunn for assault and battery and false imprisonment, contending that the Constitution gave no power to Congress to punish for contempt.

The argument before the Supreme Court raised the old issue between strict and broad construction. Justice Johnson, giving the opinion of the Court, came directly to the question. The issue here was whether Congress might punish nonmembers for contempt, and he admitted that the Constitution gave no such power to either house and that the judiciary article did not mention the power. "Shall we, therefore, decide," he asked, "that no such power exists?"[42] The asserted power could be supported only by impli-

[39] See below, p. 222.
[40] 6 Wheat. 264 (1821).
[41] 6 Wheat. 204 (1821).
[42] Ibid., p. 225.

cation, and the spirit of American institutions was hostile to the use of implied powers.

Nevertheless, implied powers were essential. Johnson put the case in strong terms. Had it been possible, the framers would have created a constitution which left nothing to implication. He echoed the words of Marshall in the Bank case:

> But what is the fact? There is not in the whole of that admirable instrument a grant of powers which does not draw after it others, not expressed, but vital to their exercise; not substantive and independent, indeed, but auxiliary and subordinate.[43]

Johnson repeated his demand for discretion in the lawmaking body and pointed out the leading barrier to a usurpation of power. Individual liberty could be in little danger, he insisted, "Where all power is derived from the people, and public functionaries, at short intervals, deposit it at the feet of the people, to be resumed again only at their will." The great end of our institutions, he went on, was the safety and happiness of each citizen. Yet the relation between means and this end was often hard to determine. Said he:

> The science of government is the most abstruse of all sciences; if, indeed, that can be called a science which has but few fixed principles, and practically consists in little more than the exercise of a sound discretion, applied to the exigencies of the state as they arise. It is the science of experiment.[44]

William Johnson had turned his back on strict construction. The former speaker of the powerful assembly of South Carolina deemed discretion essential for a government that would act.[45] Yet the remedy he prescribed for preventing an excess of power was Jeffersonian, an appeal to the people. The process of election was the cardinal restraint on the national officers. On this he would rely, rather than on a narrow limiting of discretion. Since the safety of the people was the supreme law, public functionaries needed power adequate to guard that safety.

Counsel for Anderson had expressed fears of unlimited powers. If the power to punish for contempt were conceded, they had warned, then it might be carried to excess. Other departments, even the

---

[43]*Ibid.*, pp. 225-26.

[44]*Ibid.*, p. 226.

[45]The Constitution of South Carolina, like those of other states, expressly empowered the legislature to punish for contempts. The relevant section provided, "Each House may punish, by imprisonment, during sitting, any person not a member, who shall be guilty of disrespect to the House, by any disorderly or contemptuous behavior in its presence—or who, during the time of its sitting, shall threaten harm to the body or state of any member, for any thing said or done in either House. . . ." (Constitution of 1790, Art. 1, sec. 13) —*Constitutions of the Sixteen States which Compose the Confederated Republic of America* (Boston, 1797), p. 231.

executive, might assert the power, and the government might assume to itself in exercising it the "most tyrannical licentiousness." Individual liberty would perish in the melee.

Johnson, however, had no sympathy for this exaggerated individualism. "The unreasonable murmurs of individuals against the restraints of society," he declared, "have a direct tendency to produce that worst of all despotisms, which makes every individual the tyrant over his neighbor's rights."[46] Every individual stood in dependence on an effectively functioning legislature. Johnson paid a glowing tribute to the importance and prestige of his favored branch of government:

> That a deliberate assembly, clothed with the majesty of the people, and charged with the care of all that is dear to them; composed of the most distinguished citizens, selected and drawn together from every quarter of a great nation; whose deliberations are required by public opinion to be conducted under the eye of the public, and whose decisions must be clothed with all that sanctity which unlimited confidence in their wisdom and purity can inspire; that such an assembly should not possess the power to suppress rudeness, or repel insult is a supposition too wild to be suggested.[47]

This power, he went on, was essential to public deliberative bodies. The executive could never require it since that branch, Johnson thought, would never operate through such bodies.[48] (The judge, one may interject, thus failed to foresee the growth of administrative tribunals.) Of necessity this congressional contempt power was broad in scope. To define all conceivable offenses which it might embrace would be impossible. Limits there were, however, to the punishment; a term of imprisonment that would end with the adjournment of Congress was all the case required.

Other restraints besides election operated on the lawmakers. One of these was tradition. In England long practice had fixed in custom the bounds of the asserted power, and in America legislatures lacked the legal omnipotence of the British Parliament. ". . . the Constitution," Johnson continued, "was formed in and for an advanced state of society," and rested "at every point on received opinions and fixed ideas."[49]

Not only had long experimentation established the rules of the game, but in addition a moral sense constrained those to whom they applied. Even under tyranny there was a need of confidence in the officers of government; and that need was still greater in a government which had no other basis than the "sound morals, mod-

[46] 6 Wheat. 227.
[47] *Ibid.*, pp. 228-29.
[48] *Ibid.*, p. 234.
[49] *Ibid.*, p. 232.

eration, and good sense" of those composing it.[50] Strict construction was thus inappropriate for Congress. Significantly, Johnson's opinion at no point discussed judicial review as a restraint on that body.

In our own time Congress has increasingly made use of the power to punish for contempt, and the Anderson opinion has provided a leading precedent. In Johnson's mind, the citizen had more to gain from confiding to Congress this discretion than from having judges scrutinize alleged abuses of that discretion. The traditional nature of the Constitution and the moral sense of those elected to office offered important restraints; the ultimate check was resort to the electorate. The judge had bowed with deference to the "Supreme Legislature."

Yet the circumstances which produced the decision in Anderson v. Dunn were of slight import and qualify its significance. At stake here was no great substantive power such as the incorporation of a bank, but only the authority of the legislature to preserve itself against interference or corruption in the transaction of its business. The succeeding year gave Johnson his third opportunity to speak, this time in support of a primary governmental power.

On the 4th of May, 1822, President Monroe vetoed the Cumberland Road Bill. That road had been planned and initiated during the administration of Jefferson and Madison as a means of linking the seaboard with the West. After its completion it had fallen into disrepair, and the bill of 1822 had sought to appropriate sums for its improvement and authorize tolls for its maintenance. The country clamored for the measure. Within the President's cabinet, Adams, Calhoun, and Crawford all favored national construction of internal improvements. For years, Henry Clay had combined this measure with the Bank and tariff protection as ingredients of his American System.

Monroe, however, thought the Constitution raised an insuperable obstacle. Although he desired internal improvements as a means of strengthening the Union, this Virginian could find in Congress no authority to construct roads or assume control of their operation. Only a constitutional amendment could, in his opinion, furnish the necessary power.

To buttress his veto message Monroe sent Congress a voluminous treatise on the constitutional issue. His "Views on the Subject of Internal Improvements" dealt exhaustively with the clauses under which the power had been asserted.[51] Monroe considered in turn five of the enumerated powers—those concerned with establishing post offices and post roads, waging war, regulating commerce, tax-

[50]Ibid.
[51]Writings, ed. S. M. Hamilton (7 vols.; New York, 1898-1903), VI, 216-84.

ing and appropriating for the general welfare, and regulating territory and property of the United States. None of these did he deem sufficient to support the bill. Nor was the "necessary and proper" clause of any avail; the framers had introduced that clause into the document, according to Monroe, "on a principle of greater caution to secure the complete execution of all the powers which had been vested in the General Government."[52] The clause had really been unnecessary, since the grant of specific powers carried with them the selection of those means which were "well adapted to the end." Yet the framers had shown wisdom in leaving nothing to implication which might be made explicit.[53]

This pamphlet Monroe circulated widely among his friends. Among the recipients were the members of the Supreme Court. From three of the judges came replies. The Chief Justice evaded the issue, although he said the President had "thought deeply on the subject."[54] Justice Story welcomed the thorough consideration which this important subject was receiving; yet he, too, refused to express an opinion on the point of constitutionality.[55]

The third reply was more explicit. Justice Johnson had long agitated for roads, canals, and improved navigation, and here was an opportunity to repudiate the argument of unconstitutionality. In putting forth his views to the President, Johnson transmitted what was virtually an advisory opinion:

Judge Johnson has had the honour to submit the President's argument on the subject of internal improvements to his brother-judges and is instructed to make the following report.

The judges are deeply sensible of the mark of confidence bestowed on them in this instance and should be unworthy of that confidence did they attempt to conceal their real opinion. Indeed to conceal or disavow it would be now impossible as they are all of opinion that the decision on the bank question completely commits them on the subject of internal improvements as applied to post-roads and military roads. On the other points it is impossible to resist the lucid and conclusive reasoning contained in the argument.

The principle assumed in the case of the Bank is that the grant of the principal power carries with it the grant of all adequate and appropriate means of executing it. That the selection of those means must rest with the general government and as to that power and those means the Constitution makes the government of the U.S. supreme.

[52]*Ibid.*, p. 266.
[53]*Ibid.*, pp. 266-67.
[54]Marshall to Monroe, June 13, 1822, Monroe Papers (MSS; Library of Congress).
[55]Story to Monroe, June 24, 1822, *ibid.*

J. J. would take the liberty of suggesting to the President
that it would not be unproductive of good, if the Sec'y of
State were to have the opinion of this Court on the bank
question printed and dispersed through the Union.

J. J. is strongly impressed with the President's views of the
difficulty and delicacy attendant on any effort that might be
made by the U.S. to carry into effect any scheme of internal
improvement through the states, and as a question of policy
or expediency sees plainly how prudent it would be to prepare
them for it by the most conciliatory means.[56]

If this letter, couched as it was in formal style, was intended as
in any sense official, it received no such treatment by Monroe. The
President made no evident use of it in the controversy over the
legislation for improvements. That Johnson sent it, however, was
noteworthy. Although ostensibly directed by his associates to make
this reply, he must have been the principal in the action. Moved
by his own concern for improved transportation, he sought to
dispel any apprehensions which the President might feel regarding
the attitude of the Court. The Chief Justice, insistent always on
judicial isolation, had remained in the background. The South
Carolinian, who in time would concede openly the political nature
of much of the Court's work, had freely confided to the executive
a collective judgment of the Court. The action was unorthodox
then, and today would be deemed highly exceptionable.

More important, the letter gave clear evidence of Johnson's well-
defined position on implied powers. Here, at last, he expressed positive approval of the McCulloch opinion, an opinion so meritorious
that the President should give it a nationwide circulation! Here
was proof of Johnson's awareness of the attacks against broad construction; broadcasting Marshall's opinion might serve to counteract those attacks.

The letter stated the same demand for a wide choice of means
which the case of Anderson had elicited. President Monroe had
been willing to tolerate only those means that were "well adapted
to the end." Johnson swept within the discretion of Congress "all
adequate and appropriate means." By attributing to the federal
government alone the selection of means, Johnson cut the ground
from under the extreme state rightists. It was not the state, but
the federal authorities, bound as they were by the electorate, that
had the last word on the extent of implied powers.

[56]This letter, bare of date and of place of writing, appears in the Monroe
Papers in the Library of Congress. Monroe, who evidently kept this letter in
his confidence, recorded the following note concerning it: "Judge Johnson
Paper relative to Internal Improvements—. It appears by this, that I have
committed to him, the view [illegible words] which was presented to Congress
but at what time is not shown. The object appears to have been to take the
opinions of the judges. This paper has no date."

In construing broadly the powers of Congress William Johnson sided with John Marshall. The young justice who had called publicly for support of the Union in 1809, who had upheld the national arms in the war, and who had recited in 1815 for his fellow-citizens the advantages that might flow from improved communications, had taken his stand for broad construction. In the Hudson opinion he had tentatively spoken of implied power as sound theory; in the Anderson opinion and the letter to Monroe he declared it to be sound constitutionalism. The development was one of growth rather than of substitution. The appointee of 1804 had in time emerged a nationalist.

Yet his nationalistic construction applied only to the legislature. Congress was the central organ and dominated the scene. The executive and the courts held somewhat subordinate positions. His narrow reading of the jurisdictional clauses set Johnson apart from his fellow-judges. His concern for state autonomy, his esteem for the popularly elected Congress, whose powers were inalienable, led him to apply the rule of strict construction to the powers of the coordinate branches, both executive and judicial. Congress was subject to frequent elections; hence, in it, the people could safely entrust a liberal grant of power.

These views, however, were sufficient to brand Johnson as a traitor in the eyes of the Virginia school. In supporting implied powers, that chief weapon in the armory of the consolidators, Johnson had strayed from the Jeffersonian creed. Soon he would be explaining to Jefferson himself his defection. But in the meantime events at Charleston were making Johnson's position there increasingly untenable.

Chapter VIII

"THE MELANCHOLY EFFECT OF POPULAR EXCITEMENT"

THOMAS JEFFERSON'S first recruit for the high bench had gone nationalist. Beginning in 1819 he had swept within the orbit of federal power the authority to enact economic regulations and to provide reforms in transportation. All of these he had calculated as salutary for national well-being.

In 1815 he had preached a nationalism in which his home state shared. In 1822, however, that state was beginning to reverse its position, and its graying federal judge spoke the sentiments of a dwindling minority there. One by one, the Bank, the tariff, the doctrine of broad construction itself, would lose the adherence of the leaders of South Carolina. Economic depression hung like a pall over the state and the port of Charleston. The smoldering discontent awaited only a spark to ignite an explosion that would help produce a radical alteration of state policy.

The moment came in June, 1822. In Charleston, a loyal slave had blurted out the story of a mass insurrection soon to break out: the Vesey uprising was to take place in the middle of June. The news brought panic to the ruling elements in Charleston, and the authorities moved swiftly to expose and crush the revolt. William Johnson would attack in print the hysteria that ensued, and thereby become enmeshed in a heated public controversy. And before a twelvemonth had passed his acrid pen would involve him in another public dispute. This judge wore the judicial robe with evident impatience, and Adams' characterization of him as "restless, turbulent, hot-headed," will gain weight from both incidents.

Yet the two local controversies of 1822-1823 do more than reveal character and power of invective. The views which Johnson struck off in the course of them expose his conceptions of a crucial area of constitutionalism. From the Revolution to the present moment, the problem of civil rights has bulked large in American governmental experience, and the individual's claims to freedom have absorbed the attention of statesmen and citizens.

126

With civil liberty is ever linked the name of Jefferson, Johnson's party leader. The author of the Declaration of Independence had given top priority to inalienable rights and had declared the purpose of government to be the securing of them. In his first inaugural he had pledged himself to protect equal justice, freedom of religion, freedom of the press, freedom of the person under habeas corpus, and trial by jury. The words were general and called for specific definition. What attitude would Johnson adopt toward these rights and toward the South's "peculiar institution"?

The first inkling of the imminent slave uprising came to Charleston at the end of May, 1822.[1] The authorities at first greeted the reports of the informing slave with incredulity, but their mood turned quickly into determination as the evidence accumulated. The night of Sunday, June 16, was to be the date of the attack; slaves from the region, it appeared, were to overwhelm the whites, sack the city, and establish a Negro republic or perhaps escape with their booty to Santo Domingo.

The disclosures brought instant action by the constituted officials. Armed patrols surrounded the city on the appointed night, at their head the young and able Colonel Robert Y. Hayne, attorney-general of the state, who was soon to be elected United States Senator.[2] Despite the terrors of the citizenry, the night, however, passed without incident. Within two days a court of two magistrates and five freeholders had been constituted, and on Wednesday, the 19th, this body, in accordance with the rigorous law for the trial of slaves, met to determine procedure, arraign the accused, and take testimony.[3] The court would continue to sit for several weeks, only to be succeeded by another like tribunal. By the close of proceedings in August, a total of one hundred thirty-one persons would have suffered arrest; of these, thirty-five would pay with their lives, and thirty-two others would be deported. At the head of those marching to the scaffold would be Denmark Vesey, a free Negro carpenter, and two slaves owned by the governor, Johnson's brother-in-law, Thomas Bennett. The ingenuity, courage, and de-

[1] Details have been taken in the main from official accounts of the subsequent trials, the one by the intendant of Charleston, the other by the two presiding magistrates of the first court. See James Hamilton, *Negro Plot. An Account of the Late Intended Insurrection Among a Portion of the Blacks of the City of Charleston, South Carolina* (2d ed.; Boston, 1822); and Lionel H. Kennedy and Thomas Parker, *An Official Report of the Trials of Sundry Negroes, Charged with an Attempt to Raise an Insurrection in the State of South-Carolina* (Charleston, 1822). For a valuable recent study of the Vesey plot, see John Lofton, "Denmark Vesey's Call to Arms," *Journal of Negro History*, XXXIII (1948), 395-417.

[2] Theodore D. Jervey, *Robert Y. Hayne and His Times* (New York, 1909), pp. 81, 132, 143.

[3] On the slave law in South Carolina, see H. M. Henry, *The Police Control of the Slave in South Carolina* (Emory, Va., 1914).

termination of the ringleaders would win them commendation even from the judges who tried them.[4]

That such severe sentences seemed necessary reflected a deep concern on the part of the white rulers. South Carolina had by this time acquired a population predominantly Negro. In 1790 the state had shown fourteen whites for every eleven blacks; by 1820 the ratio had been almost reversed, twelve whites to fourteen blacks.[5] The cotton gin had, in large part, worked this change. That invention had spurred cotton culture and had induced South Carolina, in 1803, to repeal its prohibition of the importation of slaves. By 1808, when the legal trade came to an end, 39,075 new recruits to slavery had flooded the state.[6] The figures for Charleston and the surrounding country were staggering. By 1820 that area had 57,221 slaves against 19,376 whites; and this vast servile population had before it as a constant irritant some 3,615 free Negroes, whose numbers since 1790 had increased almost fivefold.[7]

Such was the demographic setting for the revolt of 1822. The court which conducted the trials discovered more immediate causes. The intendant (mayor) of Charleston, James Hamilton, blamed Vesey's mad ambition and hatred for the whites, the misguided benevolence of masters who had indulged their slaves by freedom of movement and instruction, the religious fanaticism which flourished among a clandestine Negro Methodist sect, and the Missouri Compromise debate in Congress. That famous discussion of 1820 had, he said, aroused discontent through its "beautiful propositions of civil and natural freedom, which were sported with a wanton recklessness of their consequences, as applied to the condition of a certain portion of our common country."[8]

Hamilton's diagnosis had support in the facts. The debate over the admission of Missouri, with its heated comments on the ethics of the slave system, had furnished Denmark Vesey with useful texts in his agitation among the Charleston blacks. Thomas Jefferson himself had perceived the threat in 1820. Deploring the Missouri discussion, he confessed that his long-held hopes for emancipation

[4]Kennedy and Parker, pp. 24, 41-44.

[5]Census figures, cited in Wallace, *History of South Carolina,* III, 503, Appendix IV.

[6]Henry, pp. 103-4. At that hour of enthusiasm Judge Johnson took occasion to register unqualified praise for Eli Whitney and the prosperity which his device had brought the South and the nation. In upholding Whitney's patent rights in a suit in the Circuit Court, Johnson described at length how the cotton gin had benefited not only southern agriculture, but also northern manufacturing and shipping. See Whitney *v.* Fort (1807), quoted in Whitney *v.* Carter, 29 Fed. Cas. 1070, 1072, No. 17,583 (C.C. Dist. of Ga.; 1808).

[7]U. B. Phillips, "The Slave Labor Problem in the Charleston District," *Political Science Quarterly,* XXII (1907), 416-39, 426.

[8]Hamilton, *Negro Plot,* pp. 31-32.

and resettlement of slaves were fading. To a friend he wrote, "we have the wolf by the ears, and we can neither hold him, nor safely let him go. Justice is in one scale, and self-preservation in the other."[9]

In South Carolina, however, many planters had been slow to take alarm. Many continued to mitigate the iron severity of the police system through kind and considerate treatment of their slaves and opportunities for instruction.[10] Here and there, voices had arisen to put to question the institution itself.[11] The white few were unaware of the revolutionary potential latent in the black many.

The revelations of June, 1822, brought a change of attitude. Wrote the intendant in his subsequent account, "there is nothing they are bad enough to do, that we are not powerful enough to punish."[12] The procedure followed by the specially constituted court tipped the scale against justice and toward self-preservation.

Because of William Johnson's subsequent comments, it is important to depict in some detail this procedure. The laws under which the trial court functioned were rigorous in the extreme. The magistrate (or justice of the peace) who first learned of an accusation was free to choose at will his fellow-judges of the court, provided they be drawn, one from the other magistrates, and the remainder (between three and five) from freeholders of the place. This meant that the judges at capital trials might be wholly ignorant of the law and of court procedure and perhaps easily swayed by popular clamor. The accused Negro had no opportunity to challenge rulings or appeal to higher tribunals. Trials took place in seclusion, and even the slave's master had, as of right, no part in the trial. The "Black Code," in short, gave little evidence of due process of law.[13]

Of the shortcomings in that procedure Vesey's judges were evidently aware. Within the range of their discretion, which incidentally was considerable, they sought a more just procedure. No slave should be tried except in the presence of his owner or counsel; and notice to the owner should precede trial by at least one day. A sentence of death should not be imposed where testimony was that of but one witness, unsupported by additional evidence or circumstances. The accused should be confronted by witnesses against him, except—and this was an important qualification—where witnesses had received a pledge that their names would be withheld.

[9]Jefferson to John Holmes, April 22, 1820, Jefferson, *Writings,* ed. Ford, X, 157-58.
[10]Phillips, "Slave Labor Problem," pp. 427-29.
[11]Wallace, II, 414-15.
[12]Hamilton, *Negro Plot,* p. 2.
[13]Henry, pp. 58-61. Henry (pp. 63-65) goes on to detail certain improvements in the procedure subsequent to 1831.

Counsel might appear if the owner requested it, and the accused might make statements in his own defense and examine witnesses. Yet frequently during the Vesey trials prisoners were held incommunicado, and witnesses were promised anonymity. The whole proceeding was conducted in strictest secrecy. These practices the court later defended on the grounds of public policy.[14]

Under such a process the Court of Magistrates and Freeholders began its deliberations on Wednesday, the 19th. At this moment Justice Johnson entered the case; and his recourse was unorthodox, to say the least. On Friday, the 21st, the conservative *Charleston Courier* carried a "Communication," bearing the title "Melancholy Effect of Popular Excitement." The statement, although unsigned, was from Johnson's pen. It purported to be a recital of events occurring in the Edgefield District in the up country a dozen years earlier.[15] Word of an impending disturbance, it stated, had led the governors of Georgia and South Carolina to mobilize the militia and institute armed patrols in the area adjacent to Augusta. An unnamed gentleman from Charleston called on the governor and disclosed that the evidence prompting these precautions was pure hoax. The governor of Georgia, however, could not brook the "mortifying discovery that he had been duped"; and, accordingly, the entire countryside on the appointed night was kept in "agitated motion." No disturbance took place.

Nevertheless, the affair had a tragic ending. When, from his hiding-place, a half-drunk cavalryman in a prankish mood blew a blast on his bugle, the mounted militia took it to be the signal for the uprising. After many hours their search netted them a "poor half-witted negro" whom they suspected of sounding the call. After whipping their victim and threatening him with instant death, the troops extorted a charge against another slave, named Billy. An armed force soon found Billy asleep in his master's house and near him the horn described by the witness. Billy was put on trial for his life:

> The Court of Magistrates and Freeholders was selected from men of the first respectability in the neighborhood; and yet it is a fact, although no evidence was given whatever as a motive for sounding the horn, and the horn was actually found covered and even filled with cobwebs, they condemned that man to die the next day!—and, what will scarcely be believed, they actually received evidence of his having been once charged

[14]Kennedy and Parker, pp. v-vii.

[15]Johnson probably learned of the incident firsthand. That he resided for at least a part of the year in the Edgefield District at that period is shown by two letters sent from there to officials of the American Philosophical Society. The letters relate to his election in 1810 to that society. See Johnson to Thomas C. James, October 27, 1810 and Johnson to John Vaughn, April 28, 1811 (Archives of the American Philosophical Society, Philadelphia).

with stealing a pig, to substantiate the charge upon which he then stood on trial.[16]

Johnson proceeded—with evident analogy to the 1822 affair and to efforts by Governor Bennett to intercede in behalf of his slaves. Billy's owner, an eminent citizen of the neighborhood, failing to gain a more deliberate hearing, sought the aid of his friends. These, including a "judicial character in the neighborhood," arranged a new meeting of the court, where they argued the injustice and precipitancy of the sentence. The effort was fruitless:

> The presiding magistrate actually conceived his dignity attacked, and threatened impeachment against the judge, who, as an individual, had interfered only to prevent a legal murder and interfered upon the witness, retracting all he had testified to.
> Billy was hung amidst crowds of execrating spectators;— and such appeared to be the popular demand for a victim, that it is not certain a pardon could have saved him.[17]

Thus ended Johnson's brief anecdote. As its title suggests, he had sought to put his community on guard against hysteria and rumor-mongering. In a republic where public opinion ruled, there was danger to individual rights in exaggerated or unfounded reports, especially in times of crisis.[18]

The statement would have been innocuous enough in normal times. With trials in progress and with charges and procedures conforming in many particulars to the earlier controversy, the publication could be expected to arouse resentment. At the least, it was a warning to proceed cautiously; at the most, an accusation of arbitrary conduct on the part of the mayor and the presiding court.

The court itself adopted the latter interpretation. The tribunal inserted in the *Courier* of the 29th a statement attacking Johnson's anecdote. The author had insinuated, it said, that the court under the influence of prejudice was "capable of committing perjury and murder." The court felt itself "injured and defamed." Johnson had promised, the statement went on, to publish a denial of an intent to imply bad motives or unfair procedure on the part of the court. The court would leave the verdict with the public, but they were unable to reconcile Johnson's conduct with "that which ought to influence a gentleman respecting his solemn promise, and sensible

---

[16]*Charleston Courier,* June 21, 1822.

[17]*Ibid.*

[18]Johnson continued to look on the public fears of 1822 as largely the fruit of hysteria. Two years later, he was writing John Quincy Adams as follows: "The whole of the alarm of 1822 was founded in causes that were infinitely exaggerated. A few timid and precipitate men managed to disseminate their fears and their feelings, and you know that popular panics spread with the expansive force of vapor." Letter dated July 3, 1824 in *Free Colored Seamen —Majority and Minority Reports,* House Committee on Commerce, 27 Cong., 3 Sess., House Rep., No. 80 (1843), p. 15.

of the obligations of decency and propriety."[19] This indignant blast called for a reply.

The same page of the *Courier* carried Johnson's signed retort. The public should withhold judgment; Johnson promised in time to present his case and thus to prove the court's publication "one of the most groundless and unprovoked attacks ever made upon the feelings of an individual."[20]

The federal judge kept his promise. A pamphlet, bristling with injured pride throughout its sixteen pages, was his medium.[21] The piece narrated Johnson's relations with the assembled court, after the publication of his anecdote. His opening appeal for a fair hearing by the community attests to the widespread resentment he had incurred:[22]

> It is not until I have composed my feelings from the severe attack of last Saturday, to a state which will enable me to address you with perfect calmness, that I undertake to redeem the pledge into which I have entered, to restore myself to your good opinion. . . .
>
> My misfortune is, that I have presumed too much upon the hope, that the censures cast upon me would be repelled, by a community with whom I was born and raised, among whom I have spent a life now looking downward in its course, whose confidence and kindness I have many reasons to be grateful for, and whom I can confidently say, I have faithfully served, and never dishonoured.[23]

He went on to plead that he had no interests and held no opinions different from those of the community. All his relatives lived there, he said, and depended on their native city for protection.

Johnson then set about repairing his damaged reputation by explaining the anecdote. He said he had written it to illustrate the danger of spreading false rumors and to quiet the alarms of the weaker sex. The *Courier* had printed it on its own initiative, in the belief that it taught a valuable moral lesson. Furthermore, Johnson

[19]*Charleston Courier,* June 29, 1822.

[20]*Ibid.*

[21]William Johnson, *To the Public of Charleston* (Charleston, 1822).

[22]In a letter to Langdon Cheves, John Potter, of Charleston, deplored the "imprudent tendency" of Johnson's anecdote. He continued: "It was a serious reflection on the court composed of members as highly reputable as he was . . . . You will see a serious recrimination on the judge by the members of the court in which the whole community seems to concur and his stout reply!!!

"I believe he thought that Bennett's Negroes were innocent and possibly his publication was intended to have a bearing on this supposition—a moment's reflection must have shown, it would and must have had a contrary tendency." Letter dated June 29, 1822, Langdon Cheves Collection (MSS; South Carolina Historical Society; courtesy of the Society). Cf. the anonymous pamphlet, *Caroliniensis* (Charleston, n.d.), p. 63.

[23]Johnson, *To the Public,* pp. 3-4.

argued, he had been unaware of the establishment of the court and had actually doubted that such a court would be necessary.

Yet the court, he continued, had called repeatedly and in the bluntest terms for an apology. The harried judge had complied by submitting several drafts to the papers, only to have these returned with requests for withdrawal or suggestions for alteration. The Magistrates and Freeholders had daily pressed him for a disclaimer. When, at last, a city constable had handed him a peremptory demand from the court for satisfaction, Johnson's mood turned from conciliation to defiance. The terse publication of the 29th was the result.

The narrative closed with a summation for the defense. The evidence, he argued, proved that he had had no intention to interfere with the state authorities. He could have meant no reflection on the character or reputation of the judges, who were men of "unqualified respectability." But no true freeman could tolerate the highhanded behavior of the court; and, Johnson said, he took the case of the "humblest citizen" and made it his own. "He would deserve to be disfranchised, who could submit" to such treatment. The judge said he had not broken his word, for he had made no binding promise to retract. It was incomprehensible to Johnson how the court could have discovered defamation in a "mere reported case, an historical fact."[24]

Finally, the judge returned to his appeal for an unbiased hearing and ended on a note of confidence:

> My reputation is the property of the United States. It is in safe hands, and defies scrutiny. But I wish to live in harmony with those who surround me. The smiles of my fellow citizens are dear to me. They will read and consider my defence; and though for a time a cloud may intercept the beams of their favour, I fear nothing. Persecution against an individual cannot triumph long: every one will feel that it may become his own turn next; and though misrepresentations may prevail awhile, the weapon finally recoils upon the hand that would have inflicted the wound. Man was not always the erring being he is now; there is a natural sympathy between his soul and truth, a tact by which he still discovers and instinctively delights in it.[25]

That brought to an end Johnson's relations with the Vesey trials and the court conducting them. His closing allusion to his national reputation gave fresh proof of his continuing drive toward nationalism. Would his standing at Charleston ever recover? The wordy attempt at self-vindication reflected undue sensitiveness and pride

[24]*Ibid.*, p. 15.
[25]*Ibid.*, pp. 15-16.

of reputation. Perhaps as a federal officeholder he should have maintained a scrupulous neutrality toward affairs in his home state. But if the pamphlet sprang from an exaggerated pride, the earlier discourse on the dangers of rumor-mongering reflected the instincts of a judge. The proceedings of the *ad hoc* courts for the trial of Negroes contravened one of Johnson's cardinal tenets, the right to a fair trial.

The justice's action in the Vesey affair was no isolated instance of his concern that legal processes protect the individual. In the case of Hudson and Goodwin he had insisted that federal criminal statutes be precise in defining crimes, designating courts, and prescribing penalties,[26] and in 1818 he had rebuked the majority of the Supreme Court for loosely construing a congressional law so as to take the life of the accused.[27] In this case, the statute was ambiguous as to the penalty;[28] in dissenting, Johnson acidly remarked that the lives of the accused here depended on a comma and on grammatical uncertainties.[29] Where life was at stake any doubt about construction should be resolved in favor of the prisoners. Johnson would rather resign than accede to the majority's construction.

Johnson called for the same sort of strict construction in behalf of accused persons in cases of jury trial. His opinion for the Court in Bank of Columbia v. Okely serves to highlight his position.[30] The State of Maryland, in incorporating the Bank, had expressly authorized it to sue by summary process defaulters on notes made negotiable at the Bank. Congress had thereafter adopted the existing laws of Maryland for a portion of the District of Columbia. When Okely failed to make good a note to the Bank, that institution sought an execution by the summary remedy provided. Defendant urged that the process followed violated a Maryland constitutional provision for jury trial and trial by the law of the land, and likewise the Seventh Amendment of the United States Constitution.

Despite the fact that the Court decided for the Bank, on the ground that the defendant had waived his right to jury trial by making his note negotiable at the Bank, the Court castigated the law in question. "We readily admit," stated Johnson, "that the provisions of this law are in derogation of the ordinary principles of private rights, and, as such, must be subjected to a strict construction. . . ."[31] Johnson's trenchant opinion here was noteworthy on three counts.

[26]See above, p. 79.
[27]Dissenting opinion in United States v. Palmer, 3 Wheat. 610, 635.
[28]*Ibid.*, p. 626.
[29]*Ibid.*, pp. 636-37.
[30]4 Wheat. 235, 240 (1819).
[31]*Ibid.*, pp. 241-42.

First, he called for a strict construction of statutes in the interest of jury trial. Second, he set forth in sweeping terms the purport of "law of the land," or, in modern parlance, due process of law; those words were intended, he said, "to secure the individual from the arbitrary exercise of the powers of government, unrestrained by the established principles of private rights and distributive justice."[32] And, third, he evidently assumed that the Seventh Amendment applied not only to Congress but also to the states. If such was Johnson's conception of the nature of the Bill of Rights, then his solicitude for individual guarantees had swept him far beyond even Marshall's nationalistic views.[33]

Johnson steadily maintained his esteem for jury trial. It was a solicitude for such trials as incidental to common-law courts that in part impelled him to resist extensions of the admiralty.[34] And in 1823 he spoke out separately in Green v. Biddle; there he insisted that insofar as it affected practice in federal courts, a Kentucky law substituting trial by commissioners for trial by jury in cases on land title violated a "fundamental" right.[35] A decade later, he acceded to the rule of Barron v. Baltimore that the Bill of Rights served to restrict only the federal government; yet he insisted that throughout the states jury trial was among the "most inestimable privileges of a freeman."[36] Although an auxiliary to the administration of justice, the jury of twelve stood as an indispensable guarantee of personal liberty.[37]

The prisoner at the bar was thus entitled to trial procedure scrupulously fair. That procedure had little in common with the working of the special courts for the trials of Negroes in South Carolina.

Yet of the thirty-five who paid the supreme penalty following the Vesey trials all but one were slaves. Was not the slave, after all, in a special category and, as such, stripped of the safeguards provided for the freeman?

As a lifelong slaveholder, Johnson at no time advocated abolition.[38] In his discourse on agriculture he spoke of such talk as

[32]*Ibid.*, p. 244.

[33]In 1820, Johnson intimated that the double jeopardy provision of the Fifth Amendment might apply both to the federal and to the state governments; see his separate opinion in Houston v. Moore, 5 Wheat. 1, 34; not until 1833 did the Court through Marshall hold the Bill of Rights inapplicable to the states, Barron v. Baltimore, 7 Pet. 243; Johnson was absent from that session of the Court.

[34]See above, pp. 81-82.

[35]8 Wheat. 1, 106-7.

[36]Lessee of Livingston v. Moore, 7 Pet. 469, 552 (1833).

[37]During the Nullification controversy in South Carolina Johnson elaborated his views on the subject. See below, pp. 271-72, 276.

[38]Johnson discussed the question of slavery in a confidential letter to John Quincy Adams. He there denounced the program of the American Colonization Society as dangerous and impractical. He would have sent slaves to Haiti,

fanatical.[39] He regarded slavery as an evil, but the economy and climate of South Carolina made the institution necessary. "If it is an evil," he told his fellow-planters, "it is one which must be submitted to, until we find, like our more philanthropic neighbors of the north, that our lands can be more beneficially cultivated by free hands, than by those of the slave."[40] Like Jefferson before him,[41] he refused to assume the existence of marked differences between the white and Negro races, pending scientific observation and proof. Slavery being what it was, a system of military discipline was essential, with obedience exacted in return for kindness and affection.[42] The whole matter called for careful study; and Johnson thought the need urgent:

> I cannot but flatter myself that a free communication of opinion and experience among our enlightened farmers, would lead us in time, to adapt the government of our slaves to those general principles, which are found to influence the life and conduct of man. This would be a curious, interesting and instructive employment to the student of physiology; it would teach him to distinguish the vices of the slave from the vices of the man, and lead to a solution of the question, whether the vices of the black man be those of his condition or of his nature.[43]

Yet Johnson was fully cognizant of the deep hold which the institution had taken on the consciousness of the Southerner.[44] As a planter, Johnson would justify slavery on grounds of economic necessity; as a historian he would ascribe its origin to shortsighted colonial proprietors and avaricious merchants and shippers.[45] But

then under John Pierre Boyer, where they would be freed. He said they would at least be transformed from the "state of brutes to that of men." Some might become soldiers, a condition which this pessimistic judge said awaited man in every country and period.—Letter dated June 12, 1821, Miscellaneous Letters, Records of the Department of State (MSS; National Archives).

[39]*Nugae Georgicae* (1815), pp. 33-34; see above, pp. 000-00.

[40]Johnson doubted that this would ever occur unless freemen from the West Indies be brought in or unless some new crop be raised.—*Nugae Georgicae*, p. 34.

[41]See Dumas Malone, *Jefferson the Virginian* (Boston, 1948), pp. 267-68.

[42]See *Nugae Georgicae*, p. 35.

[43]*Ibid.*, p. 36.

[44]In 1821, Johnson wrote Secretary of State John Quincy Adams, urging that American cruisers be ordered to refrain from bringing slave ships into the southern country. Because of the demand for slaves, it was almost impossible to get rid of them once they had entered, and he stressed the difficulties of enforcing a law "opposed to the feelings, interests, or even prejudices of a whole people."—Johnson to Adams, June 12, 1821 (see above, note 38). He called the Southerner's attitude concerning slaves a "strong, deep-seated feeling, nurtured from earliest infancy. . . ."—*Life of Greene*, II, 275.

[45]*Greene*, II, 472-73, Appendix E. Johnson here asserted that slavery weakened the nation since armies could not be formed where workers could not be trusted with weapons. Yet he insisted that slaves, instead of being hostile, were usually devoted to their masters.—*Ibid.* Cf. *Greene*, II, 451-52.

as a judge, he felt himself constrained to put aside personal preference and moral considerations where national law clearly set forth the status of slaves. In 1821, he met for the first time on circuit the question whether the slave trade was illegal under international law.[46] Off Florida an American ship had captured a vessel with a cargo of two hundred and fifty slaves. In the courts various parties, including Spanish and Portuguese owners, had filed claims. When the captors set up American and British prohibitions of the slave trade as proof that the law of nations banned the trade, the judge rejected the contention. He felt no inclination to justify or palliate the trade and thanked God he had lived to see it abolished. He said no one, except those who believed that national wealth was the highest national good, would deny that slavery was a national evil. Yet the British ban, however meritorious, was purely unilateral and could give no universal effect to the prohibition. The rule to apply was this: "however revolting to humanity may be the reflection, the laws of any country on the subject of the slave trade are nothing more in the eyes of any other nation than a class of the trade laws of the nation that enacts them."[47]

When the same question appeared in Justice Story's circuit, that judge gave a contrary holding, on grounds of moral and natural law.[48] On appeal, the Supreme Court, through John Marshall, upheld the ruling of Johnson.[49] Johnson consistently strove for a humane treatment of slaves;[50] but he gave the law its way where the law was to him clear.

Small wonder then, that when principles of both humanity and legality were involved, the federal judge took offense at the treatment meted out to Vesey and his accomplices. Even slaves were entitled to decent treatment; and on trial for their lives they should receive the rudiments of a fair process. The abhorrence which Johnson felt over the affair of Vesey and the court of magistrates ap-

[46]The *Antelope*, Minutes C.C. Dist. of Ga. (1821), Bk. E, p. 192.
[47]*Ibid.*
[48]*La Jeune Eugénie*, 2 Mason 90 (1822), quoted in W. Story, *Life and Letters of Joseph Story*, I, 348-56.
[49]The *Antelope*, 10 Wheat. 66 (1825).
[50]In a lower court ruling, he read the law of salvage to the advantage of slaves. Several slaves had been saved from a wrecked boat on which they had been engaged in carrying wood for their owner; the rescuer claimed salvage. The owners replied that salvage was assignable for the rescue only of things, not human beings. Johnson emphasized the difficulties of the case, and did not find the law settled that slaves when serving as mariners were subjects of salvage. In guarded language, however, he decided to err on "the side of humanity," and awarded one hundred dollars to the rescuers.—Webber v. Four Slaves, Minutes C.C. Dist. of S.C. (1823), Bk. C, pp. 120, 124.

In making out his will, Johnson inserted two provisions aimed at preventing the break-up of families among his slaves. Will dated June 17, 1834, Will Book H, Probate Judge's Office, Charleston.

pears vividly in a passage to Thomas Jefferson which he set down
the following winter:

> I have now passed my half-century, and begin to feel lonely
> among the men of the present day. And I am sorry to tell you,
> particularly so in this place. This last summer has furnished
> but too much cause for shame and anguish. I have lived to see
> what I really never believed it possible I should see,—courts
> held with closed doors, and men dying by scores who had
> never seen the faces nor heard the voices of their accusers. I
> see that your governor has noticed the alarm of insurrection
> which prevailed in this place some months since. But be as-
> sured it was nothing in comparison with what it was magnified
> to. But you know the best way in the world to make them tract-
> able is to frighten them to death; and to magnify danger is to
> magnify the claims of those who arrest it. Incalculable are the
> evils which have resulted from the exaggerated accounts cir-
> culated respecting that affair. Our property is reduced to noth-
> ing—strangers are alarmed at coming near us; our slaves
> rendered uneasy; the confidence between us and our domestics
> destroyed—and all this because of a trifling cabal of a few ig-
> norant pennyless [sic] unarmed uncombined fanatics, and which
> certainly would have blown over without an explosion had it
> never come to light.[51]

Governor Thomas Bennett, Johnson went on, had expressed a
similar view of the plot. Bennett had gone to Attorney-General
Hayne for a legal opinion:

> When the Court of Magistrates and Freeholders who tried the
> slaves implicated, were pursuing that course of sitting in con-
> clave and convicting them upon the secret ex parte examina-
> tion of slaves without oath, whose names were not I believe
> revealed even to the owners of the accused, the governor, whose
> feeling revolted at this unprecedented & I say, illegal mode of
> trial, consulted the attorney general . . . on the legality of
> their proceedings, and you will be astonished to hear that he
> gave a direct opinion in favour of it. If such be the law of
> this country, this shall not long be my country. But I will first
> endeavour to correct the evil.[52]

The incidents of June and July had struck this Jeffersonian
judge with a crushing impact. He was convinced that the severity of
the local tribunal grew out of hysteria, which in turn sprang largely
from rumor. To him the whole trial was shot through with illegality;
for whatever reasons, constitutional or statutory, he felt that the
accused slaves and their masters had been subjected to an arbitrary
exercise of power.

[51]Johnson to Jefferson, Dec. 10, 1822, Jefferson Papers (MSS; Library of
Congress).
[52]Ibid.

Others shared Johnson's distaste at the proceedings. When Governor Bennett gave the legislature an account of the trials and his own connection with them, that body tabled his message by a vote of 80 to 35. This unpublished message described the procedural deficiencies of the trials. Bennett conceded the ability and integrity of the judges, but insisted on the rule of law. The wording of the message and the understanding of the nature of law that it reflected suggest that Judge Johnson had a hand in its framing. Said Bennett of the importance of rules of procedure:

> The rules which universally obtain among civilized nations, in the judicial investigation of crime, are not merely hypothetical, or simply matter of opinion, but the result of the highest intelligence, instructed and matured by experience. They are given as guides, to assist the imperfections of human reason, and to enable it to combine and compare the various circumstances and probabilities, which occur in every case. Few minds are competent without these aids, to develope the intricate affections of the heart.[53]

Nevertheless, Johnson's appeal to the public had in all likelihood fallen on deaf ears. The Charleston of July was a very different community from the Charleston of May. Of the transformation there is graphic proof. After the trials a group of citizens memorialized the state legislature for stern measures of protection.[54] The signatories deplored the opportunities for free association, comfortable circumstances, and intellectual improvement, which they said the great majority had approved of as proper for slaves; they sought the expulsion from the state of all free persons of color and the rule of slaves on the basis of fear—the only basis on which slavery, in their opinion, could be maintained.[55] Public opinion had veered away from liberalism, toward a grim defensiveness on the subject of slavery.[56] Judge Johnson had cause to feel lonely.

[53]Message No. 2, South Carolina House of Representatives, Nov. 28, 1822 (MSS; Historical Commission of South Carolina, Columbia), p. 6. Johnson had earlier written to Secretary of State John Quincy Adams concerning various candidates for the post of United States District Attorney in Charleston, and had advised against Bennett's appointment. Besides being no speaker, he said, Bennett had not engaged in the necessary studies. Bennett, he added, would have to depend on others for help on legal points.—Letter dated Sept. 28, 1820, Adams Manuscripts (Massachusetts Historical Society). For a letter by Bennett on the trials, see *Niles Weekly Register*, XXIII (Sept. 7, 1822), 10-11.

[54]"Memorial of the Citizens of Charleston to the Senate and House of Representatives of the State of South Carolina," Charleston, 1822, printed in full in John R. Commons and others (eds.), *A Documentary History of American Industrial Society* (10 vols.; Cleveland, 1910-1911), Vol. II (ed. Ulrich B. Phillips), pp. 103-16.

[55]*Ibid.*, pp. 110-11.

[56]Cf. Phillips, "Slave Labor Problem," p. 433.

The legislature met in a mood of determination. Even Governor Bennett confessed the helplessness of the South in the face of danger. The time for alleviating the slave problem had long since passed, he declared, and the situation called for stern measures.[57] One result was passage of a law excluding Negro seamen from ports of the state, a law which, as we shall see, Johnson would meet in the Circuit Court.[58]

Whatever may have been its true dimensions, the Vesey plot had wrought a striking change in popular feeling. In the words of a leading historian of South Carolina:

> The tragedy was already begun of the South's expending such vast talent and effort in defending, instead of seeking to eliminate, a doomed institution and striving to maintain an impossible position, a waste which, independent of the clog of a semi-barbarous laboring population, was sufficient to retard intellectual and economic progress.[59]

And as fear of an uprising became the dominant mood, leaders in South Carolina came inevitably to associate the protection of slavery with state rights. In search of protection the state, as we shall see, would enact severe laws concerning slavery; in the case of the Negro Seamen Act at least, state law would encroach on federal powers. As a result, nationalism and national power would acquire in the eyes of many Carolinians, the appearance of a threat to slavery and, hence, to life and property. When in 1824 President Monroe would remonstrate over the Seamen Act with Governor Bennett's successor, that official would respond by a defiant appeal for resistance and preservation of the state's sovereignty and independence. In the extremity, he would say, "there would be more glory in forming a rampart with our bodies on the confines of our territory than to be the victims of a successful rebellion or the slaves of a great consolidated government."[60] Johnson would watch with mounting dread the kindling of the flame of state rights. The Vesey affair helped light a smoldering fire that would flare forth in Nullification and even more momentous events to come. Many of the participants in the trials, James Hamilton, Robert J. Turnbull, and Robert Y. Hayne among them, would play stellar roles in the drama of 1832 and 1833.[61]

It was not only in Charleston that Johnson was to meet opposition. From Columbia, the state capital, a blast was soon directed

---

[57]Message No. 2, p. 22.
[58]See below, pp. 192-96.
[59]Wallace, II, 418.
[60]Message to the Legislature, Dec. 1, 1824, quoted in Warren, *The Supreme Court in United States History*, I, 627. Cf. *Caroliniensis*, p. 41.
[61]Hamilton was intendant of Charleston; Hayne, in addition to commanding the troops and serving as attorney-general, sat as a member of the second court; and Turnbull was a member of the first court.

at him and his part in the Negro trials. In the interchange that ensued, Johnson would express himself heatedly on additional facets of the problem of civil liberty. This time the assailant was Thomas Cooper, president of the state college Johnson had helped establish. This British-born scientist, educator, legal scholar, and general agitator had recently come to the state from the North; as a noted victim of a sedition prosecution, as a member of the Pennsylvania bench driven from office for unpopular views, as a materialist and free-thinker, as an avowed friend of Jefferson, Cooper had proved a turbulent figure of American politics and thought.[62]

An adverse comment by the Charleston judge provoked the attack. In response to a request for information, Johnson, it seems, had earlier dispatched to a Kentucky legislative committee a brief account of public education in South Carolina.[63] The state college, he said, had fallen short of his hopes, and he ascribed this to two causes: first, a want of "energy and zeal" in its faculty, and, second, the character of its presidents. Although men of acknowledged learning, these last had lacked "the talent of directing and governing, and that energy of character, and knowledge of the science of government, without which, a president may be very learned and very worthy as a man, but very useless as a president."[64] As for the county schools, these received aid from a state fund, on a principle which Johnson approved: "educate the poor, and the rich will be compelled to educate themselves." He found the system generally popular throughout the state, and here Johnson ventured an unguarded comment: "Mr. Cooper, the present President of the College, I am sorry to observe, has done too much to render it otherwise."[65]

This cut wounded the pride of President Cooper. In February he sent the press a heated retort, taking note of the charge and dis-

[62]See Dumas Malone, *The Public Life of Thomas Cooper, 1783-1839* (New Haven, 1926), and the article on Cooper by Dr. Malone, in *Dictionary of American Biography*, IV, 414-16.

[63]Letter to the Committee, dated Aug. 27, 1822, *Journal of the Senate of the Commonwealth of Kentucky* (Frankfort, 1822), pp. 199-203. The request for information with accompanying questions appears in the same volume, pp. 191-92. Replies were also received from John Adams, Thomas Jefferson, James Madison, Henry William DeSaussure, William Duane, A. Bourne, and Robert B. [*sic*] Hayne. For this material, the author is indebted to Mrs. Mary T. Moore, librarian of the Kentucky Collection, Western Kentucky State Teachers College, Bowling Green.

[64]*Ibid*. Johnson went on to make this suggestion for college administration: "I have often thought, that it is a grand desideratum in our institutions, to discover a plan for separating the governing and teaching departments of our Colleges, so as to preserve them from clashing, yet impose the duties upon distinct persons."

[65]*Ibid*.

claiming any antipathy to the common schools.[66] Although he felt the system open to abuses, he had never, he asserted, written a word on the subject. As a judge of the highest national court, and as the author of two "ponderous quartos" on the life of Greene, Johnson ought to have demonstrated greater skill in the weighing of evidence. Since he had never injured the judge—although he had spoken, as everyone else had spoken, with amazement at the judge's "want of common sense and common decency" in his behavior toward the court for the trial of the insurgents—the president could only attribute Johnson's statement to an innate love of slander, to a "mischievous obliquity of disposition," and to an "idiosyncrasy of moral temperament." Johnson possessed a "morbid soreness about his own character, and a perfect carelessness about the character of others." Cooper caught up Johnson's closing utterance in the pamphlet addressed to the public: if Johnson thought his reputation was the property of the United States, then "God forbid the value of the public property should be judged of from this sorry sample!" Cooper said he had ignored the worst parts of Johnson's Kentucky letter; and he warned that circumstances would determine whether he would resume the unpleasant topic.[67]

Cooper had been quick to take offense. He had charged his opponent with malignity, sensitiveness to criticism, and lack of objectivity. Instead of a reasoned defense of his position, Cooper, in the style of the day, had resorted to invective, to assailing the character of his enemy. But Thomas Cooper had met his match for irony, sarcasm, and sardonic humor. The editor of the *City Gazette* had prefaced Cooper's attack with a pious desire to see a calm reply from the justice. He had badly misjudged his man, for in two subsequent issues he carried a lengthy and blistering reply from Johnson.[68] In his own defense Johnson said he had sent his letter to Kentucky in the expectation that it would be held confidential; its publication, he contended, had been a breach of trust. He admitted his error in attributing certain views to Cooper, and explained that error on the basis of a misleading article in the *North American Review*.[69] Nevertheless, Cooper's own testimony convinced Johnson that the president was hostile to the public schools. Those institutions Johnson declared of greater political

[66]Letter dated Feb. 28, 1823, reprinted in the Charleston *City Gazette,* March 8, 1823, from the *Columbia Telescope.*
[67]*Ibid.*
[68]Letter "from the Hon. William Johnson to Thomas Cooper, M.D., President of the South Carolina College," dated March 26, *City Gazette,* April 8 and 9, 1823.
[69]See "Education in South Carolina," *North American Review,* XIV (April, 1822), 310-319, which reviews together a pamphlet on the plan of education in the state and an address by Cooper to the graduates of the college in such a way as to convey the impression that Cooper was the author of both.

importance than any others, for they brought the means of instruction to the humblest citizen, and they enlightened those who sat on juries, voted at elections, and fought wars.

As for Johnson's part in the slave trials, Cooper himself had displayed a want of intelligence and tact in alluding to it:

> It might perhaps have been thought more consistent with "common sense and common decency" in the President of the South-Carolina College, M.D. to have meddled less with an affair which did not concern him, and which still remains to pass the ordeal of public investigation and judicial scrutiny. As competent Judges as Thomas Cooper . . . have viewed that subject with very different impressions from those you see proper to claim patronage for.[70]

Cooper had also derided Johnson's biography of Greene, and its author now poured ridicule on the literary taste of the rotund educator: "The cushion on the head of Falstaff," Johnson declared, "would as soon have created him King of England, as the title of President of a College, make a liberal critic of Thomas Cooper, M.D."[71] In his Kentucky letter Johnson had called his opponent "Mr. Cooper"; and at the omission of the title "Dr.," Cooper had taken offense. This attitude Johnson derided. The judge, who himself now held honorary degrees from both Harvard and Princeton,[72] said that diplomas were "as cheap as dog's meat," and magnanimously conceded: "I would not pluck a feather from the cap of a ideot [sic], if it afforded solace to his harmless vanity."[73] He expressed disgust at the cunning which Cooper had displayed in treating Johnson's role in public controversies.

So much for the president's charges and the judge's innocence. In his second installment, Johnson resorted to Cooper's own tactics and carried the attack to the enemy. In the process he touched at length on two vital personal liberties. The one was religious freedom, the other freedom of the press.

The biography of Greene had dwelt on the value of religion and importance of its freedom. In recounting the history of colonial and Revolutionary South Carolina, its author had found much to condemn in the activities of the Established Church. Through the Society for the Propagation of the Gospel, that church, he had said, had disguised an attack on religious freedom under a pretext of promoting religion. The effect of such a policy could only be to

[70]*City Gazette,* April 8, 1822.
[71]*Ibid.*
[72]Johnson was awarded the LL.D. at Princeton and Harvard in 1818. *Harvard University Quinquennial Catalogue of the Officers and Graduates, 1636-1930* (Cambridge, 1930), p. 1156. For an account of the Harvard exercises, at which Justices Livingston and Johnson received the LL.D., see *New England Palladium and Commercial Advertiser* (Boston), Aug. 28, 1818.
[73]*City Gazette,* April 8, 1823.

harm religion itself. "He is no friend to religion," Johnson had declared, "who will tempt man to hypocricy [*sic*], deprive him of the sacred right of conscience, or withdraw the oracles of the Christian religion from the severest scrutiny that the human mind can subject it to."[74] Although he himself was an Episcopalian, and preferred the low-church or "republican" wing of that denomination,[75] he had praised the sect to which his hero, General Greene, had belonged. The religion of the Quakers, when shorn of its impractical tenets, Johnson had asserted to be the "political religion" of the United States. The "stern morality, and simplicity of character" of the Quakers and their leading doctrines, "universal benevolence, and unbounded toleration," won Johnson's unqualified approval.[76]

Moreover, Johnson had found religion of considerable importance politically. In relating how the British invaders had sought to suppress dissenters in Charleston and elsewhere, he had put the point with force. The enemy had forgotten that "religion, which looks to another world for its recompense or enjoyments, becomes the most formidable enemy that can be raised up in this."[77]

In assailing Cooper, Johnson now recurred to that subject. Cooper's unorthodox ideas on religion and open contempt for the clergy, particularly of the Presbyterian faith, were already arousing resentment; a decade later the opposition would force his resignation from the presidency.[78] Not without craftiness, Johnson selected this weak point as the target for his major thrust. He pointed to statements in Cooper's scientific writings which expressed disdain for discussions of doctrinal beliefs, asserted that atheists could be good citizens, and affirmed that without resorting to religious sanctions society itself could furnish adequate controls of conduct by means of positive institutions.[79] In spite of his regard for science, the judge stated that humility was a prime requisite for the scientist: "The region of arrogance," he said, "lies just within the threshold of science."[80]

[74]*Greene,* I, 245.
[75]*Ibid.,* I, 257.
[76]*Ibid.,* II, 464.
[77]*Ibid.,* I, 287-88.
[78]See Malone, *Cooper,* especially Chapters VIII and XI.
[79]Johnson cited especially Cooper's edition of *Memoirs of Dr. Joseph Priestley* (Northumberland, Pa., 1806).
[80]The whole passage is worthy of quotation: "But *you* would have us surrender the belief of a God rather than the belief in our own capacity to detect the means of production of the meanest insect. The region of arrogance, sir, lies just within the threshold of science: Locke and Newton advanced in her temple on bended knees; and a greater man than Mr. Cooper, M.D. has observed, 'that he just knew enough to know that he knew nothing at all.' If the veriest insect that crawls, or any single blade of grass that bends beneath cannot teach us humility, nothing can." *City Gazette,* April 9, 1823.

Furthermore, Cooper was wrong in denying religious sanctions. For proof Johnson referred to the constitutional requirements of oaths for public officers:

> When the worthies who framed our constitutions required that oaths should be administered to all who should be trusted with authority, they gave their unequivocal assent to the necessity of oaths to the purposes of civil society. But oaths necessarily imply the existence of a Searcher of Hearts, and a future state of rewards and punishments. These vain theories however, it is hoped, will all vanish before a generation of lawgivers formed under your precepts; and the poor fanatic, who fancies this world not worth living in but for the hope of a better, will be taught the folly of these vain imaginations, and find, in an *enlightened philosophy,* a full indemnity for those hopes which he now fondly reposes in heaven.[81]

Morality, Johnson went on, did not rest on positive institutions. The Christian religion furnished not merely *some,* but *all,* of the sanctions of morality.

As a private individual, Cooper might hold any opinions he wished. Johnson expressed general agreement with Cooper's statement, "It is with our actions, with our conduct, with our demeanor, in all our domestic and civil relations that society has to do; and not with our opinions." This was true, said Johnson, in relation both to the right of the individual and the power of human tribunals to punish. That William Johnson raised the religious issue was regrettable; in doing so, he violated his own announced preference for "unbounded toleration." Yet his apology was technically correct. Society might rightly concern itself with the publicly expressed opinions of a college president.[82]

After this stroke, Johnson closed with a resounding threat. He was concerned over freedom of the press. He said his motive was not to vindicate his own reputation but to safeguard that right:

> I venerate the freedom of the press; I solemnly believe it to be the palladium of our freedom. He, therefore, who deprives it of public respect and confidence, by prostituting it to the purposes of private malice, is a bad citizen and ought to be punished. And if his elevated situation be such as to bloat him with the idea that he may scoff in safety, he is the more properly an object of the law's notice.
>
> When I say the liberty of the press, I would be understood to mean its unrestrained capacity to disseminate information

[81] *Ibid.*

[82] Said Johnson: "His [a college president's] opinions will be sought after, and received with deference by those who are under him. His elevation to that station implies the sanction of his known opinions, given by those who elevate him; and in proportion to their high respectability will be the currency given to the opinions of the man of their choice."—*Ibid.*

and discuss principles and measures. I am far from intending the present shameless abuses to which it is applied, and which are no more like a rational idea of its freedom, than anarchy is like liberty.

If ever the American people become disgusted with their freedom, that disgust will be produced by licentiousness and abuse of the press.[83]

For this reason, Johnson warned that he would prosecute Cooper for libel. But this blow he never struck. Whether or not he had ground for a lawsuit, and it is likely that he did, a forthcoming and circumspect reply by Cooper probably satisfied the indignant judge.[84]

That brought to a close the second of these two local sorties of 1822-1823. In his tussle with Thomas Cooper, Johnson had proved his skill at the dubious art of invective. He had employed devices of attack that he himself deprecated, and the spectacle of one disciple of Jefferson taking to task another of the same persuasion for his religious views must have affronted many, especially the statesman of Monticello.[85] Johnson's impetuous pen had ensnared him in two affairs that a more moderate man would have shunned.

Yet the tangle of motives that had prompted the actions contained some of genuine significance. Johnson's concern for fair treatment for the accused and his conception of fair trial as a sacred right had moved him to protest, virtually alone, the conduct of the Court of Magistrates. The subsequent barrage against Cooper was not devoid of justification. The president had assaulted publicly the reputation of the judge by insinuation and indirection. Although far from blameless himself, the judge had responded by insisting on a free and pure press. If fair trial was an inestimable privilege of the individual, the liberty of the press—and that of religion, too, for that matter—had implications for social health and political freedom. Those rights had definite and known limits, and courts of law existed to maintain them.

His convictions concerning the rights of the individual, his mounting concern for strong federal power, and his precipitancy of temperament were estranging Johnson from his own community. The tide of state-rights sentiment was rising. This first and most embattled of Republican justices would welcome an opportunity to unbosom himself to the founder of the party.

[83]*Ibid.* Cf. Johnson's comment: "I feel no compunction, in hastening by my example, the time when the press shall govern the world, provided, that candour, benevolence and urbanity, shall govern the press."—*Greene,* I, xi.

[84]Letter to the Editor, *Columbia Telescope,* reprinted in *City Gazette,* April 19, 1823. See also Cooper's reply to an anonymous attack.—Letter to the Editors, Columbia *State Gazette,* reprinted in *City Gazette,* April 26, 1823.

[85]The affair was not lost on Jefferson, nor on his friend, Madison. See below, p. 162.

Chapter IX

REPORT TO MONTICELLO

THE years 1822 and 1823 marked a turning point in the career of Justice William Johnson. The bold independence of the Mandamus decision had returned. In Charleston, citizen Johnson had cried out against what he took to be a gross infraction of justice to individuals. From the bench, Judge Johnson had declared to the President that the Supreme Court found no constitutional obstacle to national internal improvements. Soon he would be repudiating a state law which many in Charleston thought vital to social order. Yet in state and nation men were attacking the federal judiciary, and Johnson was growing increasingly uneasy.

William Johnson was seeking a sound philosophy. In 1817 he had written Thomas Jefferson of his eager desire to keep alive the "sacred flame" of 1776; and in reply, Jefferson had commended him and had spoken with pride of the sound principles which the Republican party had applied to the government of the new nation. The term "Republicanism" contained, to Johnson's mind, the essence of political and constitutional wisdom. But what precisely did the term connote? In his search for an answer Johnson, by rare good fortune, entered upon a correspondence with Thomas Jefferson, and in the course of it, explored with him the true meaning of the movement which Jefferson had headed thirty years before.

Within ten months seven letters had passed between the two men. With frankness, the leader and the disciple set down their convictions on parties, on constitutional interpretation, and on the inner workings of the Supreme Court. The judge submitted his own reading of the Constitution to the President who had placed him on the bench, and drew open the curtain on the working of the Marshall Court. Politely yet firmly Jefferson replied; and he tendered the judge some timely words of advice. The interchange was to influence Johnson's conduct to the end of his career. Here the discussion of constitutional construction will be uppermost; in the ensuing chapter, that of the workings of the Court itself.

It was Jefferson who opened the exchange of letters. Now in his eightieth year, the retired President was watching from his seclusion the currents of politics with mounting anxiety, and the federal judiciary was his chief concern. Keeping his pen in action, he advised, encouraged, and warned his associates, old and new, to resist the march of broad construction and to repel attacks by the judges on state powers. John Marshall was his chief target, and the victory of implied powers he saw as a victory of Federalist principles. The McCulloch and Cohens decisions aroused the greatest hostility; in the former, Marshall had asserted implied legislative powers in Congress and implied limitations on the state power to tax; in the latter, he had exalted the Supreme Court as the ultimate arbiter of the federal system. The doctrines of both decisions irritated the Virginians and drew from them their most acrid attacks.[1]

Unquestionably Johnson, like his brothers on the Supreme Court, detected Jefferson's strategic part in the campaign. During this very period John Marshall and Joseph Story were exchanging letters which deplored the machinations of the Virginia group.[2] The state-rights and strict construction arguments of Jefferson, Roane, and others they deemed a threat to the Union. Story, the Republican, was shocked at Jefferson's part in the matter. Such opinions, coming from the aged Jefferson, filled him "alternately, with indignation and melancholy." "Can he wish yet," Story asked, "to have influence enough to destroy the government of his country?"[3] The Chief Justice was in full agreement, but he ascribed Jefferson's hostility to the judiciary to ambition and vindictiveness.[4] Since that conception of the party leader was one not shared by Johnson, his awareness of Jefferson's ire must have intensified Johnson's uneasiness in 1822.

The South Carolinian had other causes for distress of mind. In the spring of 1822 Johnson published at his own expense his two-volume biography of Nathanael Greene.[5] His researches for the work, which runs to near one thousand pages, had extended over

[1] 4 Wheat. 316 (1819); 6 Wheat. 264 (1821); Warren, *The Supreme Court in United States History,* I, 514 ff., 545 ff. Especially bitter were the anonymous press attacks of Judge Spencer Roane. See his letters signed "Amphictyon," in *Richmond Enquirer,* March 30, April 2, 1819; "Hampden," *Enquirer,* June 11-22, 1819; and "Algernon Sydney," *Enquirer,* May 25-June 8, 1821—all reprinted in *John P. Branch Historical Papers of Randolph-Macon College,* ed. W. E. Dodd and C. H. Ambler (5 vols.; Ashland, Va., 1901-1918), II, No. 1, 51-76, 77-121, No. 2, 78-183.

[2] See Charles Warren, "Story-Marshall Correspondence, 1819-1831," *William and Mary College Quarterly Historical Magazine,* 2d series, XXI (1941), 1-26.

[3] Story to Marshall, June 27, 1821, *ibid.,* p. 8.

[4] Marshall to Story, July 13, 1821, *ibid.,* p. 13.

[5] The title page reads as follows: *Sketches of the Life and Correspondence of Nathanael Greene, Major General of the Armies of the United States, in the War of the Revolution. Compiled Chiefly from Original Materials, by William Johnson, of Charleston, South-Carolina. in Two Volumes . . . .* Charleston: Printed for the Author, by A. E. Miller, no. 4, Broad-Street, near the Bay, 1822.

several years;[6] they had entailed the writing of many letters[7] and an excursion into New England in the summer of 1818.

Why did the judge produce this massive work? In his preface he set forth two objectives: first, he wished to acquaint the reader with the character of his hero; second, he sought to shed light on the history of Greene's times and of his country.[8] Doubtless, the author found in this project a means of indulging a desire for literary fame, a penchant for history, and a wish to propagate his political creed.

Johnson had received from Greene's family the General's papers and accordingly had become the official biographer;[9] and John Marshall's earlier life of Washington made it appropriate for the younger justice to take up the story of Washington's second in command. Also, the subject of the work held a peculiar fascination for its author. Greene, like Johnson, had risen to fame and power from humble circumstances, largely through his own determination and ability. In the narrative Johnson discovered a valuable moral for the "young and lowly":

> They [the incidents of Greene's life] show with certainty, that there is no condition which may not be improved by virtue and perseverance—that the acquirement of knowledge leads directly to eminence—and that the most persevering labour is not inconsistent with the improvement of the mind, when the mind is steadily bent upon its own improvement. And let no discouraging inferences be drawn from the persecutions which he underwent from envy and detraction.
>
> They will fasten on eminence; and to quote the general's own language, "every one but an idiot will have his enemies." These are among the trials incident to human life; and they will attack those most severely, who raise themselves from obscurity.[10]

The arduous rise to fame of the son of the industrious Rhode Island blacksmith must have captivated the son of the Charleston

[6]Johnson was at work as early as March, 1818. See Boston *Centinel*, March 14, reprinted in *City Gazette* (Charleston), March 27, 1818. In March, 1821, he sought the advice of Mathew Carey, of Philadelphia, concerning publication of his work. He said the manuscript had been completed almost five months. Johnson to Carey, March 5, 1821, Lea and Febiger Collection (MSS; Historical Society of Pennsylvania).

[7]E.g., Johnson to Pendleton, Aug. 19, 1818, Dec. 29, 1818, Jan. 2, 1819, Oct. 17, 1819, Dec. 5, 1819, (Miscellaneous MSS. Pendleton; New-York Historical Society); Johnson to Williams, Oct. 18, 1818, Maryland Historical Records Survey Project, Calendar of the General Otho Holland Williams Papers, in the Maryland Historical Society, Baltimore, 1940 (mimeographed), item 1127; Johnson to John Vaughn, Nov. 10, 1818, Gratz Collection, (MSS; Historical Society of Pennsylvania).

[8]*Greene*, I, vii.

[9]*Ibid.*, I, v.

[10]*Ibid.*, II, 463.

patriot. The most interesting passages of the book were those recounting the military campaigns which Greene directed in the South, and it was for these portions and for the ground they broke that the book was to win commendation.[11]

Thomas Cooper had called these volumes "ponderous." For much of the work that description is apt. There is drama, however, in the narrative of military campaigns, and, what is more significant, the whole sheds light on the mind of the author. This voluminous work, in fact, sparkles with the observations of an incisive intellect on a vast array of subjects. And Johnson illuminates most of all his favorite theme, the American Revolution. That movement had made a powerful impact on his childhood; in praise of its heroes he had risen to oratorical flights in 1812. Now he dedicated his major work to the surviving veterans of the Revolution; in his younger days, he confessed, he had had but a "faint idea of their virtues and sufferings."[12] His high estimate of the political importance of the struggle for independence gave Johnson a solicitude to preserve and carry forward the heritage of self-government and what he called Republicanism.

Furthermore, he related with pride Greene's efforts for constitutional reform. Greene was one of the earliest to call for a firmer union, with a power in Congress to mobilize the strength of all the states for the defense of the whole. The Congress and the people of the United States, Johnson remarked, had been compelled in time to resort to the improvements Greene had advocated; and results had been wholly fortunate.[13] The Constitution Johnson evidently regarded as the happiest fruit of the Revolution.

In addition, the struggle of contending factions during the Revolution had awakened in Johnson a lively interest in the origins of the political parties. To designate the particular party bias of the biography would be difficult. Those portions might be termed Federalist which dealt with the weakness of the Revolutionary central government and deprecated state jealousies. Other parts were more favorable to the Republicans. Johnson thought he had uncovered a bond of interest between the public creditors and the army and suggested that the Republicans had organized to counteract the efforts of these groups to concentrate power in the executive.[14]

[11]See Edward McCrady, *History of South Carolina in the Revolution, 1780-83* (New York, 1902), p. 56 n. Cf. comments of Jefferson below. Randolph G. Adams describes Johnson's work and a later biography of Greene as "*ex parte*" and urges care in the use of them.—Article on Greene, *Dictionary of American Biography*, VII, 573.
[12]*Greene*, I, iii.
[13]*Ibid.*, II, 447. Cf. *ibid.*, II, 204, 441-46.
[14]*Ibid.*, p. 398.

This theme he elaborated in an appendix.[15] Taking his cue from a statement in Marshall's *Washington*, he asserted that fear of monarchy and of Great Britain as a potential ally of the friends of monarchy had played a prominent part in the forming of the party. He hammered on the point that state rights were not the chief ingredients in Republicanism, although some sincere men, and others of a more designing sort, might work on state feeling for their own ends. He said the Republicans were not satisfied when forming the Constitution to set up guarantees against the national government alone; they also pledged the strength of the whole to protect the security and liberty of each individual against the state governments. Every effort to break the bond uniting the people would prostrate that security at the feet of the one or the other government.

His solicitude for the individual led Johnson boldly to declare:

> State rights, or United States' rights are nothing, except as they contribute to the safety and happiness of the people. For them, both governments are formed and made mutually to check and control each other, that they may work solely to the one end, the happiness of the individual.[16]

By 1822, then, the welfare of the individual had moved to the forefront of Johnson's political thinking.[17] So convinced was he of the soundness of his delineation of Republican principles that he closed his long work on Greene with a hint of another to come. A book on parties, he said, might one day be offered to the public.[18]

Whatever hopes Johnson may have held for literary fame and a wide circulation of his work were soon to expire. He had stated, not without sense, that sound history could be written only after a century had elapsed from the events treated and that he would endeavor to imagine himself a hundred years away from his subject.[19] But this plea of objectivity fell on deaf ears. Sales were discouragingly slow, and he reduced the price from ten to six dollars a set.[20] Of the original one thousand copies, paid for out of his own purse,[21] more than four hundred remained unsold after four years.[22]

---

[15]*Ibid.*, p. 474, Appendix F.

[16]*Ibid.*, pp. 475-76.

[17]Cf. Chapter VIII and statements in Anderson *v.* Dunn, 6 Wheat. 204, 226-27 (1821).

[18]*Greene*, II, 476.

[19]*Ibid.*, I, x.

[20]Johnson, however, explained the reduction on the basis of securing a wider circulation and combatting the "calumnies" being uttered against the book.—*City Gazette,* Nov. 20, 1822.

[21]Johnson to Mathew Carey, Aug. 11, 1822, Yates Snowden Collection (MSS; South Caroliniana Library, University of South Carolina).

[22]Johnson to Mathew Carey, Jan. 17, 1826, Chamberlain Collection (MSS; Boston Public Library). In disgust, Johnson sought to unload the residue at any price; see *ibid.*, and Johnson to Carey, April 17, 1826, Miscellaneous Papers (Johnson Folder) (MSS; New York Public Library).

A series of hostile reviews must have contributed to the lag in sales. In the course of his work Johnson had made serious charges against several leading personalities of the Revolution. He had accused Gouverneur Morris, the Federalist, of complicity in the affair of the Newburg letters. He had expressed doubts of the veracity of memoirs from the pen of Colonel Richard Henry Lee of Virginia. And he had charged Count Pulaski with negligence at Germantown. Defenders of all three went into print with indignant replies.[23]

The critics assailed the author both for the language in which his work was couched and for its content. When the *North American Review* took him to task on both counts, Johnson sent to the press a vindication of his work.[24] The reviewer had described the author as the inhabitant of a "very remote part of the nation"[25] and had gone on to accuse him of party prejudice. Johnson replied by saying his book was intended as a national work[26] and that his purpose throughout had been to demonstrate the importance of the Union and the need of harmony and forbearance in the conduct of Americans toward one another.[27]

[23]See H. Lee, *The Campaign of 1781 in the Carolinas; with Remarks Historical and Critical on Johnson's Life of Greene* (Philadephia, 1824); Anon. (probably Louis Hue Girardin), *Pulaski Vindicated from an Unsupported Charge, Inconsiderately or Malignantly Introduced in Judge Johnson's Sketches of the Life and Correspondence of Major Gen. Nathanael Greene* (pamphlet; Baltimore, 1824) (reviewed in *North American Review*, XX [1825] 375-92); William Johnson, *Remarks, Critical and Historical, on an Article in the Forty-seventh Number of the North American Review, Relating to Count Pulaski. Addressed to the Readers of the North American Review, by the Author of the Sketches of the Life of Greene* (pamphlet; Charleston, 1825); Paul Bentalou, *A Reply to Judge Johnson's Remarks on an Article in the North American Review, Relating to Count Pulaski* (pamphlet; Baltimore, 1826); and a review of these last two in *North American Review*, XXIII (1826), 414-40. For additional comments, see A. J. Levin, "Mr. Justice William Johnson, Jurist in Limine: The Judge as Historian and Maker of History," 46 *Michigan Law Review* (1947), 131, especially p. 137 n. Johnson had also written critically of James Wilson, of Pennsylvania; for this he later apologized.—See his letters to W. Bird Wilson, Nov. 15 and Dec. 30, 1822, and letters from Wilson to Johnson, Oct. 1 and Dec. 11, 1822, Wilson MSS (Historical Society of Pennsylvania).

[24]*North American Review*, XV (1822), 416-31. The name of Edward Brooks is entered in the copy at the Harvard College Library as that of the author of this review; the same collection attributes to Jared Sparks the reviews cited in note 23 above. Johnson's reply appeared under the title, "The Reviewer Reviewed," in the *City Gazette*, Nov. 14, 15, 16, 18, 19, 1822.

[25]See the retort of the editor of the *City Gazette*, Nov. 12, 1822.

[26]*City Gazette*, Nov. 19, 1822.

[27]He listed his aims as follows: "1, to trace out and to adhere to the historical truth. 2, to impress on my countrymen the necessity of hugging to their bosoms the bond which unites us to each other, by exhibiting the toil and hazard to which we were exposed from a want of combined operation and continental feeling in the revolutionary war. 3, to inculcate the wisdom of for ever preventing an enemy from passing our threshold, whatever be our private dissensions or discontent, by exhibiting pictures of the misery and distraction and corruption, necessarily consequent upon it—and lastly

Such he implied was sound Republicanism, for the followers of Jefferson were no more like the Anti-Federalists than the "pure" Federalists were like the monarchists and consolidators.[28] As for party feeling, on what ground was that to be charged, he exclaimed, "of one who is equally out of favor with both parties?"[29] But the *Life* was palatable to neither political party. Surviving Federalists would construe it as a partisan assault on venerated founders, and Republicans would see in it the apology of a renegade.

By November, 1822, then, Johnson's plight had reached the extreme. The plea for the slave insurgents had alienated many fellow-townsmen. His venture into historical writing had let loose from North and South a barrage against his literary skill and objectivity. His acquiescence in nationalistic opinions of the Court had aroused the ire of all those leaders who shared in the revival of state-rights sentiments. This was the moment for the counsel of a sympathetic friend.

The friend appeared. A letter arrived from Thomas Jefferson.[30] The writer had read with extreme satisfaction the copy of the *Life* which Johnson had sent him; he said he rejoiced to see, at last, a fair account of the campaigns in the South.

Moreover, Jefferson looked forward anxiously to the history of parties. He hoped for a repudiation of the "invidious libel on the views of the Republican party, and on their regeneration of the government. . . ,"[31] a reference no doubt to Marshall's *Life of Washington*. He himself was too old to do justice to the party's efforts to ward off monarchy and to ground the government on the only safe foundation, "the elective will of the people." So he wished the younger man to undertake the task.

But the Virginian also had other purposes in writing. After broaching the subject of the Court and its practice of unanimous opinions, he asked for Johnson's ideas on the contemporary parties. The Federalists, he thought, in abandoning that appellation in 1815, had joined the Republicans in name only. They had forsaken monarchy as hopeless and now were seeking a consolidated government. Their aim was "to break down the rights reserved by the Constitution to the states as a bulwark against that consolidation. . . ."[32] Hence, the new Republicans in Congress (Jefferson refrained from adding,

---

the wisdom of mildness and forbearance in our conduct toward each other, should we ever unhappily be distracted by civil discord, by exhibiting the views of the rancour and bloodshed which necessarily grow out of a contrary conduct."—*City Gazette*, Nov. 15, 1822.

[28]*Ibid.*, Nov. 16, 1822.

[29]*Ibid.*

[30]Jefferson to Johnson, Oct. 27, 1822, Jefferson, *Works*, ed. P. L. Ford (Federal ed.; 12 vols.; New York, 1905), XII, 246-52.

[31]*Ibid.*, p. 247.

[32]*Ibid.*, p. 251.

in the Court) were preaching the views of the old Federalists. Jefferson scarcely knew which might entail the greater horrors—a consolidation or a dissolution of the Union.

Whatever umbrage these views gave Johnson, Jefferson's warm closing salutation must have brought balm to the wounds inflicted by the assailants. Jefferson said his own opinions might be taken as "the dreams of a superannuate about things from which he is to derive neither good nor harm." Johnson should, however, accept them as a proof of the writer's complete confidence in "the rectitude of your mind and principles."[33] Although he had had motives of his own for writing, Jefferson had judged his man well; his professions of friendship and trust brought a response.

On December 10, the grateful recipient sent off his reply.[34] This twenty-one page letter is easily Johnson's most revealing statement. Here at last, after eighteen years on the Court, he discloses to the former President the difficulties he faced there and explains his nationalistic decisions.

He welcomed Jefferson's praise of his work. He had feared that his comments on Lee and other topics might have alienated Virginia. Because of his reflections on Morris, the whole remainder of the Federalist party was leagued against him, and accordingly, Johnson never felt "in greater need of the countenance of my friends."[35]

Would he publish his work on parties? Not without bitterness he catalogued the difficulties he had encountered already:

> My recent experience of the hostility which such a work must bring upon me, of the poor return that national or party gratitude would make for the vexations which certainly arise from the making of enemies; of the feeble patronage which the American people as yet bestow upon American productions; of the mortifications inseparable from the carelessness or ignorance of printers, and the villainy & extortions of book sellers; all conspire to deter me from publishing tho' I should proceed to complete another work.[36]

The judge had little taste for attempting another publication, but heartily agreed that the Republican party needed a champion to defend it before posterity. He observed that it was the same libel which Jefferson had mentioned that had first suggested to him the need of a public vindication. Judge Todd had told him Madison was at work on a treatise on the period, and this gave cause for

[33]*Ibid.*
[34]Jefferson Papers (MSS; Library of Congress).
[35]*Ibid.*
[36]He continued, however: "I have advanced far in it and my notes and extracts by far the most laborious part of the undertaking would enable me to finish it the next summer."—*Ibid.*

pleasure, but Jefferson himself should take care to leave in the hands of a friend a record of events as a proof of the purity and patriotism of the Republicans. Said Johnson:

> We were always under the impression that you would not publish any work on the subject; but while we should piously deprecate the event that put us in possession of it, you cannot be insensible that we have looked up to you as our common father, and will believe me when I assure you that we have hoped for a rich legacy of history from your pen.[37]

In the mind of the disciple, only the master could properly defend the movement from its maligners.

Johnson agreed with Jefferson that the old political parties remained, but he delineated the surviving Federalists in terms very different from those of Jefferson. Party politics were in a state of flux and confusion, and Johnson felt affairs had reached a crisis. In an atmosphere heavy with calumny and intrigue many were contending for the Presidency; the earlier enthusiasm for Crawford had now waned, as Johnson found none of the candidates to his liking. To fill the place of the old parties he hoped for new ones: "When the population of a free state," he declared, "has been once divided into two parties, by an acknowledged line of demarkation, the annihilation of one party seems necessarily to imply the extinction of the other." Yet things could not long remain so; new parties would arise and these should be desired. Many good men had left the Federalist party in disgust, and their leaders had grudgingly followed. But they would reappear, and Johnson pondered over the course a restored Federalism would pursue:

> The acquisition of Louisiana in my opinion put down among the thinking ones, all idea of ever establishing a general monarchy; the extent of our territory and the scope given to the propagation of that class of men who never can be yoked to the car of despotism, ought to have satisfied them that such a project was ridiculous. The same cause also, I am inclined to think, produced an abandonment of the project of general consolidation; and I fear caused the adoption of a plan as pregnant of evil as either of the others—a separation of the states as the only means of restoring the predominance of Massachusetts within the section that she might draw off with her. Hence the unprincipled and ungrateful separation of her views and interests during the late war—capped by the Hartford convention.[38]

Rightly or wrongly, Johnson had come to associate disunion with Federalism. In 1812 he had warned his fellow-patriots of New England's dissidence and had preached the cause of national unity. Now he recited for Jefferson how Louisiana had saved the Union.

[37] *Ibid.*
[38] *Ibid.*

Its rich commerce and carrying trade had captured support in the East and spiked the guns of the Federalists. National power was important; whatever might be the outcome of the next Presidential election, he felt it his part "to endeavour to persuade every one that . . . it is the duty of every good citizen, freely to resign himself to the public will constitutionally expressed."[39]

Certain recent occurrences, the judge went on, had alarmed those who sought to preserve the Union in the true spirit of the Constitution. A number of states had displayed "symptoms of antifederal feeling," among them, Massachusetts, Georgia, Pennsylvania, and Kentucky.[40] These and other like occurrences, he said, had converted some Republicans into "qualified Federalists." Actually, the "pure" men of both parties never had been in principle far removed.

All of this, he asserted, had produced an excessive "leaning to that bane of our civil tranquillity—the assertion of implied powers."

The passage helps explain the bold statement in Anderson v. Dunn and the confidential opinion written for President Monroe. He was now in evident discomfiture over these actions and likewise over his faltering rulings on the contract clause of the Constitution, which a later chapter will examine.[41] In a brief paragraph he revealed his perplexity and indicated the proper remedy for any incorrectness in the Court's reading:

> I wish the people of the United States could feel as sensibly as I do, the necessity for a calm and patient review of those two Articles of the Constitution which relate, the one to the obligation of contracts, and the other to the general legislating power of Congress. We should have very little to be uneasy about if those two clauses could be adequately explained and modified. But it is in vain to hope to bring any human system to perfection. Our security must be found at last, in the virtue and intelligence of the people, and in the firmness and purity of their rulers.[42]

If the Court had erred, and Johnson's call for clarifying amendments suggested doubts on the point, the final resort lay with the people. Such a final appeal was, in essence, Jeffersonian. Had not the former President himself spoken of "the elective will of the people" as the only sound footing for government?

[39]Johnson continued cryptically: "But I see a curious game going on around here which I may one day amuse you with a developement of."—*Ibid.*

[40]Said he: "The conduct of Massachusetts was unequivocal; Georgia, sometime since levelld a provision of one of her stop-laws at our Marshall; Pennsylvania openly by law instructed all her public officers to resist the United States; the recent manouvre of Kentucky to force her depreciated paper upon creditors, and evade the article of the Constitution which prohibits the states from making anything but gold and silver a legal tender, would have disgraced the times of our paper money."—*Ibid.*

[41]For Johnson's handling of this clause, see below, Chapter XII.

[42]Johnson to Jefferson, Dec. 10, 1822.

After deploring the panic he had witnessed during the insurrection scare in Charleston and the arbitrariness of the trials, Johnson closed his long letter. There was no one living, he exclaimed, whose good opinion he valued above Jefferson's.

Johnson had put the cards on the table; how would Jefferson play them? Not until March did Jefferson reply.[43] He began in a friendly vein. The biography was a highly valuable work and Johnson should ignore the reviewers. They were mere "insects." The party was in need of defenders from the "five-volumed libel" and other Federalist writings to come. Madison would leave some materials on the early period, and Jefferson's own letters would appear in due course.[44] But the more Republican defenders the better; and, accordingly, Johnson, in case he did not publish, ought at least to leave copies of his manuscript in the hands of trusted friends.

Jefferson's tone altered as he turned to the matter of constitutional construction. Johnson's apology for the resort to implied powers had made no impression. It was centralization of power that Jefferson feared most, and the Supreme Court bore a heavy burden of blame:

> . . . in truth there is no danger I apprehend so much as the consolidation of our government by the noiseless, and therefore unalarming, instrumentality of the Supreme Court. This is the form in which federalism now arrays itself, and consolidation is the present principle of distinction between Republicans and the pseudo-republicans but real federalists.[45]

The Court, he said, was itself responsible for public disfavor, and the judges should seek to restore confidence through recourse to separate opinions.

The epithet "pseudo-republican" Jefferson had once attached to Story, as we have shown; he now applied it by implication to Johnson. The inference was clear: under the rule of the Federalist Chief Justice, the South Carolinian had abandoned true Republican doctrine.

Johnson, however, stood his ground. His letter of April dealt at length with the mounting literature on the two conflicting parties

[43]Jefferson to Johnson, March 4, 1823, Jefferson, *Works* (Federal ed.), XII, 277-80. Jefferson had submitted Johnson's December letter to Madison. In doing so he had called Johnson's views there expressed "serious and sound" and had disclosed them to Madison only because of the intimacy of the two elder statesmen.—Jefferson to Madison, Jan. 6, 1823, *ibid.*, pp. 274-76. Madison replied that a good work on the parties by Johnson would be an antidote to Marshall's *Washington*, which had been "poisoning the public mind and gaining a passport to posterity."—Madison to Jefferson, Jan. 15, 1823, Madison, *Letters and other Writings* (4 vols.; Philadelphia, 1865), III, 294.
[44]The reference doubtless was to Madison's notes on the proceedings of the Philadelphia Convention, which were first published in 1840.
[45]Jefferson to Johnson, March 4, 1823, *Works* (Federal ed.), XII, 279.

of the 1790's.[46] That Jefferson would leave his letters for posterity brought him satisfaction. Yet the Federalists were busily at work documenting their cause. Marshall's book had had a wide circulation in Europe, and was doing much harm there; and a hand-picked collection of Washington's papers and a biased life of Hamilton would in time appear and furnish fresh weapons for the opponents of the Republicans. Hence, Johnson would persevere with his own treatise. Whether it would ever appear in print would depend on the question

> whether I have to my own satisfaction and that of the few friends to whom I may submit it, supported the position . . .— that the distinguishing characteristic of the Republican Party was, to check the intemperance of both Democrats and Federalists and administer the government agreeably to the true views of the Constitution, equally uninfluenced by the pretensions of the states or the United States.[47]

Such was Johnson's firm conviction, and he sought from Jefferson a definite opinion of its correctness. The Republicans, he continued, had required the support of the "Democrats"—an allusion doubtless to the early advocates of state rights; to capture that support sacrifices had been essential; but these were the means, not the end, of the party's program.

After some contemptuous remarks on Pickering and the two Adamses, Johnson approached the subject of the Court. He accepted Jefferson's advice on separate opinions and deplored dicta that had dropped from the bench. Yet he was convinced that the points actually decided, apart from opinions expressed by the Court, had public support, and he asserted that every decision in which he had concurred measured up to constitutional standards. Indeed, he would even argue the point. Could we, he asked, "amicably and confidentially examine the question how far the Supreme Court has yet trespassed upon their neighbours territory, or advanced beyond their own constitutional limits?"[48] His primary motive in asking the question, he said, was to have his own opinions tested, although he would like to convert Jefferson, "not for the triumph, but for the support it would afford me. . . ."[49] The points of cleavage between the founder and the follower in 1823 were emerging into the open.

In spite of two crippled wrists, Jefferson, on June 12, penned a long and remarkable statement for the South Carolina judge.[50] He

[46]Johnson to Jefferson, April 11, 1823, *S.C. Hist. and Gen. Mag.*, I (1900), 207.
[47]*Ibid.*, p. 207.
[48]*Ibid.*, p. 209.
[49]*Ibid.*, pp. 209-10.
[50]Jefferson to Johnson, June 12, 1823, *S.C. Hist. and Gen. Mag.*, I (1900), 3.

scarcely noticed the pain, he said, when unbosoming himself to friends who harmonized with him in principle. The octogenarian leader had lost little if any of the old clarity and grace of expression. He repudiated the Federalist taunt that the Republicans had been mere office-seekers, and set down in classic terms the political faith of the party. In the time of the government's origins, many had shunned novel theories out of preference for the practices of Europe. The elite of Europe sought security in privileged orders and in a policy of grinding down the people and extracting from them most of the fruits of their labors. The people, in turn, submitted humbly to the rule of these superior beings. In the Philadelphia convention some had accordingly tried to tighten the cords of power "to lessen the dependence of the general functionaries on their constituents, to subject to them those of the states, to weaken their means of maintaining the steady equilibrium which the majority of the convention had deemed salutary for both branches general and local."[51] The enduring object of the Federalists was to regain the powers which the people had refused and to bend to their own desires the powers that were given. By contrast, Jefferson recited the aim of his own party:

Ours . . . was to maintain the will of the majority of the Convention, and of the people themselves. We believed with them that man was a rational animal endowed by nature with rights, and with an innate sense of justice, and that he could be restrained from wrong, & protected in right, by moderate powers, confided to persons of his own choice, and held to their duties by dependence on his own will. We believed that the complicated organization of kings, nobles, and priests was not the wisest nor best to effect the happiness of associated man; that wisdom and virtue were not hereditary; that the trappings of such a machinery consumed, by their expense, those earnings of industry they were meant to protect, and, by the inequalities they produced, exposed liberty to sufferance. We believed that men, enjoying in ease and security the full fruits of their own industry, enlisted by all their interests on the side of law and order, habituated to think for themselves and to follow their reason as their guide, would be more easily and safely governed than with minds nourished in error, and vitiated and debased, as in Europe, by ignorance, indigence, and oppression. The cherishment of the people then was our principle, the fear and distrust of them that of the òther party. Composed, as we were, of the landed and laboring interests of the country, we could not be less anxious for a government of law and order than were the inhabitants of the cities, the strongholds of federalism. And whether our efforts to save the prin-

[51]*Ibid.*, p. 5.

ciples and form of our constitution have not been salutary, let the present republican freedom order and prosperity of our country determine.[52]

Such was the core of Jeffersonianism. Johnson must have read it with pleasure, since he, too, had fallen back at last on the people on whose "virtue and intelligence" he was now pinning so much trust.

Jefferson then returned to the attack on consolidation, the present aim of the Federalists, aided by "unsuspecting, or apostate" Republicans. The Jefferson of 1823 like the Jefferson of 1793 took the state-rights ground. He asked whether any state would have approved the Constitution had it given all powers to the national government; whether the whole opposition to the new government did not spring from the fear of each state that its own policy would be subjected to other states; and whether the states would be any more willing now than then to submit to a "general surrender of all their rights and powers to a consolidated government, one and undivided."[53]

He made it abundantly clear that he held Marshall's Court largely responsible for federal aggressions on state power. He was too old, he said, to undertake the task of stating, as Johnson had asked, how far the Court had trespassed on state authority. Yet he referred the inquiring judge to articles by Judge Spencer Roane on the case of Cohens v. Virginia.[54] That decision, in which Johnson had acquiesced, Jefferson bitterly denounced. As was his wont, the Chief Justice had gone out of his way, said Jefferson, to assert federal power and depreciate that of the states. If Johnson would take the trouble he would find in writings by Roane and others a complete answer to his inquiry.[55]

Nevertheless, Jefferson did set down a general formula which might serve to guide the judge in cases of that sort. The formula consisted of two canons. The first of these he phrased as follows: "The capital and leading object of the Constitution was to leave with the states all authorities which respected their own citizens only, and to transfer to the U.S. those which respected citizens of foreign, or other states; to make us several as to ourselves, but one as to all others." In the former case, he said, interpretation should favor the states, and in the latter, the central government. Jefferson could think of only one matter arising between citizens of the same state which the framers had shifted from the states to the nation: namely, "where anything but gold or silver is made a lawful tender or the obligation of contracts is any otherwise impaired."

[52]*Ibid.*, pp. 5-6.
[53]*Ibid.*, p. 7.
[54]*Ibid.*
[55]*Ibid.*, pp. 7-8.

Jefferson stated his second canon in these terms:

On every question of construction, carry ourselves back to the time when the Constitution was adopted, recollect the spirit manifested in the debates, and instead of trying what meaning may be squeezed out of the text, or invented against it, conform to the probable one in which it was past.[56]

The state should retain control over its home concerns, and the judge in reading the Constitution should attend to the history of the times when the Constitution had its framing. The advice would not be lost on Mr. Justice Johnson.

Jefferson warned that a broad construction of federal power might provoke a broad construction of state power and the Union be destroyed in the melee. He opposed the withdrawal of all offices to Washington where, further removed from the eyes of the people, they might more readily be bought and sold. If conflicts arose, the ultimate arbiter was not the Court, or any agency of either state or federal government, but the people of the nation, assembled in convention. The people should decide; and, Jefferson declared, "it has been the peculiar wisdom and felicity of our Constitution, to have provided this peaceable appeal where that of other nations is at once to force."[57]

As always, Jefferson closed on a friendly note. He and Johnson might occasionally differ on details of small consequence (a generous understatement), but their general aims were the same: "to preserve the republican form and principles" of the Constitution, and to maintain the distribution of powers it had provided. These were the two "sheet-anchors" of the Union.[58]

Yet the ex-President and his judicial appointee stood further apart than this polite remark might suggest. Admittedly, both agreed on the first objective; Johnson had long stressed the supremacy of Congress, the representative organ, and had even clashed with Jefferson on the accountability of the executive. Both men in the last analysis cherished the people as the ultimate resort. On the question of the division of power between federal and state governments, however, they had discovered a wide gulf between them. The Virginia planter, managing his debt-ridden estate and developing plans for the new state university, had in a sense come back to the state as the chief reliance of the people for the government of their intimate concerns. The South Carolinian had followed a different course. A childhood racked by the disruptions of war and a score of years in national office, much of it passed at the center of the nation, had convinced Johnson of the importance of the bond of union and had

[56]*Ibid.*, p. 10.
[57]*Ibid.*, p. 12.
[58]*Ibid.*

awakened him to the potentialities of national measures of improvement. To him, Congress was the key; held in check by the test of election, that body might serve the cause of union through measures of economic and social improvement. As for the Court, Jefferson's assault on nationalistic opinions must have revived Johnson's uneasiness; and, indeed, the justice's effort to distinguish actual decisions and *obiter dicta* had testified to his misgivings, as well as to a latent uncertainty concerning the soundness of the Court's pronouncements.

Some weeks after the June discourse on political theory Jefferson in a brief note brought his part in the correspondence to a close.[59] In the meantime, the Republican leader had submitted his June letter to his friend Madison, and had received from Montpelier an incisive commentary on it.[60] The deliberate and mild-mannered Madison agreed with Jefferson's epitome of Republicanism. He went on, however, and his reasoning would have gratified Johnson, to lecture his old associate on the true nature of the federal system. There was need, he declared, of a more convenient mode for resolving conflicts than resort to conventions. The Supreme Court served that purpose; and even though that tribunal had abused its power by magnifying federal at the expense of state authority and by inflating its own jurisdiction, that did not disprove the existence of the revising power.

Madison, however, cautioned Jefferson on Johnson's judgment. "With all his good qualities," he warned, "he has been betrayed into errors which shew that his discretion is not always awake." Madison cited Johnson's charge against Morris, his comment on Cooper in the Kentucky letter, and particularly the invoking of "religious prejudices" to which Johnson in his excitement had resorted against Cooper.[61] Jefferson moreover was soon to receive from Charleston a fresh reminder, not only of the judge's forthrightness, but also of his deviation from Jefferson's own state-rights convictions.

Before Johnson's next letter to Jefferson, a new incident had occurred in Charleston. As a later chapter will show, the state had tried to prevent agitation among its slaves by excluding Negro mariners; a private association had secured enforcement; and Judge Johnson in the Circuit Court had declared the law invalid under

[59]Jefferson to Johnson, July 31, 1823, Jefferson Papers (MSS; Library of Congress). Jefferson explained the delay by describing a fever of three weeks' duration. He enclosed the articles by Roane mentioned earlier, and added some others.

[60]Jefferson to Madison, June 13, 1823, *Works* (Federal ed.), XII, 295; Madison to Jefferson, June 27, 1823, Madison, *Letters and Other Writings*, III, 323-28.

[61]*Ibid.*, pp. 324, 325. See above, pp. 144-45.

the federal commerce power and a treaty.[62] Four days after the decision, Johnson scrawled a bitter and impassioned note and sent it off to Monticello.[63] He acknowledged the treatise by Roane which Jefferson had sent him and said he would study it and reply on that subject later on. The letter of June 12 contained "invaluable" material which Johnson wished might be published over Jefferson's signature. Events in Charleston had evidently confirmed Johnson in his fears. "I acknowledge to you my dear sir, that I have sometimes some gloomy doubts crossing my mind respecting the destiny of our beloved country."[64] His recent encounter with state-rights extremism led him to fear that those who could not govern the nation might succeed in dividing it. Disunion, "that greatest of evils," seemed, in Charleston at least, to be losing its terrors. He enclosed with his letter a copy of the recent opinion on the state exclusion law and predicted, no doubt accurately, that it would excite some surprise.

Those of his fellow-townsmen who were mooting a recourse to disunion Johnson regarded as Federalists. He said this of the private group which had taken the field to enforce the obnoxious local law: "The very men who not long since made such an outcry against self-created societies are now heading a most formidable one in this place. How far they will go God knows." The debate over the Missouri question had shown its results in blood the previous year and would continue long to excite persecution. Once again the federal judge was incurring public criticism and once again considering an exodus:

> If it be true that *"quem Coelum perdere vult prius dementat"* I have received a warning to quit this city. I fear nothing so much as the effects of the persecuting spirit that is abroad in this place. Should it spread thro' the state & produce a systematic policy founded on the ridiculous but prevalent notion that it is a struggle for life or death, there are no excesses that we may not look for—whatever be their effect upon the Union. They are really exemplifying your observations on their general principles of government. They now pronounce the Negros the real Jacobins of this country, and in doing so shew what they meant when they honored us with the same epithet.[65]

The emotion of this brief letter betrays Johnson's alarm. Rightly or wrongly, he saw at this early date the birth of the movement for state sovereignty in South Carolina. The rumored insurrection,

[62]Elkison v. Deliesseline, decided Aug. 7, 1823, 8 Fed. Cas. 493, No. 4366 (C.C. Dist. of S.C.); see below, pp. 192-96.

[63]Johnson to Jefferson, Aug. 11, 1823, Jefferson Papers (MSS; Library of Congress).

[64]*Ibid.*

[65]*Ibid.*

coupled with the federal government's opposition to the state's protective measure, had furnished momentum to the retreat from nationalism. The judge would live to see Nullification, if not the war of 1861. His "gloomy doubts" concerning the Union were well founded.

In spite of the pledge contained in this letter, no further correspondence exists between William Johnson and Thomas Jefferson. What purpose could it serve? The two Republicans had reached an impasse. To one the greatest danger lay in federal centralization, to the other, in state excesses and disunion.

What effects on Johnson's subsequent conduct did the correspondence with Jefferson produce?[66] In his attitude toward the substantive powers of the national government, Johnson did not swerve. As a matter of fact, the interchange evidently confirmed him in his assumption that Congress needed and possessed powers to effect national improvements. Many circumstances explain his resolute stand—the affiliations with business interests in Charleston, the belief that national fiscal and communicational measures would serve to bind together the parts of the Union, the conviction that government to prove effective requires a broad range of discretion in selecting alternative means, and perhaps above all, the perturbation he felt over the mounting state-rights fervor in Charleston.

Doctrines of state sovereignty had shifted from New England to South Carolina, and despite Jefferson's admonitions, Johnson continued boldly to support broad construction of congressional powers. Two decisions at the 1824 sitting of the Court furnished media for a public declaration of his views.

One of these involved the controversial Bank of the United States.[67] "A state of things," he declared in his separate opinion in the Osborn case, "has now grown up, in some of the States, which renders all the protection necessary that the general government can give to this bank."[68] Many states by law had assailed the Bank, and Johnson doubtless looked on these attacks as fresh instances of the mounting state pretensions. The judge went on to depict in sweeping terms the services of the Bank in the conduct of national finances.[69] Indeed, the Bank served other purposes. Here

---

[66]The effect on Jefferson was negligible. He continued to express apprehension over the drive toward centralization which he traced to the Marshall-dominated Court. See Jefferson to Robert J. Garnett, Feb. 14, 1824, in which he advocated a constitutional amendment on internal improvements and renewed the cry against consolidation through decisions by the Supreme Court; that branch, he said, was in essence Federalist "almost to a man . . . ." —Jefferson, *Writings* (ed. Ford), X, 294.

[67]Osborn v. Bank of the United States, 9 Wheat. 738 (1824).

[68]*Ibid.*, pp. 871-72.

[69]For Johnson's tribute to the services rendered by the Bank see *ibid.,* p. 872.

the Republican Johnson went even beyond the Federalist Marshall in asserting federal powers, and Jefferson's first canon of construction received an unintended application. Johnson asserted that the closing of the first Bank in 1811 had flooded the country with a "new description of bills of credit," against which it was clear the Constitution furnished no adequate barrier. Accordingly the government had set up a second Bank. Thus,

> A specie-paying bank, with an overwhelming capital, and the whole aid of the government deposits, presented the only resource to which the government could resort, to restore that power over the currency of the country, which the framers of the constitution evidently intended to give to Congress alone.[70]

Not for decades would the Court as a whole sanction so broad a reading of the currency power.[71] Yet contrary to Jefferson's implication, Johnson did not find Congress unchecked in its choice of measures. In a passage that is virtually a rebuttal of Jefferson's argument, Johnson gave the clue. He admitted that Congress might have exercised a latitude of construction not foreseen when the Constitution was adopted. Then, after enumerating cases of such an excess of power, he came to his point:

> . . . all this, being within the range of their discretion, is aloof from judicial control, while unaffectedly exercised for the purposes of the Constitution. Nor, indeed, is there much to be alarmed at in it, while the same people who govern the States, can, where they will, control the legislature of the United States.[72]

Unless the broad purposes for which the Constitution had been established should be exceeded, the judiciary must accordingly bow to the electorate. It was the people of the nation who should apply the test.

While this was true of the substantive powers of the national legislature, procedure was another matter, and Johnson, it should be noted, dissented from the majority here, on the ground that the implied powers of Congress did not extend to giving the courts jurisdiction over suits involving the Bank. "No one branch of the general government," he declared, "can new-model the constitutional structure of the other."[73] To admit the contention would, he thought, grant the judiciary an excessive control over the state functionaries. Although reflecting Jefferson's suspicions of the judicial

[70]*Ibid.*, p. 873.
[71]Juilliard *v.* Greenman, 110 U.S. 421 (1884).
[72]9 Wheat. 895-96. Cf. *ibid.*, pp. 873-74.
[73]*Ibid.*, p. 896.

prerogative, the position followed the line of Johnson's earlier convictions concerning the jurisdiction of courts.[74]

In another opinion this very year Johnson set forth what he took to be those "purposes of the Constitution."[75] His separate opinion in the Steamboat case, to be described later, breathes defiance of strict construction. He had never found much benefit, he announced, in pursuing the inquiry whether the whole, or any part, of the Constitution "is to be construed strictly, or literally."[76] The language of the document—"simple, classical, precise, yet comprehensive"—left little room for construction. The main question was what were its intent and meaning as willed by the framers? In Johnson's mind, the chief purpose of the Constitution was to unite the nation for the protection of the individual. This was the end; all else were only means.[77]

The Carolinian judge had moved far. In the *Life of Greene* he had attributed to the Jeffersonians the aim of promoting individual security and happiness; now he predicated the same aim of the Constitution itself. The mounting concern for individual rights had prompted him to protest the public alarm over the slave plot and to denounce the ensuing trials; and this concern was to involve him in further controversies in the future. In 1824 he grounded his respect for the individual on the Constitution itself. Congress, the elective organ of the nation, possessed power to cope with many matters. Courts of law were to withhold judgment. The people, the safest reliance, were in most instances the proper judges of infractions by Congress of its substantive powers.

The letters from Jefferson had produced no diminution in Johnson's respect for congressional power; he supported implied powers to the end.[78] On other issues, however, the exchange of sentiments

[74]See above, Chapter V.
[75]Concurring opinion in Gibbons v. Ogden, 9 Wheat. 1, 222 (1824).
[76]*Ibid.*, p. 223.
[77]For Johnson's full statement see below p. 203.
[78]Thus, in 1827, Johnson supported the power to acquire and govern territory. His lower court opinion in American Insurance Co. v. Canter, reproduced by Peters in a footnote accompanying the later decision of the Supreme Court, spoke at length on the point. He found no express provision in the Constitution for acquiring or governing territories, but held that the power to acquire was implied in the treaty-making power and possibly the power to admit new states into the Union. The power to govern grew out of the power to acquire and was vested to a vast extent in Congress. His position that it lay with the public functionaries to prescribe the extent to which the Constitution and laws should apply in acquired territories, was typical of his general approach to congressional power, and also prophetic of the much later distinction between incorporated and unincorporated territories.—(C.C. Dist. of S.C., 1827), 1 Pet. 515 ff., n.
The decision was affirmed in American Insurance Co. v. Canter, 1 Pet. 511 (1828), in which Marshall, for the Court, inferred the power to acquire and govern from a variety of sources, including the power of a sovereign

did affect his views. Although no further mention was made of the projected work on parties, and no record of such a work has yet appeared, Johnson continued to venerate the party founder.[79] Jefferson had cherished the states, as well as the people, and had seen in those units a primary means of coping with internal problems. To this conception of the states William Johnson would pay special heed in subsequent years. Finally, the young Republican took to heart the leader's precepts on another point—the procedures of the Supreme Court itself.

nation. Although not ruling on the point, Johnson seemed to regard a protective tariff as constitutional during the Nullification controversy. See below, Chapter XIV.

[79]See especially his *Eulogy on Jefferson*, discussed below, pp. 187-88, 298.

Chapter X

THE ORIGIN OF DISSENT

DESPITE the correspondence with Jefferson, Mr. Justice Johnson clung resolutely to his Federalist heresy, the doctrine of implied congressional power. Yet the interchange of views between the former President and the embattled judge explored another subject of no small importance. The letter which reached Charleston in the late autumn of 1822 broached the matter of Supreme Court practice. Notwithstanding his words of friendship and commendation, Thomas Jefferson had a bone to pick with his first recruit for the high bench.

Jefferson approached the subject with delicacy. He said he had pondered it long and for some time had considered writing to Johnson concerning it.[1] He thought highly of Johnson's "candor and devotedness to the Constitution in its true spirit" and accordingly would unbosom himself. The cause of his uneasiness was the mode by which the Court made up and delivered its opinions.

Ancient English practice set the correct model:

> You know that from the earliest ages of the English law, from the date of the year-books, at least, to the end of the IId George, the judges of England, in all but self-evident cases, delivered their opinions seriatim, with the reasons and authorities which governed their decisions. If they sometimes consulted together, and gave a general opinion, it was so rarely as not to excite either alarm or notice. Besides the light which their separate arguments threw on the subject, and the instruction communicated by their several modes of reasoning, it shewed whether the judges were unanimous or divided, and gave accordingly more or less weight to the judgment as a precedent. It sometimes happened too that when there were three opinions against one, the reasoning of the one was so much the most cogent as to become afterwards the law of the land. When Ld. Mansfield came to the bench he introduced the habit of caucusing opinions. The judges met at their chambers, or elsewhere, secluded from the presence of the public, and made up what was to be delivered as the opinion of the court. On

[1] Jefferson to Johnson, Oct. 27, 1822, Jefferson, *Works,* ed. P. L. Ford (Federal ed.), XII, 246-52.

168

the retirement of Mansfield, Ld Kenyon put an end to the practice, and the judges returned to that of seriatim opinions, and practice it habitually to this day, I believe.[2]

In Virginia, he continued, Judge Edmund Pendleton, taking Mansfield as his model, had instituted the secret, unanimous opinion in the state bench; but his successor, Judge Spencer Roane, had abolished the practice.

As for the Supreme Court, Jefferson was aware that the seriatim mode had prevailed until 1800. The reports for later years he did not have, but he understood that the practice of Mansfield and Pendleton prevailed there. Whether "the present C. J.," or some other, had reversed the earlier procedure, and when the change had come, he could not say. But he left no doubt about his attitude. Cases of high importance had been disposed of in this fashion, and the people, many of whom resented the decisions, were entitled to clear evidence of the vote and reasoning of each judge. The prevailing practice fostered irresponsibility:

The Judges holding their offices for life are under two responsibilities only. 1. Impeachment. 2. Individual reputation. But this practice compleatly withdraws them from both. For nobody knows what opinion any individual member gave in any case, nor even that he who delivers the opinion, concurred in it himself. Be the opinion therefore ever so impeachable, having been done in the dark it can be proved on no one. As to the 2d guarantee, personal reputation, it is shielded compleatly. The practice is certainly convenient for the lazy, the modest & the incompetent. It saves them the trouble of developing their opinion methodically and even of making up an opinion at all. That of seriatim argument shews whether every judge has taken the trouble of understanding the case, of investigating it minutely, and of forming an opinion for himself, instead of pinning it on another's sleeve. It would certainly be right to abandon this practice in order to give to our citizens one and all, that confidence in their judges which must be so desirable to the judges themselves, and so important to the cement of the union.[3]

Lazy, modest, incompetent! Did this description fit John Marshall's associates and, particularly, William Johnson? Had Johnson acquiesced without a murmur in Marshall's opinions in order to hide from the public eye? If this veiled taunt had come at such a time from someone else, the judge would likely have replied either

[2]*Ibid.*, p. 248.

[3]*Ibid.*, pp. 249-50. Jefferson went on to describe a bill drawn up by Attorney-General Edmund Randolph requiring seriatim opinions to be recorded in an official report. Congress had lacked time to consider the bill, "but such a volume would have been the best possible book of reports, and the better, as unincumbered with the hired sophisms and perversions of Counsel." *Ibid.*, p. 250.

with a chilly silence or with an indignant denial. Coming from the venerated Jefferson, and accompanied by professions of confidence and affection, it called inescapably for an explanation, and perhaps even for action.

Jefferson had shrewdly judged his man. William Johnson did reply at length and in time resorted to action. The discussion in which he engaged with Jefferson and the record of his judicial pronouncements illuminate the inner working of the Marshall Court. The evidence of Johnson's voice and pen throws in clearer perspective the aims and methods of the great Chief Justice himself.

Furthermore, the testimony of Jefferson and of Johnson highlight the role and procedures of that uniquely American institution, the Supreme Court. In our day that tribunal has come to symbolize the power and unity of the nation and the majesty of the Constitution. Proposals of reform and the publication of hostile interchanges among the judges have shocked those who look to the Court as to an Olympus. Judicial dissent has become the rule, rather than the exception,[4] and to many this internecine squabbling represents weakness and a betrayal of the lofty serenity of the high court. The Supreme Court, however, is a profoundly human institution, devised by human hands for human purposes; and John Marshall was its leading builder, if not its architect. An account of his relations with his coworkers will lend realism to the appreciation of its structure and functioning, then and now.

As a preliminary to the recital of Johnson's disclosures and subsequent conduct, it is essential to examine in some detail the charges which in 1822 were circulating concerning the Court, and to analyze the policy which Marshall had to that date maintained. By its own actions the Court had provoked the criticism. At the 1819 and 1821 terms, it had handed down five epochal decisions; their effect was on the one hand to expand national power—legislative and judicial—and on the other, to assert a power to review the acts and judicial decrees of the states.[5] The doctrines expressed and the power exercised here promptly brought retorts and de-

---

[4]For the first time in the record of the Court, the justices, at the October, 1943, term, were in disagreement more often than in agreement in cases with opinions.—C. Herman Pritchett, "Dissent on the Supreme Court, 1943-44," *American Political Science Review*, XXXIX (1945), 43. Cf. the same author's *The Roosevelt Court: A Study in Judicial Politics and Values 1937-47* (New York, 1948), pp. 25-26.

[5]McCulloch v. Maryland, 4 Wheat. 316 (1819); Sturges v. Crowninshield, 4 Wheat. 122 (1819); Dartmouth College v. Woodward, 4 Wheat. 518 (1819); Cohens v. Virginia, 6 Wheat. 264 (1821); and Green v. Biddle, 8 Wheat. 1, 11 (1823) in the last-named case, Story delivered an opinion for a unanimous Court in 1821, after which the case was reargued and new opinions given in 1823.

mands in Congress for reform of the Court and for diminution of its revising authority.[6]

Not merely the content but also the form of the decisions exasperated the Court's assailants. Four of the five appeared as the decrees of a unanimous Court; in none was there a reasoned dissent.[7] In all but one, and notably in the most irritating of the series, the Bank and Cohens cases, John Marshall expounded the opinion of the Court. In accordance with his wont, he grounded his argument primarily on general principle and only secondarily on the words of the fundamental law.[8]

It was two decades since the electorate had repudiated the Federalist party, yet a member of that party continued to direct the high tribunal and from that rostrum to declaim his doctrines. What was equally bad, the Court had been, in numbers at least, overwhelmingly Republican for half that period. Had the five recruits from the party of Jefferson and Madison completely succumbed to the doctrines of their chief?

The Virginia group had no doubt about the answer. On the heels of the Bank decision, Judge Spencer Roane, of the state's highest court, rushed into print under the pseudonym "Amphictyon"; then, and later as "Hampden" and "Algernon Sydney," he assailed the Republican judges for their silence and drew the conclusion that they had abandoned their principles.[9] Few men, he asserted, came out from high office as pure as when they had entered it; it was only the elect who could "pass unhurt through a fiery furnace."[10] Even the equable James Madison had endorsed Roane's views. Besides deploring the resort to general principles, Madison had pointed to the remedy—the use of seriatim opinions.[11]

But the bitterest complaints came from Thomas Jefferson. Marshall's great antagonist of 1801 had never felt warmly toward his fellow-Virginian, and the years seemed only to deepen the antagonism.[12] In 1819 he deplored the persistence of Federalism in

[6]See Charles Warren, *The Supreme Court in United States History*, I, 657 ff.
[7]In the Dartmouth College case concurring opinions were filed by Washington and Story; Duvall dissented without opinion.
[8]Story spoke for the Court in Green v. Biddle.
[9]See above, Chapter IX, note 1.
[10]Article signed, "Hampden," *John P. Branch Historical Papers*, Vol. II, No. 1, p. 118.
[11]Such a practice, he said, "might either, by the harmony of their reasoning, have produced a greater conviction in the public mind; or, by its discordance, have impaired the force of the precedent, now ostensibly supported by a unanimous and perfect concurrence in every argument and dictum in the judgment pronounced."—Madison to Roane, Sept. 2, 1819, Madison, *Letters and Other Writings*, III, 143.
[12]In 1810 Jefferson had excoriated Marshall's "cunning and sophistry" and lamented the tendency of Marshall's associates to surrender their intellectual independence.—Jefferson to Madison, May 25, 1810, Jefferson, *Writings*, ed. P. L. Ford, IX, 275.

the judiciary. After twenty years, he said, the principles of 1800 had yet to penetrate that branch; the leaven of the old Federalist mass had assimilated the new Republican matter.[13] A judiciary independent of the will of the people, he insisted, was in republics a "solecism."[14] Marshall was clearly the villain in the piece. Said Jefferson of Marshall's practice: "An opinion is huddled up in conclave, perhaps by a majority of one, delivered as if unanimous, and with the silent acquiescence of lazy or timid associates, by a crafty chief judge, who sophisticates the law to his mind, by the turn of his own reasoning."[15]

Since impeachment had long since failed as a mode of control, the only other remedy for the abuse was the seriatim, or separate, opinion. Mr. Justice Johnson was not the first of Jefferson's friends to listen to the proposal. In a long series of letters the planter-statesman had repeatedly pressed the point with ireful force.[16] Bombardment of the Court came from all directions, but the heaviest fire came from Monticello.

Behind the curtain the leading actors in the play were evidently agitated by the hubbub in the galleries. Johnson, Washington, and Story all gave expression to their concern.[17] The conservative Story lamented the weakness of the judiciary. That branch, he said, would always thwart the wishes of "demagogues" and muster support only from "the wise and the good and the elevated in society."[18]

In the hour of crisis, Story turned characteristically to his beloved Marshall. Beseeching Providence for the Chief Justice's long

[13]Jefferson to Roane, Sept. 6, 1819, Jefferson, *Works* (Federal ed.), XII, 136.
[14]Jefferson to Thomas Ritchie, Dec. 25, 1820, *ibid.*, p. 178.
[15]*Ibid.*, pp. 177-78.
[16]Jefferson to Thomas Ritchie, Dec. 25, 1820, Jefferson, *Works* (Federal ed.), XII, 175-79; to Archibald Thweat, Jan. 19, 1821, *ibid.*, pp. 196-97; to Spencer Roane, March 9, June 27, 1821, *ibid.*, pp. 201-2 n.; to Nathaniel Macon, Aug. 19, 1821, *ibid.*, p. 206; and to James Pleasants, Dec. 26, 1821, *ibid.*, p. 213. Jefferson evidently assumed that once the opinions of each judge had been officially recorded, Congress by joint protestation would denounce opinions it deemed unconstitutional and then resort to impeachment as the ultimate remedy.—Jefferson to Macon, Aug. 19, 1821, *loc. cit.*
[17]In 1821, Johnson wrote Secretary of State Adams, criticizing a system whereby district attorneys engaged copartners in their professional practice. As a result, the public had come to feel that patronizing the copartner would promote their standing with the prosecution in federal actions. Said Johnson of this suspicion, "True or false, it is a great misfortune to us that such a surmise should ever be whispered; for the reputation of purity is of vast importance to a judiciary which needs public confidence as much as we do."—Johnson to J. Q. Adams, June 12, 1821, Miscellaneous Letters, Records of the Department of State (MSS; National Archives).
". . . we hold ourselves answerable," cried Washington, in setting aside a state law, "to God, our consciences and our country, to decide this question according to the dictates of our best judgment."—Opinion for the Court, Green v. Biddle, 8 Wheat. 1, 93 (1823).
[18]Story to Jeremiah Mason, Jan. 10, 1822, W. Story, *Life and Letters of Joseph Story*, I, 411-12.

life, he dispatched to Marshall a glowing tribute to his leadership in the cause of the Constitution.[19] In acknowledging the praise of his younger associate, John Marshall gave evidence of his own malaise over the general outcry. He said he was glad that his esteem for his brothers was reciprocated. "The harmony of the bench," he hoped, would "never be disturbed. We have external & political enemies enough to preserve internal peace."[20]

On another occasion, Marshall took his case to the public. For once he descended from the heights and, as "A Friend to the Union," defended not only the doctrine, but the procedure of the Court as well.[21] Insisting that his eminent associates were not the men to sit by silently while their chief expounded views which they disapproved, he argued:

> The course of every tribunal must necessarily be, that the opinion which is to be delivered as the opinion of the court, is previously submitted to the consideration of all the judges; and, if any part of the reasoning be disapproved, it must be so modified as to receive the approbation of all, before it can be delivered as the opinion of all.[22]

Furthermore, he maintained that differences of opinion had existed on the Court, and that this had appeared in the published reports.[23]

Yet this effort by Marshall to whitewash the conduct he had pursued on the Court did violence to the facts. The judges had diverged on important issues; and at times these divergences had escaped the public eye. Marshall, as we shall see, was largely to blame for these and other dubious practices.

The cause lay in Marshall's own overriding objectives. First of all, the Chief Justice visualized a high role for the judiciary. In 1801

[19]Said Story, "I trust in God . . . that the Supreme Court will continue fearlessly to do its duty; & I pray that your invaluable life may be long preserved to guide us in our defence of the Constitution. Will you excuse me for saying that your appointment to the Bench has in my judgment more contributed under Providence to the preservation of the true principles of the Constitution than any other circumstance in our domestic history?"—Story to Marshall, June 27, 1821, Warren, "Story-Marshall Correspondence, 1819-1831" (cited in note 2, Chapter IX), p. 7.

[20]Marshall to Story, July 13, 1821, Massachusetts Historical Society, *Proceedings*, 2d ser., XIV (1900-1901), 328.

[21]Philadelphia *Union*, April 24, 1819. Marshall was here replying to Roane's "Amphictyon" articles in the *Enquirer;* see above, Chapter IX, note 1.

[22]Philadelphia *Union*, April 24, 1819.

[23]Marshall cited the *Nereide*, 9 Cranch 388 (1815), as an instance of separate concurring opinions, and Olivera *v.* Union Insurance Company, 3 Wheat. 183 (1818), as an instance of the presentation by the judge who delivered the Court's opinion of the "contrariety of reasoning on which the opinion was formed." In the former case Marshall delivered the opinion of the Court; Johnson submitted a concurring opinion; and Story, joined by another, gave a dissenting opinion. In the latter, Marshall, in delivering the opinion of the Court, briefly summarized the diverse opinions held by four unidentified justices.

he had assumed command of a tribunal which was regarded by his political foes with distrust, and by the public at large with indifference. Housed in a basement below the Senate chamber because the Capitol architect had forgotten it in his plans, scorned repeatedly by eminent nominees who preferred public office in their own states, and regarded apathetically even by its own members, the Supreme Court at that hour had evoked little respect as an organ of government.[24] John Marshall had set about with determination to construct out of these poor materials a judiciary equal to the legislature and the executive in dignity and strength. From Marbury to Cohens, his decisions had steadily asserted power in the courts. As an arm of the national government, as a bulwark against popular excesses, as a shield to the rights of property, the Supreme Court would occupy a front-rank position in the constitutional order. It was Marshall's aim to build a fortress out of a hut.

This first aim would in turn promote his second. In repudiating a strict construction, he denied that the document of 1787 was a mere legal code: "we must never forget," he declared, "that it is a constitution we are expounding."[25] Whatever hopes the framers may actually have attached to their handiwork, Marshall assumed that they had meant it to last "for ages to come."[26] In consequence he took it as his task to fix for all time the basic meanings of the Constitution, to establish the constitutional system so clearly and so authoritatively that attempts at deviation would prove futile. Convinced that he was right, he sought, through the medium of a reinvigorated Court to freeze for the far future his own conceptions of constitutionalism.

In his campaign to enthrone the Court and reveal sound doctrine, Marshall set out with many advantages. Not the least was his personality and ability. Amiable, unassuming, considerate of others, he was capable of winning the loyalty of the coldest associate. Keen in his perceptions and logical in his argument, he could persuade the recalcitrant with subtle skill: "it was both hard and

[24]Beveridge, *Life of John Marshall*, III, 120, n. 2. In little more than a decade five members resigned from the Court and two others declined appointments already confirmed. Chief Justice Jay resigned his office to run for governor of New York, and Justice Rutledge to become chief justice of South Carolina.

[25]McCulloch v. Maryland, 4 Wheat. 316, 407 (1819).

[26]4 Wheat. 415. Cf. his comment two years later: "a constitution is framed for ages to come, and is designed to approach immortality as nearly as human institutions can approach it."—Cohens v. Virginia, 6 Wheat. 264, 387 (1821). Did Marshall unconsciously borrow the expression from Johnson, who said, in 1818, "That the members of the American family possess ample means of defence under the constitution, we hope ages to come will verify"?— Opinion for the Court, in Burton's Lessee v. Williams, 3 Wheat. 529, 538 (1818).

unpleasant to differ with him," concludes Beveridge, "and both easy and agreeable to follow his lead."[27]

Such was the character and charm that Marshall brought to his office. The office in turn bestowed additional benefits. Even in our own time the Chief Justice enjoys special prerogatives in directing the high court. At public sessions he presides; in private conferences he directs the order of business, canvasses the considered reasoning of the other judges, and after the voting, assigns the writing of opinions. He may, if he will and if group morale will bear it, write all the opinions of the Court, when he is with the majority. Only when he votes with the minority may another, the senior among the majority justices, determine who shall speak for the body.[28] These tools, which Marshall himself doubtless helped to fashion, served him well during his long career on the Court.

The men who collected under Marshall's gracious rule constituted in a real sense a family; or to vary the figure, since wives remained at home, a monastic order. By 1811 all but Washington of the old Federalist associates had left the scene; henceforth, Marshall could claim, with only one exception,[29] the place of Father Superior on the basis of age as well as of rank. Each day the brothers tramped through the mud-filled streets of Washington to their courtroom in the Capitol basement or (during a brief interval) in the court clerk's private home.[30] At the close of the day's ritual, they returned to their common quarters, a boarding house. There, led by their benign abbot, they conversed on affairs of the day; there they interspersed, between remarks about counsel and gossip of the bumptious young capital, a running commentary on the cases before them. In this informal and altogether pleasant manner, they reached common agreement on decisions. Admittedly, regular consultations did take place at the court chamber, and frequently far into the evening, but these, it would appear, were auxiliary to the cheerful sessions at the dinner table or in the parlor.[31]

If the discipline which the Chief Justice imposed on his associates was agreeable, it was none the less rigid. To promote his first aim, an exalted judiciary, Marshall applied all his forces to achieve harmony and unity. Whatever divergences of view might exist within the cloister, the Court should present to the world a united front.

[27]*Marshall,* IV, 90.
[28]Charles Evans Hughes, *The Supreme Court of the United States* (New York, 1928), pp. 56 ff. Cf. Felix Frankfurter, *The Commerce Clause* (Chapel Hill, N.C., 1937), pp. 6-7.
[29]That was Gabriel Duvall, who was almost three years older than Marshall. Washington was Marshall's junior by six years; Johnson, by sixteen years; Livingston, by two; Todd, by nine; and Story, by twenty-four.
[30]Beveridge, *Marshall,* IV, 130, nn. 2, 3.
[31]*Ibid.,* pp. 86-88.

Difference of opinion must be sacrificed on the altar of authoritativeness and prestige. The Court should speak with a single voice;
and in order to establish on firm footing a sound construction of
laws and particularly of the Constitution, the voice should, on most
occasions, be Marshall's.[32] The policy produced results; by 1819
the Supreme Court stood at a pinnacle of public veneration.[33]

For the most part the Court meekly accepted the rule of "united
we stand, divided we fall." To a surprising extent the other judges
came to share Marshall's distaste for public dissent and proved
their compliance by word and deed.[34] In fact, with the sole exception
of William Johnson, no member of the Marshall Court during the
years prior to 1823 spoke out in separate opinions, whether concurring or dissenting, in more than eight cases.[35] To a considerable
degree, Marshall's unanimous and univocal opinions, launched so
auspiciously at a time when Federalists monopolized the bench,
had withstood the advent of successive Republican appointees.

That alone would explain much of the hostility to the Court
which grew increasingly after 1819. Moreover, in pursuit of his
objectives Marshall had committed errors well calculated to incur
resentment. At one point he rushed into a decision without first

[32]Of an estimated 1,106 decisions with opinion handed down during Marshall's entire tenure, the Chief Justice reportedly wrote the opinion of the
Court in 519.—Charles Grove Haines, *Role of the Supreme Court in American Government and Politics, 1789-1835* (Berkeley, Calif., 1944), p. 649. Of
more than 60 cases involving constitutional questions, Marshall spoke for
the Court in some 36.—*Ibid.*, pp. 649-50, citing studies by Henry Hitchcock
and Vincent Barnett, Jr. From 1801 to 1822, inclusive, Marshall delivered
the opinion of the majority in some 314 out of a total of 556.—Figures
compiled by the author.

[33]That year Hezekiah Niles described it as "a tribunal so far removed
from the people, that some seem to regard it with a species of that awful
reverence in which the inhabitants of Asia look up to their princes."—*Niles
Weekly Register*, XVI (March 20, 1819), 65.

[34]Marshall, in 1827, said it was his policy, when differing from the Court,
"to acquiesce silently in its opinion."—Dissenting opinion in Bank of the
United States *v.* Dandridge, 12 Wheat. 64, 90. Cf. Story's comment stating
that the Court regretted those occasions on which Marshall abstained from
writing the opinion in constitutional cases.—John M. Shirley, *The Dartmouth College Causes and the Supreme Court of the United States* (St. Louis,
1879), p. 395. Story says Washington believed that delivering dissenting
opinions on ordinary occasions weakened the "authority of the court" and
served no public benefit.—Story to Henry Wheaton, April 8, 1818, Story,
Story, I, 303-4. Story himself had swallowed his convictions in the case
of Hudson and Goodwin in 1812 (see above, pp. 77-79) and later said it
was his "usual practice" to "submit in silence to the decision" of his brethren
when he differed from them.—Dissenting opinion in Inglis *v.* Trustees of the
Sailor's Snug Harbor, 3 Pet. 99, 145 (1830).

[35]Livingston rendered separate concurring opinions in five cases, and dissenting in three; Story, concurring opinions in three cases, and dissenting in
five. These figures exclude opinions delivered seriatim in a few early cases.
(Statistics are based on figures compiled by the author). See below, Appendix II.

assuring himself of the support of a majority and afterwards had to make an ignominious admission that only one other judge had approved his action.[36] On other occasions he moved on to the merits of the case, despite the Court's lack of jurisdiction or the absence of a genuine adverse interest between the contending parties.[37] All of this revealed a lamentable lack of scruple concerning orderly legal procedure. Nor was Marshall above resorting to an artificial construction of constitutional verbiage quite apart from its historical frame.[38] Presumably such tactics appeared to him "necessary and proper" means for the establishment of sound principle.

Small wonder, then, that foes of the Court had arisen. By trampling on state laws and decisions, in its unanimous decrees of 1819 and 1821, the Court had evoked enmity; but that enmity was heightened by suspicion concerning the true views of the Republicans on the Court. Marshall's inattention to orderly legal procedure must have intensified the suspicion and given a hollow ring to the protestations which he published in the press.

This helps explain why Jefferson went to the extreme length of broaching to a member of the high court a cogently argued appeal for a change in procedure.

The man who received that appeal in November, 1822, had long since shown irritation over the tactics of his brothers. As early as 1809 William Johnson gave as his reason for submitting a separate opinion "to avoid having an ambiguous decision hereafter imputed to me, or an opinion which I would not wish to be understood to have given."[39] He alone of all the judges had suggested doubts about the bona fide character of Fletcher v. Peck; because of the community of interests between plaintiff and defendant, the controversy appeared to him strongly to resemble a "mere feigned case." "It is our duty to decide on the rights," he declared in his concurring opinion, "but not on the speculations of parties."[40] At the 1818 term Johnson's exasperation reached its climax; twice he publicly disassociated himself from what he regarded as *obiter dicta,* and in another case where the justices took up no fewer than eleven questions which had been certified from Story's court below, he protested bitterly: "We are constituted to decide causes, and not

[36]Hudson v. Guestier, 6 Cranch 281, 285 (1810), in which Marshall confessed his error in Rose v. Himely, 4 Cranch 241 (1808). Marshall made a similar mistake in the Bollman case.—Shirley, p. 310.
[37]The cases of Marbury and Cohens exemplify the former contingency; that of Fletcher v. Peck, 6 Cranch 87 (1810), the latter.
[38]See especially his construction of the contract clause, below, pp. 211, 214-15.
[39]Marine Insurance Company v. Young, 5 Cranch 187, 191 (1809) (added by errata).
[40]6 Cranch 87, 147 (1810). See below, pp. 213-14.

to discuss themes, or digest systems."[41] These statements, coupled with his record on court jurisdiction, disclose Johnson as the lone protestant against the irregularity of Marshall's procedures.

The early reports reveal Johnson struggling manfully for independence of expression. Hardly had he appeared on the high bench than he found himself in partial disagreement with Marshall in Huidekoper's Lessee *v.* Douglass, which concerned land titles under a grant of the Pennsylvania legislature; consequently he announced his own views in a concurring opinion.[42] From that time on, Johnson sought to articulate his own reasons for decisions and by 1822 had concurred separately on twelve occasions.[43] The majority of these decisions were of constitutional importance.[44]

Not until his third term, however, did he muster the courage to deliver a dissenting opinion. In the case of Aaron Burr's accomplices, counsel had expatiated on the dangers of executive tyranny. In contending that the Court lacked jurisdiction, Johnson regretted the "misfortune" of his divergence from the Court.[45] He said he had objected to a similar holding by his brothers the previous year, but had remained silent because the attorneys had confined their arguments to strict legal issues. Now one of his brothers agreed with his views, and that spared him "the painful sensation" which would result from a solitary dissent.[46] That was only the beginning; for during the next seventeen years Johnson would stand out in lone dissent no fewer than fifteen times. Again, many of his separate utterances occurred in crucial cases.[47] By an odd coincidence, William

[41]Dissenting opinion in United States *v.* Palmer, 3 Wheat. 610, 641 (1818): "As the opinion delivered in this case goes into the consideration of a variety of topics which do not appear to me to be essential to the case, I will present a brief view of all that I consider as now decided."—Concurring opinion in Gelston *v.* Hoyt, 3 Wheat. 246, 333 (1818). "It has long been with me a rule of judicial proceeding, never, where I am free to act, to decide more in any case than what the case itself necessarily requires; and so far only, in my view, can a case be considered as authority."— Dissenting opinion in the *Atalanta,* 3 Wheat. 409, 419 (1818).
[42]3 Cranch 1, 72 (1805).
[43]In 1816 Johnson explained a separate concurring opinion on two grounds: first, "Few minds are accustomed to the same habit of thinking, and our conclusions are most satisfactory to ourselves when arrived at in our own way"; and second, "the momentous importance" of the question involved.— Martin *v.* Hunter's Lessee, 1 Wheat. 304, 362, 363.
[44]These included, *inter alia,* Huidekoper's Lessee *v.* Douglass (see above, note 42); Fletcher *v.* Peck, 6 Cranch 87 (1810); Town of Pawlet *v.* Clark, 9 Cranch 292 (1815); The *Nereide,* 9 Cranch 388 (1815); Martin *v.* Hunter's Lessee (see above, note 43); Gelston *v.* Hoyt, 3 Wheat. 246 (1818); Houston *v.* Moore, 5 Wheat. 1 (1820).
[45]*Ex parte* Bollman and Swartwout, 4 Cranch 75, 101 (1807); for further details see above, p. 56.
[46]4 Cranch 107.
[47]Rose *v.* Himely, 4 Cranch 241 (1808); Yeaton *v.* Bank of Alexandria, 5 Cranch 49 (1809); Mills *v.* Duryee, 7 Cranch 481 (1813); Fairfax's Devisee *v.* Hunter's Lessee, 7 Cranch 603 (1813); The *Atalanta,* 3 Wheat.

Johnson contributed exactly half of the concurring and half the dissenting opinions delivered by all the judges between his advent and the close of the 1822 term.[48]

Furthermore, Cranch's reports of the early Court suggest that Johnson wrung from Marshall not only a grudging tolerance for individual expression, but in addition a greater opportunity for others to speak for the Court. Prior to Johnson's advent, it will be remembered, the Court had appeared of one mind and of one voice.[49] The practice of Marshall's speaking for an ostensibly undivided Court had in four years hardened into a custom. It has been suggested that Marshall remained the sole mouthpiece of the Court until 1812, following the appointment of Joseph Story.[50] But William Johnson had evidently undermined Marshall's monopoly even before that date.

At his initial term, the restless Johnson had upset the harmony of the brotherhood; not only did Johnson himself speak out in the case of Huidekoper, but one of the other associate justices had the temerity to dissent, the first instance of its kind since Marshall's appointment in 1801.[51] When the cat was away the mice did play, for Marshall's brothers twice took advantage of his absence to render opinions seriatim.[52] This insurgency extended into the next term, when in three cases the judges spoke in separate opinions, and in a fourth case Paterson dissented.[53] Marshall continued, however, to state the Court's opinion in all cases at which he was present. But by the 1807 term Marshall had quelled the revolt. Despite the arrival of the Republican Livingston, Johnson alone of the

409 (1818); United States v. Palmer, 3 Wheat. 610 (1818); The Amiable Isabella, 6 Wheat. 1 (1821). In all of these Johnson was alone in his dissent.

[48]Johnson gave 12 of 24 concurring opinions, and 16 of 32 dissenting opinions handed down between 1805 and 1822 inclusive. (Figures compiled by the author).

[49]See above, pp. 46-47. Marshall had given all the opinions of the Court but two, and from these Marshall had absented himself; the one instance of a separate utterance had been a concurring opinion by Chase.

[50]William Draper Lewis, article on Marshall in Encyclopedia Britannica (1952 ed.), XIV, 968-71.

[51]In United States v. Fisher, 2 Cranch 358, 397 (1805), Washington delivered a dissenting opinion.

[52]Lambert's Lessee v. Paine, 3 Cranch 97 (1805), and Marine Insurance Company of Alexandria v. Wilson, 3 Cranch 187 (1805). In contrast to later practice, the judges gave their opinions according to the order which was followed before Marshall's term; thus, Johnson, as junior justice, gave the first opinion at the Lambert ruling. At the second decision, he gave no opinion.

[53]Seriatim opinions were delivered in Marine Insurance Company of Alexandria v. Tucker, 3 Cranch 357; United States v. Heth, 3 Cranch 399; and Randolph v. Ware, 3 Cranch 503 (1806). In each case Johnson gave one of the opinions. Paterson submitted a brief dissenting opinion in Sims and Wise v. Slacum, 3 Cranch 300 (1806).

other judges expressed himself at length on decisions.[54] Not for twenty years would Johnson succeed in reviving the seriatim practice.

Nevertheless Johnson's campaign for free expression brought results. He himself was not to be silenced. At the next term he spoke out separately in four cases, and two other judges followed his example.[55] And by 1809 Marshall had surrendered his supreme prerogative—delivering the opinion of the Court. At three cases that year and at one the succeding year, Marshall relinquished that privilege to others.[56] When the Court next met, with Story and Duvall sitting alongside their three Republican associates, Johnson, Livingston, and Todd, Marshall had definitely abandoned his claim to be exclusive mouthpiece.[57]

Yet beginning in 1819 Johnson virtually relinquished the right he had earlier secured. At four terms he merged his voice with the others and nodded his approval of Marshall's nationalizing opinions.[58]

Why this sudden silence? Although he had decided by 1819 not to resign, there may have lingered some dissatisfaction with his judicial post and the modest salary it afforded. By the same year, his researches for the *Life of Greene* were well launched, as we have seen, and this project absorbed much of his attention for three more years. These considerations furnish a partial explanation. Also, economic and political views and his fears of state excesses probably led him to endorse many of the Court's conclusions —those conclusions which Jefferson found so offensive. Although there is evidence that he extracted a *quid pro quo* from his brothers in the language of the reported opinions,[59] he surrendered his in-

---

[54]Johnson, besides dissenting in the Bollman case, gave the opinion of the Court in Marshall *v.* Currie, 4 Cranch 172 (1807). Although the reports are silent on the point, John Marshall may have absented himself on account of his relationship with the plaintiff—Humphrey Marshall, of Kentucky.

[55]In 1808 Johnson wrote concurring opinions twice and dissenting opinions twice; Washington and Livingston each submitted one concurring opinion.

[56]Washington spoke for the Court in Pierce *v.* Turner, 5 Cranch 154 (1809); Cushing, in Marine Insurance Company of Alexandria *v.* Young, 5 Cranch 187 (1809); and Livingston, in Keene *v.* United States, 5 Cranch 304 (1809), and Hudson *v.* Guestier, 6 Cranch 281 (1810). The reports give no indication that Marshall was absent from any of these decisions.

[57]At that term, 1812, Marshall gave nineteen opinions for the majority, with the writing of eleven other majority opinions distributed among five other justices. During the ensuing decade, 1813-1822, Marshall gave an annual average of about fifteen, and the remaining judges combined, of about twenty-one opinions for the Court. Todd appeared on the Court in 1808.

[58]From 1819 through 1822, he delivered only one concurring opinion (in 1820), and two dissents (1820 and 1821). This was in marked contrast to his conduct at the 1818 session, when he submitted one concurring and four dissenting opinions.

[59]Note that in several of the opinions in which Johnson acquiesced during this period, Marshall included statements explicitly delimiting the effect of the decision. Quite conceivably, Johnson insisted on these comments in the

dependence and threw the weight of his silent vote behind the Court's pronouncements.In any event, if he shared in the culpability of his silent associates, his guilt in 1822 was of recent origin.

His acquiescence in the unanimity rule must have caused Johnson to read with mixed feelings Thomas Jefferson's argument for individual expression by judges. According to Jefferson, Marshall's practice, like that of Mansfield and Pendleton, removed the judge from public scrutiny and gave decisions an authoritativeness that was hollow. Kenyon and Roane set the proper course; their liberal mode brought court differences and individual reasoning to the eye of the public. In short, that mode made for responsible government. Latent in the letter from Monticello was an uncomfortable query: Had Johnson, the Republican, betrayed the party leader and the President who had raised him to the Court?

Johnson couched his reply in a defensive, though confidential, tone. His situation on the Court had been no "bed of roses." It was necessary to be circumspect about lifting the curtain, since the Supreme Court had much of the character of a "cabinet."[60] He had often wished for advice on the course he should pursue on the high bench; but he had never found a single colleague on the Court with whom he could confer with "unlimited confidence." Part of his hesitancy in consulting with an outsider, he implied, came from his sharing of Marshall's desire for a tribunal with dignity.

> One thing, however, I resolved on at a very early period—to let no private or party feeling run counter to the great interests of the United States. If an executive, a legislative and judicial department, are necessary to the well-being of the community, it behooves those who fill those departments always to have an eye to the importance of giving a character to those departments—of preserving that respectability without which they would cease to answer the ends proposed in their institution.[61]

In a passage seldom duplicated for frankness in the record of the Court, Johnson revealed the secrets of the boarding-house clique. His disclosures tell so much of John Marshall's policy and Johnson's early endeavors for free expression that full quotation is inescapable:

> While I was on our state-bench I was accustomed to delivering seriatim opinions in our appellate court, and was not a little surprised to find our Chief Justice in the Supreme Court

---

interest of state autonomy and as a condition precedent to his endorsement. See Sturges v. Crowninshield, 4 Wheat. 122, 207-8 (1819); McCulloch v. Maryland, 4 Wheat. 315, 436 (1819); Dartmouth College v. Woodward, 4 Wheat. 518, 629, 653 (1819); Cohens v. Virginia, 6 Wheat. 264, 429-30 (1821).

[60]Johnson to Jefferson, Dec. 10, 1822, Jefferson Papers (MSS; Library of Congress).

[61]Ibid.

delivering all the opinions in cases in which he sat, even in some instances when contrary to his own judgment and vote. But I remonstrated in vain; the answer was he is willing to take the trouble and it is a mark of respect to him. I soon however found out the real cause. Cushing was incompetent. Chase could not be got to think or write—Patterson [sic] was a slow man and willingly declined the trouble, and the other two judges you know are commonly estimated as one judge.[62]

Alone of the old Federalists, only these last two, Marshall and Washington, for all their identity of views, seem to have commanded Johnson's respect.

Continuing, the South Carolinian recounted his struggles for free expression:

Some case soon occurred in which I differed from my brethren, and I thought it a thing of course to deliver my opinion. But, during the rest of the session I heard nothing but lectures on the indecency of judges cutting at each other, and the loss of reputation which the Virginia appellate court had sustained by pursuing such a course. At length I found that I must either submit to circumstances or become such a cypher in our consultations as to effect no good at all. I therefore bent to the current, and persevered until I got them to adopt the course they now pursue, which is to appoint someone to deliver the opinion of the majority, but leave it to the discretion of the rest of the judges to record their opinions or not ad libitum.[63]

Thus did William Johnson disclose the fight he had made so many years before. In the face of Marshall's charm and prerogatives, in opposition to some of his brothers who shared the passion for harmony and unity, and in order to avoid a status of innocuous volubility, he had "bent to the current." He had succeeded only in part. The result had been a compromise, between Marshall's quest for unity and authoritativeness and Johnson's for individual expression. Johnson's own testimony has support in the narrative, already given, of the early Court's practice; more than any other judge he could lay claim to having established the principle and practice of dissent.

In his letter to Jefferson, Johnson doubted that the Court would now adopt seriatim opinions. Such a change would encounter the same difficulties which Johnson had faced at the outset of his term. It would not, he felt sure, compel incompetent men to leave the bench, for "others would write their opinions merely to command their votes." The only way to get at the root of the matter was to reduce the size of the Court. A court of seven was too numerous,

[62]*Ibid.*
[63]*Ibid.*

for it would inevitably contain at least one "intriguer," and the resulting "cabals" could not be exposed. In the conviction that an appellate court should number no more than four, Johnson sketched out the main provisions of a reform bill.[64] On a tribunal of these dimensions seriatim opinions would be feasible and safe.

Johnson's lengthy attempt to vindicate his course, however, failed to convince Thomas Jefferson. In fact, the exposure of Marshall's policy and the allusion to intriguers and cabals probably proved a fresh irritant. In his reply Jefferson pointed to the prevailing hostility to the judiciary and decried the Court's advancement of consolidation through its "noiseless, and therefore unalarming" action.[65] While conceding that a reduction of the number of judges would improve matters considerably,[66] he renewed his pressure for separate opinions:

> I must comfort myself with the hope that the judges will see the importance and the duty of giving their country the only evidence they can give of fidelity to its constitution and integrity in the administration of its laws; that is to say, by every one's giving his opinion *seriatim* and publicly on the cases he decides. Let him prove by his reasoning that he has read the papers, that he has considered the case, that in the application of the law to it, he uses his own judgment, independently and unbiased by party views and personal favor or disfavor. Throw himself in every case on God and his country; both will excuse him for error and value him for his honesty. The very idea of cooking up opinions in conclave, begets suspicions that something passes which fears the public ear, and this, spreading by degrees, must produce at some time abridgement of tenure, facility of removal, or some other modification which may promise a remedy.[67]

The Court's persistent Federalism voiced through this peculiarly offensive practice had, according to Jefferson, led its opponents to call for restraints.

[64]Johnson described his plan in this wise: "I would alter the present system thus. Let the U.S. be thrown into a southern, a western, a middle, and an eastern division, and have a judge appointed to the Se. Court from each— give their circuit jurisdiction to the District Courts with a direct appeal to the Se. Court—make us hold two sessions pr. an. and confine us to the duties of the Se. Court. Let the salaries of the three judges who would be suffered to die or retire, be divided among the district judges or even a little more, and I think you would have a system cheap, adapted to our growth, and safe. Then the seriatim opinions might be required with safety." In Johnson's opinion the change would add to the work of the justices: "My circuit-duty is nothing in comparison with a second session at Washington." *Ibid.*

[65]Jefferson to Johnson, March 4, 1823, *Works* (Federal ed.), XII, 279.

[66]Said Jefferson: "Great lawyers are not over-abundant, and the multiplication of judges only enables the weak to out-vote the wise, and three concurrent opinions out of four give a strong presumption of right."—*Ibid.*, p. 280.

[67]*Ibid.*, pp. 279-80.

William Johnson in rebuttal said he was convinced that for the most part, the nation approved the Court's decisions; he had accordingly, he disclosed, urged a friend in Congress to move a repeal of the tribunal's jurisdiction over state courts in order to test public sentiment.[68] Since Congress had failed to act, the extent of public hostility was a subject only for conjecture. Occasionally the Court's reasoning had gone astray, but those actual decisions which he had endorsed he thought were sound.

Furthermore, the Court was composed of human beings, a fact which made indispensable a modicum of secrecy. No official body, he asserted, could retain even for a year the public confidence, if its actions were constantly exposed to the public eye. His observations of human nature had brought Johnson to a sad conclusion: "I never met with but one man who could absolutely leave his vanity and weaknesses at home! and have been often absolutely astonished at the predominance of little passions over men in the most elevated stations."[69] However intended by Johnson, this statement went far toward conceding Jefferson's argument.

To that argument the judge now capitulated:

> On the subject of seriatim opinions in the Supreme Court I have thought much, and have come to the resolution to adopt your suggestion on all subjects of general interest; particularly constitutional questions. On minor subjects it is of little public importance.[70]

The venerable Jefferson had made a convert. Six months after his initial appeal he had succeeded in prodding his first appointee into renewing his course of dissent. In his next communication Jefferson revealed that Johnson's earlier independence had not gone unheeded. Besides denouncing Marshall's "*obiter* dissertations" and excessively literal constructions, he rejoiced at the example Johnson had set: "I have heard it often noticed & always with high approbation." Some of the other judges might adopt the practice, and the Court at length see it as a duty.[71] In order to secure for Johnson

[68]This "friend," Andrew Stevenson, of Virginia, was a close associate of Roane and Ritchie, and a later supporter of Van Buren and Jackson.— Article by Thomas P. Abernethy in *Dictionary of American Biography*, XVII, 630-31. In April, 1822, he had introduced into the House of Representatives a motion to repeal the twenty-fifth section of the Judiciary Act of 1789; he hoped for a decision and he offered it in a spirit of "peace and forbearance."— Beveridge, *Marshall*, IV, 379.
[69]Johnson to Jefferson, April 11, 1823, *S.C. Hist. and Gen. Mag.*, I, 210.
[70]*Ibid.*, p. 209.
[71]Said he: "why should not every judge be asked his opinion, and give it from the bench, if only by yea, or nay?"—Jefferson to Johnson, June 12, 1823. *S.C. Hist. and Gen. Mag.*, I, 12.

the support of other judges, Jefferson thereupon sought to enlist the aid of James Madison.[72]

Yet Johnson's associates of 1823 were not to be jostled from their accustomed practice. They clung with the hold of addicts to the ancient Marshallian mode. Nor were the assaults in the press or the attacks in Congress sufficient to evoke reform legislation. The Court weathered the storm without injury.[73]

Mr. Justice Johnson, however, had taken Jefferson's reproaches to heart. In 1824 a statement introducing his separate opinion in Gibbons v. Ogden reflected his new resolution: "In questions of great importance, and great delicacy, I feel my duty to the public best discharged by an effort to maintain my opinions in my own way."[74] Frequently in subsequent rulings he expressed the same sentiment.[75] The very first term after receiving Jefferson's initial appeal, Johnson spoke out alone in more cases than he had in all the previous four years.[76] During his last ten terms on the Court, he would declare himself in no fewer than nine concurring, and eighteen dissenting opinions. More than half the total had constitutional significance.[77]

[72]In January Madison had told Jefferson that only a "law, or some very cogent manifestation of the public discontent" would suffice to uproot the prevailing mode of rendering opinions.—Letter dated Jan. 15, 1823, Madison, *Letters and other Writings*, III, 292. In June, Jefferson suggested that Madison press the desirability of seriatim opinions on Justices Todd and Duvall: "If Johnson could be backed by them in the practice the others would be obliged to follow suit . . . ."—Jefferson to Madison, June 13, 1823, *Works* (Federal ed.), XII, 296. In reply, Madison acknowledged the wisdom of separate opinions, but feared that an approach to other judges might be a "delicate experiment." He said that he might venture to touch on the subject with Judge Todd and through him reach his "intimates."—Madison to Jefferson, June 27, 1823, *Letters and other Writings*, III, 327.

[73]Characteristically, Story and Johnson took diametrically opposed views on the numbers desirable on the Court. Story wrote Webster that a Supreme Court of nine would be preferable to one of five members; he assigned among other reasons, the weight which numbers gave to constitutional decisions and the need of the "commercial states," in view of the expanding West, for a fair representation in the Court.—Letter dated Jan. 4, 1824, Story, *Story*, I, 436. Johnson, on his part, wrote Mathew Carey: "Increasing the members of the Supreme Court will destroy it."—Letter dated Jan. 17, 1826, Chamberlain Collection (MSS; Boston Public Library).

[74]Concurring opinion, 9 Wheat. 1, 223 (1824).

[75]In 1827 he wrote two opinions in Ogden v. Saunders and explained the second in these terms: "I . . . feel it due to myself and the community to maintain my consistency."—12 Wheat. 213, 358 (1827). In 1829 he said, in dissenting, that he entertained views different from those of the majority and that he wished generally "that my reasons for my opinions on constitutional questions should appear, where they cannot be misunderstood or misrepresented . . . ."—Weston v. Charleston, 2 Pet. 449, 470. In 1831 he said it was his practice to give an opinion on all constitutional questions.— Concurring opinion in Cherokee Nation v. Georgia, 5 Pet. 1, 20.

[76]He delivered two concurring and two dissenting opinions in 1823.

[77]Johnson concurred in five noteworthy decisions, including Green v. Biddle, 8 Wheat. 1 (1823); Gibbons v. Ogden, 9 Wheat. 1, (1824); Ramsay v. Allegre, 12 Wheat. 611 (1827); Satterlee v. Matthewson, 2 Pet. 380 (1829); and Cherokee Nation v. Georgia, 5 Pet. 1 (1831). He dissented with opinion

Those few decisions in which Johnson held his peace he probably thought either covered satisfactorily by his earlier opinions or adequately justified by the majority opinion.[78]

Thus had Jefferson driven Johnson to revive the volubility he had relinquished in 1819, and frequently during these closing years the vocal judge attacked the generality of utterance and modes of legal construction employed by the majority. On one occasion he assailed Henry Wheaton for reporting as decided a point that was mere *obiter*;[79] at other·times he sought clearly to distinguish the generalities of the judge from the point actually decided and in order to avoid embarrassment spoke his mind independently.[80] Increasingly he scanned the briefs for clear evidence that the Court possessed jurisdiction. Although he was capable of listing precedents where precedents were properly in point, he examined for himself the authorities cited by counsel and the principles on which they relied. Generally, he moved steadily away from a strictly literal

---

in Kirk v. Smith, 9 Wheat. 241 (1824); Osborn v. Bank of the United States, 9 Wheat. 738 (1824); Bank of the United States v. Planters' Bank of Georgia, 9 Wheat. 904 (1824); Governor of Georgia v. Madrazo, 1 Pet. 110 (1828); Weston v. Charleston, 2 Pet. 449 (1829); Shanks v. Dupont, 3 Pet. 242 (1830); Craig v. Missouri, 4 Pet. 410 (1830); and *Ex parte* Watkins, 7 Pet. 568 (1833). In *Ex parte* Crane, Johnson concurred with remarks in a dissenting opinion by Baldwin, 5 Pet. 190 (1831).

[78]Thus, Brown v. Maryland, 12 Wheat. 419 (1827), would fall in the former category, and Providence Bank v. Billings, 4 Pet. 514 (1830), in the latter.

[79]Concurring opinion in Ramsay v. Allegre, 12 Wheat. 611, 614, *passim*. (1827). In seeking to disassociate himself from the reported holding of an 1819 case in which he had acquiesced, Johnson said, ". . . I stand before the public as bearing my share of responsibility incurred for certain opinions expressed in the case of the *General Smith*. For the just extent of my responsibility in that case, I must rely on the repeated decisions which I have made in my circuit in hostility with that doctrine. But I am willing to treat it as my own error, and shall, on that ground, claim the privilege of treating it with a greater freedom; at least, I shall endeavor to administer the antidote if I have diffused the poison, and claim credit for an unequivocal proof of my repentance by a public acknowledgment that it was inexcusable." —*Ibid.*, p. 635. Wheaton replied to the charge in a footnote.—*Ibid.*, p. 640. For a parallel instance see Johnson's comment in Conard v. Atlantic Insurance Company, 1 Pet. 386, 451 (1828).

[80]Said he in 1828 in a lower court opinion: "the dicta of the judge who delivers an opinion are always to be weigh'd with reference to the case to be decided, and can have no weight any farther than they comport with the decision rendered—What was the question before the Court, I hold to be always a necessary consideration in order to estimate the true bearing and effect of an adjudication. For many a very sound decision has been distorted by reporters and not unfrequently rendered upon very inadequate reasons. Judges are often led to the same conclusions by very different considerations, and may sometimes mistake the reasons which influenced their brethren to concur."—Steamboat *Edgefield*, Minutes, C.C. Dist. of S.C., Bk. C, pp. 278, 281.

construction of the Constitution and toward the historical method Jefferson had advocated.[81]

If William Johnson failed to infect his ancient associates with his unorthodoxy, his example was not lost on others. In 1824, for the first time since 1812, a new face, that of Smith Thompson, appeared on the Court.[82] Three years later Robert Trimble joined the brotherhood,[83] and the new members demonstrated their power in a dramatic incident at the 1827 term. In the company of Johnson and the aged Washington, they resurrected the seriatim practice in the leading case of Ogden v. Saunders.[84] By 1830 Andrew Jackson had sent two more judges to the Court.[85] The new recruits proved sympathetic to Johnson and frequently raised their voices with him, if not in a renewal of the seriatim opinions, at least in dissent.[86] In these twilight years Johnson at last found an administration to his taste, and fellow-judges of a congenial turn of mind.

When at that time Johnson looked for new living quarters, the aged Federalist, John Marshall, confided his misgivings to Joseph Story;[87] he feared a "revolutionary spirit" that had appeared on the Court and was apprehensive lest a separation of the judges result in seriatim opinions.[88] To the last, Marshall clung to his objective—a united Court; and very possibly he gave lip service to alien opinions in order to preserve the semblance of unity.

In 1794 the precepts and example of Thomas Jefferson had swept a youthful aspirant to state office into the ranks of the incipient Republican party. Ten years passed; the party leader as President lifted the follower to the national judiciary. There the judge, on some issues at least, strayed from the leader's creed. Yet despite divergences, the admiration of the follower for the leader persisted. When news of Jefferson's death struck Charleston, William Johnson gave voice to his long-held admiration. To a formal assemblage of citizens he delivered a eulogy that relates, not without grace, the achievements and contributions of Jefferson.[89] The occasion brought together "all parties, all ages, all denominations," and Johnson

[81]See the chapters to follow. For a fuller discussion of Johnson's views on precedent and related matters, see A. J. Levin, "Mr. Justice William Johnson, Jurist in Limine: Views on Judicial Precedent," 46 *Michigan Law Review* (1948), 481-520, *passim*.

[82]Thompson replaced Livingston.

[83]Trimble was appointed in the place of Thomas Todd in April, 1826.

[84]12 Wheat. 213 (1827).

[85]John McLean replaced Trimble, and Henry Baldwin replaced Washington.

[86]From 1829 through 1833, Johnson was variously associated in the writing of separate opinions with Thompson, McLean, and Baldwin.

[87]Marshall to Story, Nov. 16, 1833, Warren, "Story-Marshall Correspondence," p. 25.

[88]Marshall to Story, May 3, 1831, *ibid.*, pp. 22-23. For Story's reply, see *ibid.*, p. 23.

[89]Johnson, *Eulogy on Thomas Jefferson* (pamphlet; Charleston, 1826).

hailed their "uniting as one loving family, in the obsequies of a
venerated parent!"[90] Jefferson's party tenets were so simple and un-
exceptionable, said Johnson, that they needed only to be explained
to win the agreement of "every candid mind." As one of the
"humblest" of Jefferson's correspondents, the judge proceeded to
quote for his fellow Charlestonians the summary of the party philosophy which Jefferson had given him in the letter of June, 1823.[91]
Johnson read that epitome of democratic theory with evident approval:

> To the remotest ages of our existence, the spirit of Jefferson
> will sound the cry from the watchtower—"Beware!" and wo
> to those days when a salutary watchfulness shall give place to
> a supine confidence or indolent inattention. . . .[92]

The speaker himself, it would seem, had relapsed for an interval
into a "supine confidence or indolent inattention" during the years
from 1819 on. He had heard the cry, and recovering himself, had
taken his judicial behavior to the supreme arbiter, the public.

The result of his vigilance, early and late, was a restless ex-
ploration of the pathways of dissent. With judicial power went responsibility; and, in seeking to discharge that responsibility, William
Johnson set up a record of separate utterance unparalleled on the
early Court.

Table 2 shows graphically the volume of his individual expressions. Although Johnson served as spokesman for the majority infrequently, as compared with Marshall and Story, his concurring and
dissenting opinions, at least until 1830, outdid those of all others.

As elsewhere, Johnson's approach to opinion-procedure was experimental. Besides expressing his views alone and agitating for
seriatim opinions, he even introduced views held privately in an
opinion rendered for the majority.[93] The outcome of his ventures
in strategy is clear: it was the establishment of that procedure for
rendering the decrees of the Supreme Court which most harmoniously
reconciled authoritativeness with intellectual freedom—the single
statement for the majority combined with separate utterances by in-
dependents. Then and now, this has proved the mode of expression
best adapted to the exigencies of the high tribunal.

[90]*Ibid.*, p. 22.
[91]*Ibid.*, pp. 23-24. See above, pp. 159-60.
[92]*Ibid.*, p. 25.
[93]In the course of an opinion for the majority Johnson introduced his own
views thus: "For myself, individually, I must use the privilege of assigning
the reasons which claim my concurrence in that opinion."—Lessee of Livingston *v.* Moore, 7 Pet. 469, 546 (1833).

TABLE 2

NUMBER AND FORM OF OPINIONS RENDERED BY SUPREME COURT
JUSTICES DURING JOHNSON'S TENURE ON THE COURT, 1805-1833.*

Name	Term	Years	Majority Opinions	Concurring Opinions	Dissenting Opinions	Seriatim Opinions	Total
Marshall	1805-1833	29	458	0	6	1	465
Paterson	1805-1806	2	0	0	1	5	6
Cushing	1805-1810	6	3	0	0	4	7
Chase	1805-1810	6	1	0	0	0	1
Washington	1805-1829	25	70	2	2	6	80
Johnson	1805-1833	29	112	21	34	5	172
Livingston	1807-1823	17	39	5	3	0	47
Todd	1808-1825	18	11	2	1	0	14
Story	1812-1833	22	171	3	6	1	181
Duvall	1812-1833	22	14	0	1	0	15
Thompson	1824-1833	10	44	0	5	2	51
Trimble	1827-1828	2	16	0	0	1	17
McLean	1830-1833	4	27	1	3	0	31
Baldwin	1830-1833	4	11	1	12	0	24
Total			977	35	74	25	1111

*From figures compiled by the author. Dissents without opinion are omitted.

Chapter XI

NATIONAL POWERS AND THE
"HUMBLEST INDIVIDUAL"

JEFFERSON had warned Johnson to resist the centralization of power in Washington and to speak his mind in crucial decisions, but within a year the judge was once again collaborating in a highly nationalistic decision. Although he spoke out this time, his language out-Marshalled Marshall in the breadth of discretion it ascribed to Congress. The case was Gibbons v. Ogden in which the Court invalidated the New York steamboat monopoly.[1] The position which Johnson took here on the commerce power, and in an analogous case which also concerned the treaty-making power, is important, for the two cases involve the scope of national powers and their relation to those which the Constitution reserved to the states.

In his biography of Marshall, Albert J. Beveridge has pointed out the importance of the Gibbons ruling. By interpreting in broad terms the power of Congress to "regulate commerce with foreign nations and among the several states," and by intimating that to some indeterminate extent the power belonged only to the national government, Marshall cleared the way for a rapid and accelerated economic expansion.[2] The decision was to have the effect of leveling a variety of state trade barriers and thus help make the United States a single economy; its result was economic integration. Marshall's language was, however, guarded, especially in its treatment of state powers over commerce in the absence of action by Congress. William Johnson, on the contrary, spoke with finality on this and other points. Beveridge accordingly conjectures that Marshall, that "master of the Supreme Court," persuaded Johnson to express the Chief Justice's true opinion.[3]

Was Johnson a tool in Marshall's hands? That role seems hard to reconcile with the known character of the younger man. Yet assuming, as we may, a degree of mutual respect on the part of the two

[1] 9 Wheat. 1 (1824).
[2] U.S. Const., Art. I, sec. 8 cl. 3; Beveridge, *The Life of John Marshall,* IV, 446-47.
[3] *Ibid.,* p. 443.

judges, might not the genial Marshall have had something to do with Johnson's separate concurring opinion?

If any one person persuaded Johnson to state his views in the Steamboat case, it was not Marshall but Jefferson. As this and subsequent chapters will disclose, Johnson was to make good use of the keys to constitutional interpretation which Jefferson had sent him. He would construe the fundamental law by the historical method and would seek clearly to distinguish the things pertaining to the nation from those pertaining to the state, in the manner Jefferson had proposed. In addition, he had determined to express his own convictions in leading cases. That resolve bore its first important fruit in Gibbons v. Ogden.

Also Johnson's Gibbons opinion expressed an economic philosophy that he had been formulating for many years. Johnson had come to qualify an early enthusiasm for free commercial enterprise. In 1808, he had defended his decision in the Embargo case on the ground of a free right of commerce; it was incontestable, he had said, that unless restricted by law, every inhabitant of the nation had a perfect right to engage in commerce.[4] And, as we have already seen, this active judge had close ties with business interests in his own community.[5] The war and its aftermath, however, had raised doubts as to the value of unrestrained profit-seeking. In his essay on agriculture, Johnson had denounced the steamboat monopoly. Similarly, in 1821, he stated that the encouragement given to privateering during the war had exerted a pernicious influence; the rapid acquisition of fortunes which this policy had facilitated had rendered the "most valuable classes of a community dissatisfied with seeking competence by the slow progress of useful labor."[6] These were "times of commerce and of lust of wealth," wrote Johnson in his biography of General Greene.[7]

Furthermore, this Republican justice found comfort in what he took to be Thomas Jefferson's conception of commerce. That leader had done much, Johnson later asserted, to stimulate international trade, for commerce between the nations strengthened the bonds of the international society, diffused among all countries the achievements of each, and propagated the truths of science and religion.[8] Yet Jefferson had regarded commerce as a means, rather than as an end of society; as an auxiliary, rather than as a superior of agriculture and the arts. The founder of Johnson's party had feared the effects of a "passion for gain" and had been apprehensive lest

[4]10 Fed. Cas. 360.
[5]See above, pp. 104-5.
[6]The *Amiable Isabella*, 6 Wheat. 1, 87-88 (1821).
[7]*Greene,* I, 25.
[8]*Eulogy on Thomas Jefferson* (1826), pp. 30-31.

the machinations of the speculator destroy a "liberal and enlightened" spirit in commerce.[9]

These sentiments might easily inspire a broad reading of the power of Congress. To correct abuses in the economic field the national organ might have to range at will over a vast area of regulation. In practice that problem would not confront Congress till the closing years of the century. In Johnson's day it was the negative aspect of the commerce clause that was uppermost. The framers had conceived of the grant of power primarily as a restraint on the states; its purpose was to remove the possibility of retaliatory measures that might stifle trade. It was in this form that the clause first came before the Court in the Gibbons case.

Finally, besides Jefferson's advice and his own revised economic outlook, another factor prompted Johnson to speak his mind in the Steamboat decision. Six months before that decision, Johnson had met with analogous issues in Charleston. Previously, he had referred to growing state aggressiveness in seeking to justify his endorsement of implied powers; what he now encountered in Charleston was in fact a most extreme form of state fervor and assertiveness. In August, 1823, he officially repudiated a South Carolina law as conflicting with the commerce power and with a treaty. His opinion, exalting national power and warning of disunion talk, had let loose a volley of criticism, which led him to explore more fully in letters to the press the scope of national power and the menace implicit in state excesses. These events had an incalculable impact on Johnson's thinking and help to explain his bold assertion of a broad commerce power in 1824.

The law with which Johnson had been confronted in the lower court—the Negro Seamen Act—had been passed by the South Carolina legislature in December, 1822.[10] As we have seen, Charleston had been thrown into a state of near-panic when the plans of Denmark Vesey, a free Negro, for a slave revolt had been exposed.[11] While Johnson had publicly and privately regretted the state of the public mind and deplored the severity of the ensuing trials, South Carolina had taken a different view of the affair. The state law, which gave expression to prevailing fears, sought to prevent the spread of subversive ideas among the slaves by prohibiting free Negroes from entering the state. The third section of this measure required that free Negroes or persons of color employed on incoming vessels from ports outside the state be seized and held in jail until the vessels departed. The ships' captains were to pay the costs of de-

[9]*Ibid.*
[10]*7 Statutes at Large of South Carolina,* ed. D. J. McCord (Columbia, 1840), p. 461.
[11]See above, Chapter VIII.

tention and in case of default were liable to fine or imprisonment. The Negro seamen in case of such a default were to be sold into slavery.

The enforcement of this provision soon produced complications. Its immediate effect was to disrupt trade in Charleston, and American shipowners and the British minister at Washington loudly protested the restraint on commerce.[12] Secretary of State Adams then conferred with congressmen from South Carolina; from one of them who was also an intimate of Johnson's, Joel Poinsett, Adams received assurances sufficiently strong to impel him in June, 1823, to dispatch a conciliatory reply to the British complaint.[13] For several months the state withheld enforcement of the Seamen Act.

Nevertheless, the statute was not allowed to sleep. Through a private organization, the "South Carolina Association," a group of citizens took up the problem of execution, and at their behest the sheriff of Charleston removed from a British vessel one Henry Elkison, a free Negro and a British subject, who, by the terms of the law, was put in jail. The prisoner then applied to Judge Johnson for a writ of habeas corpus or, failing that, a writ de homine replegiando.

In the courtroom Elkison's counsel attacked the validity of the state law. It was in direct conflict, he argued, with both the commerce power of Congress and a commercial agreement between the United States and Great Britain. No counsel appeared for the state, but two lawyers representing the Association argued at length in support of the state law. One of them, B. F. Hunt, questioned the court's jurisdiction and went on to defend the act under the state's reserve powers. The law, he said, did not exclude persons of color, but only required their detention in a "very airy and healthy part of the city."[14] The act protected health by preventing bloodshed. As a sovereign state, South Carolina could not surrender rights essential to its self-preservation. The other counsel, Isaac E. Holmes, went even further. According to Johnson, Holmes asserted that rather than see the state surrender this power, he would have preferred a dissolution of the Union. The suggestion shocked the judge. As Johnson himself described the scene: "Everyone saw me lay down my pen, raise my eyes from my notes, and fix them on the

---

[12]*Niles Weekly Register*, XXIV (March 15, 1823), 31-32; Philip M. Hamer, "Great Britain, the United States, and the Negro Seamen Acts, 1822-1848," *Journal of Southern History*, I (1935), 4.

[13]Hamer, pp. 4-5.

[14]*The Argument of Benj. Faneuil Hunt, in the case of the Person claiming to be a British Seaman, under the 3d section of the State Act of Dec. 1822, in relation to Negroes, etc., before the Hon. Judge Johnson, Circuit Judge of the United States, for the 6th Circuit* (pamphlet; Charleston, 1823), p. 6. The copy used by the author is in the library of the Harvard Law School.

speaker's face. He still proceeded, and in a style which bore evidence of preparation and study."[15]

Here was an issue to test the mettle of any judge. The police powers of the state were in conflict with the dormant power of Congress over commerce, and public opinion passionately sided with the state.

William Johnson had foreseen this collision and in fact had sought to prevent it. In January when the state had begun the enforcement of the law, American shipmasters and the British consul had applied to Johnson for protection. Johnson had then instructed the United States District Attorney to bring the question before the state judges, and to do it in the manner "most respectful to them."[16] Johnson's brother-in-law, Governor Thomas Bennett, had with some reluctance approved the initial adoption of the act, and the judge had this to say in explanation of his own conduct:

> I felt confident that the act had been passed hastily, and without due consideration, and knowing the unfavorable feeling that it was calculated to excite abroad, it was obviously best that relief should come from the quarter from which proceeded the act complained of.[17]

These negotiations had found the state officials cooperative, and the men had secured their release. Yet the state had made no pledge to withhold enforcement in the future, and this, according to Johnson, had induced the complaining parties to carry their protests to the national capital. That the state had allowed the law to rest, however, won Johnson's praise. The revival of enforcement was to him more a private than a public act.[18]

Now the judge met the issue head on. He held the Seamen Act unconstitutional. As in the Embargo Mandamus case fifteen years before, he might have escaped on the question of jurisdiction.[19] Moreover, he was aware of popular feeling and correctly predicted the public condemnation his opinion would evoke. John Marshall himself had encountered a similar case in his own circuit and had sidestepped the main issue. Taking note of Johnson's predicament,

[15]Letter signed "William Johnson," dated Aug. 20, 1823, in the *Charleston Mercury*, Aug. 21, 1823.

[16]Elkison *v.* Deliesseline, 8 Fed. Cas. 493, 494, No. 4366 (C.C. Dist. of S.C., 1823).

[17]*Ibid.*, pp. 493-94.

[18]*Ibid.*, p. 494.

[19]Johnson was somewhat more cautious than in the earlier case. He rejected habeas corpus on the ground that Congress had not authorized the Court to issue that writ to state officers. He thought that the writ *de homine replegiando* would not lie to the sheriff, but was confident it would lie to a vendee under the sheriff. He left it to counsel to decide whether to seek that writ. 8 Fed. Cas. 496-98.

the Chief Justice now confided to Story that for his part he had little taste for "butting against a wall in sport."[20]

In his opinion Johnson examined the object and effect of the state law. Its direct aim was to prohibit from Carolina ports all ships employing Negro seamen regardless of nationality. If "the color of his skin" were sufficient ground for excluding a seaman, why not "the color of his eye or his hair"?[21] The act might as readily apply to Nantucket Indians aboard the ships of Massachusetts. Retaliation might ensue and complete the destruction of Charleston's dwindling commerce.

Such a power in the state collided with the power of Congress to regulate commerce. For the first time since 1789, an American court found in the commerce clause a ground for invalidating state legislation, and this at the hands of a Jeffersonian judge! The scholar under Witherspoon, the son of the blacksmith who had cast a vote for ratification, and the law reader with Pinckney now portrayed the power in bold terms. With that description went a word of tribute for the Constitution itself:

> But the right of the general government to regulate commerce with the sister states and foreign nations is a paramount and exclusive right; and this conclusion we arrive at, whether we examine it with reference to the words of the constitution, or the nature of the grant. That this has been the received and universal construction from the first day of the organization of the general government is unquestionable; and the right admits not of a question any more than the fact. In the Constitution of the United States, the most wonderful instrument ever drawn by the hand of man, there is a comprehension and precision that is unparalleled; and I can truly say, that after spending my life in studying it, I still daily find in it some new excellence.[22]

The document itself, by implication, denied a concurrent power in the states to regulate commerce. The very words of the grant to Congress, said Johnson, "sweep away the whole subject, and leave nothing for the states to act upon." In such a case a direct prohibition was unnecessary. The states were not prohibited from regulating the value of foreign coin or determining the standard of weights and measures, for the very words implied a "total, unlimited grant" to the federal government.[23]

This was a broad conception of the power. If coinage and weights and measures were fair analogies, then Johnson conceived of com-

[20]Marshall to Story, Sept. 26, 1823, Story Papers (MSS), cited in Warren, *Supreme Court in United States History*, I, 626.
[21]8 Fed. Cas. 494.
[22]*Ibid.*, p. 495.
[23]*Ibid.*

merce as a single, indivisible whole. "If Congress can regulate commerce," he asked, "what commerce can it not regulate?"[24] The proposition if strictly followed might conceivably bring even the internal commerce of states within the scope of the federal grant; thus only Congress could enact regulations of a commercial nature. Here was an expression of what Mr. Justice Frankfurter has described as an "organic" theory of commerce.[25] In the light of Johnson's unguarded language, the subsequent distinction made between interstate and intrastate commerce would have been groundless, for both would have fallen to the lot of Congress.

Counsel for the state had argued for the necessity of the Act. That the state, however, should be sole judge of that necessity, Johnson declared, would enable the state to throw off the Constitution at will, and make the Union, "like the old Confederation," a "mere rope of sand."[26] Yet he denied that local authorities were helpless. The states actually retained all power necessary to the public safety. A properly drawn law might have confined the seamen to their ships; all that commerce required was a right to land, to load and unload cargoes, and to depart. Instead of preventing an evil, the law, in Johnson's opinion, promoted it; for by compelling sale of the stranded Negro seamen into slavery, it permanently domesticated potential agitators. Thus, while the states could not encroach on the national power over commerce, they did retain power to enact suitable police measures.

Such was Johnson's opinion in the case of Elkison. As a stroke of judicial boldness, it calls to mind the Mandamus decision of 1808. In both instances Johnson lacked clear jurisdiction; in both he hoped to settle a grave constitutional question by judicial action. Finally, in both, he met with criticism and rebuttal in the press. In 1823, as in 1808, the judge retorted—this time over a pseudonym. A study of this newspaper correspondence, unnoticed until recently, throws into clear perspective the character of Johnson's nationalism and some of the motives prompting it.

Johnson gave his opinion on the seventh of August. When the Charleston newspapers balked at printing it, he published it as a pamphlet.[27] He promptly sent a copy to Jefferson with a letter re-

[24]*Ibid.*
[25]Felix Frankfurter, *The Commerce Clause* (Chapel Hill, N.C., 1937), p. 42.
[26]8 Fed. Cas. 496.
[27]See note by the editor in Charleston *City Gazette*, Sept. 12, 1823. The pamphlet came out as *The Opinion of the Hon. William Johnson, delivered on the 7th August, 1823, in the case of the arrest of the British Seaman under the 3d section of the State Act, entitled, "An Act for the better Regulation of Free Negroes and Persons of Colour, and for other purposes" passed in December last* (Charleston, 1823). A copy is in the library of Harvard Law School.

lating the difficulties he was encountering in Charleston. He was alarmed at the mounting spirit of persecution and at the activities of the South Carolina Association. His position in the community was growing increasingly desperate; the idea of disunion, that "greatest of evils," seemed to be losing its horror.[28] One may conclude that Johnson had forsaken his customary insistence on clear jurisdiction and pronounced his pro-national opinion in the Elkison case in the hope that his argument would lop off at the ground these early shoots of state-rights extremism in South Carolina.

That hope was soon to expire. The newspapers of Charleston began to teem with letters attacking the judge and his opinion. For two full months the attacks kept up.[29] It seems likely that the South Carolina Association helped inspire these assaults. It had been established only a fortnight before Johnson's decision and doubtless had the enforcement of the Seamen Act as its immediate objective.[30] Throughout the controversy it met regularly; at one meeting it recruited over a hundred new members.[31] Its secretary, Robert J. Turnbull, who had sat as a judge at the Vesey trials, and its solicitor, Isaac E. Holmes, who had argued against Elkison before Johnson, evidently joined forces to produce the longest of the series of hostile letters. Their pseudonym, "Caroliniensis," expressed their dominant theme—an appeal to state patriotism.[32] Johnson, they asserted, had betrayed his native state by delivering and publishing to the world his Elkison opinion. The judge, they intimated, had failed to behave as an "unstained husband" to his "sweet country's sympathies."[33]

More than a dozen others joined the masked chorus of denunciation. A few argued the constitutional issues, but most took Johnson to

[28]Johnson to Jefferson, Aug. 11, 1823, see above, p. 163. Johnson also sent a copy to John Quincy Adams, who forwarded his letter to President Monroe.—J. Q. Adams, *Memoirs,* VI, 175 (entry for Aug. 19, 1823). The author has been unable to locate the letter to Adams.

[29]They appeared between Aug. 15 and Oct. 18. Only the *Southern Patriot,* of the four Charleston dailies, declined to enter the controversy.—*Southern Patriot,* Aug. 19, 1823. For a fuller analysis of this correspondence, see Donald G. Morgan, "Justice William Johnson on the Treaty-making Power," 22 *George Washington Law Review* (1953), 187-215.

[30]The Association was founded on July 24, 1823.—See letter signed "A Member," in the *Courier,* July 24, 1823. See also letter signed "An Old Man," *ibid.,* Aug. 5, 1823.

[31]*Charleston Mercury,* Sept. 19, 1823; cf. *ibid.,* Aug. 21, and Oct. 15, 1823.

[32]The thirteen numbers appeared in the *Mercury* between Aug. 15 and Sept. 11, 1823. These numbers, together with three letters by "Philo-Caroliniensis" (*Mercury,* Sept. 17-30, 1823) and one by "A Southerner" (*ibid.,* Oct. 7), were published as a pamphlet entitled *Caroliniensis* (Charleston, n.d.). The pamphlet, a copy of which is in the Library of the Harvard Law School, will here be cited. On authorship, see John B. Irving, M.D., *A Day on Cooper River* (2d ed.; Columbia, S.C., 1932), p. 63. Turnbull was named as secretary in the *Mercury,* Oct. 15, 1823; and Holmes, as solicitor in 8 Fed. Cas. 494.

[33]*Caroliniensis,* p. 64.

task for the manner in which he had released his opinion and defended himself in the press.[34] One of these critics has left this account of the character of his victim:

> There are some men who constantly defeat their own ends
> by the perverse method of pursuing them,—they create op-
> position, inflame the passions, and render it absolutely neces-
> sary to oppose that which, if sought for in another way, would
> have been cheerfully acceded. To demand a right in a blustering
> overbearing manner, renders it necessary to resist, if only to
> punish the impertinence of the demandant.[35]

Despite a keen intellect and prophetic judgment, Johnson was no
Marshall in his handling of men. Singularly, no defender came to
his aid in this hour of need.

The burden of the argument of Johnson's critics was an appeal to
the inherent rights of the state. The disclosures of the Vesey trials
had created in many Charlestonians a deep sense of insecurity. The
spectre of slave revolts led them to seek protection through a complete sealing-off of their slaves from agitation, whether from the
North or from abroad. Caroliniensis gave expression to this desire
when he declared that the greatest danger facing South Carolina
lay in "the free and uninterrupted ingress of a colored population
into this state, from the North, and elsewhere, with their known
habits, feelings and principles, animated and emboldened as they
are, by the philanthropy of the day, and by the events, which
Europe in its throes and convulsions casts upon mankind . . . ."[36]
The menace which these men feared could come about only through
federal action and only by virtue of broadly construed federal powers. Accordingly, they gave a narrow construction to the commerce
power, and, since Judge Johnson had based his decision in part on
an Anglo-American pact for freedom of commerce, to the treaty-
making power as well. The latter power, as one put it, was merely
a "mode of exercising" the other express powers.[37] No national
power, they insisted, could prevail over the state's inherent right
of self-preservation. These positions they buttressed by arguments
suggesting at many points the later doctrine of nullification. The
state had ultimate sovereignty; the federal government was merely

[34]For a dignified though earnest treatment of constitutional issues, see the
six numbers on "Municipal Laws" by "Zeno," in the *Charleston Courier*,
Sept. 3-25, 1823. For shorter and generally more abusive letters, see "Ithuriel,"
City Gazette, Aug. 20; "Citizen by Choice," *ibid.*, Sept. 10; "Wabsea," *ibid.*,
Sept. 20; "Legion," *ibid.*, Sept. 24 and 29; "Philobombos," *ibid.*, Sept. 24;
"Amicus," *Charleston Mercury*, Aug. 19; "Philo," *ibid.*, Sept. 6; "Grampus,"
ibid., Sept. 10; "American Citizen," *ibid.*, Sept. 11; "Toneluscka," *ibid.*,
Oct. 8; "An Inquirer," *ibid.*, Oct. 11; "Groeculus," *ibid.*, Oct. 18; and "G.,"
ibid., Oct. 18.
[35]Letter signed "Wabsea," *City Gazette*, Sept. 20, 1823.
[36]*Caroliniensis*, p. 41.
[37]*Argument of Hunt*, p. 16.

an agent of the states: when the agent exceeded his instructions the principal could disregard his acts. One writer suggested that a state might ignore a treaty intruding on its powers and hinted that such treaties ought to be referred to the states for ratification.[38] Another thought Johnson's opinion left to the state only two courses of action: to alter the Constitution, which he thought impossible, or to violate it.[39]

Such were the arguments which the judge's opponents directed at his opinion. As might have been expected, the judge lost no time in replying. Two letters appeared over his own signature,[40] but for his major efforts he took a pseudonym. In this he followed the example not only of his critics but also of Judges Marshall and Roane. As his signature Johnson chose "Philonimus," which he explained meant "the friend or defender of a good name."[41] There were thousands, he asserted, who held views similar to his, but who would express them only when they felt it "as safe to *speak* as to think." He warned the community against ignoring his assailants; for "if public opinion does not rally to put down such gross attacks, public decency is at an end, and bullies and duellists alone must 'judge the land.' "[42] He wished, he said, to resist calumny and circulate accurate opinions.[43] Accordingly, he plied the local papers with letters, including nine numbers answering Caroliniensis.[44]

Once again the sensitive Johnson combined close reasoning with invective.[45] Several ideas stand out clearly from his columns of

[38]*Caroliniensis*, pp. 37-38.
[39]Zeno, No. 3, *Courier*, Sept. 5, 1823.
[40]*Mercury*, Aug. 21, and *Daily National Intelligencer* (Washington), Sept. 29, 1823.
[41]*Mercury*, Oct. 7, 1823.
[42]Philonimus to Caroliniensis, No. 4, *ibid.*, Sept. 5, 1823.
[43]Philonimus to Caroliniensis, No. 9, *ibid.*, Sept. 19, 1823.
[44]See Philonimus to "Citizen by Choice," *City Gazette*, Sept. 20, reprinted on Sept. 23 and 24; Philonimus to the editor, *ibid.*, Sept. 26, 1823; Philonimus to Zeno, Nos. 1-4, *Courier*, Sept. 10–Oct. 8, 1823. See also editor's note mentioning a letter from "A Subscriber," *Mercury*, Aug. 18; a card from Philonimus, *ibid.*, Sept. 15; and note by Philonimus, *ibid.*, Oct. 7, 1823. The nine numbers in reply to Caroliniensis appeared in the *Mercury*, Aug. 26-Sept. 19; Philonimus answered Philo-Caroliniensis, in *ibid.*, Sept. 26 and Oct. 7, 1823.
[45]The following evidence of Johnson's authorship of the Philonimus papers is pertinent:
A. Johnson was in Charleston during this period.—*Mercury*, Aug. 21, and *City Gazette*, Oct. 14, 1823. Examination of court records in Charleston and Savannah shows that he was not at this moment engaged in court business. He was accordingly free to devote himself to the press controversy. In his letter to Jefferson he had expressed his revulsion at the activities of the South Carolina Association and deplored the "ridiculous but prevalent notion— that it is a struggle for life or death. . . ."—Johnson to Jefferson, Aug. 11, 1823, see above, p. 163.
B. The letters signed by Philonimus express ideas similar to those in Johnson's writings. Philonimus displayed the same independence, forthrightness, legal erudition, pugnacity, sensitiveness, and impetuosity characteristic

explosive argument. One was antipathy to the notion of disunion toward which he thought his critics were moving. The words suggesting that the state might have to violate the Constitution, he exclaimed, "thrill thro' my frame with an indescribable sensation."[46] The state sovereignty argument he deemed all revolutionary; it converted the Constitution into a mere "letter of attorney."[47] Here was fresh evidence of Johnson's distress over the mounting disunion talk.

Another idea reappears in these papers. This was Johnson's concern for the individual. Thus, he detailed the summary procedure by which innocent seamen like Elkison could be sold into slavery.[48] This strange solitary figure, so inept in many of his dealings with others, was often moved nonetheless by compassion for the weak and oppressed. He would soon be voicing the same respect for the individual in the Steamboat case.

Again he gave an expansive interpretation to national powers. On the matter of the commerce power, he added but little to the earlier analysis. Commerce he called a "coy damsel," whom laws like the state act under question would drive from Charleston.[49] If states were to exclude seamen, what would become of Congress' power "to regulate, to foster, to encourage commerce"?[50] He here

---

of Johnson. There are many similarities in style. The terminology of Philonimus closely parallels that used by Johnson: compare the following statement from Philonimus to Zeno, No. 1, with the above comment to Jefferson: "Men have worked each other up to a belief that (as it is common to hear them express it) it is a case of life and death . . . ." So intimate was Philonimus with Johnson that he was able to assert, concerning an idea ascribed to Johnson, that it "never entered his [Johnson's] mind."—Philonimus to Caroliniensis, No. 6.

C. Many of his press critics identified Philonimus with Johnson. Thus, "An Inquirer" described the character of Philonimus in terms that might as well apply to Johnson; he suggested that Philonimus's first impulse was always to "differ from the majority." Zeno, No. 4, spoke of Philonimus as having "passed his life in studying the Constitution," an allusion to Johnson's statement in the Elkison opinion.—See above, p. 195. "A Southerner" drew a comparison between a statement made by Philonimus with one made by the Judge "in propria persona." (Caroliniensis, p. 75.) "Grampus" said Philonimus tried to "screen himself, (I beg pardon, the Judge I mean) from the public indignation . . . ." (Mercury, Sept. 10). Others identified the two as one and the same person through allusions to Johnson's Life of Greene. Cf. "Citizen by Choice," and "Philo."

D. These insinuations Philonimus at no time denied. On the contrary, much of his increasing violence of tone resulted, it seems probable, from the realization that his critics had seen through his disguise.

[46]Philonimus to Zeno, No. 2, Courier, Sept. 13, 1823.

[47]Philonimus to Caroliniensis, No. 8, Mercury, Sept. 15, 1823.

[48]Philonimus to Caroliniensis, No. 3, Aug. 29, 1823: "From the law of human will," he concluded, " 'Good Lord deliver us.' " Slaves, he contended, were persons, and not things, in the eyes of the Constitution.—Philonimus to Caroliniensis, No. 7, Mercury, Sept. 13, 1823.

[49]Philonimus to Caroliniensis, No. 4, Mercury, Sept. 5, 1823.

[50]Philonimus to Caroliniensis, No. 7, ibid., Sept. 13, 1823.

set forth the power in language soon to be elaborated at Washington.[51]

But the treaty-making power he now portrayed with bold strokes. The Constitution gave that power to the President, acting with the "advice and consent of the Senate, . . . provided two thirds of the Senators present concur"; it further constituted treaties made "under the authority of the United States" part of the supreme law of the land.[52] What was the nature and scope of this power? With an explicitness seldom duplicated in the writings of other judges, Johnson examined the power. It had lain, originally, he said, with the thirteen states; and they had relinquished it to the federal government by the Constitution. Because of the unpredictable nature of foreign relations and the need of flexibility in negotiations, it would serve the nation best to leave a wide discretion to treaty-makers. Johnson anticipated by a century the stand of the Supreme Court in asserting that the treaty-making power took in subjects not embraced by the normal congressional powers to legislate.[53]

He made it abundantly clear, however, that there were limits to the power. He found these in the express provisions of the Constitution and gave illustrations. Yet state rights were not among such barriers, for in case of conflict the treaty power was paramount. Turning to history, he said no fewer than thirty-six treaties dating from 1778 on had intruded on reserved powers. Several of these he cited at length. Early expositions, long usage, and acquiescence by the states had established the power on a firm basis. In his effort to assure the nation ample powers to cope with the complexities of foreign affairs for the good of all the people, Johnson had carried broad construction to the delicate matter of treaty-making.[54]

Finally, Johnson sought to calm the fears of his antagonists. Most of those fears he thought groundless. Within its own territory, South Carolina had ample power to control its colored population. Forbearance in the exercise of powers and steady cooperation between

[51]Said he: "The navigation of shipping appertains to the regulation of commerce, and has been, by universal acquiescence, so held by the states from the time of the adoption of the constitution, without any express words transferring it to the United States.

"The number, qualities, description and regulation of seamen, have been, by the consent and practice of all the world, and of our own government from its earliest commencement, recognized as coming within the incidents to regulating navigation." Philonimus to Zeno, No. 3, *Courier,* Sept. 22, 1823.

[52]Const. Art. II, sec. 2, cl. 2; Art. VI, cl. 2.

[53]Missouri v. Holland, 252 U.S. 416 (1920).

[54]See especially Philonimus to Caroliniensis, Nos. 6-7, *Mercury,* Sept. 11 and 13, 1823. A more detailed treatment of Johnson's analysis of the treaty-making power and related matters is presented in the author's "Justice William Johnson on the Treaty-making Power," cited in note 29 above.

national and state governments were the keys to the harmonious working of the federal system.[55]

Judge Johnson had spoken frankly. His disguise had fooled few, if any, of his adversaries, and yet it had freed him to take a firm stand on controversial issues. Fear of a break-up of the Union and the devastation that would accompany it had driven him to expound national powers in sweeping terms and at the same time to support state autonomy. He failed in his campaign to destroy the Seamen Act and pacify the extremists,[56] but his warnings that acts like this would disturb the diplomatic relations of the United States were to be borne out.[57] The whole affair of the autumn of 1823 helped Johnson clarify his position on national powers and prepared him for his role in the great case of Gibbons.

Six months after the Elkison decision, some of the foremost lawyers of the country were disputing similar questions in the Supreme Court.[58] At stake in the case was the existence of the monopolistic franchise which New York had granted for steam navigation on its rivers—the system which Johnson had earlier denounced as rendering a whole community "liable to be severely assessed by the cupidity of a few individuals."[59] Aaron Ogden had secured protection for his exclusive right from the highest state court; Chancellor James Kent himself had issued the injunction which restrained Thomas Gibbons from operating between New York City and New Jersey in competition with Ogden. Gibbons now sought relief from the order on several grounds—among them, first, the exclusive power of Congress over interstate commerce, and, second, a coasting license granted him by virtue of an act of Congress.

A month later the Court rendered its decision holding the state monopoly unconstitutional.[60] The opinion of John Marshall dealt

[55]See especially Philonimus to Caroliniensis, No. 9, *Mercury,* Sept. 19; Philonimus to Philo-Caroliniensis, No. 2, *ibid.,* Oct 7; and Philonimus to Zeno, No. 4, *Courier,* Oct. 8, 1823.

[56]In December the legislature somewhat moderated the terms of the law, although arrest and detention were retained.—*7 Stat. at L. of S.C.* 461. For Johnson's comments on the amended law and his own inability to assist one accused under it, see Johnson to John Quincy Adams, July 3, 1824, in *Free Colored Seamen—Majority and Minority Reports,* House Committee on Commerce, 27 Cong., 3 Sess., House Rep. No. 80, pp. 14-15 (1843).

[57]The British ministers continued to protest the operation of the Negro Seamen Acts of the southern states. They failed to obtain redress at Washington and after 1850 directed their consuls to seek relief at state capitals. This of course put the states in the business of diplomacy and defeated the intention of the framers of the Constitution. See Philip M. Hamer, "British Consuls and the Negro Seamen Acts, 1850-1860," *Journal of Southern History,* I (1935), 138-68, *passim.*

[58]Daniel Webster, William Wirt, and David B. Ogden appeared for Gibbons; Thomas Addis Emmet and Thomas J. Oakley for Ogden. See Warren, *Supreme Court in U. S. History,* I, 599-608.

[59]*Nugae Georgicae,* p. 40. See above, pp. 102-3.

[60]Gibbons *v.* Ogden, 9 Wheat. 1 (1824).

at length with the commerce power. That opinion was a landmark in American history; the exposition would serve as the fountainhead for a vast stream of constitutional law. Yet the Chief Justice refused to rest his decision solely on the ground of the exclusiveness of the power of Congress. The licensing act he construed as an expression of the will of the national legislature that no state regulations should be tolerated. Even Daniel Webster, who as counsel had stressed the exclusive nature of the constitutional grant, had in the end seen fit to bring in the license.

But William Johnson went beyond them both. The seventeen pages of his separate concurring opinion dealt clearly and forcefully with the voluminous arguments of counsel. Three points emerge from his statement.

In the first place, the power to regulate commerce was the exclusive possession of Congress. The simple classical language of the framers must be construed in the light of the purposes of the Constitution. Those purposes Johnson put in these terms:

> The great and paramount purpose was to unite this mass of wealth and power, for the protection of the humblest individual; his rights, civil and political, his interests and prosperity, are the sole *end*; the rest are nothing but the *means*. But the principal of those means, one so essential as to approach nearer the characteristics of an end, was the independence and harmony of the states, that they may the better subserve the purposes of cherishing and protecting the respective families of this great republic.[61]

Here at last Johnson wrote into a leading pronouncement his regard for the "humblest individual." Behind the phrase, used here to safeguard the material interests of a steamboat operator, one senses his concern for the physical liberty of the Negro seaman. The Constitution furnished a protecting shield, not only for planters and merchants but also for the Elkisons of the world. This he deemed its primary purpose, but the second and subordinate purpose also had crucial importance. The biographer of Greene found in the early history of the country evidence that the framers had intended an exclusive grant. The immediate cause for the forming of a new Constitution had been the threat which the hostile commercial regulations of the states had produced to their own harmony and to their common interests abroad. Since its purpose was to eliminate these evils, the power granted was commensurate with that which the states had formerly held. Furthermore, the states had acceded to this notion, for they had allowed their various restrictive laws to fall of their own weight. The sustaining power they had transferred to Congress.

[61] *Ibid.*, p. 223.

Additional support for his contention Johnson found in international law. That law, he said, regarded man as a "social animal," and deemed all commerce legitimate in peacetime unless limited by positive law. A sovereign state could restrain commerce at pleasure. The power was exclusive in a single authority, for "the power to prescribe the limits to its freedom necessarily implies the power to determine what shall remain unrestrained. . . ." The grant of the power to Congress had withdrawn a similar power from the states.[62]

Commerce was thus a unit which could be properly regulated only by a single authority. The argument here paralleled Johnson's earlier allusion to coinage and the standards of weights and measures. Whether foreign or interstate, that commerce, he now insisted, was subject to the same rule of exclusiveness.

The opinion of the majority had leaned heavily on the federal license. In Johnson's view, Congress had granted the license in order to confer on American vessels privileges in the coasting trade which were withheld from foreign vessels. Hence, the license bespoke no intention to remove ships from state cognizance. Even though Johnson conceded some merit to the argument based on the license, he thought this ground largely irrelevant.[63]

On the question of exclusive power the Gibbons opinion was merely an extension of that of Elkison. On a second point it broke new ground. This concerned the scope of the commerce power. The matter involved here—navigation—was more than a mere incident of commerce; it was "the thing itself; inseparable from it as vital motion is from vital existence."[64] Other subjects, too, might come within the grant with the passage of time:

> Commerce, in its simplest signification, means an exchange of goods; but in the advancement of society, labour, transportation, intelligence, care, and various mediums of exchange, become commodities, and enter into commerce; the subject, the vehicle, the agent, and their various operations, become the objects of commercial regulation.[65]

This was a dynamic concept of commerce. Social change, which Johnson, the historian, had observed, and in which as promoter

[62]*Ibid.*, p. 227.

[63]He had previously stated, "if the licensing act was repealed tomorrow, the rights of the appellant to a reversal of the decision complained of, would be as strong as it is under this license."—*Ibid.*, pp. 231-32. Further on, however, he admitted that the practice of the government on many subjects had been to occupy only as much of the field as it thought the public interest required. The fact that Congress had passed the licensing act might be taken to indicate its intention that the states should abstain from regulating the subject.—*Ibid.*, pp. 233-34.

[64]*Ibid.*, p. 229.

[65]*Ibid.*, pp. 229-30.

of sundry improvements he had participated, called for an expanding field of national regulation. Johnson's concept of the subject was in a sense unique for his day. Half a century was to elapse before the Supreme Court began the long process of adapting the commerce clause to the progress of invention and economic consolidation.[66]

Finally, Johnson took this opportunity to explore further the issue which the case of Elkison had raised so acutely. Might the states exercise their police powers over commerce, and to what extent?[67] The question was novel, and the passage of time would render it complex, but Johnson had a forthright answer:

> The same bale of goods, the same cask of provisions, or the same ship, that may be the subject of commercial regulation, may also be the vehicle of disease. And the health laws that require them to be stopped and ventilated, are no more intended as regulations on commerce, than the laws which permit their importation, are intended to innoculate the community with disease. Their different purposes mark the distinction between the powers brought into action; and while frankly exercised, they can produce no serious collision.[68]

Yet Johnson acknowledged, and this from bitter experience, that collisions between the respective powers were inevitable. He had tried to avoid open conflict in the instance of the Seamen Act by negotiations with state officials; that same remedy he now prescribed for others—a "frank and candid co-operation for the general good."[69] Such, ultimately, was the only effective recourse where two governments exercised distinct powers over the same individual and the same object.

The concurring opinion in Gibbons v. Ogden ranks as one of Johnson's best. The logical sequence of the argument and the precision and grace of the language reflect the time and thought that Johnson devoted to its preparation. In it he was defending before the public his extreme assertion of national power. Jefferson's insistence on judicial responsibility had had its effect. So had Jefferson's analysis of the line separating state from national powers. Johnson had grasped the twofold formula; he had consulted the time of the framing and had read as national the powers pertaining to foreign

[66]See especially Pensacola Telegraph Co. v. Western Union Telegraph Co., 96 U.S. 1 (1877).

[67]Johnson had by now abandoned the idea, which he had earlier intimated, that the states had lost a power to regulate internal commerce. See his treatment of a New York tax on passengers as possibly warranted by that state's control of "personal intercourse, as incident to internal commerce . . . ."— 9 Wheat. 231.

[68]Ibid., p. 235.

[69]Ibid., p. 238.

affairs. His conclusions differed from those of Jefferson, but not because of any pressure from John Marshall.

Forces other than the Chief Justice's dominance had been at work on William Johnson. He had assigned both the treaty-making and commerce powers exclusively to the national authorities. Great Britain had protested the Seamen Act under a treaty, and South Carolina's intransigence had embarrassed the Monroe administration. The collision of state law with national treaty had demonstrated to Johnson that in the making of treaties as in the control of foreign commerce the nation must have power commensurate with its responsibility. Thus, Johnson commented in the Gibbons opinion:

> The states are unknown to foreign nations; their sovereignty exists only with relation to each other, and the general government. Whatever regulations foreign commerce should be subjected to in the ports of the Union, the general government would be held responsible for them; and all other regulations, but those which Congress had imposed, would be regarded by foreign nations as trespasses and violations of national faith and comity.[70]

This position on the commerce power resulted likewise from Johnson's confidence in the civilizing effects of trade. On the subject of exclusive power, it was Elkison rather than Marshall that had furnished the lesson.

Furthermore, Johnson had read both the treaty-making and commerce powers as broad in scope. His readings in history had prepared him for this by bringing home the reality of social change. Accordingly, he had urged an ample discretion for treaty negotiators so that the nation could meet unforeseen contingencies. To keep step with what Johnson called the "advancement of society," Congress required a commerce power wide in its sweep. In this, Johnson had hewn out a path of his own.

Thomas Jefferson had cherished the people and had deemed the states the primary agents for the achievement of social well-being. Johnson agreed with him on the end but deviated on the means. His recent historical researches had corroborated the lesson of a war-ravaged childhood—the vital necessity of national unity. So he concluded that the Constitution was meant not just to ally, but to "unite" the states; the ultimate aim was not the welfare of a class or section, but the protection of individuals, even the "humblest." Here was that esteem for the people which Jefferson had ascribed to the Republicans; here was that "universal benevolence" which Johnson so admired in the Quakers. If his conclusions on national powers were unorthodox, his major premise was Jeffersonian.

[70] *Ibid.*, p. 227.

Chapter XII

VESTED RIGHTS AND
SOCIAL INTERESTS

IT WAS at the 1827 session of the Court that Thomas Jefferson's advice to William Johnson produced its most dramatic single result. The bankruptcy case, Ogden v. Saunders, evoked the first set of seriatim opinions in two decades; the Chief Justice was this time with the minority, and for the first and only time in a leading case, he stated his convictions at length in a dissenting opinion.

The question at stake in that case had lasting importance. It presented the issue whether a state might under the Constitution enact measures to grant relief, through a process of settlement and discharge, to insolvent debtors. William Johnson, who, as shown earlier,[1] had spoken out in behalf of personal rights, here faced the related issue of property rights. Specifically, the problem concerned the power of the states to regulate the making of contracts and the remedy for their enforcement. Yet the issue at bottom embraced the status of private property in relation to government. On the subject Johnson spoke his own matured convictions.

Furthermore, this judge's separate opinion in the case was prophetic of things to come. The Court of John Marshall has acquired a reputation for extreme solicitude for vested rights. Its steady effort to shield from government interference the interests of property holders has become a byword to historians. The justice from Charleston has more than once shared the credit or the blame for this program.[2] Yet at many points this first dissenter resisted the trend of his associates. In the Ogden and other opinions he not only decried the policy of the Marshallians, but, more constructively, pointed a new way for the Court.

By 1827, Johnson's views on property had come to a full ripening. Several years before that, during the grim winter of 1822-1823, his thinking had undergone a change. The confession he tendered to Jefferson and the advice it elicited contributed heavily to the shift.

[1]See above, Chapter VIII.
[2]See, for example, Edward S. Corwin, *The Twilight of the Supreme Court* (New Haven, 1934), p. 58, and Charles Grove Haines, *The Revival of Natural Law Concepts* (Cambridge, 1930) pp. 90-91.

Since, however, even earlier he had dropped hints of his future course, it will be well to survey Johnson's rulings concerning property prior to 1822, before relating his change of heart at that time.

From the outset, the young Jeffersonian judge had looked with deference on the rights of property. In some of the cases those rights felt the impact of national power. Such, indeed, was the Embargo Mandamus decision, in which Johnson struck down Jefferson's order on the ground that only positive legislation would suffice to delimit the all-important right to engage in commerce.[3] In 1814, although he upheld a wartime seizure of goods imported from enemy territory, he did so with obvious reluctance.[4] That same year, however, he declared forfeit a shipment of coffee where a non-importation statute expressed clearly the will of Congress.[5] In this last case, two justices joined Story in dissent; the New Englander took the side of the innocent purchaser of the goods and applied common-law analogies in construing the act. In Story's mind, the majority's ruling would work grave injury to the "commercial interests" of the land.[6] But Johnson found that the public, too, had important interests in the law. Brushing aside Story's argument with the statement that administrative remedies afforded relief in hardship cases, he declared:

> In the eternal struggle that exists between the avarice, enterprise and combinations of individuals on the one hand, and the power charged with the administration of the laws on the other, severe laws are rendered necessary to enable the executive to carry into effect the measures of policy adopted by the legislature. To them belongs the right to decide on what event a divesture of right shall take place. . . .[7]

Provided its voice was clear and unequivocal, the national legislature might pass "severe laws" in protecting the public interest. This early reliance on what he called "positive law" would deepen with the years.[8]

On several occasions Johnson showed a like respect for governmental power in the states. His very first opinion, in fact, voiced a regard for the power of the Pennsylvania assembly to regulate land grants.[9] Again, when the majority, through Story, upheld the title of a British claimant to the Fairfax lands in Virginia on the ground

[3]See above, p. 62.
[4]The *Rapid,* 8 Cranch 155, 160. See above, p. 113.
[5]United States v. 1960 Bags of Coffee, 8 Cranch 398 (1814).
[6]*Ibid.,* p. 406.
[7]*Ibid.,* p. 405.
[8]For Johnson's views on natural and positive law as applied to the question of salvage, see Fisher v. the *Sybil,* 9 Fed. Cas. 141, 142, No. 4824 (C.C. Dist. of S.C., 1816), affirmed in the *Sybil,* 4 Wheat. 98 (1819).
[9]Huidekoper's Lessee v. Douglass, 3 Cranch 1 (1805). For Johnson's statement supporting discretion in the state legislature, see *ibid.,* p. 73.

that in confiscating the lands and granting them to another the legislature of Virginia had failed to comply with a technical procedural requirement, Johnson delivered a vigorous dissent.[10] That requirement, he said, might serve as a salutary restraint on the governor, but the "supreme legislative power" might in its discretion overlook it.[11] Elsewhere he championed the power of Vermont over church lands[12] and the power of Maryland over the judicial remedies for non-fulfillment of agreements.[13]

In all of this, Johnson, while befriending property, showed a definite regard for legislative regulations dictated by public need. This was true, whether the legislation were that of the nation or that of the state.

Yet during these early years this judge pursued an irresolute course in relation to one subject of constitutional construction. Here the Court, and Johnson with it, exemplified decisively the malpractices about which Jefferson complained. The source of trouble was the contract clause. At the Philadelphia convention, the framers had placed the following among the limitations on the states: "No state shall . . . pass any bill of attainder, ex post facto law, or law impairing the obligation of contracts. . . ."[14] Preceding this passage are prohibitions against state legal tender laws, the cause of so much irritation prior to the convention; the contract clause occurred to the framers almost as an afterthought.[15] Although evidence is meager, it is likely that the framers intended to protect from state interference only contracts between private individuals; public contracts, those to which the state itself was a party, probably lay outside the prohibited sphere of state regulation. Presumably they also felt antipathy toward laws which referred back to con-

[10]Fairfax's Devisee v. Hunter's Lessee, 7 Cranch 603 (1813).

[11]In Britain, according to Johnson, this procedural requirement (inquest of office) had served as a beneficial restriction on the Crown, and in Virginia, it might serve as a corresponding check on the governor. There was, he asserted, nothing magical about it nor indispensable about it, and the British Parliament had at times dispensed with it. Johnson asked what prevented the legislative power of Virginia from setting it aside.—*Ibid.,* p. 631.

[12]Town of Pawlet v. Clark, 9 Cranch 292 (1815).

[13]Bank of Columbia v. Okely, 4 Wheat. 235 (1819); see above, pp. 89, 134. In speaking for the Court, Johnson denied that the state, by including in the charter of a bank the right to sue on notes through summary process, had thereby parted with power to regulate the administration of justice; this was part of the remedy. The forms of administering justice and the jurisdiction of courts were, he felt, wholly subject to legislative control and that control was inalienable.—*Ibid.,* p. 245. Although speaking here of Congress, Johnson made this assertion in a context that showed it was applicable also to state legislatures.

[14]Art. I, sec. 10.

[15]A provision against state impairment of contracts was first moved by Rufus King on August 28, 1787.—Benjamin Fletcher Wright, Jr., *The Contract Clause of the Constitution* (Cambridge, 1938), p. 8.

tracts previously made, but not to laws applying only to subsequent contracts.[16]

In but one case prior to 1810, Calder v. Bull, did the Supreme Court deal at length with the whole clause.[17] There, the three majority judges opined that the *ex post facto* clause, like that concerning bills of attainder, related only to criminal matters.[18] By this somewhat dubious decision, the early Court relegated statutes concerning civil matters to the vague coverage of the ban on contract impairments. To the Marshallians it fell to define the meaning of that portion of the clause.

The leading case of Fletcher v. Peck at last elicited from the Court its first decision under the contract clause proper and from Justice Johnson a loud protest.[19] In the year 1795 the Georgia legislature had granted to four land companies the title to some thirty-five million acres of western lands in exchange for the trifling sum of half a million dollars.[20] When the people of that state awoke to the magnitude of the transfer and the wholesale bribery which had prompted it, they swept the lawmakers from office. In 1796 the new legislature rescinded the grant and destroyed all official evidence of the earlier statute. Third parties, however, had already begun to make purchases.[21] In Boston, one Robert Fletcher purchased from one John Peck some fifteen thousand acres of these Yazoo lands for three thousand dollars. Thereupon Fletcher brought action in the federal court to "contest" the transaction and to recover the purchase money. Could a state legislature revoke a previous grant of land?

The Supreme Court held the repeal invalid. Speaking for the majority, John Marshall adjudged it void on two grounds. First, it violated natural law, or what Marshall called "certain great principles of justice whose authority is universally acknowledged." Second, the repeal act conflicted with the contract clause. Georgia's

[16]*Ibid.*, pp. 15-16. Professor Wright finds in the following provision from the Northwest Ordinance of July 13, 1787, the leading precedent for the constitutional provision: "And, in the just preservation of rights and property, it is understood and declared, that no law ought ever to be made or have force in the said territory, that shall, in any manner whatever, interfere with or affect private contracts, or engagements *bona fide,* and without fraud previously formed."—*Ibid.*, pp. 6-7.

[17]3 Dall. 386 (1798).

[18]For a detailed analysis of the Calder decision and the interpretation of the clause prevailing at the time of the framers, see William Winslow Crosskey, "The True Meaning of the Constitutional Prohibition of Ex-Post-Facto Laws," 14 *University of Chicago Law Review* (1947), 539-66.

[19]6 Cranch 87 (1810).

[20]Warren, *The Supreme Court in United States History,* I, 392 ff.

[21]In time, the resulting confusion induced the federal authorities, under Jefferson's lead, to obtain title from Georgia and to draft a settlement recognizing alike the rights of the public and those of innocent purchasers.

grant of land had been a public contract—one whose terms had long since been executed. By virtue of a technical definition of contracts, Marshall was able to force the grant within the scope of the contract clause, and by inferring a duty on the part of the state to respect its own agreements, to confer immortality on the provisions of the grant.[22]

Johnson alone of the other judges stated his views. He concurred in holding the law invalid only on the first ground. He did not hesitate to declare that a state lacked the power to revoke its grants; but he did this "on a general principle, on the reason and nature of things: a principle which will impose laws even on the Deity."[23] He admitted that where power, or the right of jurisdiction, was concerned, a legislature could not bind its successors; to part with such essential accompaniments of sovereignty was "a species of political suicide." Yet where interest, or the right of soil, was involved, a state might make a binding contract. Possessions of that sort were not necessary to its political existence; these might be parted with in every respect. Once vested in an individual, such property became intimately blended with his existence, "as essentially so as the blood that circulates through his system."[24]

"The reason and nature of things!" Was Johnson setting up his own notions of natural justice as a transcendental barrier to governmental regulation? If natural law might restrain the Deity, a fortiori, it would certainly limit the actions of legislators merely human. This one notable appeal by Johnson to natural law has aroused the critics of later times. It should be noted, however, that in another statement at this period Johnson intimated that eternal principles of justice were subject to positive legislation.[25] Also, in view of his later conduct, it is likely that Johnson's reliance on natural law in the Fletcher case grew out of his hostility to the retrospective character of the state action and the total absence of compensation to the grantees. At this very period, Jefferson himself was denouncing retroactive civil laws, as violations of natural right.[26]

[22]6 Cranch 133, 135; ibid., pp. 136-37. Cf. Robert L. Hale, "The Supreme Court and the Contract Clause," 57 Harvard Law Review (1944), 512-57, 621-74, 852-92, at 634. Marshall also alluded to the ex post facto clause, 6 Cranch 138-39.

[23]6 Cranch 143.

[24]Ibid.

[25]Dissenting in 1813, in a case concerning the "full faith and credit" clause, he said: "There are certain eternal principles of justice which never ought to be dispensed with, and which courts of justice never can dispense with but when compelled by positive statute."—Mills v. Duryee, 7 Cranch 481, 486 (1813). See below, pp. 233-34.

[26]In 1813, Jefferson wrote of the retrospective application of a congressional patent law: "The sentiment that ex post facto laws are against natural right, is so strong in the United States, that few, if any, of the state constitutions have failed to proscribe them. The federal constitution indeed inter-

Yet if Johnson here gave currency to ideas drawn from the law of nature, he rejected the effort to apply the contract clause. He conceded the difficulties which enveloped the construction of that clause, but was emphatic that here it could be of no avail. That the framers had failed to use words of a "less equivocal signification" was a matter of regret.

To the majority's ruling he raised three objections. First, the contract clause could scarcely be held to embrace executed contracts. No grant or conveyance could create any continuing obligation, for obligation implied an existing moral or physical necessity; after execution a grant was merely evidence that a particular act had been done.

Again, Marshall's construction might operate in such a way as to stifle certain important powers of the states. Said Johnson:

> The states and the United States are continually legislating on the subject of contracts, prescribing the mode of authentication, the time within which suits shall be prosecuted for them, in many cases affecting existing contracts by the laws which they pass, and declaring them to cease or lose their effect for want of compliance, in the parties, with such statutory provisions. All these acts appear to be within the most correct limits of legislative powers, and most beneficially exercised, and certainly could not have been intended to be affected by this constitutional provision; yet where to draw the line, or how to define or limit the words, "obligation of contracts," will be found a subject of extreme difficulty.[27]

The problem which faced Johnson here was to apply a restricted interpretation to words which, when divorced from their origins, were susceptible of a broader application. His effort to safeguard a power in states to regulate the process of making and enforcing contracts, a system which he would later call the "administration of justice," was a solitary quest.

In the third place, Johnson was fearful lest Marshall's construction might paralyze the state's power of eminent domain. This all-important power he defined as follows:

> That right which every community must exercise, of possessing itself of the property of the individual, when necessary for public uses; a right which a magnanimous and just government will never exercise without amply indemnifying the individual, and which perhaps amounts to nothing more than a

---

dicts them in criminal cases only, but they are equally unjust in civil as in criminal cases, and the omission of a caution which would have been right, does not justify the doing what is wrong."—Letter to Isaac M'Pherson, Aug. 13, 1813, *Writings*, ed. H. A. Washington (9 vols.; Washington, 1853-1854), VI, 176.

[27] 6 Cranch 145.

power to oblige him to sell and convey, when the public necessities require it.[28]

Such a power in the state was in no sense incompatible with ownership by the individual.[29] To prevent misconduct by their rulers, the people should rely on a "frequent recurrence to first principles" and the establishment of "adequate constitutional restrictions."[30] In spite of his distaste for the Georgia repeal law, Johnson evidently found the people a safer reliance in these matters than the Supreme Court. The sentiment would in time deepen into a conviction.

In short, William Johnson rejected Marshall's expansive reading of the contract clause as incorrect in its treatment of executed public contracts, and as dangerous in its bottling up of governmental power. His concurrence rested altogether on the principle of natural justice; the legislature had destroyed rights which had previously been created by an act that the Court must assume to have been valid.[31] Such retrospective laws he deemed intrinsically unjust, and in time he would find a constitutional provision under which to annul them.

In closing, Johnson charged that the cause strongly resembled a fictitious case. He had abandoned his scruples, he wryly stated, because of his confidence in the eminent lawyers who had argued the cause; they would never, he was sure, have imposed such a case on the Supreme Court.[32] With this cryptic explanation Johnson closed

[28]*Ibid.*

[29]Johnson said the government could demand of the individual his property or his life, "not because they are not his, but because whatever is his is his country's."—6 Cranch 143.

[30]6 Cranch 144.

[31]He found "insuperable difficulties" in the idea that the grants of a legislature might be void because that body was corrupt: "The acts of the supreme power of a country must be considered pure for the same reason that all sovereign acts must be considered just; because there is no power that can declare them otherwise."—6 Cranch 144.

[32]These "unctuous sentences" Beveridge attributes to a political motive. Johnson, he says, wished to avoid affronting Jefferson and Madison, who were at this time devising a federal solution for the Yazoo land controversy and whose plans required that Georgia's original title be upheld.—*Life of Marshall*, III, 592 ff. Counsel included Luther Martin for Fletcher, and J. Q. Adams, Robert G. Harper, and Joseph Story for Peck.

It would be more plausible to ascribe the statement to naïveté or irony. Were politics behind it, it would have been easier to have kept silent altogether than to have irritated the Chief Justice by talking out.

Johnson himself doubted that Georgia, because of Indian claims, originally had full title to the lands.—6 Cranch 145-46. Furthermore, the youthful judge expressed on several other occasions the same curious esteem for the judgment and motives of counsel. Thus, in 1808, he took jurisdiction of the Gilchrist Mandamus petition because the District Attorney had entered no objection: "The high respect in which that gentleman's talents and information are held would be at least an apology for any court's proceeding in that mode, upon his acquiescence."—"Judge Johnson's Remarks," 10 Fed. Cas. 359, 361; see above, pp. 62-64. In 1812, he denied that the federal courts could assume jurisdiction over crimes at the common law, partly because

his opinion. In spite of his bow to natural law, he had strongly protested the effort to expand the contract clause into an impenetrable
shield for property.

Not for thirteen years would Johnson again express himself in a
case under the contract clause. In the interim the Court broadened
the scope of the clause in three great cases. In each of the three
it is likely that Johnson approved the decision and perhaps also
Marshall's opinion.[33]

The first case came up in 1812. Was New Jersey's grant of land
to Indians under terms expressly exempting the lands from future
taxation a contract? The Court held that it was, and that a subsequent act repealing the exemption provision violated the contract
clause.[34] Despite shortcomings in the presentation of the case,[35]
it is evident that Johnson supported the decision and, accordingly,
a capacity in states through contract stipulations to restrict the
important power of taxation.

The remaining two cases fell during Johnson's silent years. At
the 1818 session, counsel argued the actions of New Hampshire
in altering the fifty-year-old charter of Dartmouth College. Was the
charter incorporating the college a contract within the meaning of
the Constitution? Marshall, Washington, and Story, it would seem,
were agreed that it was. Duvall and Todd took the side of the
state. Johnson and Livingston were undecided.[36] While Marshall re-
putedly set to work on an opinion not yet accepted by a majority,
Mr. Justice Johnson embarked on a trip north. There, besides scour-
ing New England for Greene papers, he sought out Chancellor James
Kent in Albany. Daniel Webster's argument for the college had

"the general acquiescence of legal men shows the prevalence of opinion in
favor of the negative of the proposition."—United States v. Hudson and
Goodwin, 7 Cranch 32.

After the Fletcher decision, a Savannah newspaper reprinted from the
Richmond Enquirer, this jibe at Johnson: "They! The lawyers! And pray,
from what romantic bar were the ideas of judge Johnson extracted? Are the
lawyers of South-Carolina so many Wythes? Will they never vindicate cases
which their consciences do not approve?"—Republican and Savannah Evening
Ledger, Aug. 18, 1810.

[33]The views expressed by Story in 1815 in an opinion invalidating a confiscation of church lands by Virginia as violative of "the principles of natural
justice, . . . the fundamental laws of every free government, . . . the spirit
and the letter of the Constitution of the United States, and . . . the decisions
of most respectable judicial tribunals . . ." cannot be attributed to Johnson.
He was listed as absent from the decision, which was stated to be that only
of a majority.—Terrett v. Taylor, 9 Cranch 43, 52, 55.

[34]New Jersey v. Wilson, 7 Cranch 164 (1812). Johnson was probably
present, although he reached Washington ten days after the beginning of
the session.—Warren, I, 423, n. 2.

[35]Cf. Wright, p. 37, discussing Given v. Wright, 117 U.S. 648 (1886).

[36]Beveridge, Marshall, IV, 255.

helped win over that eminent jurist, and the New Yorker's opinion doubtless influenced his visitor from the South.[37]

In considering Johnson's role in the decision, it is important to recollect attitudes he had expressed in his essay on agriculture in 1815. He had there warned his fellow-planters against inducing the state to adopt a reckless practice of granting charters in connection with internal improvements. Fearing that the public interest might suffer, he had urged that South Carolina either buy up or legally vacate charters she had sold for river clearance.[38] The statement would suggest that, in 1815 at any rate, he attributed to states a power, by condemnation or otherwise, to terminate such contracts.

In any event, when the Court next met, Chief Justice Marshall was able to brush aside counsel Pinkney's request for a rehearing, and to state the opinion of the Court in the Dartmouth College case.[39] The corporation charter, he held, was a contract; the contract clause removed public contracts of that sort from state interference. In reaching this result, Marshall pushed still further the literal reading of the clause.[40] The Chief Justice, however, included in his opinion statements conceding a power in the states to control public institutions. Whether or not the concession was aimed at winning Johnson's approval, that justice endorsed this epochal opinion without remark.

Finally, at this same 1819 term, Johnson submerged his voice in the common opinion in Sturges v. Crowninshield.[41] Here the Court considered the validity of an act of New York to relieve insolvent debtors as applied to a debt formed prior to its passage. The act authorized under special process the discharge of debtors from their obligations. Speaking for the Court, John Marshall held the act a violation of the contract clause. Although the case did not call for it, Marshall spoke in such general terms as to convey the impression that all insolvent debtor laws would be voided, whether

[37]Shirley asserts that Kent "agreed to draw up an opinion for Johnson."— J. M. Shirley, *The Dartmouth College Causes* . . . , p. 253. For correspondence relating to Johnson's interview with Kent, see Haines, *The Role of the Supreme Court in American Government and Politics*, pp. 420-22. The date of the meeting is furnished by Kent himself, who recorded the following in his copy of 1 Wheaton: "August 27th, 1818—I had the pleasure of seeing Judge Johnson at Albany."—Information furnished by Miss Frances D. Lyon, Librarian, New York State Law Library, Albany. Beveridge assumes that Justice Livingston also followed Kent's advice.—*Marshall*, IV, 256-58.

[38]*Nugae Georgicae*, p. 40. See above, p. 102.

[39]Dartmouth College v. Woodward, 4 Wheat. 518 (1819). Washington and Story delivered separate concurring opinions, Livingston concurred in all three opinions, and Johnson concurred in Marshall's opinion. Todd was absent, and Duvall dissented without opinion.

[40]For his comments, see 4 Wheat. 644-45. Cf. Wright, p. 44.

[41]4 Wheat. 122.

retrospective or prospective in their effect. And once again, he found in the words of the constitutional clause no reason for making an exception in behalf of such state laws.[42]

The appearance of solid unity on the Court was in fact wholly false. Only three of the seven justices fully approved of the opinion.[43] Eight years later, Justice Johnson would cut away the façade and call the judgment as much a "compromise" as a legal decision.[44] The court was actually greatly divided:

> The minority thought it better to yield something than risk the whole. And, although their course of reasoning led them to the general maintenance of the state power over the subject, controlled and limited alone by the oath administered to all their public functionaries to maintain the constitution of the United States, yet, as denying the power to act upon anterior contracts could do no harm, but, in fact, imposed a restriction conceived in the true spirit of the constitution, they were satisfied to acquiesce in it, provided the decision were so guarded as to secure the power over posterior contracts, as well from the positive terms of the adjudication, as from inferences deducible from the reasoning of the court.[45]

As an exposure of the methods of the Marshall Court, the statement has interest. As a revelation of the process by which the contract clause was expanded, under the guise of unanimity, it is important. Johnson's opposition to Marshall's reading evidently led him to persuade the Chief Justice to place at the end of his opinion comments limiting the reasoning to the facts of this case, a qualification which Johnson pointed out later.[46] Yet the effect of the Sturges opinion was to forestall all efforts by states to provide relief, through discharge, for debtors.[47]

What caused Johnson to lapse into silence? That he had openly resisted the expansion of the contract clause in the Fletcher case makes his subsequent conduct enigmatic. Contrary to his early convictions about the narrow meaning of the clause and the need of safeguarding state power, he signed his name in 1819 to opinions stating in sweeping terms restrictions on the power of government. As late as January, 1822, Johnson was telling a friend that the judges were acting in the spirit of the framers; they were seeking to

[42]Ibid., pp. 205-6.
[43]See Chapter VII, note 33.
[44]Separate opinion Ogden v. Saunders, 12 Wheat. 213, 272-73 (1827).
[45]Ibid., p. 273.
[46]Ibid.
[47]In another case the same year, Marshall was reported as having decided: "That the circumstances of the state law, under which the debt was attempted to be discharged, having been passed before the debt was contracted, made no difference in the application of the principle."—M'Millan v. M'Neill, 4 Wheat. 209, 212-13 (1819). See Johnson's comment on this.—12 Wheat. 272.

protect the citizen from the "tyrannical and corrupt" laws of some of the states.[48]

Johnson had stood meekly by while the majority erected out of the contract clause a formidable barrier to state legislation affecting property. Whatever may have been his true convictions, he had tolerated the sanctification of vested rights at the expense of social interests.

The South Carolinian was soon to repent his conduct. In December, 1822, he expressed to Jefferson his wish to see a patient study and modification of implied powers and of the contract clause. No system could be perfect, and, accordingly, he had come to rely on the uprightness and intelligence of the people and the firmness and integrity of their governers. The next June, Jefferson went to some pains to denounce judicial abuses—among them, the resort to a merely literal interpretation. Instead of consulting the framers, the Court had, he complained, devoted itself to finding what meaning could be "squeezed out of the text or invented against it."[49] The advice was in point.

Even before that, in February, Johnson finally broke his long silence. At last he voiced in a leading decision, Green v. Biddle, his concern for the requirements of society. The case grew out of efforts by Kentucky to inject order into a chaos of conflicting land titles.[50] The Occupying Claimant Law of 1812 had sought to exempt occupants of lands from damage claims and to reimburse them for improvements, in case title was found to vest in others. The majority of the Supreme Court, speaking through Justice Washington, held that this law conflicted with a compact between Kentucky and Virginia safeguarding the rights of original holders in Kentucky lands.[51] Taking Marshall as his model, Washington held that this interstate agreement was a contract in the meaning of the Constitution and reached this result through a simple definition of contracts.[52] Such an extension of the contract clause verged on the fantastic.[53]

[48]Johnson to J. R. Poinsett, Jan. 3, 1822, Poinsett Collection (MSS; Historical Society of Pennsylvania); for Johnson's full statement, see below, pp. 236-37.

[49]Jefferson to Johnson, June 12, 1823. For a fuller discussion, see above, pp. 160-61.

[50]8 Wheat. 1 (1823).

[51]The compact provided "that all private rights and interests of lands within the said district . . . derived from the laws of Virginia, . . . shall remain valid and secure under the laws of the proposed state, and shall be determined by the laws now existing in this state [Virginia]."—8 Wheat. 3.

[52]See 8 Wheat. 92.

[53]Cf. Wright, pp. 46 ff. Significantly, by 1831, when Johnson's views had prevailed, an opinion which he rendered for the Court under this same compact made no mention of the contract clause.—Hawkins v. Barney's Lessee, 5 Pet. 457, 463.

To these lengths Johnson would not go. In spite of his silent acquiescence in an opinion given earlier in this same case by Story, prior to Henry Clay's arguments for Kentucky,[54] he now set forth a separate opinion differing sharply from Washington's. He scrupulously avoided reliance on the contract clause, for he found that the Kentucky constitution, of which he said the compact formed a part, furnished an adequate sanction.[55]

In this opinion Johnson at last renewed his appeal for the maintenance of power in the legislature. Virginia, he assumed, had intended to concede the usual powers of a sovereign state to Kentucky. Essential to a sovereign, he said, was a right to exercise unlimited legislative power within its own territory. In a passage that was prophetic of the position later to be adopted by the Court, he asserted that every restraint on the exercise of this power was a restraint on the intended grant and should be rigorously construed. A contrary construction would, he feared, threaten the state's power of eminent domain and its power over property transfers.[56] If forced to choose between the challenged exercise and the total extinction of the power of Kentucky, he would favor the former alternative.

Johnson thereupon denounced the course which his brothers were pursuing. He, at least, found urgent social concerns threatened by the decision:

> I cannot admit that it was ever the intention of the framers of this constitution, or of the parties to this compact, or of the United States in sanctioning that compact, that Kentucky should be forever chained down to a state of hopeless imbecility—embarrassed with a thousand minute discriminations drawn from the common law, refinements on mesne profits, set-offs, &c., appropriate to a state of society, and a state of property, having no analogy whatever to the actual state of things in Kentucky—and yet, no power on earth existing to repeal or to alter, or to affect those accommodations to the

[54]Story's opinion was rendered in 1821.—8 Wheat. 10.

[55]"While the constitution continues unrepealed," he said, "it is putting a fifth wheel to the carriage to invoke the contract into this clause. It can only eventuate in crowding our dockets with appeals from the state courts."—8 Wheat. 97.

[56]". . . who can doubt that where private property had been wanted for national purposes, the legislature of Kentucky might have compelled the individual to convey it for a value tendered, notwithstanding it was held under a grant from Virginia, and notwithstanding such a violation of private right had been even constitutionally forbidden by the State of Virginia? Or who can doubt the power of Kentucky to regulate the course of descents, the forms of conveying, the power of devising, the nature and extent of liens, within her territorial limits?"—8 Wheat. 101.

ever-varying state of human things, which the necessities or improvements of society may require.[57]

Technically, Johnson's was a concurring opinion. He deemed the Kentucky law inoperative insofar as it abridged the right to trial by jury in federal courts. But in spirit it was a dissent. However belatedly, he here deplored the condition of "hopeless imbecility" into which the state governments were sinking under the blows of the majority.

The "ever-varying state of human things" demanded a power in government to make the necessary adjustments. Johnson had altered his course. Four years later, he would make his major statement on the problem of property rights in another controversy over insolvent debtor legislation.

What had produced this dramatic shift? Doubtless public criticism of the Court and Jefferson's exhortations played a part. The business depression which persisted in Charleston and the plight of many debtors there probably also contributed, for Johnson several times during these years advocated broad-gauge bankruptcy laws.[58]

Whatever the cause, he was now re-evaluating the status of property rights. The republican form of government to which he had long ago dedicated himself was exhibiting disturbing tendencies. The individualism which it inspired now seemed to promote a ruthless acquisitiveness, at the expense of social health.[59] This theme he advanced in his *Eulogy on Jefferson*. There he set down with evident approval the views of the fallen leader:

> He knew that avarice was the besetting sin of a republican government. That the very security with which property was

[57]8 Wheat. 104. In 1824, Johnson, in dissenting from Marshall, refused to read into the terms of a Pennsylvania confiscation act an implied exemption of certain lands of the colonial proprietor.—Kirk v. Smith, 9 Wheat. 241, 294.

[58]See above, pp. 118-19.

[59]In his *Life of Greene* (I, 255), Johnson wrote nostalgically of colonial Charleston during the years before 1763. The social health and contentment of the city at that period he ascribed to a considerable equality of possessions and privileges: "The luxuries of the day were within the reach of a moderate fortune, and few could be said to be elevated above one common level. Hence social happiness was not disturbed by the workings of envy, or the haughty demeanour of upstart pride. The party in power felt and acknowledged that they had been called to the government by the voice of the people; and the people blended with a respectful deportment, the elevating consciousness of those who have conferred the power to which they submit. Indeed, with all the high and just pretensions of republicanism, it will ever be a question, whether that state of things which tempts all to ambitious pursuits, although it developes the powers of man, and expands his bosom with a conscious dignity not to be exchanged for life or happiness either, does not intrench much upon that tranquillity of mind, without which much may be possessed, but little enjoyed." Johnson disparaged the Fundamental Constitutions of Carolina and called their reputed author, John Locke, a "profound metaphysician," who was "miserably deficient as a practical politician."— *Ibid.*, I, 225.

possessed, not less than the influence which it confers; operating with some of the leading propensities of our nature, fostered a devotion to its acquisition, which he would have directed to more exalted objects. He dreaded the noxious and baneful influence of a passion for gain—in its progress degrading to national character; dangerous to the tranquillity of the world; fatal to every ennobling sentiment; destructive to every social feeling; and when become the ruling principle of a government, converting man into a ferocious animal.[60]

This concern over an exaggerated deference to property underlay Johnson's pronouncements in the great case of Ogden v. Saunders.[61] A citizen of Kentucky sued a citizen of Louisiana on bills of exchange drawn up in New York. The defendant raised as bar to the action a discharge he had obtained under a New York bankruptcy law passed prior to the contracts. Did the contract clause prohibit insolvent debtor laws when applied to subsequent contracts? Lawyers first argued the cause in 1824, but significantly, a division among the judges forced its postponement until 1827. After a new argument, the court gave its decision. The majority upheld the act; the venerable Federalist, Bushrod Washington, the aging Republican, William Johnson, and two recent appointees, Smith Thompson and Robert Trimble, spoke with seriatim opinions.

Johnson's own separate opinion ranks among his longest. Its length and likewise its vigor of expression probably sprang from its author's revulsion at views expressed by the Chief Justice. For once in his career, Marshall delivered in a leading constitutional case a full-blown dissenting opinion. With the silent approval of Story and Duvall, the old Federalist denied that the laws of a state controlled the obligation of contracts. Daniel Webster, in arguing against the law, had contended that obligation depended not upon the laws of the state, but upon the approval of the parties and the "sanction of universal law"; the contract clause, cried Webster, stood as a "great political provision, favorable to the commerce and credit of the whole country."[62] To the minority judges those views must have had the ring of truth.

Marshall still clung to a verbal reading of the clause; but he went even further. His economic conservatism, in which Story shared, appeared with severe clarity in this opinion. The appeal to natural law, natural rights, and the social compact, which had once in-

[60]Johnson continued: "He dreaded the possible growth of that most degrading of all aristocracies, which, having its basis in the distribution of pecuniary favours, like the wand of Circe, converts men into swine: that power, before which the stately port of the freeman shrinks into the cringe and smile of the knave, or more degraded sycophant."—*Eulogy on Thomas Jefferson* (1826), p. 30.
[61]12 Wheat. 213 (1827).
[62]*Ibid.*, pp. 240, 247.

spired the revolutionists at the Liberty Tree and the author of the Declaration of Independence, now assumed a different guise. John Marshall sought to convert it into a barrier against laws for the relief of stranded debtors. Individuals, he said, enter society with a right to form contracts. Such agreements, regardless of intervening conditions, it is the plain duty of government to enforce.[63]

The net result of this brand of individualism was to enshrine the rights of the creditor and to paralyze the power of state governments to cope with economic crises.

Against this doctrine Mr. Justice Johnson directed his best efforts. Although in a second opinion he declined to give an out-of-state application to the New York law, his first opinion left no doubt of his belief in its validity as applied locally.

If Marshall had resorted to natural law as a support for vested rights, Johnson now forsook his former deference to that law as a guide to judges and turned instead to positive law.[64] The states might act through their concurrent power over bankruptcy; their legislatures operated under restraints that were more effective and salutary than the law of nature as revealed by the judges at Washington.[65]

The contract clause, Johnson was convinced, was inapplicable. He laid his finger on the difficulties produced by this controversial provision when he called those difficulties "factitious" and the "result of refinement and technicality; or of attempts at definition, made in terms defective both in precision and comprehensiveness."[66] The core of the problem lay in the term "obligation." Johnson asserted that right and obligation were correlative; both originated in the actions of contracting parties. And here he reflected his dislike for the appeal to a transcendent law of nature. The needs of society were not to be overlooked:

> The obligation of every contract will then consist of that right or power over my will or actions, which I, by my contract, confer on another. And that right and power will be found to be measured neither by moral law alone, nor universal law alone, nor by the laws of society alone, but by a combination of the three—an operation in which the moral law is explained and applied by the law of nature, and both modified and adapted to the exigencies of society by positive law. The constitution was framed for society, and an advanced state of society, in which I will undertake to say that all the contracts of men

[63] *Ibid.*, pp. 346-47.
[64] In 1824, he had referred to the operation of positive national law, in asserting the power of Congress over commerce to be exclusive.—Concurring opinion in Gibbons *v.* Ogden, 9 Wheat. 1, 227.
[65] 12 Wheat. 279, 280. See below, pp. 248-49.
[66] *Ibid.*, p. 281.

receive a relative, and not a positive interpretation: for the rights of all must be held and enjoyed in subserviency to the good of the whole. The state construes them, the state applies them, the state controls them, and the state decides how far the social exercise of the rights they give us over each other can be justly asserted. I say the social exercise of these rights, because in a state of nature, they are asserted over a fellow-creature, but in a state of society over a fellow citizen.[67]

Mr. Justice Johnson, at least, had discovered society. Because of social change and complexity, he now attributed to the governments of states, as earlier he had to Congress, a power commensurate with the need. He here repudiated an unqualified freedom of contract—a concept of singular vitality.[68]

In a state of nature, Johnson continued, a party to a contract could be excused from performance when prevented by sickness or some other unavoidable cause. In society the laws of the community controlled parties; government served both to construe and to enforce contracts. Thus, the nature and form of contracts, and the remedies for enforcing them, lay within the sphere of governmental power. He assailed an exclusive preoccupation with the interests of the creditor, for society must enforce the rights of "humanity," and both the debtor and society had a stake in the administration of justice and the general well-being. Johnson put it this way:

The debtor may plead the visitations of Providence, and the society has an interest in preserving every member of the community from despondency—in relieving him from a hopeless state of prostration, in which he would be useless to himself, his family, and the community. When that state of things has arrived in which the community has fairly and fully discharged its duties to the creditor, and in which, pursuing the debtor any longer would destroy the one, without benefitting the other, must always be a question to be determined by the common guardian of the rights of both; and in this originates the power exercised by governments in favor of insolvents. It grows out of the administration of justice, and is a necessary appendage to it.[69]

Marshall's conception of creditor's rights, Johnson implied, suited only a primitive or barbarous state of society.[70] And Johnson could find no objection, moral or political, to applying here the maxim, "*Lex non cogit ad impossibilia.*"[71] Presumably Johnson was not opposed to a power to enact bankrupt laws retrospective in applica-

[67]*Ibid.*, p. 282.
[68]The notion of an absolute freedom of contract would appear under new auspices later on and again encounter the judicial ax in our own century. See West Coast Hotel Co. *v.* Parrish, 300 U.S. 379, 391 ff. (1937).
[69]12 Wheat. 283-84.
[70]*Ibid.*, p. 284.
[71]*Ibid.*

tion. Despite the "unanimous" opinion in the Sturges case, Johnson said he had held this position then, and saw no reason to abandon it now. In suggesting that a bankrupt law might apply even to prior contracts, he stood out alone among the seven judges.

Furthermore, he raised serious objections to a contrary construction of the clause. It was important, he thought, to regard the remedy for enforcing contracts as something strictly separate from the obligation; otherwise, the state's power would be unduly restricted. It was correct to presume that one who entered into a contract thereby registered his agreement to obey the rules of remedy furnished by the state where the contract was formed. A knowledge of these laws might likewise be presumed.

Again he assailed the idea that contractors might exact a literal fulfillment of their agreements. He cited many examples to show how society controlled the several stages in the life of contracts, including inception, construction, fulfillment, and enforcement. Giving sanctity to the letter of contracts might endanger all these controls and even statutes of limitations—laws which Johnson deemed indispensable to society. Not only could a state in his view prohibit parties from contracting for payment by future acquisition on the part of debtors, but it might prohibit men from "running in debt altogether. . . . A measure a thousand times wiser than that impulse to speculation and ruin, which has hitherto been communicated to individuals by our public policy."[72]

Here, then, was a partial retreat from the law of nature. To a considerable extent, Johnson had found in positive law a corrective of that authority. In reply to the charge that his views involved artificiality and complexity, he asserted: "All the notions of society, particularly in their jurisprudence, are more or less artificial; our constitution nowhere speaks the language of men in a state of nature. . . ."[73]

Yet Johnson retained his old distaste for certain retrospective laws. Characteristically, he now based his opposition on constitutional rather than natural law. He here revealed his considered view of the general purpose of the whole clause forbidding states to pass "any bill of attainder, *ex post facto* law, or law impairing the obligation of contracts." Shunning a merely literal reading, he said that the general object of this provision was to prohibit "arbitrary and tyrannical legislation over existing rights whether of person or property." The *ex post facto* clause, he was convinced, interdicted not only criminal but also civil acts, retrospective in effect. The real gist of that clause, he declared, was that "the states shall pass

[72] 12 Wheat. 290.
[73] *Ibid.*

no law, attaching to the acts of individuals other effects or consequences than those attached to them by the laws existing at their
date; and all contracts thus construed, shall be enforced according to
their just and reasonable purport."[74]

In closing, Johnson recurred to the needs of society.[75] As in his
Eulogy on Jefferson, so again Johnson warned of the dangers latent
in an unlimited sway of property. His parting words proclaimed his
stand on the age-old issue between the individual and the state:

> What we contend for is no more than this, that it is equally
> the duty and right of government to impose limits to the avarice
> and tyranny of individuals, so as not to suffer oppression to be
> exercised under the semblance of right and justice. It is true,
> that in the exercise of this power, governments themselves may
> sometimes be the authors of oppression and injustice; but,
> wherever the constitution could impose limits to such power,
> it has done so; and if it has not been able to impose effectual
> and universal restraints, it arises only from the extreme dif-
> ficulty of regulating the movements of sovereign power; and
> the absolute necessity, after every effort can be made to govern
> effectually, that will still exist to leave some space for the
> exercise of discretion, and the influence of justice and wisdom.[76]

This was Johnson's matured conviction. The concern for power
in government first suggested in the Fletcher case he had reiterated,
after a lapse, in Green *v.* Biddle. But the Ogden opinion stands as
his major essay on property. To prevent economic oppression, the
legislature required a wide range of power within which to effect reform; the judge should practice the virtue of restraint. Only where
laws clearly trod on existing rights should he intervene. It was the
purpose of the law that provided the test of its validity.[77]

By 1827, Johnson had moved to firm ground. He had put to the
test his own basic assumptions about society. As a result he had
changed his course. For all his pugnacity, this judge had the happy
faculty of self-examination. This appears from a letter which Johnson wrote to Mathew Carey during these years of re-evaluation.
Speaking of the schools and certain readings which the teachers were
then introducing, he exclaimed:

> Old fellows are apt to croak and therefore I rather distrust
> my sentiments. But really when I look 'round upon the super-

[74]12 Wheat. 286.
[75]It was the right of the government, he said, "to limit and define the
power of contracting, and the extent of the creditor's remedy against his
debtor; to regard other rights besides his, and to modify his rights so as not
to let them override entirely the general interests of society, the interests of
the community itself in the talents and services of the debtor, the regard due
to his happiness and to the claims of his family upon him and upon the government."—*Ibid.,* pp. 291-92.
[76]*Ibid.,* p. 292.
[77]*Ibid.,* p. 291.

ficial group who are soon to wield this government, I tremble. Yet how can it be otherwise? Do they read anything besides novels and reviews? What an admirable preparation for receiving law from others is it to accustom ourselves to taking all our opinions from others![78]

The passage suggests more than skepticism of self and the crabbedness of age. It reveals fears for the future of self-government. The whole effect of Johnson's opinions was to throw the burden of wise government on the shoulders of the people; that in turn called for a citizenry informed, discriminating, and vigilant. The positive law to which Johnson deferred was the product of republican institutions; if the people were to rule, the people must be just and wise.

The Ogden opinion expressed Johnson's new convictions; to these he continued to adhere. Subsequent opinions did little more than apply or elaborate the positions he had adopted in the essay of 1827. Four of these later rulings, however, deserve mention.

In 1829 Johnson declared his matured view on the *ex post facto* clause.[79] After a state court had held a title bad, the state legislature had in effect decided it good. Was this action an impairment of a contract? The majority said no, since the Constitution nowhere prohibited a state from creating contracts. Johnson agreed that there was no impairment here; yet the doctrine of the majority he wholly disapproved. For a state to endow a void contract with obligation would be to violate the real intent of the framers of the Constitution.[80] To combat the majority's doctrine Johnson turned in a learned commentary on the Calder decision of 1798.[81] In ruling that *ex post facto* laws extended only to criminal matters the early judges, he said, had stated an unsound dictum. As a result the Court of Marshall had had to "toil uphill" to bring within the contract clause retrospective state laws applying to civil matters. The Court should avoid that necessity by adopting Johnson's own construction; that is, it should read the *ex post facto* clause as applying to civil as well as criminal matters. It were better to reverse an old decision than to stretch the words of the Constitution beyond their evident meaning.[82] The judge had lived to repent his conduct

[78]Letter dated Nov. 14, 1825, original in possession of Mr. Charles Feinberg, of Detroit. The author is indebted to Mr. Feinberg, and to Mr. A. J. Levin, who brought this letter to his attention.

[79]Satterlee *v.* Matthewson, 2 Pet. 380.

[80]Johnson concurred here, on the ground that the state statute was merely declaratory of the law on a point on which the courts had fluctuated in their decisions. The latest decision ought to furnish the precedent.—*Ibid.*, p. 415.

[81]*Ibid.*, p. 681.

[82]*Ibid.*, p. 687.

in the Sturges case. Although a reversal of the generation-old precedent was by now beyond hope, Johnson's point was well taken.[83]

Two years later, Johnson grasped an opportunity to root statutes
of limitation in firm constitutional ground.[84] He now spoke for a
unanimous court in saying that a state might pass such laws through
its control over the administration of justice. Such laws were valid
even though they might produce a complete divestiture of right.[85]

On another occasion this Republican judge repelled a strong effort to curb the power of the states over remedy.[86] Pennsylvania
had discovered that one of its officials had committed wholesale defalcations. Existing laws gave the state a claim to his lands for
satisfaction of its losses, but provided no mode of enforcement. The
state had then set up commissioners and outlined the procedures
they should follow in enforcing its lien. In spite of the retrospective
application and the unorthodox nature of the procedure, the remedy
adopted received Johnson's full blessing.

In these three cases Johnson reaffirmed the dominance of positive law. The vindication of limitation laws and laws on remedy
generally comported with this stand. Where the Constitution was
silent the positive enactments of the state were entitled to respect.
Where the state's measures bore down arbitrarily on existing rights,
then it was the express terms of the *ex post facto* clause of the
Constitution, the highest form of positive law, that should control.

In all of this Johnson had traveled far from that early reliance
on natural law. By 1830 he was setting down important qualifications on the political theory of the Revolution. His dissenting opinion
in Shanks *v.* Dupont[87] gives us his ripened philosophy of the obligation of the individual to society.

Ann Shanks, a citizen of South Carolina, had married a British
officer during the wartime occupation of Charleston and had left
the country with him before the signing of peace. Had she become
a British subject and accordingly entitled under treaties to sue for
recovery of lands she had owned in the state? The majority, speaking through Story, thought she had. Johnson disagreed.

Counsel for Mrs. Shanks had argued that individuals possess a
right to elect to change their allegiance. This was that natural right

---

[83]In later years the Court would covertly bring within the contract clause
state acts not impairing, but rather enlarging, the obligation of contracts.—
See Hale, "Supreme Court and the Contract Clause," pp. 514-16. Johnson's
construction, however, would have raised two difficulties: first, it would
have left the contract clause with no very important reason for being; second,
it would have extended the ban on retrospective civil statutes, by analogy,
to the federal government through the medium of Art. I, sec. 9.

[84]Hawkins *v.* Barney's Lessee, 5 Pet. 457 (1831).

[85]*Ibid.*, p. 467.

[86]Lessee of Livingston *v.* Moore, 7 Pet. 469 (1833).

[87]3 Pet. 242.

of expatriation so popular with the early Jeffersonians. If Justice Johnson had ever believed in such a right he now thought otherwise. His confession is significant:

> I had this question submitted to me on my circuit some years since, and I then leaned in favor of this right of election. But more mature reflection has satisfied me that I then gave too much weight to natural law and the suggestions of reason and justice in a case which ought to be disposed of upon the principles of political and positive law, and the law of nations.[88]

He thought it clearly expedient that states should extend this right to individuals. Governments ought to allow individuals to use their talents and to seek their fortunes wherever they wished. A wise government would extend the right up to the limit of its own security. Yet to assert this as an inalienable right was a different matter. South Carolina had adopted the common law of England, and that law had denied the existence of the right. Moreover, the course of legislation in that state before the Revolution showed that the right of election belonged to the state alone, and that an election to leave its territory was a crime in the individual.

This he thought determined the question. The right was not inherent or beyond the laws of society. It was no more inherent or inalienable, in fact, than the power "to hold, devise, or inherit the lands or acquisitions of an individual." The community had claims of its own. These Johnson emphasized:

> The right to enjoy, transmit, and inherit the fruits of our own labor, or of that of our ancestors, stands on the same footing with the right to employ our industry wherever it can be best employed; and the obligation to obey the laws of the community on the subject of the right to emigrate, is as clearly to be inferred from the reason and nature of things, as the obligation to use or exercise any other of our rights, powers, or faculties, in subordination to the public good.[89]

The principle Johnson discovered in the law of nations.[90] It was a subject for community action; the security of the individual lay in "exerting his influence to obtain laws which will neither expose the community unreasonably on the one hand, nor restrain one individual unjustly on the other."[91] Nor did Johnson give much cre-

---

[88]*Ibid.*, p. 258. Johnson had evidently failed to vote in an earlier decision indirectly involving the right of expatriation.—M'Ilvaine v. Coxe's Lessee, 4 Cranch 209, 211 n. (1808).

[89]3 Pet. 261-62.

[90]Writers on international law, he said, showed that when an individual proposed to move, a question of right or obligation arose between himself and the community which had to be decided somehow, and how else than by a "reference to the positive legislation or received principles of the society itself?"—*Ibid.*, p. 262.

[91]*Ibid.*

dence here to the theory of the social contract. To trace the origin
of government to compact and individual will was fallacious; only
two governments, he contended, Massachusetts and the United
States, rested on such an origin, and there only a fraction of the
population had participated in the compact. In vigorous terms, Johnson pictured the debt which the individual owed to society:

> If the moral government of our Maker and our parents is
> to be deduced from gratuitous benefits bestowed on us, why
> may not the government that has shielded our infancy claim
> from us a debt of gratitude to be repaid after manhood? In the
> course of nature, man has need of protection and improvement
> long before he is able to reciprocate these benefits. These are
> purchased by the submission and services of our parents; why,
> then, should not those to whom we must be indebted for ad-
> vantages so indispensable to the development of our powers,
> be permitted, to a certain extent, to bind us apprentice to the
> community from which they have been and are to be pro-
> cured?[92]

Thus did Johnson seek to counteract the anarchistic tendencies in
the Lockian and Jeffersonian theory of natural rights and social
compact. The weakness of that doctrine lay in its exaggerated stress
on individual will and individual capacity and in its neglect of the
function of society. Thus, the doctrine of election, said Johnson, left
only a "shadow of a tie" to society.[93] To insist on such a right was
to bring man back to a state of nature, where he could herd with
whomever he pleased and where his link with society would depend solely on his own caprice.

Johnson denied that in taking this stand he was abandoning moral
law. Moral obligations were, he said, universal and unchanging.
Here he was considering only political obligation, which he insisted
"must frequently vary according to political circumstances."[94] Problems such as fixing the age of legal majority required positive enactment.

By 1830, then, Johnson had formulated his philosophy in detail.
At bottom there remained the respect for the individual, whose happiness was the object of the Constitution. His civil rights and liberties—jury trial, criminal procedure generally, freedom of speech
and freedom of religion—rested not alone on natural justice, but
on the express provisions of the fundamental written law. Furthermore, all rights, whether of person or of property, merited protection from retrospective laws; Johnson had reread and redefined the
purport of the *ex post facto* clause. In enforcing such rights as
these the judge might overrule the legislature.

[92]3 Pet. 262-63.
[93]*Ibid.*, p. 265.
[94]*Ibid.*, p. 263.

Yet this judge learned to exercise restraint where matters called for government action. Under the impact of popular criticism, Jefferson's admonitions, economic distress, and his own discoveries in the origins of the Revolution and Constitution, Johnson came to the conviction that social change demanded social measures; security lay not in any "system," but in the uprightness and wisdom of the people and the rulers. His comment in 1823 epitomized his change of outlook; legislatures must have the power to make those "accommodations to the ever-varying state of human things, which the necessities or improvements of society may require." Government, he declared in the Ogden case, was the "common guardian" of all. That decision proved a turning-point in the history of the contract clause.[95] Furthermore, Johnson's pronouncement supporting a state power to combat the maladjustments of an economic crisis was to serve a century later as a beacon to the Supreme Court when during a national depression the states struggled to adjust the claims of property to the exigencies of society.[96] His conception of the dynamics of society and the resulting demands for positive legislation set Johnson apart from his contemporaries on the Court.

His concern for society led him to attribute broad and inalienable powers to government. He steadily maintained his support of the power of eminent domain. Control over the administration of justice was another vital power which he defended. It embraced the mode of acquiring, and the legitimate character of property rights and the remedy for their enforcement.[97] The notion of the state's police powers would emerge during later decades; yet Johnson's insistence on the state's power to regulate the "social exercise" of rights would seem to suggest his attitude toward such powers.

The gospel of laissez faire had little appeal for Mr. Justice Johnson.[98]

[95]Professor Wright states that prior to the Ogden case, in only one decision under the contract clause had the state act been sustained—Goszler v. Georgetown, 6 Wheat. 593 (1821). Subsequent to it the Court of Marshall took up nine contract cases in all, and in none was the state law held unconstitutional. Wright, pp. 52-53.

[96]Home Building & Loan Association v. Blaisdell, 290 U.S. 398, 428-29, 444 (1934).

[97]His position on the power to tax is less clear. In 1812 he probably concurred in an opinion acknowledging the possibility of its relinquishment by a state.—See above, p. 214. Very possibly, however, it was pressure from Johnson and the new appointees that led Marshall, in 1830, to admit the vital importance of that power and to refuse to rest relinquishment on anything short of an express statutory provision.—Providence Bank v. Billings, 4 Pet. 514, 561.

[98]For another interpretation of Johnson's position in many of the cases dealt with in this chapter, see A. J. Levin, "Mr. Justice William Johnson and the Common Incidents of Life," 44 Michigan Law Review (1945), 59-112, 243-93, passim. See also Oliver Schroeder, Jr., "The Life and Judicial Work of Justice William Johnson, Jr.," 95 University of Pennsylvania Law Review (1946-1947), 164-201, 344-86, especially 344-60.

Chapter XIII

THE REPUBLIC AND ITS FAMILIES

THE case of Ogden and Saunders gave William Johnson other matters for thought besides the status of property. By the 1820's, state rights had become a war cry of American politics. The problem which that slogan suggests was to plague Johnson for the rest of his life. This and the succeeding chapter will tell the story. The judges at Washington stood in the thick of the fight and, among them, Jefferson's first appointee.

The third President had himself long preached the doctrine of state rights. In his inaugural he had insisted on "the support of the state governments in all their rights, as the most competent administrations for our domestic concerns and the surest bulwarks against anti-republican tendencies. . . ." That declaration had followed on the heels of the Virginia and Kentucky Resolutions; the assemblies of two states had served Jefferson and Madison as rostrums from which to assail unconstitutional federal laws. The extreme theory of state rights has accordingly often been associated with Jefferson. Would Johnson in his closing years follow that lead?

As elsewhere, the years of Johnson's service on the high bench had a crucial import for the formulation of the role of the states in the American system of government. After a century and more has elapsed, the federal structure is a familiar and accepted form of political organization. The division of powers between distinct and coordinate governments, general and regional, in which the United States pioneered, has received successful application in at least three other nation states.[1] Proponents of the scheme would extend it not merely to such regions as Western Europe and Central Africa but to the very globe itself. If the system which combines autonomy for local matters with union for general concerns has won recruits abroad, at home it has entered upon a new phase. Within this oldest of federations the growth of federal-state cooperation in

[1] Dr. K. C. Wheare defines the principle as "the method of dividing powers so that the general and regional governments are each, within a sphere, coordinate and independent," and gives Canada, Australia, and Switzerland as examples of its successful operation. See his *Federal Government* (New York and London, 1947), pp. 11, 33.

meeting common problems has partially displaced the traditional pre-occupation with legal distinctness.

Yet when William Johnson took his judicial oath in 1804 the federal principle was little more than a novelty, vaguely comprehended and variously interpreted. In the years that ensued, the Court on which he sat would meet and dispose of many an issue affecting the operation of the dual system. Federalism was an experiment. Judicial decrees of that epoch would establish the fundamentals; to later judges it would remain only to elaborate the earlier decrees.

Those early pronouncements, however, would not go unchallenged. These were matters of violent public controversy. However solemn, however unanimous might be the voice of the Court, the judges would more than once hear defiant shouts of protest and disagreement. Not only would states, North and South, denounce decisions restrictive of their powers, but the ultimate recourse, whether nullification or secession, would be threatened at one time or another from every quarter of the Union. In such an atmosphere, the youthful judge approached his task of helping to expound the status of the members of the Union.

The circumstances under which he proceeded to the task were unique and uncomfortable. He stood in fact at the center between two extremist forces. At least until his last years on the bench, most of the judges shared a strongly nationalistic bias. John Marshall's solicitude for property rights and antipathy to democratic forces made him fearful of power in states; his unremitting effort to expand the contract clause gave evidence of his apprehensions regarding state power.[2] Justice Story saw more danger in anarchy among the members than in tyranny at the center of the Union; hence, as we have seen, he urged the establishment of imposing national institutions.[3]

It is fair to say that on the whole this was the spirit which motivated the majority during the first two decades of Johnson's tenure. Alexander Hamilton had long before proposed at Philadelphia that the framers transform the states into mere districts of the central government. The advice went unheeded, but the Supreme Court under Marshall kept a suspicious eye on exertions of the powers which the states retained. The climax came in 1821, when a unanimous Court rendered decision in Cohens v. Virginia.[4] Although finally deciding the cause for the state, the Chief Justice asserted in boldest

[2]Marshall wrote to Story, "It would seem as if the state legislatures (many of them at least) have an invincible hostility to the sacredness of charters."— Letter dated July 31, 1833, W. Story, Life and Letters of Joseph Story, II, 150. Cf. Haines, The Role of the Supreme Court in American Government and Politics, pp. 623-30.
[3]Letter to Pinkney, 1816, Story, Story, I, 293, 296.
[4]6 Wheat. 264.

terms a jurisdiction in the Court to hear appeals from state courts where state laws seemed to conflict with federal.

If the Court at Washington pressed inexorably for centralization, Johnson's own state furnished an opposing centrifugal force. In 1823 Johnson had collided, inside and outside the Circuit Court, with the extremist South Carolina Association. From that time on, leaders in South Carolina continued to assail federal measures. The time had come, cried Thomas Cooper in 1827, the year of the Ogden case, "to calculate the value of the Union."[5] Five years later, the state was preparing to oppose by armed force the execution of what it deemed unconstitutional federal laws. Johnson watched these developments with growing misgivings.

Between judicial dictation and forcible state resistance, was there no middle road?

Such a course William Johnson evidently sought to pursue. In his *Life of Greene* and in his letters to Jefferson, he allied himself with the attitude he there ascribed to the Republicans.[6] The framers had limited both governments, federal and state, in the interest of the individual. Johnson liked this neutral attitude and challenged Jefferson to tell him at what point his conduct on the Court had departed from true doctrine.

Jefferson complied by laying down his two canons of interpretation. The first called for power in the states to control matters affecting their own citizens exclusively and a power in the United States to control matters respecting citizens of other states and foreigners; the second insisted that the judges, in interpreting the Constitution, consult the attitudes prevalent in 1789.[7] Jefferson emphasized the importance of state autonomy and condemned the judges for violating his formula. The aging planter of 1823 retained the same belief in the primary role of the states which, as President, he had proclaimed in 1801. For the conduct of domestic affairs, the people must rely on their state governments.

Johnson took this advice seriously. As described earlier, he applied the first canon in such a way as to amplify the powers of Congress; both treaties and commercial regulations, for example, he deemed vitally important to citizens of all the states. The powers to adopt them he accordingly construed broadly.[8] Yet he was able simultaneously to approve broad state powers over internal matters. He likewise preferred a historical to a literal construction of constitutional clauses.

[5]Wallace, *History of South Carolina*, II, 425.
[6]For a fuller treatment of the subject, see above, Chapter IX.
[7]See above, pp. 160-61.
[8]See above, Chapter XI. Cf. pp. 164-66.

The attitude which Johnson adopted toward the states of the Union appears in the opening passages of his opinion in the Steamboat case. The Constitution had as its primary purpose the protection of individuals. Yet a subsidiary purpose was the promotion of the "independence and harmony" of the states in order that they might the better cherish and protect "the respective families of this great republic."[9] Johnson was ready to treat the Union to a degree as a single community, a "republic"; in the same breath he acknowledged the states to be vital and essential ingredients of the system; to them he gave the intimate name "families." "There is, and perhaps ought to be," he declared in his *Greene*, "a clannish spirit in the states of the Union. . . ."[10] In his subsequent treatment of the federal system he shunned a severely legalistic approach and dealt with the relationship as one between a community and its component family units.

That was the conception which increasingly impelled this Jeffersonian judge, especially after 1823, to acknowledge power in the states. All too aware of the ominous talk of disunion in Charleston, Johnson pursued a judicial course at several points diverging from that of the Court majority. Johnson would hew out a path of his own most notably in his treatment of the rules which governed the interpretation of state powers over internal affairs—the true sphere of state autonomy. His statements on those rules as declared in a series of leading cases will furnish the substance of this chapter. Yet two preliminary subjects call for analysis. Here, too, Johnson broke with the majority.

First, to what extent should state laws and state decisions be given an extraterritorial, that is, out-of-state, application? As early as 1813, Johnson split with the majority on the question. In behalf of the Court, Justice Story read the constitutional "full faith and credit" clause and a statute of Congress implementing it in such a way as to require that binding effect be given a New York judgment for debt in courts elsewhere. Johnson, in dissenting, gave a narrow reading to the statute in the interest of interstate harmony. Only explicit positive law could suffice to justify the judges in parting from what Johnson regarded as a basic principle, i.e., that "jurisdiction cannot be justly exercised by a state over property not within the reach of its process, or over persons not owing them allegiance or not subjected to their jurisdiction by being found within their limits."[11] Although Johnson seems to have accepted the

[9] Concurring opinion in Gibbons *v.* Ogden, 9 Wheat. 1, 223 (1824). See above, p. 203.
[10] II, 181.
[11] Mills *v.* Duryee, 7 Cranch 481, 486 (1813). Here, one who had obtained a judgment for debt in a New York court sought execution in a court in the District of Columbia. What effect must the latter court give to the

majority's position later,[12] his early divergence was noteworthy. The majority chose in the interest of a national uniformity of laws, to read broadly both Constitution and statute. Johnson would maintain the exclusive hegemony of each state over its territory and citizens until Congress should clearly command enforcement there of the policies of other states. The judges of later years would pursue consistently neither the one nor the other course and, in consequence, would produce endless confusion and complexity, especially in the matter of divorces.[13]

If Johnson had met with defeat in his initial effort to thwart an out-of-state application of state decisions, he had smoother sailing in 1827. With Jefferson's admonitions behind him, he approached the case of Ogden v. Saunders.[14] His response was unique. As we have seen, his separate opinion defending the New York Insolvent Debtor Law from the operation of the contract clause appeared in the company of those of Washington, Thompson, and Trimble. This cause, however, presented an additional issue. Might original defendant, Ogden, set up in the federal court in Louisiana, the state

decree of the former? Congress had implemented the "full faith and credit" clause (Art. IV, sec. 1) by providing that the records and judicial proceedings of the state courts, when properly authenticated, should have the same faith and credit in federal courts as they had by law or usage in the courts of the states from which they were taken. Did this mean that one state's judgments should be received in other states merely as evidence or, alternatively, that they must be carried into effect there? The majority chose the latter alternative. Johnson chose the former. In a concise opinion he revealed his concern for harmony among the states and his debt to that body of international law which he thought should often control, by analogy, the relations among the states. He construed the Constitution and the statute not as requiring enforcement, but merely the receiving as evidence, of the New York judgment. Nothing could tend more to arouse interstate jealousies than to enforce judgments of other states. "Faith" and "credit," he said, were terms applicable only to evidence.

[12]Hampton v. M'Connel, 3 Wheat. 234 (1818). There was no indication of a dissent here. The case was not, however, entirely analogous to the Mills case. In 1822, Johnson, on circuit, again restricted the application of the "full faith and credit" clause. Anticipating his stand in Ogden v. Saunders, Johnson here declared the New York Insolvent Debtor Law altogether "municipal," incapable of an extraterritorial operation. Said he, "The effort in the present instance is to give an extra-territorial operation to the law of New York and in fact to make it prevail here against an express law of this state, regulating the mode of instituting suits. This would produce direct hostility between the various codes of law of the different states, instead of that peace and amity which the clause of the Constitution now relied on was calculated to enforce."—Garesche v. Cowing, Minutes C.C. Dist. of S.C. (1822), Bk. C, pp. 67, 69.

[13]E.g., see Williams v. North Carolina, 325 U.S. 226 (1945). For commentary see Edward S. Corwin, "Out-Haddocking Haddock," 93 University of Pennsylvania Law Review (1945), 341, 346, referring to Johnson's dissent in Mills v. Duryee. See also Sherrer v. Sherrer, 334 U.S. 343 (1948), especially a statement by Mr. Justice Frankfurter, dissenting, ibid., p. 364.

[14]12 Wheat. 213. For a discussion of Johnson's opinion in the case relative to the contract clause, see above, pp. 220-25.

of his citizenship, a New York discharge as a bar to a suit instituted by a citizen of Kentucky? On this second point, Johnson switched sides; the judges associated with Johnson on the first point now lapsed into silent dissent. In refusing to give the discharge effect in another state Johnson now spoke with the support of Marshall, Story, and Duvall. The opinions which he expressed on the point, however, were for the time at least, solely his own.[15]

The question, said Johnson, was "whether a discharge of a debtor under a state insolvent law would be valid against a creditor or citizen of another state, who has never voluntarily subjected himself to the state laws, otherwise than by the origin of his contract."[16] Despite British practice to the contrary, Johnson was convinced that no rule of international law required enforcement of a discharge obtained in one nation against a creditor residing in another. The Constitution had wisely adopted a corresponding practice for the Union. Said Johnson by way of summary:

> My opinion on the subject is briefly this: that the provision in the constitution which gives the power to the general government to establish tribunals of its own in every state, in order that the citizens of other states or sovereignties might therein prosecute their rights under the jurisdiction of the United States, had for its object an harmonious distribution of justice throughout the Union; to confine the states, in the exercise of their judicial sovereignty, to cases between their own citizens; to prevent, in fact, the exercise of that very power over the rights of citizens of other states, which the origin of the contract might be supposed to give to each state; and thus, to obviate that *conflictus legum,* which has employed the pens of Huberus and various others, and which any one who studies the subject will plainly perceive, it is infinitely more easy to prevent than to adjust.[17]

Thus, while confirming the state's sovereign power over conflicts between its own citizens, Johnson sought to promote the harmony of the several families of the republic. In regulating contracts, states might pass arbitrary laws or turn aside the "course of distributive justice"; this might in turn become the subject of "jealousy, irritation, . . . or retaliation." The anxiety to promote harmony which had prompted the early dissent, reinforced now by the words of caution from Monticello drove Johnson to pursue

[15]Said Johnson: "I am instructed by the majority . . . finally to dispose of this cause."—12 Wheat. 358. Not until 1832 did the majority, through Marshall, express definite concurrence with Johnson's opinion here.—Boyle *v.* Zacharie, 6 Pet. 348.

[16]12 Wheat. 358: Johnson said the "full faith and credit" clause did not apply, since the question went "to the invalidity of the discharge altogether. . . ."

[17]*Ibid.,* p. 359.

a unique course in the Ogden case.[18] Yet he was perfectly aware that his ruling imposed hardship on individuals and thwarted a uniform application of bankruptcy laws. A power other than that of the states existed, as we shall see, capable of coping with that problem. Meanwhile the state might act. As long as its action remained a family affair, there could be no danger of a blood feud and a disruption of the peace of the great community.

A second preliminary question is pertinent. To what extent was the Supreme Court properly the grand censor of the federal system? Was that tribunal the most appropriate recourse for settling all the conflicts that might arise between the nation and the states? Here, too, Johnson's concern for harmony and state autonomy caused him to deviate from the majority.

In 1821, Johnson had concurred in the Cohens decision and presumably in Marshall's opinion exalting the role of the Court as final arbiter.[19] As late as January, 1822, in fact, Johnson was sure that that decision had been correct. In a frank letter to a friend he breathed his confidence and revealed his hostility to the state laws over which the Court was exercising its reviewing power:

> I have no uneasiness on the subject of these attacks upon us. Only let us give the people time to read and think. In the Virginia case, you perceive we have the popular side. Our decision is that the United States will prevent the states from trampling on individual rights and in all the other wrangles we are engaged in with the state authorities, it is demonstrable that we are defending the rights of the citizens of other states from tyrannical and corrupt legislation of those states that are so much in debt as to find it to their interest to prevent the recovery of debts by due course of law; or in which the legislatures have taken the side of their own citizens in opposition to the legal claims of other citizens to lands in possession of the former or in which the states have become largely interested in the state-banks or greatly under the influence of those who are, and find it inconvenient to be checked in this new issue of paper-money by the necessity of paying specie

---

[18]But cf. Clay v. Smith, 3 Pet. 411 (1830), wherein Johnson, for the Court, held that a Kentucky citizen, by voluntarily participating in bankruptcy proceedings in Louisiana under the law of the latter state, had relinquished his "extra-territorial immunity from the operation of the bankrupt laws of Louisiana."—*Ibid.,* p. 412.

[19]Cohens v. Virginia, 6 Wheat. 264. Two points were made by the Court: first, that under the 25th section of the Judiciary Act, it had jurisdiction. Cohens had been convicted in the Virginia courts for violating a state law against lotteries; Cohens contended that laws of Congress for the District of Columbia authorized sale of the lottery tickets in Virginia. The existence of this federal question, the Court decided, brought the case within appellate jurisdiction under the Constitution and statute. Second, that rightly construed, congressional laws did not authorize sale of tickets outside the District in violation of state laws.

for their bills. Take these views together and you find exactly that state of things which made it necessary to frame the Constitution such as it now is. Some clever fellow will I hope take the subject up and give a proper exposé of it.[20]

The passage is significant: it reflects a strong distaste for economic measures of some of the states and it presumes the Court to be the proper authority for annulling them. In his letters to Jefferson, Johnson was soon trying to vindicate his conduct by disassociating himself from some of the views expressed by the Court and by asserting that the people supported the Court in its role of umpire.[21] But Jefferson was unimpressed. He thought the only suitable arbiter for most conflicts was a national constitutional convention. He applied his two canons of interpretation directly to the Cohens opinion and found it wanting under both.

The advice evidently hit home. The South Carolinian soon began to swallow his contempt for economic reforms in the states and to lose some of his former assurance about the utility of judicial review of state laws, and he began to speak out in behalf of judicial restraint.

His renewed volubility was nowhere more evident than in cases testing the validity of state laws. Before the 1823 term he had participated in no fewer than eight decisions setting aside state legislation.[22] In none of these had he spoken out in clear dissent; in but one had he spoken at all.[23] From 1823 on, Johnson was present at eight similar decisions; and in only two of these did he fail to speak his mind.[24] In half of the remaining six, Johnson dissented

[20]Johnson to J. R. Poinsett, Jan. 3, 1822, Poinsett Collection (MSS; Historical Society of Pennsylvania; courtesy of the Society).

[21]See above, pp. 154–58. In Buel v. Van Ness, 8 Wheat. 312 (1823), decided shortly before the April, 1823, letter to Jefferson, Johnson, speaking for the Court, rejected arguments tending to restrict the scope of the appellate jurisdiction authorized by the 25th section of the Judiciary Act of 1789. Johnson here emphasized the wording of the act. He went on to insist that the cases embraced by the section were "noticed only for their national importance" and were thought appropriate for an appellate court because of the principles involved.—Ibid., p. 323.

[22]Johnson was absent at Terrett v. Taylor, 9 Cranch. 43 (1815). The cases here discussed are listed in 131 U.S., cclviii (Appendix).

[23]Johnson concurred without opinion in United States v. Peters, 5 Cranch 115 (1809); New Jersey v. Wilson, 7 Cranch 164 (1812); Sturges v. Crowninshield, 4 Wheat. 122 (1819); M'Millan v. M'Neill, 4 Wheat. 209 (1819); McCulloch v. Maryland, 4 Wheat. 316 (1819); Dartmouth College v. Woodward, 4 Wheat. 518 (1819); Farmers and Mechanics Bank v. Smith, 6 Wheat. 131 (1821). Johnson gave a concurring opinion in Fletcher v. Peck, 6 Cranch 87 (1810). He delivered a concurring opinion in Town of Pawlet v. Clark, 9 Cranch 292 (1815), a case whose inclusion in this list is questionable.

[24]Johnson concurred without opinion in Brown v. Maryland, 12 Wheat. 419 (1827). His concurrence in the second case, Society for the Propagation of the Gospel v. New Haven, 8 Wheat. 464 (1823), is not certain, since that was stated to be the decision only of the majority. Not included in this

with opinion; in two others he regarded the state law as valid in relation to its own citizens in its own courts, but refused to give the law an extraterritorial effect; in only one did he concur in invalidating the state law as internally applied.[25] The transformation that took place in 1822 and 1823 affected not only Johnson's outspokenness but also his willingness to strike down judicially the laws of the states. Only the New York steamboat franchise and the Maryland tax on importers met with his flat repudiation, and both clashed with the commerce power.

By 1830, on the eve of Nullification, Johnson had adopted a restricted conception of the Court's role. Just as he had sought to confine to its own territory and citizens the control of the state, so, too, he had tried to delimit the sphere of judicial action where state internal policy was concerned. Local decisions on state laws[26] and the practices prevailing in local courts were entitled to respect. This point he had put clearly in 1828. Where two governments, each with its system of courts, existed side by side, it was the duty of the national judges "to yield rather than encroach"; the duty was reciprocal and doubtless state judges would show the same spirit of "moderation and comity."[27] The next year, when the majority had approved issuance of a writ of prohibition to state officials, Johnson had dissented; both the Constitution and governmental policy, he declared, had sought to prevent the direct action of the national government on the officials of the states.[28]

discussion are the following decisions, from which Johnson was absent: Boyle v. Zacharie, 6 Pet. 348 (1832); Worcester v. Georgia, 6 Pet. 515 (1832); and Bryne v. Missouri, 8 Pet. 40 (1834).

[25]Johnson dissented with opinion in Osborn v. Bank of the United States, 9 Wheat. 738 (1824); Weston v. Charleston, 2 Pet. 449 (1829); and Craig v. Missouri, 4 Pet. 410 (1830). He concurred on grounds of extraterritoriality in Green v. Biddle, 8 Wheat. 1 (1823), and Ogden v. Saunders, 12 Wheat. 213 (1827). He concurred with opinion in Gibbons v. Ogden, 9 Wheat. 1 (1824).

[26]The latest state adjudication should, he insisted, serve as guidepost to the Supreme Court.—Concurring opinion in Satterlee v. Matthewson, 2 Pet. 380, 415 (1829).

[27]Opinion for the Court, Fullerton v. Bank of the United States, 1 Pet. 604, 614 (1828). Cf. his indignant separate opinion to the same effect in Elmore v. Grymes, 1 Pet. 469, 472 (1828).

In 1824 Johnson diverged from his associates in declaring unsuable a state bank where the state itself was both corporator and stockholder of the bank. The state, he thought, could appear in no other than a sovereign capacity, and hence was immune under the Eleventh Amendment from suit.—Bank of the United States v. Planters' Bank, 9 Wheat. 904, 910 (1824). Subsequently, Johnson capitulated to the majority's holding that the state might divest itself of sovereign immunity but explicitly saved the state law in question from the operation of the constitutional ban on bills of credit.—Bank of Kentucky v. Wister, 2 Pet. 318, 324 (1829). Cf. Johnson's self-conscious separate opinion in Governor of Georgia v. Madrazo, 1 Pet. 110, 124 (1828).

[28]Weston v. Charleston, 2 Pet. 449, 471 (1829). Here Johnson construed the Judiciary Act narrowly in the interest of state judicial autonomy.

Where state laws or decisions appeared to encroach on the federal sphere, there might be a need for review. But the federal judges, in exercising the power to review, could proceed only by express constitutional or statutory authorization. In much of this sphere the judicial power was formidable, especially since Congress, the elected representatives, lacked an ultimate control.[29] The national judges had a duty to proceed with mildness and forbearance, in the interest of the harmony of the republic.

So much for the preliminaries. It is important now to consider this question: How should the judges proceed in those numerous controversies of conflict of power where the Court's jurisdiction was clear and where no extraterritorial application of the contested state laws appeared? Here, again, William Johnson pursued his own course.

From the start the nation and the states, as elements of our dual system, have met in conflict. In the exercise of their reserved powers the states inescapably ran head-on into powers delegated to the federal government, or into limitations imposed on the states.

In approaching these conflicts of power, the majority exhibited most clearly its conception of the Court as ultimate arbiter of the

[29]Chapter V, above, has already analyzed most of Johnson's rulings on the point of jurisdiction. A few of his rulings should be mentioned here, however. As early as 1816, he had fought an effort to confirm in the Court a power to issue compulsory process to state tribunals. Like national vessels on the high seas, the two governments could both act on individuals, but must refrain from issuing commands to each other. For this reason, and because of its regard for the state courts, so important to the "equality and security" of the states, Congress had provided the mild device of removal of cases to federal courts. Only over the lower federal tribunals might the Supreme Court assume the posture of a superior.—Concurring opinion in Martin v. Hunter's Lessee, 1 Wheat. 304, 363, 374 (1816).

See his comments on the role of the Court in interstate controversies.— Opinion for the Court, Burton's Lessee v. Williams, 3 Wheat. 529, 534, 538 (1818).

In 1824, Johnson broke with his brothers by opposing a right in the national bank to sue originally in federal courts. Manifesting a confidence in the states, the Constitution had intended such cases to come up through the state courts; the majority, he said, had resorted to a fiction in attributing a federal question to the case.—Dissenting opinion in Osborn v. Bank of the United States, 9 Wheat. 738, 886 (1824). Cf. his earlier comment to the same effect.—1 Wheat. 380. "The Constitution," he said in the Osborn case, "presumes that the decisions of the supreme tribunal will be acquiesced in; and after disposing of a few questions which the Constitution refers to it, all the minor questions belong properly to the state jurisdictions, and were never to be taken away in mass."—9 Wheat. 887.

In deciding cases before them the judges of the states might on many occasions construe the Federal Constitution, laws and treaties; over these decisions the Supreme Court wielded a revising power. In this broad area of power the Congress and the President had no part. Accordingly, by way of compensation to the states, Johnson sought to delimit the number and variety of cases originating in the lower federal courts. Johnson employed both of Jefferson's canons in supporting this position.—9 Wheat. 896-97, and 885-86.

federal system. The issues assumed many guises. First, the state law under attack would be read as colliding with a power which the Constitution had granted to Congress. The majority would tend to construe the federal power as exclusive—that is, as one which, even in the absence of a congressional exercise, was totally withdrawn from the states. Second, the state law would be interpreted as conflicting with a law of Congress. The judges might concede a concurrent power in the state over the subject, but would read the action of Congress as intended to shut out the states from dealing with the subject. Third, the state law would be read as a violation of a prohibition in the Constitution. The majority's treatment of the contract clause illustrates its tactics here, as shown in the foregoing chapter.

In dealing with all of these—exclusive power, concurrent power, and express or implied prohibition—the Marshallians applied themselves, not so much to expand federal, as to contract state power. This was the mode of judicial prescription. It reflected not merely a hostility to the states but also the belief that the whole problem was essentially legal. The judges took it as their mission to delineate precisely the boundaries separating the two sovereignties for ages to come.

From the start, Johnson chose a different course. Viewing the states as families, each with its peculiar problems and vital needs, he held suspect a purely legalistic conception of the problem. How he would dispose of these conflicts and to whom he would assign the principal task of resolving them will furnish the material for the remainder of this chapter.

The issues arose in seven major decisions of the Supreme Court. The cleavage in the Court first came to light in a case concerning the distribution of judicial power. In Martin v. Hunter's Lessee,[30] the judges pondered the question whether the judicial power of the United States was exclusively vested in the federal tribunals, or whether, in the absence of congressional laws to the contrary, state courts might entertain federal cases originally.

Joseph Story spoke for the majority and by his own testimony with the full approval of Marshall.[31] The judicial power of the nation ought, he said, to be regarded as exclusive. Article III had granted certain powers to the United States and thus imposed on Congress a duty to implement the article by creating courts and vesting in them the whole range of federal jurisdiction. With eyes riveted on the document, and scarcely so much as a glance at the views current in 1789, Story saw there a command to Congress to

[30] 1 Wheat. 304 (1816). See above, pp. 86-88.
[31] Story to George Ticknor, Jan. 22, 1831, Story, *Story,* II, 49.

create federal courts and lodge in them all this power. He proceeded from the assumption that the Constitution was a national compact created by the people of the nation as a unit. Said he of the language of Article III:

> It is the voice of the whole American people solemnly declared, in establishing one great department of that government which was, in many respects, national, and in all, supreme. It is a part of the very same instrument which was to act not merely upon individuals, but upon states; and to deprive them altogether of the exercise of some powers of sovereignty, and to restrain and regulate them in the exercise of others.[32]

The moderate course which Congress had actually pursued, however, forced him to temper his zeal. Congress, he admitted, might have a modicum of discretion in regulating power and jurisdiction.[33]

In concurring, Johnson acknowledged that certain power had been totally relinquished by the states. He referred especially to cases in admiralty and mentioned also the bankruptcy power, although on the latter he did not commit himself. Yet the burden of his argument went to assert the concurrent nature of most of the judicial power. Deploring a purely verbal construction, he found support for his position in the actual practice of Congress.

Instead of envisaging federal and state authorities as essentially foes and hence requiring a meticulous insulation, he repeatedly voiced confidence in the state judiciaries. When the need arose for protecting federal interests, Congress might devise the appropriate safeguards. It was for Congress to decide in what manner to distribute the judicial power.

Until the federal government should decide to assume the ceded power, states might continue to exercise it. Johnson set forth his views on concurrent power in these terms:

> But does it not then follow that the jurisdiction of the state court, within the range ceded to the general government, is permitted, and may be withdrawn whenever Congress think proper to do so? As it is a principle that every one may renounce a right introduced for his benefit, we will admit that as Congress have not assumed such jurisdiction, the state courts may, constitutionally, exercise jurisdiction in such cases.
>
> Yet, surely, the general power to withdraw the exercise of it, includes in it the right to modify, limit, and restrain that exercise.[34]

The defender of state concurrent power found further support in the analogy of international law.[35] The national legislature, he was sure, had acted in this spirit.

[32] 1 Wheat. 328.
[33] *Ibid.*, pp. 336-38.
[34] *Ibid.*, pp. 375-76.
[35] See *ibid.*, p. 376

Johnson was aware of the "sensitive irritability of sovereign states, where their wills or interests clash,"[36] and accordingly here sought to justify modes of safeguarding national interests without judicial dictation to state judges. Characteristically, he insisted that this was a task for Congress, and accordingly sketched out measures Congress might adopt to attain the desired end.[37]

Thus did Story and Johnson lay the groundwork for two rival theories for resolving these conflicts. The majority's theory of judicial prescription not only made the Court the judge in such matters, but subtracted important power from the states, however convenient a concurrent power might prove. Johnson's, on the contrary, was one of congressional selection and regulation. It left power with the parts of the Union until the supreme legislature should find it necessary to withdraw it for the good of the whole. The South Carolinian had lost his first skirmish, but he stood his ground.

Three years passed. In Sturges v. Crowninshield,[38] the judges for the second time faced the issue of exclusive versus concurrent power, now in connection with bankruptcy. The New York Insolvent Debtor Law was up for review. Might the states, in the absence of federal legislation on the subject, exercise a concurrent power to pass bankruptcy laws?

One wing of the Court had already met and disposed of the issue on circuit. Bushrod Washington had emphatically called the bankruptcy power exclusive in Congress.[39] He put the theory of exclusive power in these terms:

> . . . whenever such a power is given to the general government, the exercise of which by the state governments would be inconsistent with the express grant, the whole of the power is granted, and, consequently vests exclusively in the general government.[40]

The key word in the passage was "inconsistent," for judges fearful of state excesses would tend to see all such state powers as likely to be exercised harmfully. Washington disdained the "novel" and "extravagant" doctrine of concurrent power and insisted that the judiciary, in order to avert future conflicts, should set clear

[36]*Ibid.*, pp. 373-74.
[37]See *ibid.*, pp. 381-82.
[38]4 Wheat. 122 (1819).
[39]Golden v. Prince, 10 Fed. Cas. 542, No. 5509 (C.C. Dist. of Pa., 1814).
[40]*Ibid.*, p. 545.

limits to the powers of the two governments.[41] This attitude toward state bankruptcy laws was shared by Joseph Story.[42]

In the Sturges case, however, the Court turned its back on these precedents. Speaking for an ostensibly united bench, the Chief Justice affirmed a concurrent state bankruptcy power. He agreed that in general federal powers which, by express terms or by nature, required the exclusive surveillance of Congress, should be deemed beyond state cognizance. Yet each power was entitled to examination on its own merits. Bankruptcy, he said, was a complex affair and hence required discretion in Congress to act or omit to act as circumstances dictated. To permit the states to act on insolvency, pending national regulation, was to give not a violent but rather a convenient reading to the Constitution.

On this occasion Marshall evidently saw merit in Johnson's esteem for the exigencies of the states. The South Carolinian himself would expound his own views in the Ogden case; even now, however, he felt strongly that Congress should confirm a concurrent state power over bankruptcy.[43] This power, like much of that over judicial affairs, was to him a proper field for state action, subject always to the overriding regulations of the national legislature.[44]

A year later, in 1820, the Court disposed of the third case in the series. Houston *v.* Moore concerned the respective federal and state powers over the militia.[45] During the stress of war, a Pennsylvania militiaman had ignored a presidential summons to serve. A state court-martial thereupon fined him for his dereliction. A state law had authorized these proceedings and imposed as a punishment the penalties prescribed in federal laws for failure to comply with summons. Was this state law in violation of the militia powers of Congress and the many federal statutes passed to implement them?

[41]Said he: "The sooner the limits which separate the two governments are marked by those authorities, which can alone define and establish them, the less danger there will be of serious, if not fatal collisions hereafter, arising respecting essential powers, to which a prescriptive right may be asserted by the one, in opposition to the chartered rights of the other."—*Ibid.*

[42]Van Reimsdyk *v.* Kane, 28 Fed. Cas. 1063, No. 16,871 (C.C. Dist. of R.I., 1812). District Judge Drayton, in Johnson's circuit, had accepted the rule of exclusiveness in bankruptcy cases.—Gill *v.* Jacobs, 10 Fed. Cas. 373, No. 5426 (C.C. Dist. of S.C., 1816).

[43]His model bill drawn in 1820 expressly acknowledged a concurrent power in the states. See above, Chapter VII, note 38.

[44]In 1817, the Court through Marshall assumed the power to pass laws on naturalization to be exclusive in Congress.—Chirac *v.* Chirac, 2 Wheat. 259, 269.

[45]5 Wheat. 1.

The majority approved of the state court-martial. Washington announced the judgment and proceeded to expound his own opinions.[46] He was willing to concede a power in the states over the subject. Yet this Federalist judge felt that Congress, by its statutes, had occupied the field and thereby effectively shut out the states from regulating the militia. To hold otherwise, to permit the states to supplement federal laws in the field, was to embrace a spurious doctrine. To allow both governments simultaneously to deal with the same problem was to invite conflict and to oppress the citizen.[47] Yet Washington found a way out by adopting the position Johnson had taken in the Martin case. The state, he thought, could prosecute the offender on the ground of a concurrent judicial power.

Justice Story, with the evident support of Marshall, filed a lengthy dissent.[48] He was unable to find any power in the state to support the Pennsylvania law. In his mind, Congress had monopolized the militia field through its statutes; he doubted that Congress could have delegated federal criminal jurisdiction to state courts.[49] A contrary ruling, thought he, would open the federal system to numerous hazards, among them the possibility that a citizen might twice be punished for the same offense.

Washington, Story, and Marshall had all treated the militia power as one which Congress, by occupying the field, had withdrawn from state cognizance. They had split only over the question whether the state courts under existing federal laws might punish those who disregarded a national summons to serve.

But William Johnson here struck out on his own. The efforts of his brothers to insulate the two governments from potentially harmful contacts overtaxed his patience. He thrust aside the silence which

[46]In concluding, he said: "Two of the judges are of the opinion that the law in question is unconstitutional and that the judgment ought to be reversed.

"The other judges are of opinion that the judgment ought to be affirmed, but they do not concur in all respects in the reasons which influence my opinion."—*Ibid.*, p. 32. It is therefore doubtful that the decision stands as authority for Washington's views, as intimated by Dr. J. A. C. Grant; see his valuable "The Nature and Scope of Concurrent Power," 34 *Columbia Law Review* (1934), 995, reprinted in *Selected Essays on American Constitutional Law* (4 vols.; Chicago, 1938), III, 784-829, 799-800.

[47]For his comments, see 5 Wheat. 23.

[48]The brother justice who joined in this protest was doubtless Marshall. See Meade v. Deputy Marshal, 16 Fed. Cas. 1291, No. 9372 (C.C. Dist. of Va., 1815), in which Marshall intimated that jurisdiction to try militia delinquents was exclusively vested in federal courts-martial. See also his comment in a letter to Story, dated July 13, 1819, Warren, "Story-Marshall Correspondence, 1819-1831" (cited in Chapter X, note 2), p. 3, stating that the opinion in the militia case was committed to Story and could not be "in better hands."

[49]See 5 Wheat. 68-69.

during these years he was maintaining on other issues and delivered a separate opinion. He attacked incisively the main issue.

Unlike his brother Washington, the South Carolinian saw no reason why both governments might not make punishable the same offense:

> Every citizen of a state owes a double allegiance; he enjoys the protection and participates in the government of both the state and the United States. . . . Where the United States cannot assume, or where they have not assumed, this exclusive exercise of power, I cannot imagine a reason why the states may not also, if they feel themselves injured by the same offence, assert their right of inflicting punishment.[50]

Characteristically, Johnson found examples of the exercise of a concurrent right to punish in "every day's practice."

The former captain of the Charleston Artillery then examined the militia power. The Constitution had divided that power, reserving to the states the appointment of the officers and the training of the recruits. Thus, the United States was made in fact dependent on the states for the assistance of their forces; if the states failed to do their part there was no power in the nation to make up the deficiency. The laws passed by Congress could not reach Houston since he had not entered national service, and hence he was immune from a federal court-martial.

Pennsylvania had supplemented the federal laws with its own sanctions passed by virtue of its concurrent powers. Said Johnson:

> . . . it is contended, that if the states do possess this power over the militia, they may abuse it. This is a branch of the exploded doctrine, that within the scope in which Congress may legislate, the states shall not legislate. That they cannot, when legislating within that ceded region of power, run counter to the laws of Congress, is denied by no one; but, as I before observed, to reason against the exercise of this power from the possible abuse of it, is not for a court of justice. . . .

The present case, he insisted, was an example of the "most honorable and zealous cooperation." Pennsylvania had loyally supported the nation by counteracting deficiencies in the federal laws through laws of its own; the state had shown its disinterestedness by turning the fines it collected over to the United States. Johnson praised Pennsylvania for its action: "To have paused on legal subtleties with the enemy at her door, or to have shrunk from duty under shelter of pretexts which she could remove, would have been equally inconsistent with her character for wisdom and for candor."[51]

By treating the militia power as concurrent and acts of Congress as intending no withdrawal of power, Johnson sidestepped many of

[50] *Ibid.*, pp. 33-34.
[51] *Ibid.*, pp. 45-46.

the perplexities which troubled his brothers. Facing the hard fact of war and the urgent needs it presented, Pennsylvania had cooperated valiantly with the federal authorities. And in case the states under the guise of cooperation should act so as to impede the federal government, "the absurdities that might grow out of an affected cooperation in the states, with a real view to produce embarrassment, furnish the best guaranty against the probability of its ever being attempted, and the surest means of detecting and defeating it."[52] That danger was imaginary. In his protest against "legal subtleties" Johnson here stood alone. But a century later the Supreme Court, in a curiously parallel case, would follow his steps.[53]

By 1820, then, the Court had moderated its pellmell course toward exclusive power. True, the judges seemed agreed that naturalization and certain aspects of judicial power, notably admiralty, were for Congress alone to regulate. Accordingly, Johnson's description of exclusive power as an "exploded doctrine" was an overstatement. The Court at that period took the cases as they came and determined the nature of each power in its turn. Johnson himself was convinced that the states might share in the powers over bankruptcy, federal-question jurisdiction, and militia affairs.

Paradoxically, when the Court came to construe the commerce power, the Charlestonian boldly applied the rule of exclusiveness. In 1824, in Gibbons v. Ogden, Marshall and the majority declined to rest their decision against the steamboat monopoly solely on the ground that the power to regulate commerce was totally consigned to the nation.[54] Johnson, however, felt no doubt about the point; on this score he rejected both the Carolina Negro Seamen Act and the New York monopoly. From the nature and purpose of the grant, from the analogy of commercial regulations under international law, and from the practice of the early Congresses and state legislatures, he deduced the exclusiveness of the commerce power in Congress.[55] The states had totally relinquished a power to

[52]Ibid., p. 36.
[53]"Cold and technical reasoning in its minute consideration may indeed insist on a separation of the sovereignties and resistance in each to any cooperation from the other, but there is opposing demonstration in the fact that this country is one composed of many and must on occasion be animated as one and that the constituted and constituting sovereignties must have power of cooperation against the enemies of all."—Mr. Justice McKenna, in Gilbert v. Minnesota, 254 U.S. 325, 329 (1920).
[54]9 Wheat. 1. For a discussion of the Gibbons and Elkison cases, see Chaper XI.
[55]Note that in Cohens v. Virginia Marshall had already declared, "The powers of the Union, on the great subjects of war, peace, and commerce, and on many others, are in themselves limitations of the sovereignty of the States . . . ."—6 Wheat. 264, 382 (1821). The Chief Justice evidently re-

regulate commerce. On this extreme promontory of power Johnson stood alone.

At the same time, however, he took some trouble to depict other powers which the states might exercise even over articles in commerce. If the "harmony" of the states meant that they must refrain from passing retaliatory commercial laws, this was no reason for destroying their "independence." Accordingly, in the Steamboat case, Johnson defended from assault the ordinary "municipal" powers of the states. An article of commerce might at the same time be regulated by Congress under the commerce power and by the states under these police powers. It was the purpose of the state law that marked its character; while "frankly exercised," these reserved powers could produce no serious clashing.

Once again, Johnson looked at the realities of the problem. Actual practice under the federal system disclosed the technique for avoiding conflicts:

> Hitherto, the only remedy has been applied which the case admits of—that of a frank and candid co-operation for the general good. Witness the laws of Congress requiring its officers to respect the inspection laws of the states, and to aid in enforcing their health laws; that which surrenders to the states the superintendence of pilotage, and the many laws passed to permit a tonnage duty to be levied for the use of their ports. Other instances could be cited, abundantly to prove that collision must be sought to be produced; and when it does arise, the question must be decided how far the powers of Congress are adequate to put it down.[56]

In a single opinion Johnson had assigned to Congress the whole commerce power and at the same time shielded the states in the exercise of their powers over health, safety, and related matters. In addition, he had described the method for avoiding dispute where both governments converged on the same object. The remedy was primarily political, rather than judicial. He had declared himself in lucid terms. Accordingly, he kept his silence in later controversies under the commerce clause.[57] The Supreme Court in after

treated from this stand in relation to the commerce power. See above, pp. 202-3.

For Johnson's treatment of the treaty-making power as exclusive, see above, pp. 201, 206.

[56] 9 Wheat. 238-39.

[57] Although Smith Thompson dissented in behalf of state power, Johnson evidently agreed with the majority, in Brown v. Maryland, 12 Wheat. 419 (1827), probably on the ground of exclusive federal power. In 1829, he was detained in North Carolina for two weeks, due to injuries resulting from a stagecoach accident.—*National Intelligencer*, Jan. 13, 23, Feb. 2, 1829. Doubtless he was present—*ibid.*, March 23, 1829—when the Court decided Willson v. Blackbird Creek Marsh Company, 2 Pet. 245. The language of this all-too-brief opinion mentions protection of the public health as one of the purposes of the law and also points out that the controversy was

years, however, would acknowledge a state concurrent power over certain aspects of commerce. Thereby, it would not only amplify the court's range of discretion, but produce complications for the nation and the states.[58]

Three years after the Steamboat case, the judges resolved their fifth controversy. In Ogden v. Saunders they had again to cope with bankruptcy. William Johnson struck one final and well-directed blow for concurrent power. The two new judges on the Court took a like view of the subject, but Justice Washington cast a longing backward glance at the rule of exclusiveness he had broached so long before.[59]

Johnson, as already shown, held the states impotent to extend their bankruptcy laws beyond their borders. That position furnished a rationale for construing the power of Congress. The nation possessed power to pass "uniform" laws on the subject. Hence, only through national action might laws in behalf of stranded debtors receive a nationwide application. This interpretation, said Johnson, accorded with a high end of the Constitution—"that of making an American citizen as free in one state as he was in another."[60] Thus, it remained for Congress to make up the deficiencies in a state-by-state system of legislation.

The Constitution had coupled the congressional power over bankruptcy with that over naturalization. By comparing the two powers, Johnson provided a touchstone for distinguishing exclusive from concurrent powers. Naturalization, he urged, bore heavily on foreign relations and on interstate harmony; hence, it must lie beyond state control. State bankruptcy laws, when internally applied, had no such external consequences. Here the rule of concurrence was legitimate and salutary.

Jefferson's appointee lashed out at a judicial meddling with the prerogatives of the state legislatures. The advice from the party's founder had found its mark. The same thorough inquiry into the times of the framing which Johnson had employed in the commerce cases he repeated here, but with a contrary effect. Indeed, he came near repeating Jefferson's very words in his resort to a historical construction of the bankruptcy power.[61] Again, in his

---

one between a state and its own citizens. Congress had not seen fit to enter this field through commercial regulations. For conjectures concerning Johnson's attitude toward New York v. Milne, 11 Pet. 104 (1837), see Beveridge, *Marshall*, IV, 583.

[58]Cooley v. Board of Wardens, 12 How. 299 (1851). See comment in Willoughby, *Constitutional Law of the United States* (2d ed.), II, 1004-5.

[59]12 Wheat. 213 (1827). Justices Thompson and Trimble expressly acknowledged a state concurrent power over bankruptcy.

[60]*Ibid.*, p. 274.

[61]See *ibid.*, p. 276. Cf. *ibid.*, p. 278.

zeal to protect state autonomy, Johnson repeated another rule. He said it was a key principle of the Constitution to intrude as little as possible between the citizen and his state government. Accordingly, except for a few general provisions, the governmental functions of the states had been left intact in their relation to the state population and internal matters.[62]

Six years earlier, Johnson had supported implied powers by urging the need of discretion in Congress. The same materials which made up the national government, he now insisted, made up the states.[63] If the nation required discretion, so did the states. Nor were the local lawmakers unlimited. The Court should remember that the interest of each state, public opinion, and a moral sense which would exist even in the worst times would always serve as restraints.[64]

No, the Constitution necessarily placed trust in the states. The ultimate reliance against abuse of this power was "the wisdom and virtue of the state rulers, under the salutary control of that republican form of government" which the Constitution guaranteed to every state.[65]

State officers were responsible to state citizens. To Johnson the fundamental limitation on state powers internally applied was, therefore, election. By the same token the national representative body held the rein on concurrent power; by assuming power through its own action, Congress could to that extent withdraw the corresponding power from the states. Otherwise, the citizen of the state should look to the local legislature for protection.

And the citizen owed a reciprocal obligation to lend support to the state government. That position Johnson took in the sixth case in this series, when one Plowden Weston, a fellow Charlestonian, carried to the Court his argument against a local tax on his United States Bank securities.[66] The city council had included in a general tax law an annual levy of twenty-five cents for every hundred dollars of capital value on high-interest stock of the national bank. The highest court of South Carolina had upheld the tax, and counsel Robert Y. Hayne, arguing for an exemption of the federal securities, had pressed Weston's appeal in the Court at Washington.[67]

[62]*Ibid.*, pp. 280-81.
[63]*Ibid.*, p. 279.
[64]*Ibid.*
[65]12 Wheat. 280.
[66]Weston *v.* Charleston, 2 Pet. 449 (1829).
[67]City Council *v.* Weston, 2 Harper 340 (S.C., 1824). The state court divided by a vote of four to three. Cf. Bulow *v.* City Council, 1 Nott and McCord 527 (S.C., 1819), in which the same court had upheld a somewhat similar tax by a vote of three to one.

The chief precedent against the tax was the McCulloch decision of 1819.[68] Maryland's tax had struck directly at the operations of the Bank, and Marshall had set forth in forceful terms the immunity of federal instrumentalities from state taxation. The power to tax, he said, coining a famous epigram, was the power to destroy. Although the South Carolina tax, by contrast, did not, in the view of the Court, single out federal securities, Marshall and the majority held it void. The tax burdened the borrowing power of the United States; this was an essential power, and if the state could tax at all it might tax so as to cripple the actions of the government.

Johnson and Thompson were of a different mind, and each stated his views in a dissent. The Charlestonian had endorsed the Mc-Culloch opinion, and in return had very probably brought pressure on Marshall to qualify its scope.[69] Johnson now conceded that a state law which was disguised as a tax but which actually obstructed or restrained the borrowing power of the nation would be intolerable. The ordinance, he agreed, was clumsily worded. Its true object was to impose an income tax. It exempted low-interest stock of the Bank and was apportioned to principal and not to interest; all this proved that the law was "conceived in the spirit of fairness, with a view to revenue, and no masked attack upon the powers of the general government."[70]

A generation before, the young lawmaker had cast his vote for a state income tax; now the graying justice thought such a tax "unwise and suicidal."[71] But that was no reason for holding it unconstitutional. Why should not federal securities, he demanded, when they become mixed with other investment holdings of citizens, be taxable along with other capital? Or why should the investor who enjoys a comfortable living from interest on government securities and who receives protection from government be exempted from taxation?

He continued his defense of a state power to exact support from its citizens by challenging Marshall's epigram. His comment was oddly prophetic of the words of a dissenter of later times: "No one imagines that it [the stock] is to be singled out and marked as an object of persecution, and that a law professing to tax, will be per-

---

[68]McCulloch v. Maryland, 4 Wheat. 316. See above, pp. 110, 115-16.

[69]Said Marshall at the close of the McCulloch opinion: "It [this opinion] does not extend to a tax paid by the real property of the bank, in common with the other real property within the state, nor to a tax imposed on the interest which the citizens of Maryland may hold in this institution, in common with other property of the same description throughout the state."—4 Wheat. 436.

[70]2 Pet. 472.

[71]See above, p. 33. 2 Pet. 473.

mitted to destroy. . . .">[72] The real question, he insisted, was not whether federal securities were to be exposed to abnormal burdens, but rather whether they should be assigned exemptions which directly obstructed the taxing and borrowing power of the state. It was the purpose of the state law that gave it its character. Johnson was anxious to uphold the authority of the state if he could do so. Until Congress should act so as to clarify the matter, this was his determined stand.[73]

Johnson's brief for the Charleston levy, however, went unheeded. From the seed of the Weston decision there would sprout a luxuriant growth of tax immunities. In two other federations, Australia and Canada, however, Johnson's attitude would prevail. In the United States, government securities would retain tax immunity, but the analogous exemption of official salaries would in time meet with judicial repeal.[74]

In the Weston case Marshall and Johnson exhibited sharply contrasting attitudes toward the states. The former regarded the states with suspicion, the latter with trust. In 1830, Johnson went the limit in vindicating a law of Missouri. The case was Craig v. Missouri,[75] the last of this series. In most of the previous controversies he had upheld the local measures in the absence of express congressional reservation. In the present instance, as in the contract clause cases, it was an express constitutional prohibition that called for construction.

The State of Missouri in 1821 had authorized its treasury to issue a limited amount of loan office certificates in small denominations and had made these receivable in payment of taxes and debts due the state. Did these certificates fall within the constitutional ban on "bills of credit"? Marshall and the majority held the act in violation of the "plain meaning" of the constitutional text. But

[72]*Ibid.* Cf. Mr. Justice Holmes' comment, "The power to tax is not the power to destroy while this Court sits."—Dissenting opinion in Panhandle Oil Co. v. Mississippi, 277 U.S. 218, 223 (1928). See also a discussion by Mr. Justice Frankfurter, concurring in Graves v. New York, 306 U.S. 466, 487 ff. (1939).

[73]Johnson's concise opinion lends no clue to his attitude toward the effect of a congressional declaration of tax exemption. Statements he made much earlier on circuit might imply that he would hold such an express provision binding on the Court.—Bank of the United States v. Deveaux, 2 Fed. Cas. 692, 693, No. 916 (C.C. Dist. of Ga., 1808).

In dissenting in Shanks v. Dupont in 1830, Johnson came out for congressional action to clarify the confusion in another field—that of naturalization. For his statements stressing the absolute allegiance owed their states by citizens between 1776 and 1789, calling on courts not to dictate bounds to state power in this area, and recommending action by Congress, see 3 Pet. 242, 255, 264.

[74]Graves v. New York, 306 U.S. 466 (1939). On the foreign experience, see *ibid.*, pp. 490-91, and Wheare, p. 101.

[75]4 Pet. 410 (1830).

Johnson found an important state power jeopardized by the decision. Where to draw the line between a legitimate loan and a void issue of currency was the question; Johnson found it difficult in the extreme.

To determine the meaning of the words of the Constitution, Johnson ransacked the writings of the period. He found that some features of the Missouri law brought it close to the forbidden line, yet he would give the state the benefit of the doubt. The law he found an expression of an undoubted power, although in a somewhat doubtful form. ". . . I am bound to believe that it was done in good faith, until the contrary shall more clearly appear."[76]

Here was perhaps his most extreme stand in support of state power. Had the majority decided otherwise, there would have been no power outside Missouri, save the Court itself, capable of cutting down the Missouri law.

But Johnson here remained in the minority. Only one of the two Jackson judges, John McLean, stood beside Johnson and Thompson in issuing separate dissenting opinions.[77] The four-to-three line-up was, however, portentous. The more neutral attitude of the newer men was to become the rule for the Court of the next generation. Small wonder that Marshall, a year later, complained to Story of the "revolutionary spirit" on the Court and expressed fears about seriatim opinions.[78]

In these issues of federalism, William Johnson had acquired an impartial attitude toward the states. Unlike his brothers, this judge assumed the state innocent until proved guilty. Since both the republic and its families might serve the individual and since both operated under restraints calculated to preserve harmony, each was entitled to respect and forbearance. Furthermore, since each must retain power to deal with the ever-changing condition of human life, each should retain room within which to effect reforms and work out through cooperation mutually satisfactory measures.

Accordingly, Johnson had exercised with caution the high prerogative of judicial review. Foreign intercourse or the harmony of the states might require him to act to delimit the geographical sphere of state power or to affirm an exclusive power in Congress. Elsewhere, the Court should abstain from dictating to state authorities and leave it to the supreme national legislature to make adjustments where adjustments were required. Johnson's effort to give Congress control over the states in the exercise of concurrent powers presaged

[76]*Ibid.*, p. 444.
[77]Henry Baldwin, along with Story and Duvall, acquiesced in Marshall's opinion.
[78]Letter dated May 3, 1831, Warren, "Story-Marshall Correspondence," pp. 22-23.

the law of the future. The method of judicial prescription might seem desirable in theory; but the realities of social living in our time have made necessary a different kind of control.[79] The twentieth century has brought a vast proliferation of devices for federal-state cooperation.[80] This trend, so universally accepted today, follows the pattern first sketched out judicially by Mr. Justice Johnson.

Such were William Johnson's conceptions of state rights in the American dualism. The Jeffersonian concern for state autonomy had impelled him to resist at several points the policy pressed by the Marshallians. By 1830 a menace of a different sort was looming up. In meeting it, Johnson would undergo the supreme ordeal of his career.

[79] Cf. Grant, "Nature and Scope of Concurrent Power," p. 829.
[80] See Jane Perry Clark, *The Rise of a New Federalism* (New York, 1938), *passim;* and comments in her preface, *ibid.,* pp. ix-x.

Chapter XIV

"THE HOLY TEMPLE OF OUR UNION"

THE late summer of 1830 brought to Federal Judge Johnson's home near Charleston an invitation of some interest. The leading men of South Carolina were invited to a meeting at Columbia in September to discuss "the important political topics which engage the attention of the people of this state. . . ." Those sponsoring this meeting had expressed their aim more explicitly in resolutions: since a "reckless and usurping majority" in Congress had violated the constitutional compact by adopting the Tariff of 1828, South Carolina must look to her defenses. The scheduled meeting would help "enlighten the citizens, and rouse them to a sense of their injuries."[1] By declaring that the state should take the remedy into its own hands, the letter showed itself the work of those favoring some form of nullification. The invitation came from a committee of five, headed by Johnson's old Princeton classmate, John Taylor. Would Johnson agree to attend this meeting and declare his views publicly on the doctrine of nullification?

William Johnson by this hour had become the Supreme Court's leading champion of state rights. While acknowledging broad controls in Congress, he had resisted the efforts of his brothers judicially to circumscribe the autonomy of the members of the Union. To Johnson the great republic was a community bound into a unity through a myriad of common institutions, attitudes, and interests. Because of these common elements it was safe, and because of the needs of society it was essential, to ascribe wide discretionary powers to the states. Yet some of the bonds which united the sections seemed by 1830 to be losing their strength, and the question arose, whether a federation of the American type could endure without these bonds.[2]

There was irony in Johnson's predicament. His leading associates, Marshall, Washington, and Story, had all long before watched with

---

[1] *Southern Times and State Gazette* (Columbia), reprinted in *Niles Weekly Register*, XXXIX (August 28, 1830), 3.
[2] For a discussion of a community of cultural and social institutions and values in 1787, see John C. Ranney, "The Bases of American Federalism," *William and Mary Quarterly*, 3d ser., III (1946), 1-35.

dismay similar movements for resistance in their own states.[3] The judges had recoiled from these events and had recorded their misgivings in a long train of opinions depreciating state power. South Carolina had remained true to the Union; her spokesman on the Court had accepted national power. But as Johnson's state had begun her steady retreat toward state rights, he had moderated his policy. He had maintained consistency by passing over to Congress much of the task of adjusting federal-state conflicts.

The challenge of nullification, however, was leveled at Congress itself. In pursuit of what it took to be its vital interests, a single state was assailing the acts of the national legislature and asserting the power to obstruct them within its borders. How would Johnson deal with this threat? As controversy led to crisis, and crisis by the end of 1832 to the verge of conflict, how would he regard the central issue? This voluble judge would declare his views on several occasions; he would reveal his considered opinions on the nature of the Union and the role within it of the legislator, the judge, and the citizen. His conduct would follow logically from premises he had laid down during prior years.

By the day on which Johnson received the invitation to the Columbia rally, South Carolina seethed with political ferment. Two rival parties cleft the state; their discussions quickened the public pulse to the fever point. One of these, the "States Rights" party, urged forcible resistance by the state. This group had called the Columbia meeting to help select a legislature committed to vigorous measures. The other, the "Unionist" party, held back, preferring to seek relief through remonstration and amendment of federal laws.

The immediate cause of the trouble was a congressional act of 1828, the "Tariff of Abominations." Pressure politics had secured passage of the law, its proponents showing a remarkable lack of that forbearance which Johnson had so long advocated. The act had boosted import duties in order to protect northern industry. By raising the cost of manufactured goods, it had borne down heavily on southern cotton planters, especially those in South Carolina, who were already hard pressed by the competition of new lands in the Southwest. The sense of grievance was enhanced by the way in which the national authorities had diverted revenues to improvements in the North.[4]

[3]Beveridge, *Life of John Marshall*, II, 402 ff. Cf. Story's comment in 1816, confessing that he had the most "mortifying and self-humiliating" memories of the conduct of Massachusetts during the War of 1812.—Letter to Pinkney, W. Story, *Life and Letters of Joseph Story*, I, 293, 296.

[4]The foregoing discussion has been based on the following works: David Franklin Houston, *A Critical Study of Nullification in South Carolina* (New York, 1896), Chapter III; Chauncey Samuel Boucher, *The Nullification Con-*

Because it seemed oppressive, the tariff also seemed to many unconstitutional. It rested, thought the Nullifiers, on a usurpation of power by Congress. In addition, to many it seemed to establish a precedent which menaced the system of slavery. Not only the economy but the society of the South was at stake. If Congress were allowed to stretch its powers to the point of adopting protection, it might by the same route interfere with slavery.[5]

That this concern over the slave system furnished an ultimate or perhaps subconscious motive is suggested by the leadership of the States Rights party. Among the ablest and most zealous of the movement's organizers were James Hamilton, Robert J. Turnbull, Robert Y. Hayne, and Thomas Cooper. These men had all been shocked by the exposure of the Vesey plot in 1822; most of them had been close to the prosecutions that followed; all had met rebuff or criticism at the hands of the federal judge, William Johnson.[6] One might suppose that the whole affair and the Elkison controversy that followed it had acted powerfully on their minds and led them to challenge broad national powers wherever they discovered them, as endangering the social order.

The States Rights men looked for a shield which their state might use as a safeguard to its vital interests, and John C. Calhoun provided that shield in its finished form.[7] Calhoun, like other older leaders, had earlier supported broad construction. In 1828, however, he secretly helped to draft a manifesto setting forth the theory of a state interposition. As the "South Carolina Exposition and Protest," this was published by the legislature and thereupon became the platform of the movement. The tariff it denounced as an oppressive act of the majority, which the minority, the southern planting interest, was justified in resisting. The state had in convention voluntarily acceded to the constitutional compact. In case the national government violated the compact by usurping power, the state might at another convention denounce the law in question and make arrangements for its defeat within the state. Jefferson and Madison had used parallel language in their campaign against

troversy in South Carolina (Chicago, 1916), Chapter I; Wallace, History of South Carolina, II, Chapter LXXV; and Charles M. Wiltse, John C. Calhoun, Nationalist, 1782-1828 (Indianapolis, 1944), Chapter XXIX.

[5]See Calhoun's comment in his letter to Maxcy, Sept. 11, 1830, Maxcy-Markoe Collection (MSS; Library of Congress), quoted in William M. Meigs, The Life of John Caldwell Calhoun (2 vols.; New York, 1917), I, 419.

[6]See above, Chapter VIII and pp. 197-202.

[7]As early as October, 1828, Hamilton had already used the term "nullification" and had relied on a text from Jefferson.—Wiltse, p. 384.

the Alien and Sedition Acts of 1798, and the names of both were invoked by the Nullifiers.[8]

To achieve their ends, the Nullifiers had to overcome one notable obstacle. The state constitution required a two-thirds majority of the legislature on the calling of a convention, and by the summer of 1830 the party faced a formidable opposition. The previous spring the widely travelled Joel R. Poinsett, frail yet resolute, had returned from a mission to Mexico and apprised President Jackson of his plans. He was returning to his native state, he told Jackson, to enter local politics and combat the "pernicious doctrines" which were afoot there.[9] Before long, Poinsett had drawn to his Unionist party a sizable share of the leadership of Carolina. Among his recruits were not a few of the state's judges[10] and a number of men close to William Johnson. Prominent among the latter was Dr. Joseph Johnson, formerly the local head of the United States Bank, who frequently tendered advice to Poinsett in letters, and deprecated the program of the Nullifiers.[11] Others included former Governor Bennett, Johnson's nephew Edward McCrady, and his young friend Christopher G. Memminger.

There was little liking for the tariff or belief in its validity among the Unionists. Where they diverged from the party of Hayne and Hamilton was over the appropriate remedy. They favored continued protests and appeal to the electorate and the courts, with secession a possible last resort.

Such were the parties which arrayed themselves for the struggle. The contest at this stage was almost wholly a local affair. With the factions agreed on other points, the question of nullification came more and more to the fore as they prepared to contest the October elections to the state assembly.

A prominent feature of the campaign was the public dinner, suitably enlivened by speeches and by toasts. The meeting at Columbia

[8]See *ibid.,* and "South Carolina Exposition," Calhoun, *Works,* ed. R. K. Crallé, (6 vols.; New York, 1855), VI, 43, quoting Madison's report to the Virginia legislature, 1800.

[9]Quoted in J. Fred Rippy, *Joel R. Poinsett, Versatile American* (Durham, 1935), p. 135.

[10]See Wallace, II, 437-38.

[11]A number of these letters are included in the Poinsett Collection (MSS; Historical Society of Pennsylvania). On Feb. 20, 1830, Joseph Johnson wrote Poinsett, urging him to proceed cautiously, intimating that he thought the tariff oppressive, admitting, however, that the pro-nullification group might be wrong in their interpretation of the Constitution. This same correspondent later complained of the unequal distribution of national revenues for state internal improvements.—Letter dated March 22, 1830. He also deplored allusions which the opposition had made to his own connection with the United States Bank and spoke encouragingly of prospects for redress by gradual means.—Letter dated July 17, 1830.

in September would be just such an occasion. To this gathering the States Rights leaders had invited Mr. Justice Johnson.

In pondering over what reply to make during those hot August days, William Johnson must have realized the South's vulnerable position, for he had long been aware of rival sectional interests. In 1822 in a letter to Poinsett he had privately deplored the effect of the embargo laws on agriculture;[12] and in the same year he had observed to Jefferson: "You know the characteristic selfishness to the eastward; it could grasp in its embrace wealth, fame, dominion, everything."[13] New England, it would seem, had economic interests divergent from those of the South and there was a danger that national power and resources would be employed in behalf of the former and against the latter.

In paying public tribute to the dead Jefferson in 1826, Johnson had made what was doubtless an oblique sally at the spending policy of the existing administration. Jefferson, as President, had provided a model for the proper expenditure of public funds. He had sought, in justice, to distribute the revenues equally among the parts of the nation. Although this policy had related to a navy and New England shipping, Johnson's discussion of it might easily be taken as a rebuke to John Quincy Adams.[14] Mr. Justice Johnson must have struck a sympathetic chord in his Charleston audience; the city council had thanked the speaker for his "able and eloquent" eulogy and ordered it published.[15] The judge could comprehend the sense of grievance which was mounting in his state.

Much of the difficulty lay in the preoccupation of the South with agriculture and especially cotton. Perhaps it was to counteract, in a small way at least, the dominance of cotton that Johnson had resumed his earlier interest in diversification of crops. We find Joseph Johnson telling a friend in the spring of 1829: "The judge among the rest, is holding his court. He has lately mounted another hobby, has purchased a little farm and commenced the culti-

[12]In advising Poinsett, then a congressman, concerning the appropriate tactics by which the executive might deal with pirates and smugglers in the Gulf of Mexico, Johnson complained of the ill-effects of "that wretched restrictive system," wished the Virginians might acquire some "commercial ideas," and condemned the Easterners for policies which made "the agriculture of the country nourish with its blood their manufactures and shipping."— Letter dated Jan. 3, 1822, Poinsett Collection (MSS; Historical Society of Pennsylvania; courtesy of the Society).

[13]Johnson to Jefferson, Dec. 10, 1822, Jefferson Papers (MSS; Library of Congress).

[14]See Johnson, *Eulogy on Thomas Jefferson*, p. 28.

[15]*Ibid.*, title page. Joseph Johnson may have had some agency in the Council's action, for he had then been serving as intendant.—Article by J. G. deR. Hamilton, *Dictionary of American Biography*, X, 108.

vation of sugar cane—this . . . is becoming the fashion."[16] In the midst of the ensuing crisis, this versatile planter was to take time to advise the growers of corn and potatoes on the best methods of killing crows and to prepare for others a learned note on the raising of strawberries.[17] Johnson, the citizen, was again promoting forces that might serve to resist the march toward disunion. If such was his motive, he was resisting a flood with a bucket. Cotton had long since triumphed and had enlisted a whole state in its defense. The problem now was not whether, but how, to defend it.

With regard to the legal issue, the judge had long since deprecated extremist doctrines of state rights. True, he had seldom resorted for argument to that passage in the Constitution which makes the Federal Constitution, laws and treaties, the "supreme law of the land."[18] This provision, of course, was the principal single clause in repudiation of nullification. Johnson had preferred to rely on the notion of a cooperating system of sovereignties, federal and state, each having power to deal with individuals, but neither having power to restrain directly the acts of the other.

Nevertheless, as early as 1821, Mr. Justice Johnson from the bench had deplored the "growing pretensions of some of the state courts over the exercise of the powers of the general government."[19] National officials were subject to control only by the national government. And the very next year Johnson had complained to Jefferson of an increasing "anti-federal feeling" in some of the states; among symptoms of this, he expressly noticed an action by Georgia against a federal marshal and a law of Pennsylvania requiring that

[16]Letter to Poinsett, May 23, 1829, Poinsett Collection (MSS; Historical Society of Pennsylvania; courtesy of the Society).

[17]William Johnson, "Rural Economy; On the Killing of Crows," *Charleston Courier,* April 27, 1831; Johnson delivered his treatise on the strawberry in his capacity as president of the Horticultural Society of Charleston. He praised the many uses for the strawberry, urged its wide planting as a native product, examined the origins and history of the fruit, and, in the manner of a modern Department of Agriculture bulletin, described the most effective methods of cultivation.—William Johnson, "Memoire on the Strawberry," *The Southern Agriculturist,* V (1832), 568-77.

[18]Art. VI.

[19]Opinion for the Court, M'Clung *v.* Silliman, 6 Wheat. 598. A citizen had gone to a state court for a mandamus to an official of a federal land office; the state court had taken jurisdiction, but had denied the petition on the merits. Johnson regarded this action of the state court in assuming jurisdiction as illegal. Congress, he said, had not delegated the power to issue mandamus to federal officials to its own courts; much less could such a power be contended for in state courts. The federal official could only be controlled by the power that had created his office. Johnson insisted: "Whatever doubts have from time to time been suggested, as to the supremacy of the United States, in its legislative, judicial or executive powers, no one has ever contested its supreme right to dispose of its own property in its own way."— *Ibid.,* p. 605.

state officials defy the process of federal courts.[20] All this, combined with other considerations, had driven Johnson to approve implied powers.

In his "Philonimus" papers of 1823, Johnson had taken Turnbull, Holmes, and others to task for insisting on the validity of the Negro Seamen Act. Deeming that act invalid, he had denied that the state could constitutionally exercise final judgment as to the necessity of the act and continue to enforce it. He branded the arguments of those earlier opponents as wholly revolutionary.

The judge pressed this same theme in 1828 after the appearance of Turnbull's *Crisis* papers. Over the name "Brutus," Turnbull had fulminated against the principle of protective tariff and denounced the march of broad construction generally. The interests of the North he deemed hostile to those of the South, and a southern minority might soon find itself the prey of a northern majority in Congress. Hence, the state should pursue the principles of state sovereignty and strict construction at all costs. The pamphlet would soon become the manifesto of the Nullification Movement.

In replying to Turnbull, Johnson significantly chose the name "Hamilton." The series, which originally appeared in the *Courier,* and later as a pamphlet of over one hundred pages, gave a masterly analysis of the federal system and a frank revelation of Johnson's political theory. At the outset, he laid his finger on the basic point of difference between Turnbull and himself. "My philosophy teaches me," he declared, "that he who adopts in judging his fellow men the more liberal side of the question is after all most likely to be right."[21]

Although Johnson conceded the rapid growth of northern manufacturing and even predicted that American industry would, in time, outstrip that of England, he refused to agree that the economic interests of the North were incompatible with those of the South.

---

[20]Johnson to Jefferson, Dec. 10, 1822, Jefferson Papers (MSS; Library of Congress). On the Georgia law, cf. Warren, *The Supreme Court in U.S. History,* I, 353-55. There is no reason to doubt that Johnson had concurred in Marshall's opinion in United States *v.* Peters, 5 Cranch 115 (1809), which upheld federal power against the opposition of Pennsylvania.

[21]Hamilton (pseud.), *Review of a Late Pamphlet under the Signature of "Brutus"* (Charleston, 1828) (copies at Library of Congress and Harvard), p. 7. The influence of Johnson's friend, Mathew Carey, is evident both in the argument presented in behalf of protective tariff and in the pseudonym. Carey, too, frequently chose this pen name. The numbers first appeared in the *Charleston Courier,* between Nov. 14, 1827, and Feb. 12, 1828. No. 18, on slavery, was added in the pamphlet edition, making a total of twenty-nine numbers. The minute books of the Federal Circuit Court in Savannah show that although Johnson was otherwise regular in attending the semiannual sessions of that Court, he failed to turn up for the sitting of Nov. 26–Dec. 8, 1827, preferring doubtless to remain in Charleston to work on the letters. Turnbull's *Crisis* papers were published in Charleston in 1827.

The nation would profit by a multiplicity of diverse interests, and measures injurious to one would be seen to injure all.

In theory, Johnson traced the federal system to the will of the whole people acting in the only convenient way they could act—through state conventions. The government at Washington was, therefore, entitled to a broad choice of means in pursuing national objectives. One by one, the leading powers of the national authorities—commerce, treaty-making, war, and appropriating for the general welfare—came up for treatment; all received a wide reading.

And Johnson buttressed theory with constant allusions to experience. Even if, abstractly considered, his theory might be doubted, he said, the long-sustained practice of the government furnished a sufficient justification. From 1789 on, those who had actually held the reins of power had found broad construction of national powers indispensable. Strict construction he identified as essentially a minority doctrine; even Jefferson, once in power, had had to forsake it when confronted by the realities of domestic and international politics.

Turnbull's doctrine, he insisted again and again, could lead only to sectional contention, discord, and war. It was not the tariff principle, but the system of slavery that furnished the greatest threat to the Union. The menace came less from what Congress might do to slavery than from the divergent opinions held by some Northerners and Southerners on the question. He pleaded for an end to name-calling and vituperation and a calm dispassionate discussion in the interest of mutual understanding.

As a prediction of events which his century would unfold, the pamphlet has a moving irony. As a prophetic commentary on constitutional interpretations which our century would adopt, it is startling in its accuracy.

Now, in 1830, his state was asserting to the hilt the pretensions he had complained about. Whenever it should be attempted, nullification could only result in obstructions to the enforcement of federal laws. Mr. Justice Johnson, as the superior federal judge in the state, might be the first to become enmeshed in the fracas. That was anything but a pleasing prospect.

Nevertheless, after weighing all the issues, William Johnson thrust himself into the Nullification controversy. On the last day of August, he sat down to pen a terse reply to the invitation. He told Taylor, his fellow-Princetonian of the class of 1790, that he was uncertain why he had been asked to appear. Perhaps it had been a mark of respect, perhaps a jest. Yet if given a hearing, he would appear at the dinner. He would state his case to those whose minds were still "in a state for thinking." His position he condensed into eight points:

1st. That the protection of domestic manufactures was an avowed leading and necessary object of the Constitution.

2. That it never was lost sight of, but always relied upon as the capacity of the country to produce developed itself.

3. That the late attempts on a large scale grew out of a succession of such developments and a state of things resulting from changes in the application of labor, which imperatively required of every wise government to adopt such a course of policy.

4. That Carolina has not only not been injured but really benefitted to many thousands by the tariff.

5. That no state in the Union is more deeply interested in maintaining the principles of the tariff.

6. That nullification is folly, and the peaceable course projected under it, all a silly and wicked delusion.

7. That it grows out of a deliberate conspiracy against the union, which has been steadily working upon us for the last six years, though very few are in the secret.

8. That a convention is the grand end and aim and agent of that conspiracy.

Johnson ended his brief note with a flourish:

My friend, you have much at stake, and you are not the man whom I would think to frighten or wish or hope to deceive. Before Almighty God, I declare to you that I believe all the above propositions to be true; and you have my permission, nay, request, to publish this with my name to it, for I am in earnest.

Yours affectionately, . . .[22]

This extraordinary statement is noteworthy on two grounds. On the one hand, it reveals Johnson to have ranked among the very few leaders in the state who supported the tariff. He evidently believed that protection, by furthering the industrial revolution, would expand national production and thereby benefit even languishing South Carolina. That he should have deemed protection constitutional is no surprise, in view of his expansive reading of congressional power.[23]

[22]*Niles Register,* XXXIX (Oct. 2, 1830), 98, reprinted from the *Columbia Telescope.* Niles's version of the first point has been corrected to conform with a copy appearing in the *Charleston Mercury,* Sept. 21, 1830.

[23]Johnson and Thomas Grimké have been listed as among the few Unionists who approved the tariff.—John G. Van Deusen, *Economic Bases of Disunion in South Carolina* (New York, 1928), p. 35, n. 3. Johnson's construction of the commerce clause alone would seem to cover the case of the tariff.— See above, pp. 194-96, 203-5. Although Johnson's views on the constitutional point were also held by James Madison, not for near a century would the Supreme Court rule directly on the point.—Hampton *v.* United States, 276 U.S. 394 (1928); cf. Willoughby, *Constitutional Law of the United States* (2d ed.), II, 680-81.

More significant here were his views on a second subject—the nature and origins of Nullification. The state veto on federal laws he deemed ineffectual and likely to lead to disaster. Those instigating the movement were engaged, in his view, in a conspiracy. In 1823, Johnson had encountered judicially the South Carolina Association and had deprecated its activities. By July, 1824, just six years previous to his letter to Taylor, he was deploring his inability to thwart enforcement of the revised Seamen Act. The Constitution, he then complained, was being "trampled on by a set of men who, I sincerely believe, are as much influenced by the pleasure of bringing its functionaries into contempt, by exposing their impotence, as by any other consideration whatever."[24] Presumably, it was the same men to whom Johnson now attributed the drive for nullification.

To that theme Johnson recurred in a second letter. A fortnight and more had passed, and no reply had come from Taylor. With but four days remaining before the dinner at Columbia, Johnson at last sent off a politely worded declination. To the committee on arrangements he expressed his pleasure at the honor of being invited and his confidence that this meeting, unlike others, would go off without "intemperate toasts."[25]

Although unable to attend in person, he would present his views in writing. He was entirely opposed, he said, to the theory of nullification, to use a "barbarous and novel term." As for a convention, that would prove perilous and completely ineffectual unless the state wished to secede. Johnson came back to his earlier charge:

> And while I believe that nine tenths of those who favor the measure, are as honest in being disposed to favor it, as I am in my opposition to it, yet I must be permitted to say, that I most sincerely fear, that there are among us those who press the calling of a convention, for the distinct purpose of so embroiling our relations with the general government, as to involve the latter in the dilemma, of either abandoning the reins of government altogether, or of maintaining it by force. In the latter case they flatter themselves that the states, or some of them, will take part with us, and thus in either case, a dissolution of the union would ensue. If there are any such, I trust that they are very few in number, and must think them only fit to be consigned to the care of the regent of the lunatic hospital.[26]

[24]Johnson to J. Q. Adams, July 3, 1824 (cited above, Chapter VIII, note 18).
[25]Letter dated Sept. 16, 1830, *Niles Register*, XXXIX (Oct. 16, 1830), 132, reprinted from *Charleston Courier*, Oct. 1, 1830. Johnson evidently thought Taylor was chairman of this committee. Said Johnson, referring to certain other banquets being held at this period: "I would as soon be privy to intoxicating a jury, that sat upon a case of life and death, as be partaker of a feast" of that kind.—*Ibid.*
[26]*Ibid.*

He was sure no other state would join his in a secession movement. Furthermore, he resented the charge of submissiveness and
fear then being leveled at the Unionists. Both parties could lay claim
to honesty, patriotism, and independence of mind. "Our fear,"
he exclaimed, "is the fear of God, and of disgrace, and of public
calamity; our submission, submission to our consciences."

In closing, Johnson proposed a toast for delivery at the meeting.
In it, he expressed succinctly his opinion of the doctrine and leadership of the Nullification Movement: "*The generous feelings of my
countrymen*—Elevation of character is conspicuous in its most
irregular movements. May it never be misdirected by false reasoning,
false calculations, false pride, or false men."[27] This denunciation,
one may assume, went undelivered at the dinner in Columbia.

The very next day a communication from Taylor reached Johnson. The August letter had nettled the old friend, and now this
erstwhile governor and United States Senator deplored the eight
points. Taylor said that, had he had his way, he would have withheld the invitations to the federal judges in the state. He deemed
it completely improper for those judges to "come down and mix in
the common fight, in the discussion of subjects which may, and in
all probability will, come before them for adjudication. . . ."[28]
Taylor alluded icily to the conduct of the Federalist judges during
the prosecutions under the Sedition Act. As a member of the "conspiracy," he would welcome Johnson's appearance at the dinner;
he and the others at the meeting would listen attentively in a case
in which the judge became "accuser, witness, and advocate" against
them.

After this telling rebuke, Taylor took up the main point. He was
out of public life for good, he said, but nonetheless he earnestly
wished his state to continue pursuing that "great desideratum,
a tribunal (other than that on which you sit) which shall have
power and weight enough to prove *an obsta principiis, to the usurpa-
tions of the general government, in despite of the constitution and
in despite of the rights of the states.*"[29] It was better, cried Taylor
invoking the name of Jefferson, to dissolve the Union than to sub-

[27]*Ibid.*
[28]John Taylor to Johnson, Rice Creek, Sept. 11, 1830, *Niles Register,*
XXXIX (Oct. 2, 1830), 98-99, reprinted from *Columbia Telescope.* One observer thought Thomas Cooper had drafted Taylor's reply: "It appears
Judge Johnson, who has his own way of doing things, has got into a scrape
with his old crony, Judge Cooper, and honest John Taylor, signs his name
to a cutting epistle from the old Jacobin."—Item signed "Lookers-on," *City
Gazette,* Sept. 24, 1830.
[29]Taylor to Johnson, Sept. 11, 1830, *Niles Register,* XXXIX, 99. The italics
are Taylor's.

mit to a government of unlimited powers. "If this is conspiracy," said he in closing, "make the most of it."[30]

This challenge brought a softened response from the judge. Although a spirit of friendship fought with an indignant defensiveness throughout this long third letter, the tone of it generally was moderate. Johnson said he would be willing, after the October elections, to resume the dispute in the press, but preferred to let it rest. Although he would unwillingly forego his "feeble efforts to reconvert the state" through the newspapers, he would do nothing to weaken his lifelong comradeship with Taylor.[31]

In addition, Johnson now somewhat blunted his accusation of conspiracy. He even intimated that he, too, would favor a separation if he understood the facts in the same terms as Taylor: "I would not live under a government of unlimited powers, and if I saw distinctly that nothing but a revolutionary movement could impose due restrictions, I would cry out for revolution."[32] He had meant no reproach by his charge.

The evidence of such a combination, he said, was before the public. Although legal proof might be difficult to procure, he was convinced that there had been enough published to establish the existence of a "fixed purpose and zealous co-operation among some of our citizens to get rid of the Tariff Act or get rid of the Union." Yet he attached no moral imputation to his assertion. Those who genuinely thought the national government tyrannical should take no offense at the charge. "Shall there be a Caesar and no Brutus, no Cassius, no Casca, found among us!" Only the motive could characterize the act. Continuing to pour oil on the troubled waters, Johnson suggested that there was no reason to suppose Congress would not moderate the tariff system.[33]

Taylor had wished to see an impartial umpire established over the federal system. William Johnson now showed him that such an umpire already existed. It was not the Supreme Court, but a branch of the Congress. His statement expresses eloquently the

[30]*Ibid.*

[31]Johnson to John Taylor, Sept. 22, 1830, *Niles Register*, XXXIX (Oct. 9, 1830), 120, reprinted from *Columbia Telescope*. Said Johnson of the dinner: "Where were the men who now claim to be radicals and exclusive patriots, when you and I stood shoulder to shoulder in the stormy days of ultra federalism? and more recently in that universal homage now rendered to the talents and worth of our friend Crawford, by men who revelled in the most wanton abuse of him, when you and I stood up for him almost alone."— *Ibid.*, p. 119.

[32]*Ibid.*, p. 119.

[33]Said he: "As to those who press the alternative upon the people, of either compelling a repeal of the tariff or positive resistance, if there are any such who know or believe that congress cannot and will not recede, I leave them to settle with their own consciences how near this approached to a distinct effort to dissolve the union."—*Ibid.*, p. 120.

lengths to which he was now pushing his judicial restraint and his deference to the supreme legislature of the land:

As to affording the states some more satisfactory security than the intervention of the supreme court, it is what I have been urging for years.—Rest assured that we are far from coveting jurisdiction, especially where states are concerned. Heaven save us from encountering the irritable feelings of sovereigns. But I have always been met by the question— What can the states want more than the senate? They are all there equally represented, and every law which passes that body involves a decision on its constitutionality—a decision made by a body sworn to decide impartially, and in which the smallest state has as much weight as the greatest. To this I have never been able to find but one answer, and that is, that as to one class of cases that tribunal is not accessible. I mean cases in which the constitutionality of state laws is brought in question. There I would certainly amend the constitution so as to give an appeal to the senate; and perhaps require the concurrence of two-thirds to declare the law of a state unconstitutional. At present, although we are emphatically *the men of the people,* being charged exclusively with the protection of individual rights against unconstitutional laws, yet indirectly we are compelled to pass upon the delicate question of sovereign right, from which may heaven deliver us.[34]

Under the impact of the drive toward state rights, Johnson had lost confidence in the utility of judicial review. A generation earlier, John Marshall at a moment of stress had broached to a friend the wisdom of appealing judicial decisions to Congress.[35] But the younger justice spoke out publicly on the point.

That Johnson should have attributed broad discretion to the Senate in the adoption of national laws should bring no surprise. In the Anderson case he had rested that discretion on the exigencies of government, and in 1824 he had seemed to sanction judicial review of congressional laws only where the broad purposes of the Constitution were clearly violated.[36] The appeal to the Senate of decisions against state laws, however, was another matter. This very proposal Johnson had privately rebutted, not without cogency, as late as 1822, and had termed it a "plausible, pestiferous project."[37] That he should now advocate so profound a change shows how thorough the 1823 shift of position had been.

[34]*Ibid.,* p. 119. The italics are Johnson's.

[35]Marshall to Samuel Chase, Jan. 23, 1804, Etting MSS (Historical Society of Pennsylvania), quoted in Beveridge, *Marshall,* III, 177-78.

[36]See above, pp. 120 and 165-66.

[37]In his letter to Poinsett of Jan. 3, 1822, he had described the proposal in these terms: "On the subject of the proposed amendment to the Constitution in transferring jurisdiction to the Senate in certain cases, I think the party espousing it have compleatly laid bear [*sic*] their side to the army of their

Here again Jefferson's appeal for responsible government had borne fruit. The state legislatures at that date elected the Senators and to a degree might hold them accountable. What better, then, than to assign to the Senate a final decision on the validity of state laws?

The proposal was, however, a counsel of extremity. Even if such an amendment could be procured, an unlikely possibility, South Carolina would have found it an inadequate safeguard. She sought not a protection for state laws but a defense against federal. She stood in the minority and accordingly felt her vital interest jeopardized by the majority. To give the majority, or even two-thirds, of the states a veto on state laws would fall far short of her requirements. Yet this was Johnson's major concession to the advocates of state resistance.

In this same letter, the last of his interchange with Taylor, the judge displayed some trepidation over his earlier declaration about the constitutionality of the tariff. He tried, rather lamely it must be admitted, to extricate himself from that aspect of the controversy and even denied having announced his position on the point.[38]

On the central issue he still thought he was in the right. Although he doubted that anyone else in South Carolina agreed with him in as many as seven of his eight points, he was sure all would eventually agree with him in all eight. "You know," he told his friend, "the course of my public life. I have more than once before been in a

opponents. You recollect sometime ago T. Pickering then a Senator, very gravely proposed that he and others should draw for the Presidency—That they are not the safest body in the world to trust the *salus populi* to is proved by their conduct suspending the Habeas Corpus Act at the suggestion of Mr. Jefferson in the affair of Bollman and Swartout on half an hour deliberation and now they would present us with a singular anomaly in jurisprudence; that they should constitute a tribunal when the states assent, and nearly all of their Senators admit the right of the legislatures to instruct their Senators. A curious state of things would result while a parcel of automatons were deliberating on a question involving the rights or the whims of a state, every legislature in the Union would be trying the question ex parte on some motion to instruct their Senators. But it is even worse than this, for as the resolution proposes that any state may volunteer in any question before the Senate we should at once see the floor of the Senate converted into the arena of faction and state wrangles. It is a plausible pestiferous project."—Poinsett Collection (MSS; Historical Society of Pennsylvania; courtesy of the Society).

[38]After agreeing that no invitation should have been sent him, and for the reason given by Taylor, Johnson said he thought it had been a hoax and had treated it accordingly. He continued: "There is one thing I must beg you particularly to notice. I do not mean to suffer myself to be drawn into the question of construction and constitutionality of the tariff act. I see that in my first point I have written *Constitution*, where I ought to have said *convention*: but the context will correct the lapsus. I will treat the subject historically, and no [sic] otherwise, and then if I find I have even approached the subject of construction, I will not sit judicially upon a cause arising under it."—*Niles Register*, XXXIX, 119.

minority, to all appearances as hopeless as the present, *aye even on the election of Jackson to the presidency*." The cantankerous William Johnson was by habit a dissenter; and now, no less than earlier, he would persevere in his solitary course.

The federal judge had declared himself on nullification. Deeming the whole affair essentially political, he had doubted the effectiveness of a settlement through the medium of the judiciary.[39] On the other hand he had treated the theory of a state veto as ill-considered and as dangerous in operation. Henceforth, he would hold his peace. Taylor had scolded him for his unjudicial conduct and many southern papers had echoed the criticism.[40] These reproofs must have strengthened his determination to keep silent in the future.

Judge Johnson had twice invoked Heaven to save him from the "delicate question" of sovereign power. With this request Heaven failed to comply. Twice during the ensuing struggle Johnson ran headlong into efforts by the Nullifiers to obstruct federal laws. On both occasions a right of the individual was at stake, specifically, trial by jury.

The first of these controversies came on appeal to Johnson's court in the spring of 1832. This was the celebrated Bond case.

As early as the summer of 1830 extremists in the States Rights party were considering the defeat of the tariff through the medium of juries.[41] In the October elections that year the party captured the legislature by a narrow margin. Thus, it was able to carry a set of pro-nullification resolutions, and under the new governor, James Hamilton, to set about educating the voters for the next election two years hence. The two-thirds requirement for the summoning of a nullifying convention remained its principal obstacle.[42]

South Carolina continued in turmoil during 1831. On July 4, the Unionists received the first clear intimation that Jackson would take their side if a crisis came.[43] That news must have confirmed Wil-

---

[39]It is likely that the prospect of a collision in South Carolina influenced Johnson in his treatment of the issue in Cherokee Nation *v.* Georgia, 5 Pet. 1 (1831).—See above, pp. 88-89. The Cherokee controversy he regarded as wholly political.

[40]Thus, the *North Carolina Journal* (Fayetteville), called Johnson's conduct "alarming, and highly reprehensible."—Reprinted in *Charleston Mercury,* Sept. 29, 1830. The *Georgia Courier* (Augusta) remarked, "as prejudices now run in Carolina, against the Supreme Court, it would have been much the more prudent course for him to have given a very different answer to the polite invitation he received."—*Mercury,* Oct. 1, 1830. Cf. comments from the *Camden* (S.C.) *Journal* and the *Richmond Enquirer* in *Mercury,* Oct. 1, 1830.

[41]See a comment ascribed to George McDuffie.—Thomas Ritchie to his brother, June 8, 1830, *Branch Historical Papers,* III, 207-9, quoted in Meigs, I, 416-17.

[42]Boucher, pp. 100 ff.

[43]Jackson's letter of June 14, 1831 was read at a large party rally in Charleston.—Boucher, pp. 149-53.

liam Johnson's enthusiasm for Jackson, whose administration was the first he supported wholeheartedly. In August, after toying with the idea of a visit to the France of Louis Philippe, he was attending a dinner for Jackson's new cabinet in Washington.[44] The Unionists and Johnson with them could rely on Old Hickory.

Nevertheless, the States Rights party, now with the open support of Calhoun, pressed ahead. Its present tack was to refer the validity of the tariff to a South Carolina jury. Isaac Holmes and Alexander Mazyck, two lawyers from the party's fold, imported a bale of English woolen cloth. Bonds to the amount of $137 were given as security for payment of the protective duties. When payment was refused, District Attorney Gilchrist sought execution on the bonds.[45] The case came before United States District Judge Thomas Lee in September. Before a thronged courtroom, leaders from both camps debated the propriety of presenting the tariff question to the jury.[46]

In an atmosphere tense with excitement, Judge Lee gave his decision. With dignity and learning, he ruled against summary process.[47] Liberally construing the Constitution, he let the question of the existence of the bonds go before the jury. The question of the constitutionality of the tariff, however, was not in his opinion proper for a jury to decide. Thus restricted, the jury brought in a verdict for the government.

Judge Lee warned that the case would settle but little. The government, if bonds proved insecure, could easily exact cash in payment of duties. "All this excitement . . . all these long and learned discussions" would achieve nothing. Appeal, he said, would lie only to the Circuit Court, which his brother Johnson would soon hold; but neither court could settle finally the point of law, since the smallness of the amount involved would prevent appeal to the Supreme Court. Said he:

> Why agitate this question when no possible good can result from it? It is not an accidental case, it is one avowedly made

[44]*Charleston Courier*, Aug. 26, 1831. In June, Joseph Johnson added this postscript to a letter to Poinsett: "My brother Willm talks strongly of a trip to France in a few days to see the culture of beets and grapes—I think he will go."—Letter dated June 6, 1831, Poinsett Collection (MSS; Historical Society of Pennsylvania; courtesy of the Society). But court business evidently kept the judge in Charleston, for he was holding court in July.—Minutes C.C. Dist. of S.C., Bk. C, pp. 346-55.

[45]Gilchrist's predecessor had refused to seek execution and was dismissed for his neglect.—Jackson to Van Buren, July 23, 1831, Jackson, *Correspondence* ed. J. S. Bassett (7 vols.; Washington, 1926-1935), IV, 316.

[46]Holmes and George McDuffie were counsel for defendants; Gilchrist and James L. Petigru, for the government.

[47]United States *v.* Holmes and Mazyck (Dist. of S.C., 1831), *Charleston Courier*, Sept. 24, 1831, reprinted in *Niles Register*, XLI (Oct. 8, 1831), 119. On Thomas Lee, see J. B. O'Neall, *Bench and Bar of South Carolina*, I, 87-101.

for the purpose of calling in question the constitutionality of
the Tariff Act of 1828. . . . Let a verdict in the case be one
way or the other, it must be evident to all who hear me, that it
will be unimportant, inconclusive, settling no point.[48]
This decision was anathema to the States Rights party. The very
next day, despite "tempestuous weather," that group convoked a
mass meeting in Charleston to thank defendant lawyers and denounce
Lee for depriving his fellow-citizens of a jury test of "that oppressive act under which they have long and so dreadfully suffered."[49]

One may readily suppose that such a test by a Charleston jury
would have gone against the tariff. The meeting resolved that all
hope of judicial redress was now gone; it was useless to appeal,
since the known opinion of the federal Circuit Court supported protection.

Yet an appeal to Johnson's court was made. Just why it was made
is unclear. Johnson's letters to Taylor had received wide circulation.
For example, an anonymous pamphlet, sometimes ascribed to Thomas Cooper, had taken note of Johnson's earlier stand. A certain Nullifier, went this satirical tale, was pursuing his course through a Hell
peopled mainly by cunning and greedy Yankees. At one point
he encountered sinners being roasted for the Devil's feast. There
he saw among the "unlucky wights being thus converted into roasters
. . . a high dignitary of the bench, and author of a big book, upon
a spit made expressly to suit him, with *eight points*."[50] Johnson's
outburst of the previous year had become common talk. Doubtless
defendants pressed their appeal in the belief that an adverse decision would strengthen their standing with the public.

In any event, counsel had ample time in which to prepare their
briefs. That autumn Mr. Justice Johnson fell ill and was confined in
Raleigh throughout the winter. On this account he not only missed
a full term of the Supreme Court but was detained from his circuit
duties until spring.[51]

[48]*Niles Register,* XLI, 123.
[49]*Ibid.,* p. 124.
[50]*Memoirs of a Nullifier: Written by Himself* (Columbia, S.C., 1832), p.
49. Dr. Malone contends that Cooper was not the author of the work.—See
Malone, *Public Life of Thomas Cooper,* p. 406. An anonymous writer after
the District Court decision spoke thus of Johnson's probable attitude: "It
has . . . been stated in the papers, that his opinion on this important question has been openly avowed, and that opinion is in favor of the constitutionality of the Act; nevertheless, on a fair, full and solemn argument before him, he might change his opinion and honestly and conscientiously
decide that the act is unconstitutional."—Letter signed "Cujus," *City Gazette,*
Oct. 1, 1831.
[51]The *Charleston Courier,* for Nov. 21, 1831, quoted a Raleigh newspaper to the effect that Johnson had been seriously indisposed in that place
for several weeks. Joseph Story wrote in March, 1832, that Johnson had

It was June before the Charleston papers spread Johnson's opinion in the Bond case over their pages.[52] The judge emphatically affirmed Lee's September ruling. In a long and technical opinion he explored general principles and authorities from the time of Coke to prove the weakness of the defendants' resort to the jury.[53] He sidestepped the issue of congressional power.[54] His aim was not to uphold the tariff, but to maintain that the construction of statutes belonged to the judge—and the Constitution was a "statute of the highest order."

Counsel for the States Rights side had sought to bind the Court to follow the practice of the state courts relative to pleadings and reference to the jury. With this Johnson refused to comply. The state might prescribe the *lex loci,* but the forensic law, regulating the practice of the Court, lay within the sphere of federal judicial power. The Constitution had, he said, created a separate judiciary for the nation with power to execute national laws and to protect the constitutional rights and the interests of foreigners and citizens of other states. This necessitated that in administering justice the federal courts be free from state control, legislative or judicial.

In earlier years William Johnson had stood firmly for the right of jury trial and likewise the desirability of federal judges' employing state court practices.[55] Both of those considerations he now sought to place in their true light.

Thus, he first insisted that questions of law belonged to the judge, and those of fact to the jury. This rule he deemed cardinal.[56] To assign to the jury the task of construing laws would prove fatal to the jury itself. Concerning this proposal, Johnson declared:

> It is in my opinion destructive of the first principles, and of the greatest utility of jury trials, and calculated to bring them

been absent from the Court the whole term, and said: "If half the accounts I hear of him are true, he is in a bad way in point of health. He has been confined the whole autumn and winter at Raleigh, N.C., and is about going southward, or just gone."—Story to Professor Ashmun, March 1, 1832, Story, *Story,* II, 91. By April Johnson was back in Charleston writing to Washington for his salary check.—Letter to Richard Smith, cashier of the Washington branch of the United States Bank, April 12, 1832, Conarroe Papers (MSS; Historical Society of Pennsylvania).

[52]Holmes *v.* United States (C.C. Dist. of S.C., 1832), *City Gazette,* June 9, 1832. The arguments of counsel Holmes and Gilchrist had by consent been submitted in writing on a bill of exceptions.

[53]*Ibid.*

[54]Johnson did, however, state that counsel for defendants had tried to declare it to be a fact in evidence that the bond covered a duty imposed to protect manufactures and had then argued ingeniously although obscurely in favor of a construction of the Constitution "by which the supposed spirit or intent of it was to overrule its express enactments."—*Ibid.*

[55]See above, pp. 134-35 and 238.

[56]Said he "We [the Court] will not invade the limits of the jury, nor must they be permitted to pass ours. Both innovations would equally conduce to destroy the trial by jury."—*City Gazette,* June 9, 1832.

into odium—to make them unpopular and impair their utility! They were intended to be auxiliary to the execution of our laws, and not to be the tools and instruments of casual excitements, for embarrassing the administration of those laws.[57]

Second, whatever might be the practice of the state courts, the Circuit Court, Johnson insisted, was controlled by the rules of the United States Supreme Court. Parties must present their cases according to the "forms of law." Wherever possible, it was his aim to simplify these forms. But the rule contested for was beyond consideration. He would repel it.[58]

Thus the curtain fell on the Bond case. Johnson and his brother Lee had held out for the hegemony of the federal judiciary over the construction and enforcement of federal laws. Their decisions had furnished the opposition with a pretext for the charge of judicial tyranny, and for an appeal to stronger measures. Public opinion was by now running so strong against the tariff that the very bonds in this case went uncollected.[59] During the peak of the crisis Calhoun was able to complain to the Senate, with doubtful accuracy, that the state had met frustration in its attempt to test the tariff judicially.[60]

Nullification by jury had failed. Accordingly, the States Rights party moved swiftly to attempt nullification by convention. The results of the campaign would soon present Johnson with a fresh assault on federal court processes.

Even before that, however, Johnson made one more sally in the press. The October elections to the state legislature were approaching. The issue was clear—Nullification or not. Nullifiers and Unnionists were waging a pitched campaign. At this moment Mr. Justice Johnson received another invitation to dinner; this time the hosts were to be the Unionists in Dorchester.

Once again the federal judge declined and again disclosed his stand. In June Congress had passed a compromise tariff, reducing certain levies. A majority of South Carolina's representatives had opposed it; they demanded a complete repudiation of protection. In a thinly veiled figure of speech, Johnson now denounced those States Rights leaders who had once approved the tariff, who now excoriated it, and who at the same time refused to accept reductions. Johnson said he and others had done what they could to secure a lowering of the offensive levies.[61]

[57]*Ibid.*
[58]*Ibid.*
[59]*Niles Register,* XLIII (Nov. 24, 1832), 205.
[60]See Calhoun's speech in the Senate, Jan. 16, 1833, *Register of Debates,* 22d Cong., 2 Sess., I, 102.
[61]See Johnson to Thomas Lee, Jr., Oct. 3, 1832, *Charleston Courier,* Oct. 11, 1832.

This Jeffersonian judge evidently put the Nullifiers, because of their threat to the Union, in the same class with Ultra-Federalists. He would have liked to attend the dinner, for:

> . . . I know I should have found among you many sons of the fearless whigs of Edisto, who so nobly maintained the bloody struggle of the Revolution, and also of some of those early and much valued friends of my own, with whom I had the honor, myself, comparatively but a boy, emulating their grave example, to maintain the struggles of 1798 against principles the reverse in aspect, tho' the same in consequences, with those which now threaten to prostrate the Union, or neutralize its advantages.[62]

And again Johnson closed with a toast, this time to the *"holy temple of our Union. . . ."*[63]

Yet the best efforts of Unionists were to no avail. The Nullifiers swept the elections of October by an estimated 23,000 to 17,000.[64] Nationalism was on the wane in South Carolina.

The theory of nullification could now be put into practice. With their overwhelming control of the legislature, the States Rights men carried out the program of the 1828 "Exposition." In November a state convention met at Columbia. On the 24th, after a week of discussion, it solemnly adopted the Ordinance of Nullification. The tariff was declared "null, void, and no law, nor binding upon this state, its officers or citizens."[65] To insure compliance, the Ordinance further sought to prevent appeals of cases that might arise under it to the Supreme Court; it prescribed for state officers and jurors within the state an oath of obedience to the Ordinance, a provision against which Johnson would soon be complaining. The effective date of all these measures was fixed at February 1, 1833. In case the federal government should attempt otherwise than through "civil tribunals" to use coercion to effectuate the tariff, the people of South Carolina would "thenceforth hold themselves absolved from all further obligation to maintain or preserve their political connexion with the people of the other States."[66]

---

[62]*Ibid.*

[63]The whole toast reads thus: *"The holy temple of our Union*—the fame of Erostratus to him who would destroy it."—*Ibid.* The reference was doubtless to Herostratus, an Ephesian who set fire to the temple of Artemis at Ephesus on the night Alexander the Great was born, in order to immortalize himself. The culprit was subsequently put to the torch for his act.—Smith's *Dictionary of Greek and Roman Biography and Mythology,* II, 439.

[64]Houston, p. 107, n. 1. William Johnson ran as Unionist candidate for commissioner of the poor in the Cannonsborough District of Charleston and was successful.—*Charleston Courier,* Oct. 13, 1832. His motive for this extraordinary action may have been to lend strength to the party ticket.

[65]*Register of Debates,* 22d Cong., 2 Sess., II, Appendix, p. 162.

[66]*Ibid.,* p. 163.

The legislature promptly reassembled. A series of acts was passed to carry out the Ordinance. These provided for a strengthened military force, laid down the procedure for the test oath, and prescribed regulations to frustrate the national courts and officers in their efforts to collect duties. With deft strokes the lawmakers had applied their scalpel to the long-maturing system of cooperation with the federal government.[67]

The state had thrown down its challenge. The ostensible aim of nullification was the preservation of the Union; its methods, avowedly peaceable. The presumption of peaceableness, however, was wholly predicated on compliance by the federal authorities. Either the nation would modify the tariff by February or by inaction tolerate non-enforcement of its laws in South Carolina. Any other course would be met by force.[68]

The authorities of the nation were no match for the Nullifiers in speed. In Charleston, to be sure, Poinsett was rallying his defeated Unionists and dispatching to Jackson urgent appeals for aid. At Washington, however, things were at a standstill. Jackson himself was now determined to put down nullification and preserve the Union; but it took time to mobilize political support and devise appropriate measures.[69]

At last the President took his case to Congress. His message of January 16, 1833, denounced nullification and stoutly upheld national power in the crisis.[70] To a proclamation which Jackson had

[67]For example, sections 11 and 12 of the state Replevin Act prescribe fines and prison terms for any person who assisted in providing jail space for those who might be held under tariff enforcement proceedings.—*Ibid.*, pp. 178-79. The effect of these provisions gains significance when set in juxtaposition with a comment of a Charleston paper a decade earlier. The *Courier*, for June 18, 1822, commented on a sentence passed by Judge Johnson on a convicted counterfeiter. Said Johnson to the accused: "Garcia, you are a bad fellow, and to keep you out of bad company, we send you to hard labor for seven years." The *Courier* continued: "The compliment to the jail contained in the above sentence is due from the authorities of the United States; for the prisoners of the United States are entertained in our jail solely through the hospitable courtesy of the state. Their board is paid for, it is true, but not their lodgings."

[68]Johnson was fully cognizant of the convention's temper and measures, for on Nov. 26, he was calmly holding Circuit Court in Columbia.—Minutes C.C. Dist. of S.C., Bk. C, p. 385. He was absent when the Circuit Court met in Milledgeville, Georgia, on Nov. 7, 1832, preferring perhaps to watch developments in Charleston.—Minutes C.C. Dist. of Ga., Bk. F, p. 394.

[69]Jackson and Poinsett disagreed as to the proper measures to be employed in enforcing the revenue laws. Poinsett, realizing that Jackson's plan for summoning a posse in Charleston would pit friends against friends and brothers against brothers, preferred that the President, on receiving a report from the federal judges that the laws could not be executed, should summon the militia to the defense of national law.—Poinsett to Jackson, Jan. 16, 1833, Jackson, *Correspondence,* V, 6-7. Cf. Jackson to Poinsett, Dec. 2, 9, 1832, *ibid.,* IV, 493, 498.

[70]Special Message, Richardson (ed.), *Messages and Papers of the Presidents,* II, 610.

issued in December, Governor Hayne of South Carolina had retorted in kind; Hayne had appealed to the spirit of 1776 for resistance to tyranny and the same day had issued orders for the organization of military forces.[71] Jackson now maintained that since South Carolina had called for resistance without first having exhausted all the avenues of redress, judicial and political, she was not rightfully asserting the right of revolution. Meantime the Union must be preserved and federal laws executed.

The President, to achieve this result, asked for power to employ the land and naval forces of the nation. In addition he requested new powers for the federal officers and courts in order to frustrate the recent acts of the state. The crisis was at hand. The old general invoked the memory of the founders and declared:

> They bequeathed to us a government of laws and a federal union founded upon the great principle of popular representation. After a successful experiment of forty-four years, at a moment when the Government and the Union are the objects of the hopes of the friends of civil liberty throughout the world, and in the midst of public and individual prosperity unexampled in history, we are called to decide whether these laws possess any force and that Union the means of self-preservation.[72]

Never since its founding had the American experiment stood in greater danger from internal causes. The issue at bottom was one of constitutional construction. Who finally should umpire the Union? Was it the national judiciary under suitable authorization from Congress? Or was it the individual state? Might one of the families of the republic block a federal law, even though that law had received passage through all the forms prescribed by the Constitution?

Mr. Justice Johnson here faced his supreme test. He had tried to strengthen the hands both of state and nation. He had avoided talk of national supremacy in the belief that cooperation between the two governments would alone avert collision. Yet collision was imminent. The blow would fall at Johnson's own doorstep!

The judge acted with characteristic directness. He was back in Washington for his final session of the Court. Congress was at work on two crucial measures, one, a tariff reduction bill, the other, a "Force Bill" embodying the President's proposals for the due enforcement of federal laws. At this moment, Johnson conferred with Louis McLane, Secretary of the Treasury. Next day the judge wrote McLane:

[71]Jackson's proclamation was issued Dec. 10, 1832.—*Ibid.,* p. 640. Hayne's was issued Dec. 20, 1832.—*Register of Debates,* 22d Cong., 2 Sess., II, Appendix, pp. 190-96.
[72]Richardson, II, 631.

Dr. Sir,   Jan. 1833

I have very imperfectly performed my promise to you of yesterday. Such is the effect produced upon my hands by disease that I can scarcely write legibly & you will see that I write with great difficulty. I will take the liberty of detailing a few facts to which to call the President's attention, as bearing upon the great interest which now absorbs the public attention.

And first in explanation of the view of this bill [doubtless the Force Bill]. Our jurors to be legally impanelled must be drawn by ballot by a child under ten years, from the taxables thrown promiscuously into a box. So that but for their Ordinnnance of abomina [sic] we should have been as secure from conceits on our side as they on the other. But knowing this and with a hellish malevolence for which posterity will mark them, they resolved to cripple their own courts and pack their own juries that we may not escape, while on our part they will know that we would die in our adherence to the known principle so wisely [?] introduced (and actually and historically introduced) as a security against the actual state of things now existing, introduced to save men from the madness and tyranny of packed political, fanatical selfis[h] and exasperated juries, from converting justice into forms and courts into the passive means of brute-force.

I think the counties of Spartanburg and Greenville may be relied upon—and arrests may easily be conveyed up to Wilmington, thence up to Lumberton to await trial.

On the otherwise good effects of exciting a jealousy in that quarter, the President's military eye needs no suggestion from me.[73]

Johnson went on to detail for the President some hints concerning the proper strategy in Charleston Harbor. He could say more but was exhausted.

The judge had handed the case to the political organs of the government. One may assume that he deemed this whole affair now political—well outside the appropriate sphere of judicial determination. His suggestions for legislative and military action found their way to the President and the appropriate committee chairman in Congress.[74]

As a judge, he was concerned immediately with individual rights and accordingly deprecated the state's interference with trial by

[73]Jackson Papers (MS; Library of Congress).

[74]On Friday, Jan. 25, 1833, McLane forwarded Johnson's letter to the President. McLane said he would pass the comments on juries on to "Judge Wilkins and Mr. Bell," chairmen respectively of the Senate and House Judiciary Committees, which were then drafting the Force Bill. Jackson endorsed McLane's letter as follows: Mr. McLane enclosing Judge Johnston's [sic] letter—answered and order to Sec. of War.—A. J."—Jackson Papers (MSS; Library of Congress).

jury. In its precipitate course toward nullification South Carolina had, by binding jurors to conform with its Ordinance, impaired a right Johnson deemed fundamental. The exponents of extreme state rights had thus ended by abridging an individual right. It was the protection of the lowliest individual, Johnson had said, for which the Union existed.

The danger which threatened the nation soon receded. Fortunately, the ailing federal judge was spared a direct collision with the authorities of his home state. By early March Jackson had signed two acts for terminating the struggle. One provided for a gradual lowering of the tariff and for abandonment of protection. The other, embodying reforms long advocated by Johnson, strengthened the arm of the federal judiciary in enforcing federal laws and decisions.[75]

In view of tariff reform South Carolina repealed its Ordinance of Nullification; the state had obtained redress. By way of defiance it transferred its censures to the Force Act.

Yet the tumult to which the theory of nullification had given rise within and without the state and the complexities which had arisen in the path of its enforcement produced a virtual repudiation of the doctrine. However plausible in theory, the state veto in practice would have led to violence, if not to outright war. Although factional strife would continue in the state for another year or more, public opinion there and indeed in the whole South would move inexorably toward the assertion of another right, that of secession. Judge Johnson would then have left the stage, but most of his associates, save for a few stalwarts like Poinsett and Petigru, would embrace the new position. Another convention would meet in South Carolina in 1860 to declare that state out of the Union.

As for Johnson, the end of the crisis found him again at his Charleston home. According to one early account, the beleaguered judge found the atmosphere too oppressive even for his robust character and accordingly withdrew to the North the ensuing summer.[76] If so, then Johnson was belatedly doing the thing he had

[75]Both acts were approved on March 2, 1833.—4 Stat. 629 and 632. The Force Act, entitled "An Act Further to Provide for the Collection of Duties on Imports," contained two sections of temporary duration which empowered the President to employ the militia and other forces to safeguard the jurisdiction of federal courts and to carry out their decisions; the remaining sections confirmed the exclusive jurisdiction of the federal courts over cases under the revenue laws, provided for removal of federal cases and suitors from state courts, authorized the securing or duplicating of records in state courts, authorized marshals to improvise new federal jails, and authorized writs of habeas corpus for persons detained by state courts in certain cases.

[76]O'Neall states: "When the unfortunate Nullification struggle rose to its height in the State, Judge Johnson, whose nature was earnest and whose opinions were always very decided, found himself in opposition to the sympathies of the majority of his fellow-citizens; and while his interest in the contest was of the warmest, his judicial position, especially on such a question, not

threatened a decade earlier when he first detected what he took to be a spirit of persecution and a movement for disunion emerging in Charleston.

In this final crisis of his career, Johnson had moderated the precipitancy of 1808 and 1822. Rebukes which he provoked from Taylor and others had doubtless impelled him to hold back. As a judge, if not altogether as a citizen, he had kept aside.

He had, it is true, charged some of the Nullifiers with conspiracy. In all likelihood, his lifelong sympathy for the Union caused him to minimize the mounting sectional spirit and sense of grievance in the South. The charge may likewise have grown out of Johnson's extreme moral sensitivity. That a conspiracy did exist would be difficult to prove.

What he did witness was a movement of tragic consequences. Perhaps it was slavery and not the tariff that first awoke southern fears of national power. Perhaps the Vesey affair and federal opposition to the resulting Seamen Act began a movement which reappeared in the Ordinance of Nullification and culminated in the Ordinance of Secession.

To Johnson the dominant element in federalism was voluntary cooperation. The great republic and its families rested on common traditions and common aspirations. Cooperation between the whole and its parts was thus possible, and because of social realities it was indispensable. In the end Johnson had been compelled to insist on a legal distinctness and on federal supremacy. But that had resulted from the development within a minority section of economic and social interests divergent from those of the majority of states. Under those conditions voluntarism had failed, and under those conditions the federation itself very nearly broke down after 1860. To put it in other terms, one may venture the proposition that without certain fundamental bonds of union, neither federation nor cooperation is possible, and that with them these are possible and inseparable.

In the end Johnson sided with the nation. He had forsaken the Jefferson of the Kentucky Resolutions and adhered to the Marshall of the McCulloch case. Yet, even here, one detects the hand of

only forbade interference, but imperatively commanded the most complete abstinence. He very properly, therefore, while not employed in his official duties, absented himself from the State, and during the summer of 1833 he resided in the Western part of Pennsylvania. Here, unfortunately, he contracted a bilious remittant fever from which he never entirely recovered."— J. B. O'Neall, *Biographical Sketches of the Bench and Bar of South Carolina*, I, 78. Evidently O'Neall gleaned this information from William Henry Trescot.—*Ibid.*, Preface, p. ii. Johnson did, however, sit with the Circuit Court in Charleston as late as June 13, 1833, and reappeared at Milledgeville, Georgia, when the Court met there on Nov. 7, 1833.—Minutes C.C. Dist. of S.C., Bk. C, p. 394; Minutes C.C. Dist. of Ga., Bk. F, p. 438.

Jefferson. In assigning Congress the role of supreme arbiter, Johnson was relying on the representative organ of the national majority. As in 1822, he was resigning himself to the "public will constitutionally expressed." And in resisting the march toward extreme state rights, he was defending the rights of the individual. For the individual the Union existed. At these convictions Johnson had arrived in his twilight years.[77]

[77]Available evidence suggests that Johnson doubted the existence of a right of peaceable secession. He had discussed the possibility of secession by South Carolina, alone or in conjunction with other states, in his letters to Taylor. The context, however, suggests that he treated it not so much as a constitutional right of peaceable withdrawal, as the right of revolution. He took the same stand earlier in his "Philonimus" letters. See above, p. 220, specifically, Philonimus to Caroliniensis, Nos. 6-8, *Charleston Mercury*, Sept. 11-15, 1823, and Philonimus to Zeno, No. 4, *Charleston Courier*, Oct. 8, 1823. Cf. comments on the social compact theory, the basis of the southern argument, which he made in Shanks *v*. Dupont, soon after the Webster-Hayne debate.—3 Pet. 242 (1830). See above, pp. 226-28.

Chapter XV

"A MIGHTY EXPERIMENT"

MIDWAY in his sixty-third year, William Johnson came back to the birthplace of his father. From colonial New York, the first William had embarked, seven decades earlier, for the South. Full of youthful hope and determination, he had set up his smithy in Charleston and helped launch the Revolution. Success, popularity, and domestic happiness had marked his life. In 1818, at that high point of national prosperity and harmony he had gone to his grave, confident in the future of the young republic.

Now the son was retracing the steps of the father. His mission had a very different character. The year was 1834; the month, July. In Charleston the state rights extremists maintained their control. The legislature had enacted for militia officers an oath of allegiance to the state, which Unionists deemed a fresh assertion of state supremacy and a menace to the Union. Judge Johnson's own nephew, Lieutenant McCrady, had refused to take the oath and forced his case to the state's highest court.[1]

The harassed jurist was once again combatting his recurrent illness.[2] He had just made out his will; besides providing for Sarah and his family, his slaves, and his friends, he requested that he be interred in "the same simple unostentatious manner" in which he had lived.[3] This done, Mr. Justice Johnson set out on his last journey to the North.

The end came on Monday, the 4th of August. In a time when anesthetics were unknown, he submitted to surgery. He died as he lived—resolute, courageous, alone. Next day's paper carried the story:

[1] The state court held the oath invalid by a vote of two to one. For a discussion of the case and the oath controversy, see C. S. Boucher, *The Nullification Controversy in South Carolina*, pp. 316-66.

[2] Johnson's last extant letter is dated June 28, 1834, and is addressed to Franklin Bache, Esq., of Philadelphia. Johnson explains his delay in replying to Bache's of May 16, on the basis of "serious indisposition." (Archives, American Philosophical Society, Philadelphia; courtesy of the Society).

[3] Will dated June 17, 1834. Two codicils were added in July—one in Charleston, and the other in New York. Johnson named as executors James Jervey, C. G. Memminger, Edward McCrady, John L'Engle, and Christian Breithaupt.—Will Book H (Probate Judge's Office, Charleston).

The Hon. Judge Johnson, of South Carolina, breathed his last, at Brooklyn, at one o'clock yesterday. He had arrived here some weeks ago, for the purpose of placing himself under the charge of an eminent medical practitioner of this city, having for some time suffered with an affection of the jaw, to eradicate which it required he should undergo the most painful surgical operation. Dr. Mott, of this city, was selected for the purpose, who expressed his opinion of the inability of the Judge to survive the operation. With a knowledge of the expression of the surgeon, he still determined upon placing himself under his hands; and without the aid of friends, or being bound, he submitted, with the utmost fortitude and calmness, to the most excruciating tortures; but in the course of half an hour after the completion of the doctor's labors, he died of exhaustion, produced by the sudden reaction of the nerves, which had been excited to their utmost power in buoying up his mind throughout the whole of the operation. . . .

The funeral of the Hon. Judge Johnson will take place from the house of Mr. Lewis, Corner of Columbia and Orange streets, Brooklyn Heights, at half past 4 to-morrow afternoon. The municipal and other authorities of the cities of New York and Brooklyn, the members of the bar, officers of the army, navy, and militia, and citizens and strangers generally, are respectfully invited to attend.[4]

Johnson had lost his last battle; he had fought it well. New Yorkers and Brooklynites alike, said the press, turned out in force to do honor to the eminent stranger who had died in that place under conditions so "peculiarly afflicting."[5]

A week later the Charleston bar gathered at the Circuit Courtroom to do honor to the departed jurist. There they paid tribute to the man who, without the aid of "ancestral rank, or hereditary wealth, or great family influence," had risen to the pinnacle of the profession, and who had helped bring the state to adopt the principles of Jefferson's party. After paying their respects to Johnson's talents, integrity, and independence, the lawyers predicted that his principles of the law would descend to posterity.[6] This example of the lawyers was soon followed by the Literary and Philosophical Society. After an impassioned tribute by Johnson's lifelong friend and fellow-combatant, Poinsett, the society adopted resolutions commending the private virtues and intellectual traits of one of the earliest and most zealous of its members.[7]

[4] New York *Evening Star*, Aug. 5, 1834.
[5] *New-York American*, Aug. 7, 1834. This issue gives an account of the funeral. The federal and municipal courts had closed out of respect for the deceased.—New York *Evening Star*, Aug. 6, *New-York American*, Aug. 5, and *New-York Commercial Advertiser*, Aug. 6, 1834.
[6] *Southern Patriot* (Charleston), Aug. 14, 1834.
[7] *Charleston Courier*, Aug. 18, 1834.

Later at Washington, Chief Justice Marshall for the last time opened a session of the Supreme Court. In ordering that expressions of loss drawn up by the Court's bar be published, he voiced his "respectful affection" for the departed brother.[8]

Mr. Justice Johnson's contemporaries had registered their esteem. Throughout the obsequies ran a common strand, admiration for his intellectual gifts, his honesty, and his independence. One would suppose that the memory of such a man would endure. Yet in actuality the name of William Johnson soon vanished from the records of history. The only tangible sign that Jefferson's disciple and Marshall's colleague had ever lived was a simple stone monument, which Johnson's children had caused to be erected in the churchyard of St. Philip's.[9] The man who had risen from obscurity had returned to obscurity.

Why this abrupt descent to oblivion? Had the vigorous and stormy life of William Johnson been a failure? One need not look far to discover the reasons for the neglect which befell his memory.

For one thing, the paucity of source materials has presented a discouraging obstacle to the biographer. Johnson's private papers, like those of other Unionists of his state and period, vanished during the course of the century.[10] In addition, this judge showed only a desultory interest in legal scholarship. Unlike Joseph Story, he had little taste for the publication either of commentaries or of his lower court opinions.[11] It was accordingly a bleak prospect that

[8]The resolutions were adopted on Jan. 12, 1835.—9 Pet. v, vi. Johnson was absent from the 1834 session of the Court. Marshall died July 7, 1835.

[9]The pedestal bears the following inscription: "In Memory of William Johnson, Born in the City of Charleston, So. Carolina, December 27th., 1771. Died 4th August Anno Salutis Mundi 1834. His Children who loved and valued him most dearly have caused this marble to be erected. He was at an early age a member of the State Legislature, Speaker of the House of Representatives, a Judge of the Supreme Court and in March 1804, was appointed associate justice of the Supreme Court of the United States, which station he filled at the period of his Death. His virtue pure his integrity stern his justice exact his patriotism warm and his fortitude not to be shaken in the hour of Death. Conscia Mens recti famae mendacia redit."

[10]See Lillian Adelle Kibler, *Benjamin F. Perry: South Carolina Unionist* (Durham, N.C., 1946), Preface, p. xii. Johnson's collection of papers which must have been considerable was either lost or destroyed. Some of Johnson's descendants surmise that his papers were moved to Columbia during the Civil War and suffered destruction when Sherman's forces occupied and partially razed that city.

[11]Only a relatively small proportion of Johnson's lower court opinions was published in the press or in periodicals of the time. The rest were recorded only in the manuscript journals of the Circuit Courts. There they remain. In the Circuit Court counsel had once cited as precedent a published Circuit Court opinion by Story; Johnson denied that this could serve as a precedent and declared: "Those who have observed my judicial habits will have noticed, that I seldom if ever rest my opinions upon nisi prius decisions— I think it is a public misfortune, that they are ever published, for they commit a judge to posterity, without an opportunity of correcting his errors,

presented itself to any who might have cared to resurrect the ideas and achievements of William Johnson.

And during the rest of that century few could have entertained such an intention. The towering and ingratiating figure of Marshall won a host of admirers and biographers. In their effort to spotlight Marshall these tended to cast his associates into darkness.

Because of certain traits of temperament and intellect, Johnson himself was in part responsible for this neglect. The tenacity and independence with which he maintained his views led him to attribute to those who differed from him a judgment less sound and motives less pure than his own.[12] Johnson always aspired to practice good will toward others, yet he often concealed this aspiration behind a curtain of sensitiveness and reserve. "He delighted to serve his fellow men," said Poinsett, "but from excessive delicacy he shrunk from all expression of their gratitude."[13] In his vehement pursuit of impartial justice, he was capable of striking out even against his friends; Thomas Jefferson, John Taylor, and the triers of Vesey could all bear witness to this.

Furthermore, in tracing out a course of reasoning to its logical conclusions he often left with his contemporaries an impression of obscurity. That is the testimony of those who perhaps knew his mind the best—the members of the Charleston bar:

> Possessing great power of analysis, and very acute discrimination, no sophistry could before him sustain unsound principles or weave a web, which he could not disentangle. To the consideration of every legal question he brought such an extent of learning—such an accumulation of knowledge and experience, as seldom failed, after all the arguments and illustrations of counsel, to present it in a new light, and to afford additional means for its determination. Indeed his extraordinary ingenuity sometimes caused him to refine further than most men could follow him, and to find distinctions not easily made perceptible to less gifted minds. Truth is not always so obvious to the clearest intellect; it makes its way but by slow degrees.[14]

---

add to the already enormous bulk and expense of a law library; often make business for our courts which never would have originated otherwise; and finally give a bias to legal opinions which ought to be received exclusively from tribunals of the last resort."—The *Amanda,* Minutes C.C. Dist. of S.C., 1821, Bk. C, pp. 15, 17; quoted in part in *Caroliniensis* (Charleston, n.d.), p. 27, from *City Gazette,* Jan. 18, 1822.

[12]Said a friend, Rev. John Bachman, at the time of Johnson's death: "He was not perfect—he may have been at times too strenuous in the maintenance of the opinions he had adopted, and unwilling sufficiently to allow that others, who were investigating the same subject, and sought for truth equally with himself, could come to different conclusions without the imputation of weakness or obstinacy . . . ."—*Charleston Courier,* Aug. 18, 1834.

[13]*Ibid.*

[14]*Southern Patriot,* Aug. 14, 1834.

Joseph Story expressed a similar view, for he found Johnson's opinions lacking in precision and certainty.[15] In short, William Johnson had little of the disarming charm of manner or the simple clarity of expression characteristic of the great Chief Justice. He was scarcely the man to inspire disciples. This Johnson could boast no Boswell![16]

Finally, the ideas which Johnson expressed were just as unlikely to win devotees as the manner in which he expressed them. The interests which dominated the nation throughout the nineteenth century could take little comfort in Johnson's views. South Carolina and the whole South exhausted their blood and treasure in defense of state rights; Mr. Justice Johnson had not only stood consistently for broad powers in Congress but openly resisted nullification. The North came increasingly under the control of business and industry intent on expansion under cover of laissez faire and a judiciary zealous in thwarting legislative efforts at reform or regulation; Johnson had seen dangers to the public in the sanctification of property, had tolerated regulation, state and federal, and had doubted the competence of the judge to cope with these matters. The Confederacy would resent the memory of its native son; the northern captains of industry would proclaim Marshall and Story their judicial patron saints. Notwithstanding his strenuous career, the blacksmith's son was forgotten by his own century.

With the dawn of a new century, the name of William Johnson reappeared in American writings. A new economic order had emerged. Old issues faded as the American polity underwent new strains and tensions. Government was shouldering new burdens, and men began to question precedents which had been accumulating since the time of Marshall. The long task of adapting the Constitution to a new state of things had begun.

[15]"His opinions are wanting in exactness," wrote Story, "as if he were confused and unable to put his thoughts together satisfactorily to himself."— Quoted in Joseph Cox, *United States Supreme Court; its organization and judges to 1835* (Cincinnati, 1890), Part II, p. 13. It may well be that Johnson had all this in mind when he wrote of Jefferson: "It is among the greatest misfortunes of the world, that profound men are so often misunderstood and mistrusted. We cannot keep pace with their conceptions, and are reluctant to acknowledge that superiority which humbles us."—*Eulogy on Thomas Jefferson* (1826), pp. 29-30.

[16]It is likely that the unfavorable traits noted above help to explain a damning comment made by James L. Petigru concerning Johnson's qualities as a judge. A staunch Unionist, Petigru had argued for the government in the Bond case. On Sept. 16, 1834, Petigru wrote Hugh S. Legaré respecting the latter's candidacy for the vacant judgeship as follows: ". . . I say I wrote you in July that as Judge Johnson was gone and you were the only one I knew that was fit to fill the place, for which God knows how little he was fit, I wished you were at home or had some friend near the old man to nominate you."—Quoted in James Petigru Carson, *Life, Letters and Speeches of James Louis Petigru* (Washington, 1920), pp. 158, 159.

As early as 1905, a legal scholar who was engaged in editing a collection of Marshall's opinions discovered the young dissenter. Johnson was the only member of the Marshall Court, he said, to maintain an independent mind. The author paid tribute to Johnson's "curious foresight and comprehension of the actual workings of the system which Marshall created."[17] A generation later, another observer deplored the restraining influence which Marshall wielded over his brothers and declared Johnson's social theory a century ahead of its time.[18]

In the aftermath of a calamitous depression, the Supreme Court itself began to reappraise the precedents. In revising its course it turned back for guidance to the "prophetic" ideas of Johnson.[19] A full century after his death, the name of William Johnson returned to the pages of the Supreme Court Reports and of legal publications.[20] The prediction of the Charleston lawyers at last came true.

This recent interest in the work and thought of William Johnson forms part of a larger quest. The American people have created an economy of unprecedented abundance and complexity. Men in every locality depend for employment and subsistence on the constant operation of factories, mines, farms, and carriers, at full capacity. Their pressures for regulation of the whole and protection of the parts have thrust government into the center of the stage. With an increasing momentum, state and federal functionaries have taken on

[17]Joseph P. Cotton, Jr., The Constitutional Decisions of John Marshall (2 vols.; New York, 1905), I, Preface, p. vii. Even earlier, Shirley had expressed an interest in Johnson, but had been discouraged by the difficulty of obtaining original materials about him.—John M. Shirley, The Dartmouth College Causes . . . (St. Louis, 1879), pp. 249-410 passim, especially p. 366.

[18]Ernest Sutherland Bates, The Story of the Supreme Court (Indianapolis, 1936), p. 130.

[19]See above, Chapter XII, note 96, and Chapter XIII, note 74.

[20]E. g., see comments in Felix Frankfurter, The Commerce Clause (Chapel Hill, 1937), pp. 5, 43, and Robert H. Jackson, "Back to the Constitution," 25 American Bar Association Journal (1939) 745, 749. See also Donald G. Morgan, "Mr. Justice William Johnson and the Constitution," 57 Harvard Law Review (1944), 328-61, and "Justice William Johnson on the Treaty-making Power," 22 George Washington Law Review (1953), 187-215. Cf. the many articles by A. J. Levin in the Michigan Law Review: "Mr. Justice William Johnson and the Unenviable Dilemma," 42 ibid. (1944), 803-30; "Mr. Justice William Johnson, Creative Dissenter," 43 ibid. (1944), 497-548; "Mr. Justice William Johnson and the Common Incidents of Life" (in two parts), 44 ibid. (1945), 59-112 and 243-93; and "Mr. Justice William Johnson, Jurist in Limine" (in three parts as follows)—"The Judge as Historian and Maker of History," 46 ibid. (1947), 131-86, "Views on Judicial Precedent," 46 ibid. (1948), 481-520, and "Dissent and the Judging Faculty," 47 ibid. (1949), 477-536. See Oliver Schroeder, Jr., "The Life and Judicial Work of Justice William Johnson, Jr." (in two parts), 95 University of Pennsylvania Law Review (1946, 1947), 164-201 and 344-86. See also Thomas K. Johnstone, Jr., "A Short Sketch of the Life of Mr. Justice William Johnson," 4 Year-Book of the Selden Society (University of South Carolina School of Law) (1940), 33-35.

the tasks of directing, limiting, and coordinating the activities of citizens.

To many observers this process has posed a dire threat to popular and constitutional government. The growth in governmental functions strikes many as malignant rather than benign. Laws for the dispossessed seem to threaten the rights of owners; centralization of power in Washington, the rights of the states; the mushroom growth of administrative agencies, the vitality of the legislature; the disparagement and administrative bypassing of judicial processes, the prerogatives of the Supreme Court. In combination, these apprehensions spell doom to the liberty of the individual.

This specter conveys added horror when viewed in the setting of our twentieth-century world. In the form of totalitarianism, despotism has returned in new trappings and paradoxically has appealed to its recruits in the name of democracy. To defend their institutions and to ward off a third and devastating world war, the nations committed to individual liberty have explored the paths to unity. A growing number of persons propose federation as the solution—a union for common ends that would be both energetic and democratic. That would mean more government, this time on a supra-national level—to some, an added menace to the liberty of individuals.

Ours, accordingly, is an age of crisis and political controversy. Small wonder, then, that Americans turn back for reassurance to their political traditions. Small wonder that they should explore the time of origins to determine what is most essential in their political and constitutional heritage. The investigation of the beginnings of our Constitution and of Johnson as one of its earliest and most trenchant expositors forms an appropriate chapter in that inquiry.

That, too, was an age of crisis and political ferment. Johnson's life spanned most of it. For six years Americans fought their War of Independence. For an equivalent period they debated a closer union. Throughout the entire epoch, men long inarticulate began to aspire to a share in the benefits and the responsibilities of government and to a protection from the sway of privileged orders. The discussions which these issues provoked dug to the roots of political society and explored its fundamentals. The Johnson of middle life more than once alluded to the "mental activity" whipped up by the Revolution; unquestionably the youth who grew up during these years was constantly subjected to the intellectual ferment about him.

Johnson reached adulthood on the morrow of the adoption of the Constitution. Charles Pinckney had proffered the Philadelphia charter to his fellow South Carolinians as an experiment—whose practicability time alone would disclose. The framework was there; but the process of interpretation, a significant part of the experiment, remained to be accomplished. The discussion of the appropriate rules of interpretation would absorb the minds of Americans for the next generation and more. To Marshall's Court it fell to settle most of the fundamental issues of constitutional construction; and to William Johnson, who sat beside Marshall for most of the latter's tenure, it fell to participate in the work.

To this task of constitutional implementation, the appointee of 1804 brought a mind of vigor and breadth. Witherspoon's Princeton had lit a lamp of intellectual inquiry that blazed with intensity to the end. And the many interests which that college had kindled continued to absorb him. This restless, disputatious mind shunned a narrow concentration on lawbooks and instead ranged at large over literature, philosophy, history, and science.

The thought processes which Johnson brought to his work rested on two assumptions. First, in the tradition of the Enlightenment, he regarded accumulated knowledge as so modest in scope as to permit the persevering student to acquire at least a good toehold in all the fields of inquiry. In dealing alike with the commerce clause and the cultivation of strawberries, he called on history, philosophy, and science for testimony and guidance. Second, he felt that truth could prevail only in an atmosphere of skepticism of authority and dogma. Thus, while attaching supreme importance to the Christian religion, he insisted on a rigorous testing of its doctrines. Doubtless, in his view, the law merited the same kind of treatment. Although he clung passionately to his own convictions, he believed that truth could be discovered only through the combined efforts of many observers and many critics.[21] It is of no surprise, therefore, that in general he should insist on information, communication of opinions, and discussion as essential to the correct disposition of political and constitutional problems.

Nor is it strange that Johnson took the view he did of the representative legislature. To him, the science of government was of all

[21]E.g., see his comments on the need of comparative data from many agricultural experimenters, in *Nugae Georgicae* (1815), pp. 14-15, 19, 33. Soon after his election to membership in the American Philosophical Society, he made this proposal to the Society: "Dispersed as the members of this society are & seldom having it in their power to attend your meetings would it not be promoting the views of the society if the attention of the members were from time to time directed by the vote of the society to particular objects, I take the liberty of throwing out this hint because, altho' the general enquiries proper for the attention of such an institution cannot be mistaken, yet much advantage results from drawing the minds of a number of able men to act at the same time upon any one subject. It is drawing the rays of genius to a focus."—Johnson to John Vaughn, April 24, 1811 (Archives, American Philosophical Society; courtesy of the Society).

sciences the most complex; its method was experimental. It would logically require not only discretion but also wisdom and experience in the numerous and deliberative assembly. Johnson had arrived at this conviction by his fiftieth year, after nearly a generation in public office. Six years in the state legislature and twenty on the state and federal bench had confirmed the nascent skepticism of dogma.

Yet if Johnson's reason told him to proceed with caution and to consult the opinions of others before reaching decisions, his temperament occasionally tendered a different sort of advice. A restlessness of disposition led him at times to exchange the judicial robe for the less pretentious though more utilitarian garb of the citizen. In his impatience to get on with things, he more than once plunged headlong into politics and affairs.

Perhaps there was a trace of envy in the admiration which Johnson professed for Jefferson, for we find him placing high on the list of that statesman's virtues a "philosophic calm diffused over his most ordinary actions, a perfect repose of the passions, which triumphed over persecution."[22] Johnson, it is true, gradually acquired the sense of justice and legal order of the judge. Yet to his own discomfort he never quite shook off the combativeness of the advocate.

It was a young zealot for debate who in that age of great debates ascended to the Court of John Marshall. To what extent did William Johnson capitulate to the ideas of the older jurist?

There is little doubt that Marshall, and through him the Federalist tradition, exerted a definite influence on Jefferson's appointee. Few could match the Chief Justice for geniality or intellectual acumen. For three decades the two worked at close hand; yet Johnson, so far as our records show, uttered scarcely a whisper of criticism of the presiding judge. Indeed, it may have been Marshall's integrity of character that led Johnson to assert that the "pure" men of both the parties were in basic agreement on fundamentals.

For one thing, Johnson evidently came to share the old Federalist's esteem for nationalism. In a day when one's state was one's country, the whole Court took as its mission the assertion of national power and close union. Johnson, indeed, came prepared for this role, for the experience of the Revolution and the teachings of the elder Johnson, President Witherspoon, and C. C. Pinckney had instilled a love for the more perfect union of 1787. Furthermore, Johnson saw Congress as the chief recipient of the delegated powers; the powers of the other branches of the federal government he tended to construe strictly. Nevertheless, Marshall's persistent de-

[22]*Eulogy on Thomas Jefferson,* p. 7.

mand for national power as a prerequisite of national unity doubtless had an effect. On and off the bench William Johnson worked
constantly for principles and projects that would strengthen the bonds
of union.

Again, Marshall's economic conservatism won at least a partial
allegiance from Johnson. Here, too, other forces were also at work;
the economic tracts of Mathew Carey, the intimate connections with
finance and business in Charleston, the lofty conception of the role
of commerce in society, all affected his judicial course. Yet Marshall's increasing esteem for the propertied elements of the community[23] also took its toll. Johnson appealed to natural law against
the Yazoo land-grant repealer, acquiesced in the subsequent expansion of the contract clause, and as late as 1822 complained bitterly about state laws which trod on vested rights. Later he altered
his official course of action; yet even then an income tax impressed
him personally as harmful.

If Johnson came to share much of Marshall's nationalism and some
of his devotion to the security of property, he broke away on other
issues. It was over the role of the judiciary in the constitutional
system that Johnson with growing frequency parted company from
his brothers. This defection from Marshall resulted, as we shall see,
both from personal taste and from Jeffersonian conceptions.

To John Marshall the salvation of the nation lay primarily in a
powerful, harmonious, and pretentious judiciary. The function of
the judge, he had declared in the Marbury case, was "to say what
the law is." The Constitution was law. In expounding the provisions of the Constitution the judges should maintain concord, should
rehearse in unison, and should assign the public recital of their
conclusions to a single spokesman, preferably the Chief Justice.
The resort to this solo form in the rendering of decisions would give
firmness, finality, and certainty to the fundamental law. It would
set at rest constitutional controversy and bequeath a system of order
and security to the latest ages.

This policy of Marshall's rested on three audacious assumptions.
In the first place, it assumed that questions of constitutional construction were essentially simple. Issues of constitutional law, like
those of the overriding law of nature, could be resolved through the
operation of reason. To each question there could be but one correct answer.

In the second place, Marshall deemed these questions justiciable—
susceptible, that is, of settlement through the regular processes of
litigation and adjudication. And, finally, Marshall deemed him-

[23]See especially Marshall's dissenting opinion in Ogden v. Saunders, 12
Wheat. 213, 332 (1827), and cf. Beveridge, *Life of John Marshall*, IV, 479 ff.

self and his usually tractable associates fully equipped for the task. To the seven high judges and not to the elected assembly, least of all to public opinion, these questions belonged. By training, by experience, and most of all by the permanence of tenure which shielded them from political pressures, the men of the bench were best fitted to resolve these issues.

Marshall's ultimate appeal, therefore, was to authority. In his eyes, to leave matters of constitutional dispute to elected assemblies and the public was to nourish unsound principles and to invite chaos. Such a course would expose decisions on fundamentals to ignorance, self-seeking, partisan rancor, and sectional bias. A remote and dispassionate arbiter was essential, and that arbiter was to a considerable degree a privileged order.

Marshall's application of these conceptions in the practice of his Court has exerted a profound influence. At the time of Johnson's death De Tocqueville expressed his amazement at the prestige which Americans attached to their judiciary.[24] Today many regard the high tribunal with a reverence verging on the religious.

On the other hand, the rule of judicial infallibility and judicial hegemony has on a number of occasions produced bitter public controversy. The Dred Scott, income-tax, and New Deal decisions are all in point. In carrying forward the Marshall tradition, the Court has incurred popular antipathy and has well nigh petrified the law and paralyzed government. At such times that safeguard of liberty, judicial review, has tended to become a brake on social reform and a barrier to the popular will.

William Johnson found it hard to accept Marshall's notions of the judicial mission. His own disposition and mental processes had a good deal to do with his deviation. The rule of unanimity could only have galled one with his temperament and his regard for the pursuit of truth through the expression of multiple opinions. "Few minds," he protested in a separate opinion in 1816, "are accustomed to the same habit of thinking. . . ." The complacent tone and irregular practices of the Court drew from him repeated objections. He had accordingly risked the displeasure of his associates and especially of Marshall. The lapse into silent acquiescence in 1819, although temporary, signified a limited acceptance on Johnson's part of Marshall's presuppositions.

After four years Johnson recovered his balance. During the winter of 1822-1823 he took a fresh look at the judicial function. The deceptive simplicity in which that function had appeared now faded. Issues of constitutional construction began to appear complex and

[24]Alexis de Tocqueville, *Democracy in America,* ed. P. Bradley (2 vols.; New York, 1945), I, 150-52, 278-80.

many-sided. At this very moment Johnson dropped a comment in Green *v*. Biddle that reveals his perplexity. The Court was balancing the rights of a landowner against the power of Kentucky to protect the rights of an innocent occupant. The judge had few precedents or other guideposts to direct his decision. Said Johnson, ". . . I acknowledge that I am groping my way through a labyrinth, trying to lay hold of sensible objects to guide me. . . ."[25] The dissenter was attempting to find his own way out. Johnson was struggling to recapture his intellectual integrity. However, he was supported in his quest by advice from Thomas Jefferson.

The influence of Thomas Jefferson on William Johnson was strong and deep. It is discernible in the conceptions which Johnson formed on three subjects—the role of the judge, the power of the legislature, and the place of the individual in the state. It affected Johnson's conduct during the whole of his career, but especially after 1822.

Thomas Jefferson set as his objective the liberation of men's minds. That meant in turn attacking despotism wherever it showed itself. The author of the Declaration of Independence had pointed that indictment at the irresponsible monarch of Britain. The founder of the Republican party had combatted tendencies toward monarchy and toward usurpation of power on the part of the Federalist administrations. These targets of his attacks had this in common: in his mind they endangered popular government and individual liberty. In 1822 the particular cause of his misgivings was the federal judiciary.

These fears Jefferson recounted in his letters to Johnson. Some issues of construction, such as those relating to the federal system, Jefferson thought improper for judicial determination; but it was not merely that the judges had amassed to themselves great power. It was also the manner in which the power was exercised and the absence of effective restraints that irked him. The secrecy that cloaked the Court's deliberations, the rule of unanimity that imparted plausibility and a false appearance of concord to decisions, and the oracular simplicity of Marshall's opinions drew forth his reproaches. These judges were human and liable to error. Yet the impracticability of impeachment and the single-opinion rule shielded them from the accountability exacted of other officials. The people had been cheated of the proper restraints on the national judiciary.

Jefferson planted his observations in the solid ground of Republican doctrine. Republican government meant responsible government. The Federalists, he asserted, had feared the people and had sought safety in a regime of privilege and undefined powers;

[25] 8 Wheat. 1, 101 (1823).

the Republicans had cherished the people and had sought ultimate security in the people's will. Only limitation of power, election, and freedom of expression could secure responsible government. On these principles Jefferson based his criticism of the Marshall Court. To Johnson he left it to make the appropriate applications.

Johnson took the hint. Tendencies already present in his judicial deportment then came to the fore. It is in the last decade of Johnson's career on the bench that the influence of Jefferson appears most clearly.

First of all, he became firm in his conceptions of the judge's task. In seeking to limit the power and assert the public responsibility of judges, Johnson in a sense began with himself. His was a gospel of judicial restraint. Earlier he had mused over the "frail materials" of which the judiciary was composed and had spoken of those who occupied the bench as fallible men. By 1827 he was declaring judicial power, like all power, liable to abuse and undue expansion. Note his comment in a case in admiralty: "But who is to issue a prohibition to *us,* if we should ever be affected with a partiality for that jurisdiction?"[26] The power of judges, notwithstanding its negative aspect, was nevertheless a power. Because of its impact at many points on sovereign authority, it partook of the political as much as of the legal. Hence, the individual judge should proceed with due humility and should accept the burden of accountability.

These views of the judicial role caused Johnson to persevere in the writing of dissenting opinions. Habits he had formed on the state bench, his native querulousness, and his independence of judgment prompted him to initiate his quest for freedom of expression on the Court. It was the conviction of popular responsibility that chiefly impelled him to renew it after 1822 and to continue it to the end.

The effect of Johnson's assertion of independence was a mounting discord on the Marshall Court that stands in marked contrast to the common stereotype of that tribunal. As a matter of fact Marshall's long judicial voyage was anything but serene. To be sure, Marshall had things his way during the initial phase; for four years he sailed his bark across an unruffled bay of Federalist unanimity. When Johnson climbed aboard in 1805, the seas became choppy and squall-driven. For two decades the chief breasted head winds of open criticism and accordingly often pulled in his sails to appease the gales. At this stage he more than once read opinions that bore in their patchwork form the evident marks of compromise. At last

[26]Concurring opinion in Ramsay *v.* Allegre, 12 Wheat. 611, 640. Italics are the author's.

in the mid-twenties the vessel sailed out into a storm-tossed ocean. Johnson and the recent replacements in the crew threatened open mutiny; and after the debacle in Ogden v. Saunders, Marshall, to regain harmony, presumably shifted his course. Division, rather than concord, marked this final phase of the voyage.

The grudging tolerance for dissent which Johnson exacted has by now ripened into positive acceptance. Jefferson's arguments for separate opinions have stood the test of time. The dissenters of one generation, because of their vision and the cogency of their arguments, have set the course for the majority of the next. Jefferson's standard of reason and experience has carried the day against Marshall's standard of authority.

Because of his doubts about judicial infallibility and omnicompetence, Johnson assigned to judicial review only a limited scope. Judges, he insisted, should read grants of court jurisdiction strictly. Where jurisdiction was clear, they should apply the rule of purpose in construing the substantive powers of government which the Constitution defined in general terms. It was the broad purpose of the law, whether a federal commercial or a state police regulation, that determined its character and furnished the criterion. Where doubt existed, even where the law approached the forbidden line, Johnson would presume a legitimate intent on the part of the lawmakers. Where the judges upheld the national bank charter, Johnson favored the general dissemination of their argument for power in Congress as the best method of dispelling popular doubts. When that insidious measure, a state income-tax law, was before the Court, he upheld it regardless of personal predilections. In short, the chief beneficiary of Johnson's reiterated dissents was the supreme legislature.

Exaltation of the representative assembly is thus the second manifestation of Jeffersonianism. This was the expression in constitutional terms of the esteem Johnson felt for Republicanism. Madison had long before defined a republic in the tenth number of the *Federalist* papers: to him it meant a representative government. During that fateful winter of 1822-1823 Johnson gave up the search for a perfect legal system and fell back on the "virtue and intelligence of the people and the firmness and purity of their rulers." This shift of position reflected growing doubts about restraints which were judicially devised and judicially imposed. It betokened a mounting esteem for legislative discretion and reliance on legislative judgment.

To Johnson the representative was no despot. The legislator was bound by oath to support the Constitution, was aware of moral considerations, worked under established rules of procedure, and kept a watchful eye on his reputation with mankind. The ultimate and compelling restraint was the ballot box. The lawmaker, unlike the judge, operated always under the direct checkrein of accountability.

And these assemblies voiced their decisions in positive law. Johnson time and again referred with deference to that concept. By 1827 he was willing to treat positive law as a corrective, or at least an authentic interpretation, of the universal moral order. This was not so much to deny the existence of natural and moral law as it was to doubt that judges were those best equipped for the task of revelation. Others were better acquainted with social conditions; they should play this role.

In bowing before positive law, Johnson revealed a deep concern for social exigency. His ill-fated venture into historical writing taught him one thing at least—the reality of social change. Events close to home, notably the decline of commerce and the depression of agriculture in his native state, deepened this awareness. Accordingly, we find him insisting that the "advancement of society" might in time justify broad regulations under the commerce clause. In a similar vein he was reading broadly the bankruptcy powers, federal and state, as fruitful media for social betterment. In their representative bodies the people possessed a key instrument for ameliorating the ills of society.

This conviction impelled Johnson to his unique conceptions of the federal structure. At first it was Congress that commanded his attention. In broadly construing its powers he looked on them less as interdictions on the states than as means for improving the lot of individuals and promoting national unity. Later he shifted his gaze to the states and dealt with the powers of their legislatures as tools for the remedying of social ills on the local plane.

That conflict between the general and local authorities might occur was no imaginary fear. This Johnson discovered to his own mortification. Accordingly, he sought to circumscribe state powers where these might provoke retaliation in other states, complicate foreign relations, or strike directly at the national government and its instrumentalities. Yet because both governments served the people and because cooperation presented fertile potentialities, he strove to open up a wide area for negotiation and collaboration. American federalism rested on the bedrock of common values and objectives; to make the house storm-worthy and adaptable to the needs of those who occupied it, Johnson assigned a large share of the work of construction and maintenance to the national representatives.

The same regard for the legislature brought him into that early collision with the executive. In granting Gilchrist his clearance papers, Johnson was asserting the time-honored rule of law. Yet elsewhere Jefferson's antagonist of 1808 saw in executive power an indispensable tool of government. In foreign affairs the President required a broad discretion; in domestic, his subordinates carried out measures of regulation in all their manifold and technical detail. Johnson thought that in the domestic area the judge might have to intervene to determine issues of power and motivation. In that day the functionaries of government were few, and their duties impinged only slightly on the daily life of the individual. Nevertheless, Johnson intimated that, because of the complex machinery and the technical work involved, it might be safer for Congress than for the judges to devise the most efficient brakes for the administrative steam roller.

Johnson's nationalism, in short, had at its core the dominance of Congress. Marshall sought to elevate judicial power; Johnson, the power of the national legislature. Not that he denied the existence of a power to review national statutes. Where constitutional provisions were explicit, he would have intervened even against Congress, for the Constitution he deemed positive law of the highest order. It was rather that he left to the representative body control of a large measure of the Court's jurisdiction and the initiation and implementation of national improvements and regulations.

In our own century representative bodies have at times tottered under the load of work imposed on them. Because they have dallied when conditions called for action, they have lost some of their earlier high standing with the public. Rather than strip them of power, William Johnson, one may suppose, would advocate the adoption, after empirical study, of improvements in the machinery of the legislature for the gathering and digesting of information and for the discussion of policies. He would ask the voters to examine their candidates by the standards of wisdom and experience. His ultimate reliance was on the people.

The people he thought of not as an inarticulate mass but as individuals. It was in his conception of the role of the individual in political society that Johnson made good his third debt to Jefferson. It was the "humblest individual" that the Union protected; the Constitution had his liberties, his interests, and his prosperity as its ultimate goal. The fundamental assumption was that every individual possessed intrinsic endowments and worth and therefore merited the solicitude of authority. This belief erects a sharp line of demarcation between Johnson's scheme of things and those political systems which pay lip service to majority rule and the people's welfare but neglect individual freedom and individual security.

William Johnson spelled out this conception in the sphere of civil liberty. The press, as the conveyor of information and the forum for discussing ideas and principles, was essential to liberty. Rumor and hysteria might lead the community to deal unjustly with individuals, and for that reason Johnson rushed into print at the time of the Vesey trials. The secrecy and the irregular procedure of those trials led him to cry out for fair play in behalf of the suspected insurgents. In opposition to the majority of his neighbors, he persevered in thinking that even slaves were entitled in capital cases to "due course of law." Rights of this sort, like trial by jury, had express footing in the Constitution. Johnson deemed them fundamental. These rights it was the special province of the judiciary to protect.

On the rights of property, Johnson looked with somewhat less reverence. For one thing, the relevant constitutional safeguards rested largely on implication. Provisions such as the contract clause grew up, under the ministrations of the majority, into a luxuriant hedge around property. Yet it was not merely the absence of express guarantees that plagued Johnson; his sympathies went beyond the man of property to embrace broader elements in the community. Where Marshall sought to shield the creditor, and Story the commercial man, Johnson looked beyond them to the humbler folk and to the public at large. The debtor, the farmer, even the laborer, belonged to the community; they, too, could count government as their servant. Johnson, it is true, attempted a one-man campaign to expand the *ex post facto* clause as a safeguard against certain arbitrary laws respecting property; yet this was to rest decisions on an express provision rather than an implication and was directed at the grosser abuses of power.

After 1822, Johnson forsook his cryptic silence in the contract cases. The sanctification of property rights might lead to economic oppression; the legislator might have to deal with such oppression in the interest of individual liberty and social happiness. In insisting that property rights be exercised "socially," Johnson was more perceptive than Marshall and probably more explicit than Jefferson. He was generations ahead of his time.

The lowliest individual, therefore, became in Johnson's mind both the master and beneficiary of government. That the individual was capable of filling this high role was the hypothesis on which the American experiment rested. The blacksmith had dimly perceived the possibilities of the experiment and helped launch it. The son followed its progress with watchful concern. In the long-forgotten "Hamilton" papers of 1828, he states his fundamental assumption: "I rest my hopes for the permanency of our institutions, . . . on the virtue and intelligence of the community. If these fail, no constitutional provisions . . . will avail to the preservation of the commonwealth."[27]

William Johnson, it would seem, equated America with freedom under representative institutions. In this same tract he looks at the world of 1828 and sees crises ahead for the cause of freedom:

We have seen the commencement of the *revolutionary* period; but who shall dare to affirm, that we have witnessed its close? The raging of the tempest is hushed; but who shall say, that the elements are settled into permanent repose? No, it is not so. The great antagonist principles of light and darkness, seem, even now, to be silently mustering their forces for the final struggle. Is it wise, or is it safe, to presume, that, "within the wind of this commotion," we shall, or can, remain unaffected and unmoved? I confess I have very different anticipations. I deem it not improbable, that our duty, our honour, our safety even, may call us to a very different course; a course, for which, in the use of all sober means, we are bound to hold ourselves prepared. One of these means is, to strengthen and consolidate the Union of the States; to harmonize the public feelings; to liberalize public opinion; to dispel local jealousies; to foster, with a beneficent impartiality, and with large and far-reaching views, the great interests of the country; and thus build, on a firm basis, a lofty *national* character, and a permanent national prosperity—a character and prosperity, that may abide, if need be, the shock of the sternest conflict. . . . It is a truth, which no man, worthy of the name of a statesman, can lose sight of, for a moment, that we occupy, and cannot but occupy, an important and most conspicuous position in the great community of nations. We cannot, if we would, withdraw from the part assigned us by that Almighty Providence, which controls the affairs and prescribes the duties of individuals and of nations. We must retain it, with all its advantages, its hazards, and solemn responsibilities.[28]

Johnson the prophet had spoken once again. In his convictions about the individual and representative government, he owed a heavy debt to Jefferson. Marshall had, in a sense, helped mold the

[27]Hamilton (pseudonym), *Review of a Late Pamphlet* (see Chapter XIV, note 21), p. 16. Said Johnson: "What is our security against abuse [of power] . . . ? The virtue and intelligence of the people at large—the political, and *moral* responsibility of the depositories of power—and the perfect sameness of interest that subsists between them."—*Ibid.*, p. 15. Johnson's earlier researches for a history of parties served him well, for this pamphlet is filled with quotations from speeches and documents of the first years of the national government.

[28]*Ibid.*, pp. 104-5. The italics are Johnson's. Said he: "Will it read well for us on the pages of the future historian, that the great cause of truth and freedom failed, and was borne down in the strife, because we proved recreant to our trust? Recreant because the North distrusted the South, and the South was jealous of the North."—*Ibid.*, p. 105.

form of his thinking, and Jefferson, the content. In his *Eulogy on Jefferson,* Johnson makes clear his obligation. This impassioned tribute, in fact, reveals as much of the hopes and fears, the beliefs and doubts, of the follower as it does those of the leader. The embattled dissenter speaks feelingly of the public scorn and ridicule which Jefferson incurred during his life. Words which he utters in defense of the President who raised him to the bench may as properly be applied to Johnson himself:

Look through the whole range of the political career of our departed friend, and there is not an error which had not its origin in a tremulous anxiety for the safety of that posterity, over whose interests he ever watched with paternal solicitude. Public opinion has indeed settled down into a conviction that he committed errors; and yet must not time and experience decide the question? Who knows whether our conclusions may not be the result of less profound views of the tendency of measures? National virtue, national freedom, true national greatness, the happy issue of a mighty experiment in the government of the world, these were the purposes that absorbed his attention.[29]

[29]*Eulogy on Thomas Jefferson,* pp. 28-29.

APPENDICES

Appendix I

BIBLIOGRAPHICAL NOTE

Since an extensive documentation has been afforded in notes, no effort is here made to present all the references which have been consulted in the preparation of this work. Johnson's own writings, the medium for his ideas, have appeared in such a variety of sources, however, that there may be value in enumerating both the sources and, in some cases, the writings they contain.

A. Manuscript Correspondence

Letters from William Johnson are contained in collections at the various places listed below. A numeral in parentheses indicates the number of letters, if more than one, in the collection.

American Philosophical Society, Philadelphia. Archives (3). Letters to Franklin Bache, Thomas C. James, and John Vaughn.

Boston Public Library. Rare Book Department, Chamberlain Collection (2). Letters to Rev. Ashbel Green and Mathew Carey.

Charles Feinberg, Detroit. Letter to Mathew Carey.

Harvard College Library, Cambridge, Mass. Sparks MSS. Letter to Jared Sparks.

Haverford College, Haverford, Pa. Charles Roberts Autograph Collection. Letter to Isaac Shelby.

Historical Society of Pennsylvania. *See* Pennsylvania, Historical Society of.

Library of Congress, Division of Manuscripts, Washington, D.C. Peter Force Papers. Letter to Peter Force.

———. Jackson Papers. Letter to Louis McLane.

———. Jefferson Papers (8). Letters to Thomas Jefferson.

———. Monroe Papers. Memorandum to James Monroe.

———. William C. Rives Collection. Letter to James Madison.

Massachusetts Historical Society, Boston. Adams Manuscripts (2). Letters to John Quincy Adams and William H. Crawford.

———. Pickering Papers (2). Letters to Timothy Pickering.

Donald G. Morgan, South Hadley, Mass. Letter to sister of William Johnson.

National Archives, Washington, D.C. Records of the Department of State, Miscellaneous Letter Series (9). Letters to John Quincy Adams (7), James Madison, and Richard Rush.

————. Records of the Department of State. Pardon Records (2). Letters to John Quincy Adams.

————. Records of the Solicitor of the Treasury, Letters Received. Miscellaneous (2). Letters to William H. Crawford and Richard Rush.

New-York Historical Society, New York City. Miscellaneous Manuscripts. Letter to Charles Harris.

————. Miscellaneous Manuscripts Pendleton (5). Letters to Nathaniel Pendleton.

New York Public Library, New York City. Emmet Collection. Letter to Cashier of United States Bank.

————. Miscellaneous Papers (Johnson Folder) (2). Letters to Mathew Carey and Richard Smith.

————. Monroe Papers (MSS). Letter to James Monroe.

Pennsylvania, Historical Society of, Philadelphia. Conarroe Papers. Letter to Richard Smith.

————. Dreer Collection. Letter to Charles Harris.

————. Etting Collection (2). Letters to Langdon Cheves and John Hart.

————. Gratz Collection. Letter to John Vaughn.

————. Henry D. Gilpin Collection, Poinsett Section. Letter to Joel R. Poinsett.

————. Lea and Febiger Collection (3). Letters to Mathew Carey.

————. Poinsett Collection. Letter to Joel R. Poinsett.

————. Wilson Collection (2). Letters to Rev. W. Bird Wilson.

Presbyterian Historical Society, Philadelphia. Files. Letter to Rev. George S. Woodhull.

University of South Carolina, South Caroliniana Library, Columbia, S.C. J. Rion McKissick Collection. Letter to Bank of the United States.

————. Miscellaneous (2). Letters to Col. Thomas Taylor and Smith Thompson.

————. Yates Snowden Collection. Letter to Mathew Carey.

B. Published Correspondence

A number of Johnson's letters, including many to the editors of newspapers, appeared in print either during his life or subsequently. These may be classified for convenience as follows:

1. Letters in Magazines and Newspapers

Charleston *City Gazette*. May 25, 1822. Letter to the Editor.

———. June 5, 1822. Letter to the Editor.

———. June 12, 1822. Letter to the Editor.

———. Nov. 20, 1822. Letter to Henry O'Hara.

———. April 8, 9, 1823. Letter to Thomas Cooper.

———. Sept. 20, 1823. Philonimus to Citizen by Choice.

———. Sept. 26, 1823. Philonimus to Editor.

Charleston Courier. Sept. 10–Oct. 8, 1823. Philonimus to Zeno (4 nos.).

———. Oct. 11, 1832. Letter to Thomas Lee, Jr.

Charleston Mercury. Aug. 18, 1823. "A Subscriber" to the Editor.

———. Aug. 21, 1823. Letter to the Editor.

———. Aug. 26–Sept. 19, 1823. Philonimus to Caroliniensis (9 nos.).

———. Sept. 15, 1823. Card from Philonimus.

———. Oct. 7, 1823. Note by Philonimus.

———. Sept. 26, Oct. 7, 1823. Philonimus to Philo-Caroliniensis.

National Intelligencer, Washington, D.C. Sept. 29, 1823. Letter to Gales and Seaton.

———. Dec. 5, 1826 (tri-weekly ed.). Letter to the Editors.

———. Feb. 24, 1827 (tri-weekly ed.). Letter to Gales and Seaton.

Niles Weekly Register, Baltimore. XXXIX (1830), 98. Letter to Committee on Arrangements.

———. XXXIX (1830), 119-20. Letter to John Taylor.

———. XXXIX (1830), 132. Letter to John Taylor.

South Carolina Historical and Genealogical Magazine (Charleston). I (1900), 207-10. Letter to Thomas Jefferson.

Washington Gazette. April 24, 1819. Letter to the Editor of the Raleigh *Star*.

———. April 24, 1819. Letter to Secretary of the Treasury.

2. Letters in Miscellaneous Publications

Free Colored Seamen—Majority and Minority Reports. House Committee on Commerce, 27th Cong., 3 Sess., House Rep. No. 80 (1843), pp. 14-15. Letter to John Quincy Adams.

Goodwin, Mrs. Maud Wilder. *Dolly Madison* (New York, 1896), p. 197. Letter to Dolly Madison.

Journal of the Senate of the Commonwealth of Kentucky (Frankfurt, 1822), pp. 199-203. Letter to Committee on Public Education.

Maryland Historical Records Survey Project, Calendar of the Otho Holland Williams Papers (in the Maryland Historical Society, mimeographed, 1940), item 1127. Letter to William Elie Williams.

C. BOOKS AND PAMPHLETS

All of the following except Johnson's *Life of Greene* are pamphlets. It is possible that Johnson also wrote a pamphlet entitled *Notes on the Finances of the State of South Carolina, by a Member of the House of Representatives* (Charleston: W. P. Young, 1799). A copy at the Historical Society of Pennsylvania has Johnson's name inscribed on it, though not in Johnson's hand. No clear evidence of Johnson's authorship has yet appeared.

A Bill to Establish an Uniform System of Bankruptcy in the United States. Washington: Davis and Force, 1820.

Eulogy on Thomas Jefferson, Delivered August 3d, 1826, in the First Presbyterian Church. . . . Charleston: C. C. Sebring, 1826.

Hamilton (pseudonym) *Review of a Late Pamphlet under the Signature of "Brutus."* Charleston: James S. Burges, 1828.

Nugae Georgicae; an Essay, Delivered to the Literary and Philosophical Society of Charleston, South Carolina October 14, 1815. By the Senior Vice-President. Charleston: J. Hoff, 1815.

The Opinion of the Hon. William Johnson, delivered on the 7th August, 1823, in the case of the arrest of the British Seaman. . . . Charleston: C. C. Sebring, 1823.

An Oration Delivered in St. Philip's Church; before the Inhabitants of Charleston, South Carolina, on Saturday the Fourth of July, 1812. . . . Charleston: P. Young, 1813.

Remarks Critical and Historical on an Article in the Forty-seventh number of the North American Review, Relating to Count Pulaski. . . . Charleston: C. C. Sebring, 1825.

Sketches of the Life and Correspondence of Nathanael Greene, Major General of the Armies of the United States, in the War of the Revolution. 2 vols. Charleston: A. E. Miller, 1822.

To the Public of Charleston. Charleston: C. C. Sebring, 1822.

D. Newspaper and Magazine Articles

"Communication: Melancholy Effect of Popular Excitement," *Charleston Courier,* June 21, 1822.

"Judge Johnson's Remarks on the Publication of the Attorney-General's letter to the President, on the Subject of the mandamus issued by the Circuit Court of South-Carolina to the Collector, in the Case of the Resource," *Charleston Courier,* Oct. 15, 17, 18, 1808, reprinted in 10 Fed. Cas. 359-66.

"Memoire on the Strawberry Read before the Horticultural Society of Charleston by the President . . . ," *The Southern Agriculturist* (Charleston), V (1832), 568-77.

"The Reviewer Reviewed. In four letters from the Hon. William Johnson to a Friend," Charleston *City Gazette,* Nov. 14, 15, 16, 18, 19, 1822.

"Rural Economy; On the Killing of Crows," *Charleston Courier,* April 27, 1831.

"To the Public," *Charleston Courier,* June 29, 1822.

E. Judicial Opinions

1. Opinions Delivered in the South Carolina Court of Common Pleas (1800-1804):

    2 Bay's Reports.
    1 Brevard's Reports.

2. Opinions Delivered in the United States Circuit Courts (1804-1834):

    A number of Johnson's opinions on circuit were published at the time in the Savannah and Charleston newspapers. Some of these were reprinted in legal periodicals of the time and most of them were later included in the *Federal Cases,* a collection of decisions in the federal circuit and district courts for the years 1789-1880. The remainder appear in manuscript form in the Minutes of the Circuit Courts for the Districts of South Carolina and Georgia, on file in Charleston and Savannah respectively.

3. Opinions Delivered in the United States Supreme Court (1805-1833):

    2-9 Cranch's Reports
    1-7 Peters' Reports
    1-12 Wheaton's Reports

F. Miscellaneous Writings

Probate Judge's Office, Charleston. Will Book H. Will of William Johnson (1834).

Appendix II

Number and Nature of Opinions Rendered by Supreme Court Justices Annually, 1805-1833

Year	No. of Cases	Per Curiam	Marshall M	Marshall C	Marshall D	Paterson / Livingston M	C	D	Cushing / Story M	C	D	Chase / Duvall M	C	D	Washington M	C	D	Johnson M	C	D	Todd M	C	D
1805	24	5	17																	1				
1806	28	7	18					1									1							
1807	19	9	10			*Livingston*			1									1		1		*Todd*		
1808	30	5	22		1	1	1		1			1						1	2	2			
1809	49	14	31			1	1		2						1	1			2	4			
1810	39	8	24		1	3	1	1				2			2			2	2	2			1
1811	No Session																							
1812	38	8	19			1			*Story* 1			*Duvall* 1			5			3					
1813	45	5	18			6	2		7	1		1		1	4			4		2		2	
1814	48	2	15			4		1	10	1	3	2			7			7			1		
1815	40	1	18			5		1	9		1				4			3	2				
1816	43	2	17			1		1	10						3			7	1	1	3		
1817	41	2	14						8			1			8			8					

							THOMPSON						BALDWIN						TRIMBLE			McLEAN		
1818	37	3	16		4		4		1			3				4	1	4	2						
1819	33	1	13		1		9	1	1			2	1			6									
1820	27	1	11		3	1	3					3				5	1	1	1						
1821	41	8	12		6		7									7		1	1						
1822	31	2	15	1	3		6		1			1				2	2	2	2						
1823	31	2	8		1		10		1			4				5									
1824	41		15		3		11	1	1			6				4	1	4	1						
1825	27		10		2		7					3				5	1								
1826	33	2	12		4		6		1			4				4									
1827	48	2	15	2	3	1	9					2		1		8	1	1	9						
1828	55	1	24		6		7		3			2				5	1	3	7						
1829	44	2	17		2	1	11		1			6				5	1	1	1						
1830	57	5	20		5	1	8				1	6	2			7	1	4	6						2
1831	42	2	13		4	1	7					4	1	4		5	1	2	7						
1832	56	4	20	1	9	1	13					1		6				8	1						
1833	41	3	14		6		8		1			6				4	1	6	1						

"M" indicates majority opinions; "C" indicates concurring opinions; "D" indicates dissenting opinions. Opinions delivered seriatim are omitted; no account has been taken of dissents without opinion or of concurrences by one justice in the dissenting opinions of others. For totals see Table 2, p. 189, above.

Table of Cases

Index

Adams, Henry, 5
Adams, John, 31, 38, 41, 43, 44, 141n, 158
Adams, John Quincy, 105, 116, 122, 126, 158, 193, 213n, 258; charges W.J. with hotheadedness, political machinations, place-hunting, and nepotism, 106-8
Adams, Samuel, 4
Administrative appeal, W.J. on, 67-68
Administrative law, *see* Executive power
Admiralty jurisdiction, *see* Judicial power
Agriculture, diversification of crops an aim of W.J. in 1830, 258-59; reforms in, advocated by W.J., 100-4
Alien and Sedition Acts, 34, 264, 257
American Colonization Society, 135n
American Philosophical Society, 287n
American Revolution, 161, 226, 273, 286, 288; W.J.'s father's role in, in Charleston, 3-14, 22; W.J. on, 96; aims and results of, praised by W.J. in *Life of Greene,* 150-51; political theory of, qualified by W.J., 226-28
American system, 122
American Whig Society, 20
Amory, Rev. Isaac, uncle of W.J., 7-8, 17

Bachman, Rev. John, 283n
Baldwin, Henry, 90n, 186n, 187n, 189, 252n
Bank of South Carolina, proposal for, defeated, 15; legislative bill to incorporate, supported by W.J., 32-33
Bank of the United States, 37, 126; Charleston branch of, 33, 105, 107-9, 117; exemption of securities of, from state taxation, 249-51; functions served by, lauded by W.J., 164-65; right of, to sue in lower federal courts, 83-86; upheld in McCulloch case, 110-12, 115-16
Bankruptcy power, 207, 241, 294; broad construction of, reflected in W.J.'s model bill, 117-19; as exclusive or concurrent, 242-43; states may exercise, subject to uniform national laws, 248-49
Bay, Elihu Hall (Judge), 24n, 36n
Bennett, Thomas (Governor), brother-in-law of W.J., 25, 127, 131, 138, 257

Bennett, Thomas, Sr., 24-25
Beveridge, Albert J., quoted, 174-75, 190
"Black Code," 129
Blackstone, William, 21
Borrowing power, 250
Boston Port Act, 10
Bourne, A., 141n
Boyer, John Pierre, 136n
Breithaupt, Christian, 280n
Brevard, Joseph (Judge), 36n
Burke, Mr. Justice, quoted on state of early South Carolina laws, 21n
Burr, Aaron, *see* Burr conspiracy
Burr conspiracy, 55-57, 66
Butler, Pierce, 15

Calhoun, John C., 95, 116, 122, 269, 272; elaborates doctrine of nullification, 256-57
Calhoun, John Ewing, 24n
Carey, Mathew, 116, 118, 260n, 289
"Caroliniensis" papers, 197-99
Charleston *City Gazette,* 142
Charleston *Courier,* 60, 130, 131, 132, 260
Chase, Samuel, 48, 53, 189; characterization of, by W.J., 182
Cheves, Langdon, 95n, 116
Civil rights and liberties, 126, 228, 275, 296; Bill of Rights as applied to states, 135. *See also* Criminal procedure; *Ex post facto* laws; Freedom of religion; Freedom of the press; Trial by jury
Clay, Henry, 95, 122, 218
Coke, Edward, 271
College of New Jersey (Princeton), attended by W.J., 17-20; W.J. awarded LL.D. by, in 1818, 143
Columbia, S.C., W.J.'s characterization of, in 1804, 39
Commerce power, 238, 261, 294; deemed exclusive by W.J., 246-48; importance of and W.J.'s construction of, in Elkison and Gibbons cases, 190-206; and state power, 246-48
Common Sense, by Thomas Paine, 10
Common-law jurisdiction of federal courts, *see* Judicial power
Confederacy, 284
Conflictus legum, 235
Congress, contempt power of, upheld by W.J., 119-22; control by, of jurisdiction to review executive acts, 71-73; delegation of power